CHAPTER 45 NEW COMPANION

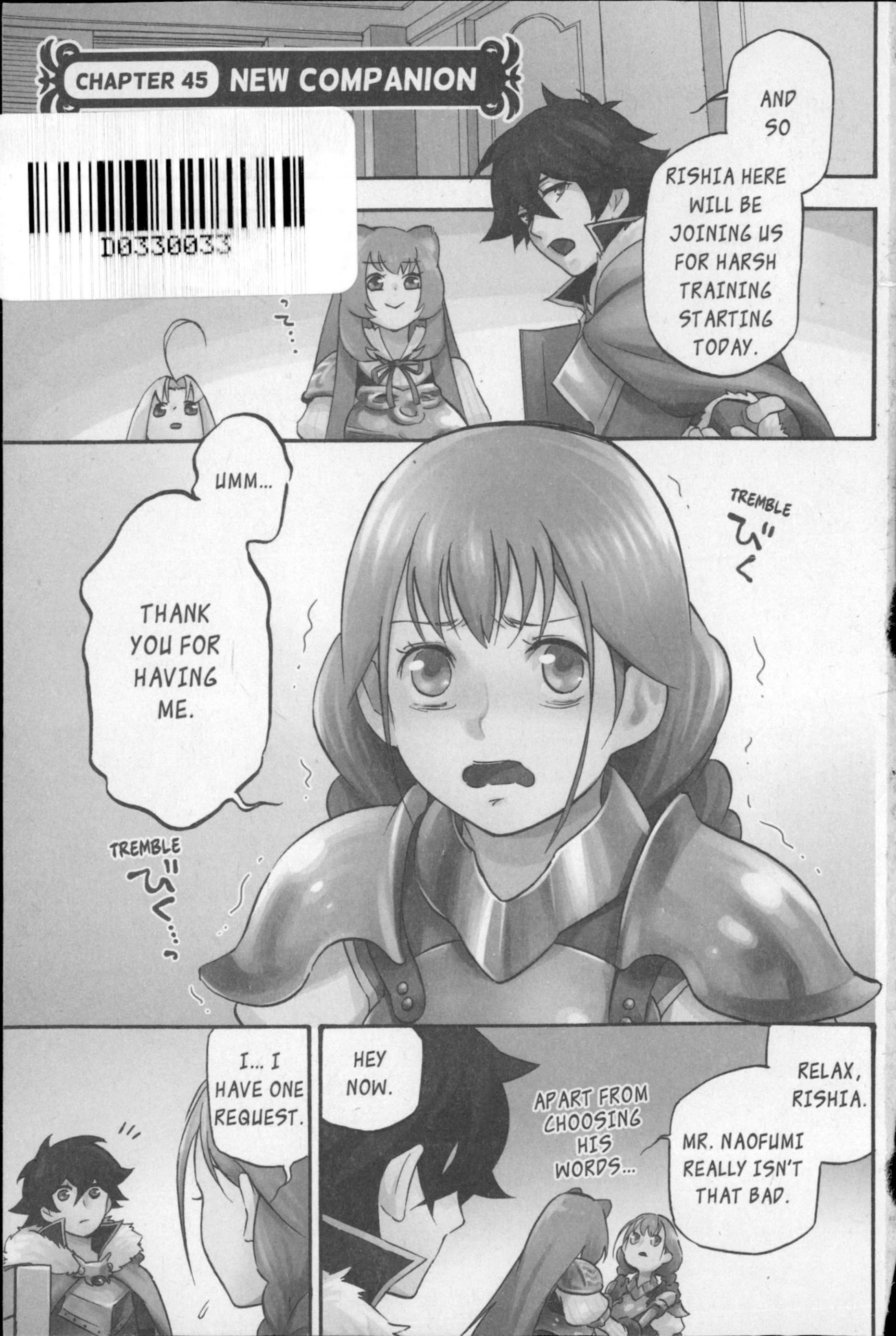
AND SO RISHIA HERE WILL BE JOINING US FOR HARSH TRAINING STARTING TODAY.
TREMBLE びく
UMM...
THANK YOU FOR HAVING ME.
TREMBLE びく...
RELAX, RISHIA.
MR. NAOFUMI REALLY ISN'T THAT BAD.
APART FROM CHOOSING HIS WORDS...
HEY NOW.
I... I HAVE ONE REQUEST.

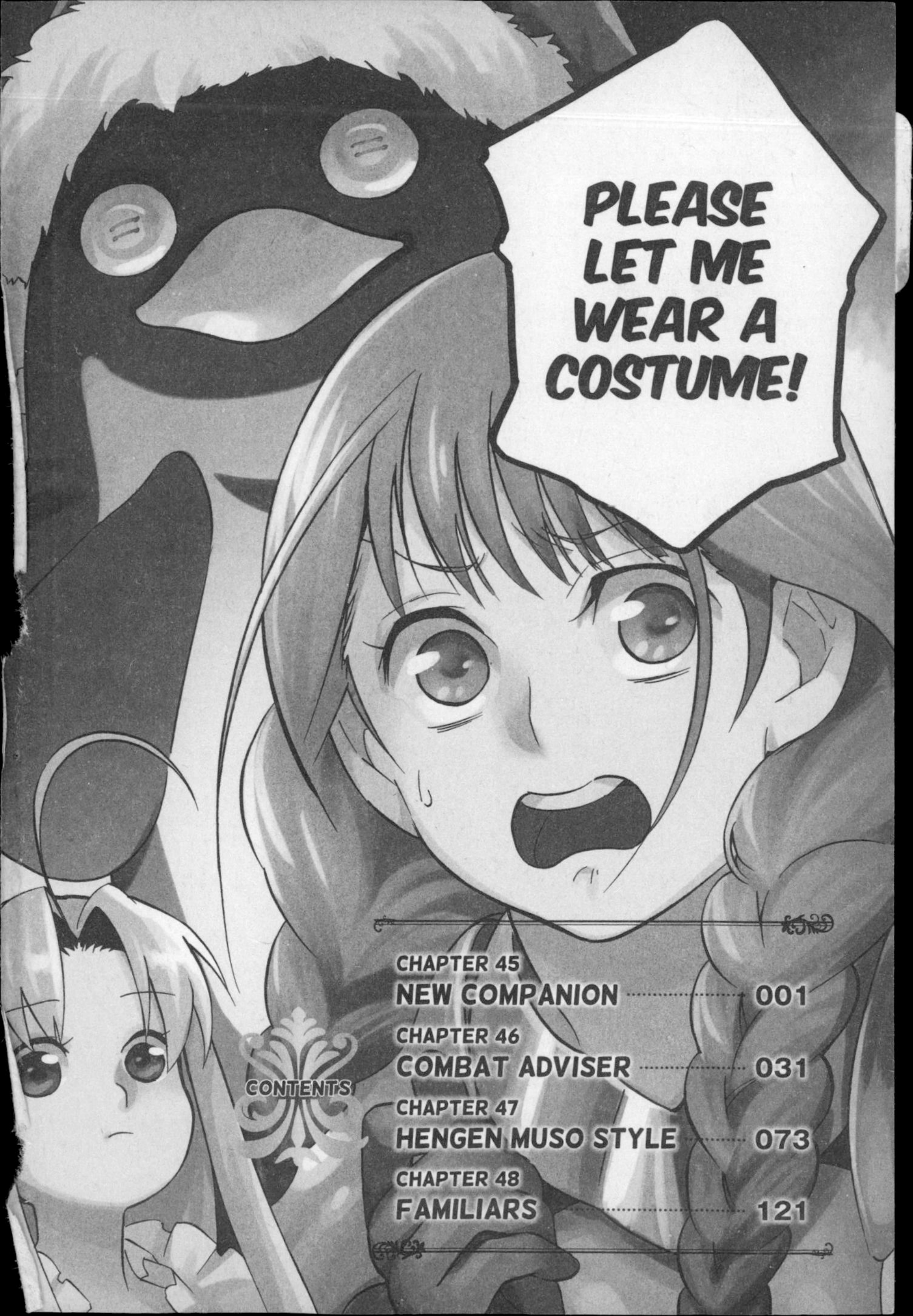
PLEASE LET ME WEAR A COSTUME!

CONTENTS

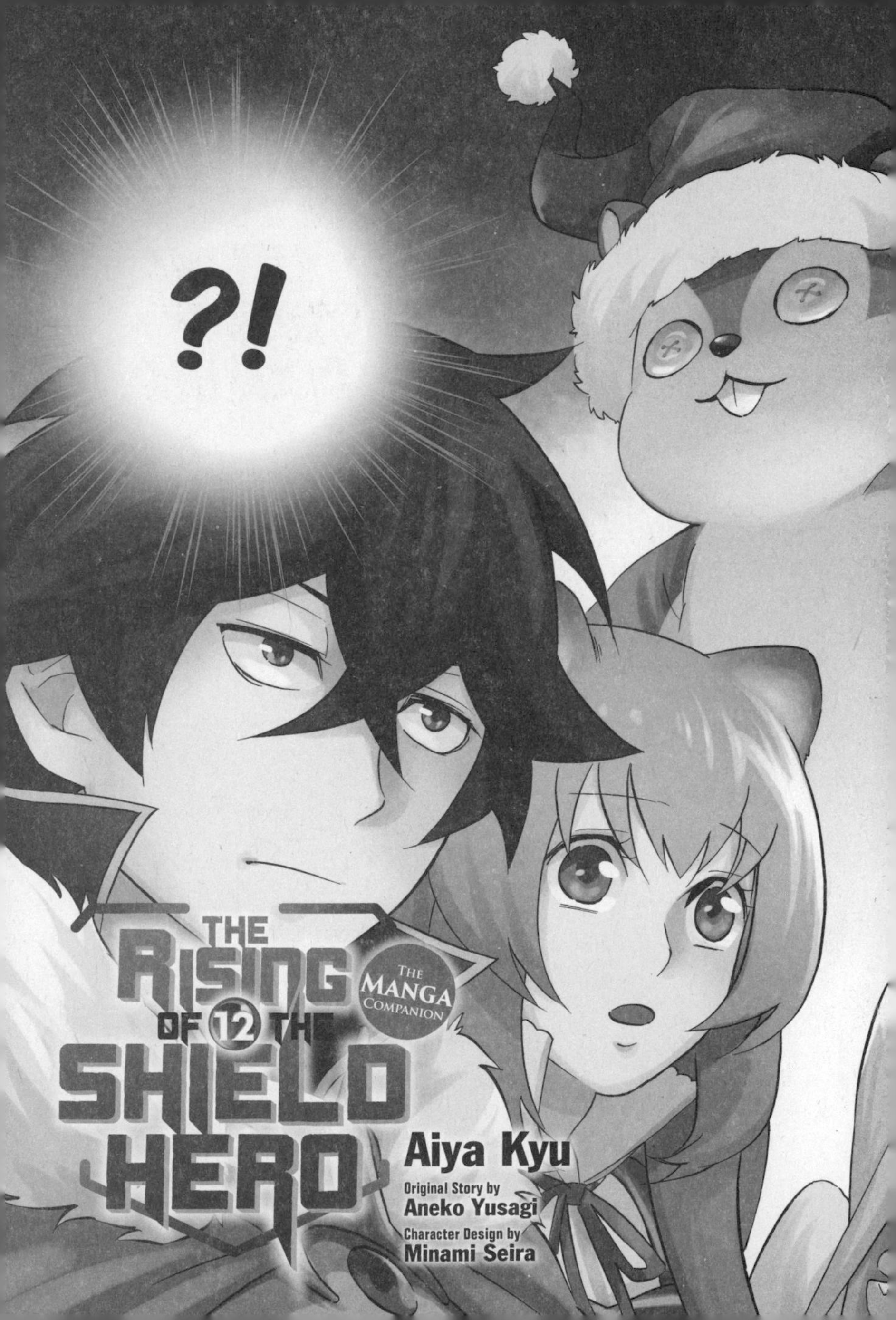
?!

THE RISING OF THE SHIELD HERO

THE MANGA COMPANION

12

Aiya Kyu

Original Story by
Aneko Yusagi

Character Design by
Minami Seira

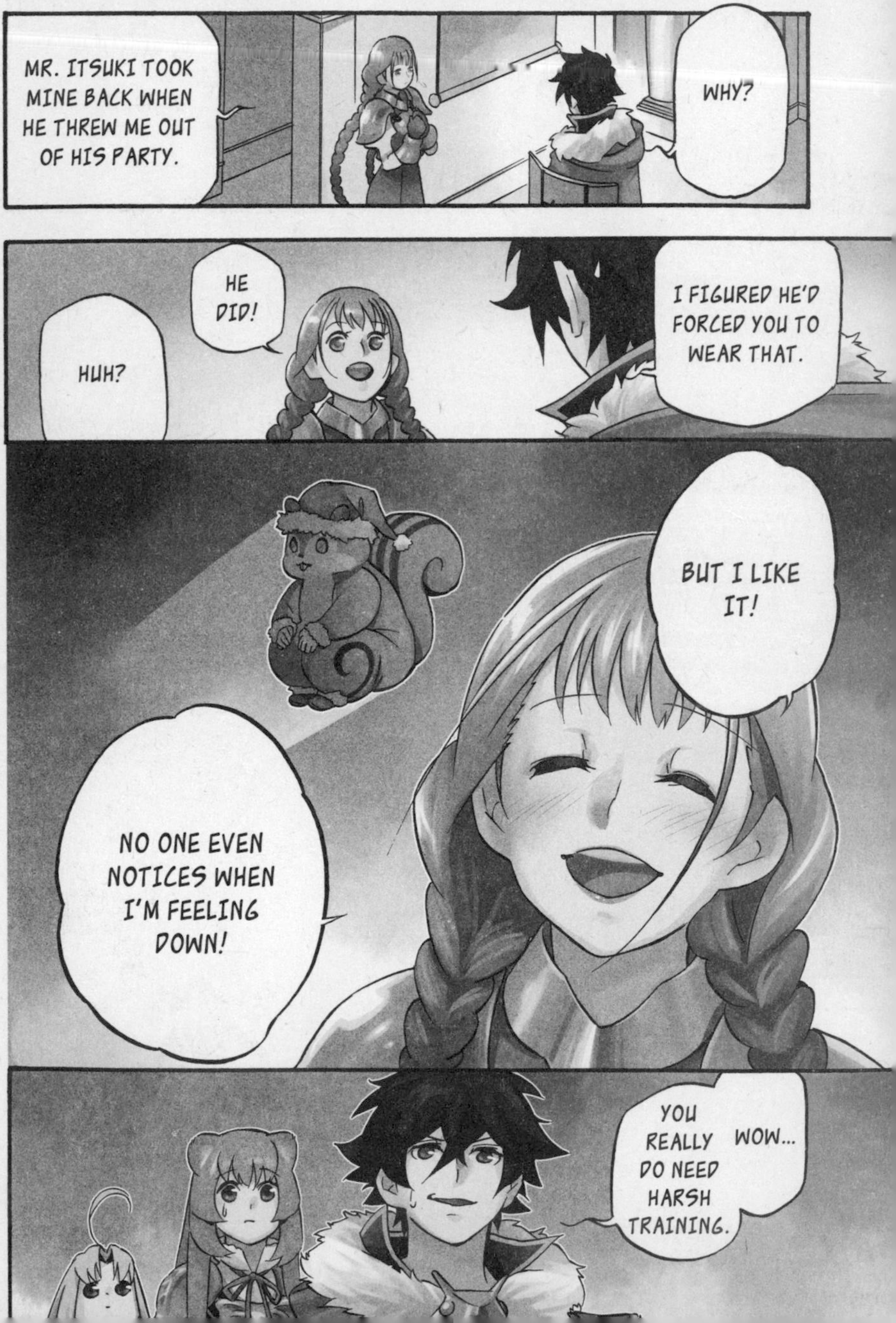
WHY?
MR. ITSUKI TOOK MINE BACK WHEN HE THREW ME OUT OF HIS PARTY.
I FIGURED HE'D FORCED YOU TO WEAR THAT.
HE DID!
HUH?
BUT I LIKE IT!
NO ONE EVEN NOTICES WHEN I'M FEELING DOWN!
WOW...
YOU REALLY DO NEED HARSH TRAINING.

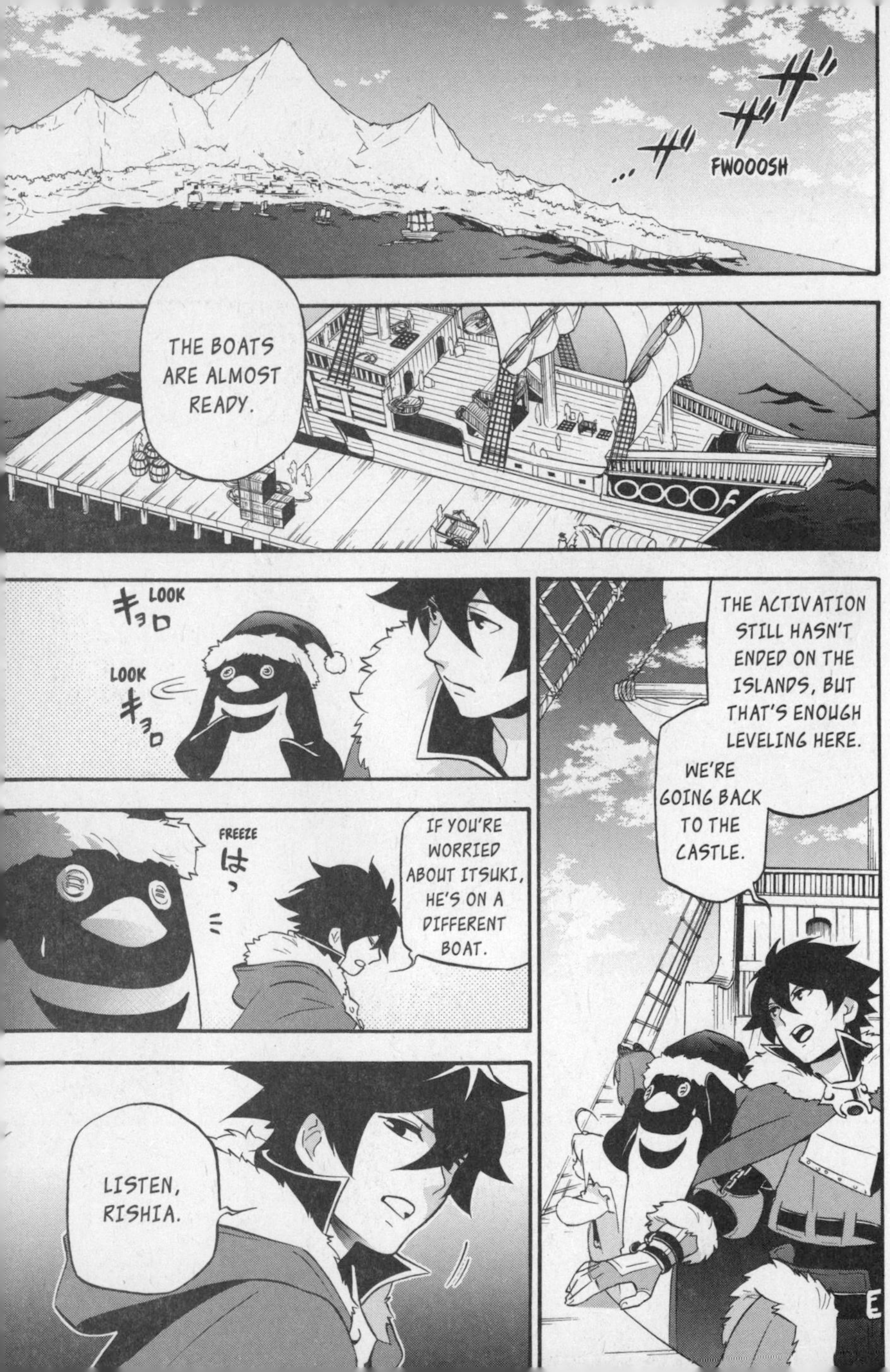
…ザザザザ
FWOOOSH
THE BOATS ARE ALMOST READY.
THE ACTIVATION STILL HASN'T ENDED ON THE ISLANDS, BUT THAT'S ENOUGH LEVELING HERE.
WE'RE GOING BACK TO THE CASTLE.
LOOK キョロ
LOOK キョロ
FREEZE は,
IF YOU'RE WORRIED ABOUT ITSUKI, HE'S ON A DIFFERENT BOAT.
LISTEN, RISHIA.

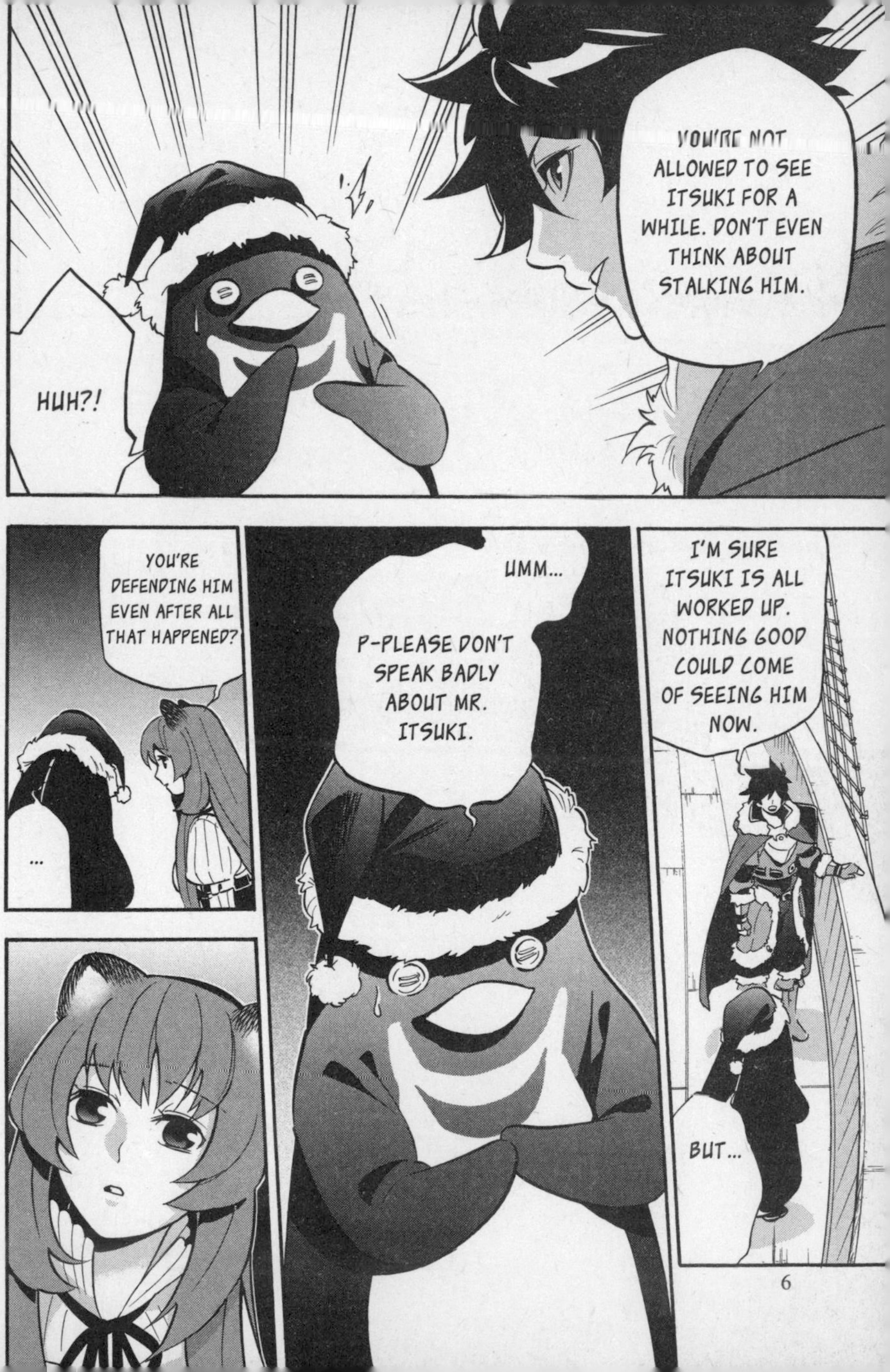
YOU'RE NOT ALLOWED TO SEE ITSUKI FOR A WHILE. DON'T EVEN THINK ABOUT STALKING HIM.
HUH?!
I'M SURE ITSUKI IS ALL WORKED UP. NOTHING GOOD COULD COME OF SEEING HIM NOW.
BUT...
UMM...
P-PLEASE DON'T SPEAK BADLY ABOUT MR. ITSUKI.
YOU'RE DEFENDING HIM EVEN AFTER ALL THAT HAPPENED?
...

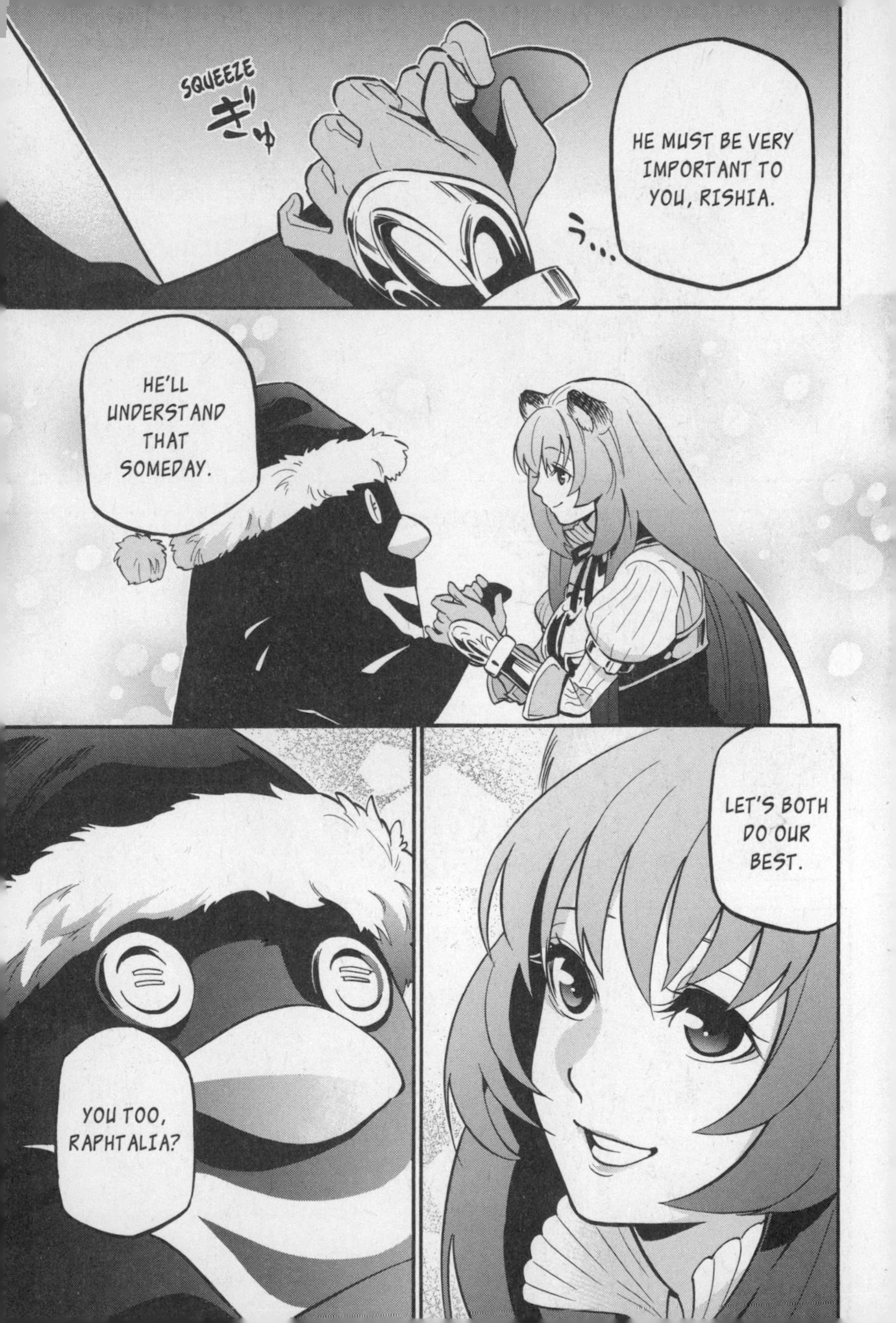
HE MUST BE VERY IMPORTANT TO YOU, RISHIA.
う…
SQUEEZE
ぎゅ
HE'LL UNDERSTAND THAT SOMEDAY.
LET'S BOTH DO OUR BEST.
YOU TOO, RAPHTALIA?

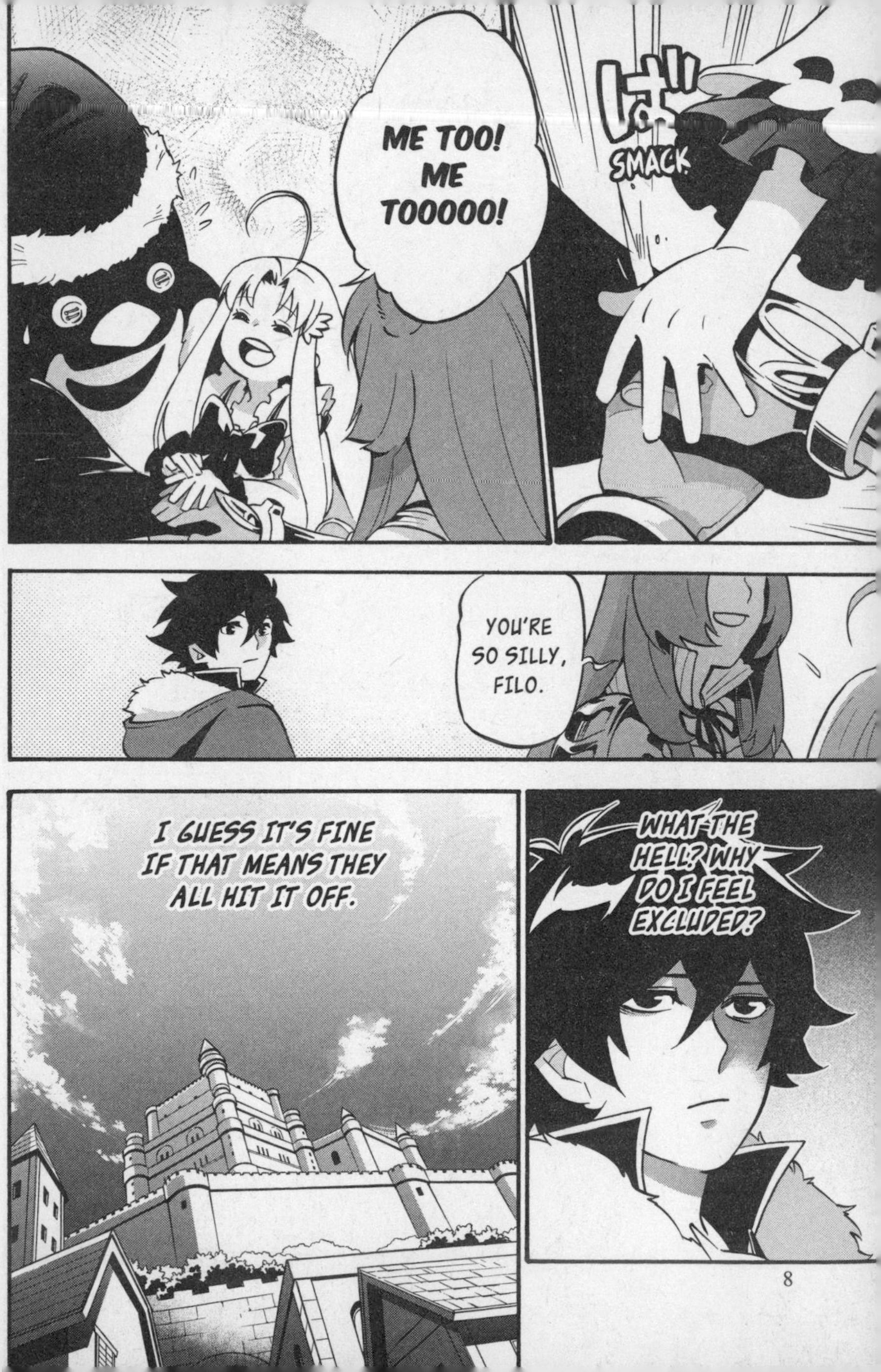
SMACK
ME TOO! ME TOOOOO!
YOU'RE SO SILLY, FILO.
WHAT THE HELL? WHY DO I FEEL EXCLUDED?
I GUESS IT'S FINE IF THAT MEANS THEY ALL HIT IT OFF.

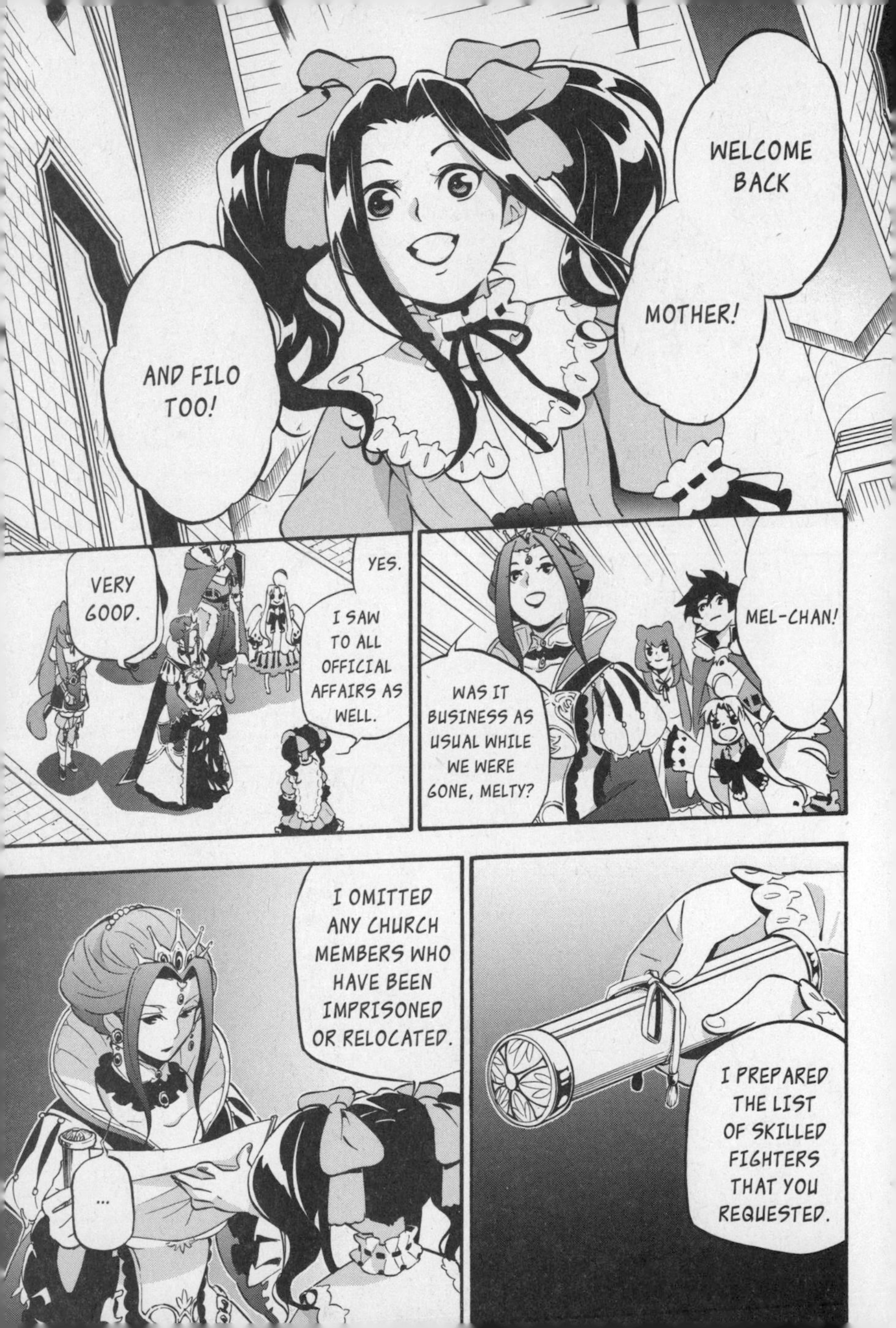
WELCOME BACK MOTHER!
AND FILO TOO!
MEL-CHAN!
WAS IT BUSINESS AS USUAL WHILE WE WERE GONE, MELTY?
YES.
I SAW TO ALL OFFICIAL AFFAIRS AS WELL.
VERY GOOD.
I PREPARED THE LIST OF SKILLED FIGHTERS THAT YOU REQUESTED.
I OMITTED ANY CHURCH MEMBERS WHO HAVE BEEN IMPRISONED OR RELOCATED.
...

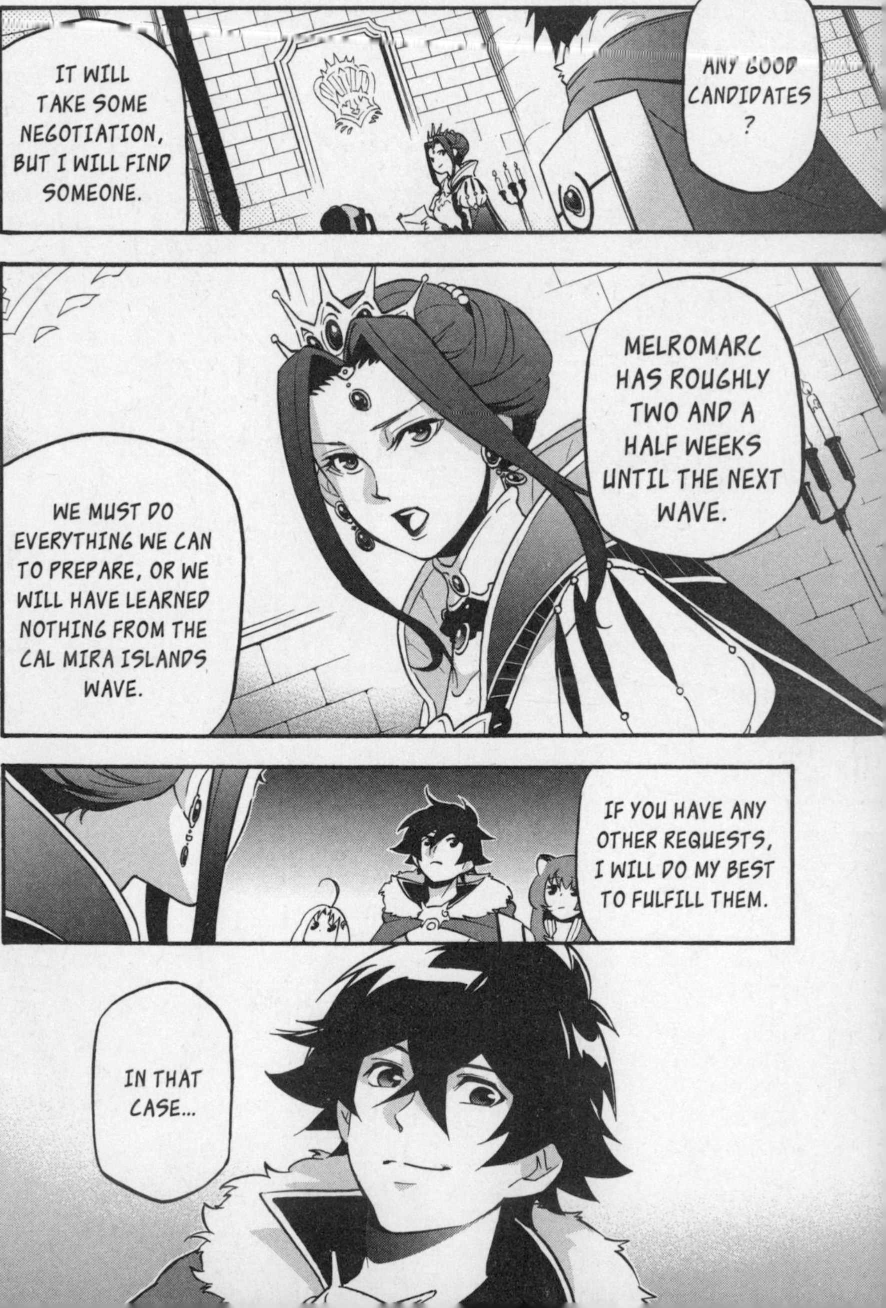
ANY GOOD CANDIDATES?
IT WILL TAKE SOME NEGOTIATION, BUT I WILL FIND SOMEONE.
MELROMARC HAS ROUGHLY TWO AND A HALF WEEKS UNTIL THE NEXT WAVE.
WE MUST DO EVERYTHING WE CAN TO PREPARE, OR WE WILL HAVE LEARNED NOTHING FROM THE CAL MIRA ISLANDS WAVE.
IF YOU HAVE ANY OTHER REQUESTS, I WILL DO MY BEST TO FULFILL THEM.
IN THAT CASE...

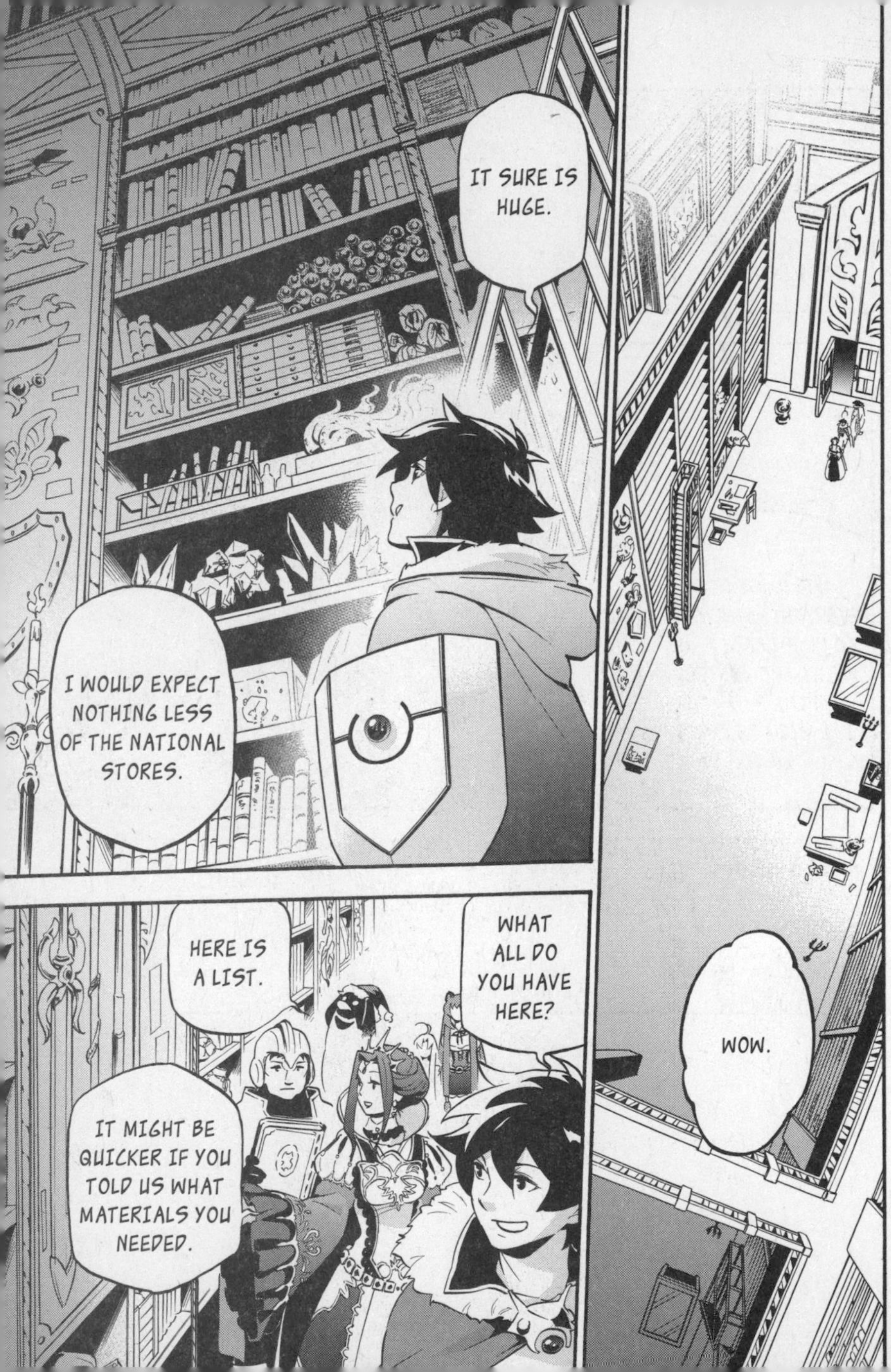
WOW.
IT SURE IS HUGE.
I WOULD EXPECT NOTHING LESS OF THE NATIONAL STORES.
WHAT ALL DO YOU HAVE HERE?
HERE IS A LIST.
IT MIGHT BE QUICKER IF YOU TOLD US WHAT MATERIALS YOU NEEDED.

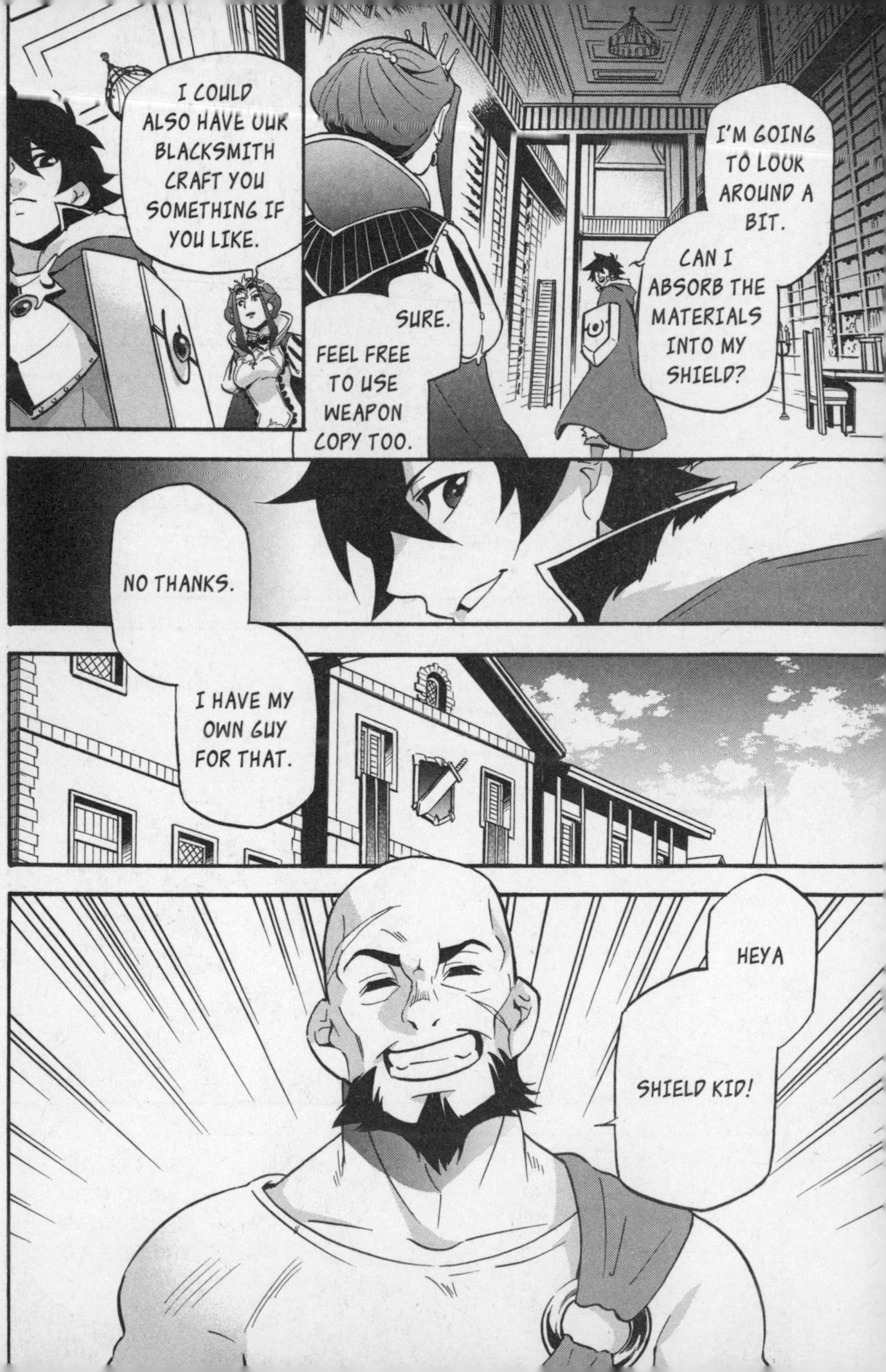
I'M GOING TO LOOK AROUND A BIT.
CAN I ABSORB THE MATERIALS INTO MY SHIELD?
SURE.
FEEL FREE TO USE WEAPON COPY TOO.
I COULD ALSO HAVE OUR BLACKSMITH CRAFT YOU SOMETHING IF YOU LIKE.
NO THANKS.
I HAVE MY OWN GUY FOR THAT.
HEYA
SHIELD KID!

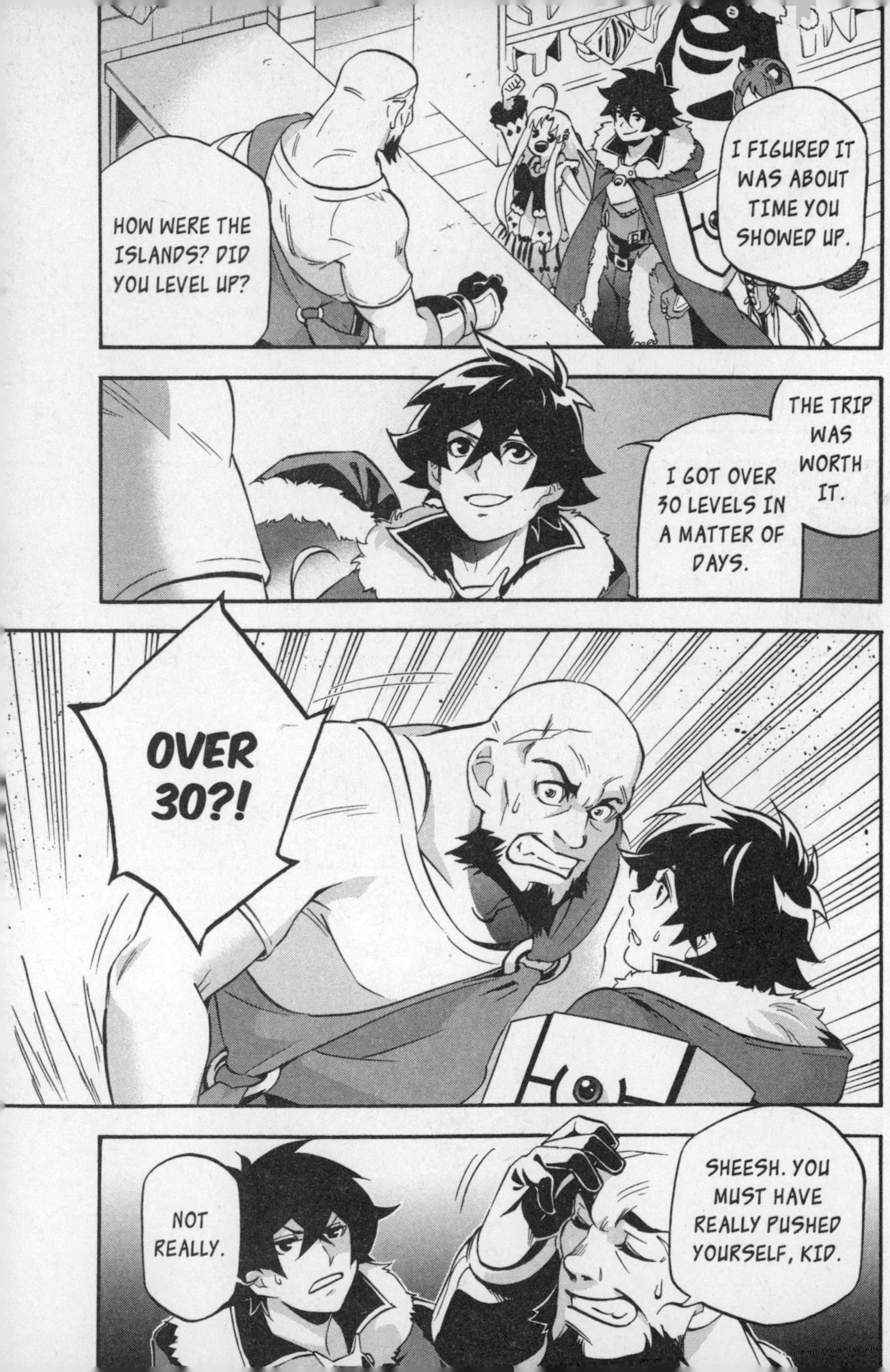
I FIGURED IT WAS ABOUT TIME YOU SHOWED UP.
HOW WERE THE ISLANDS? DID YOU LEVEL UP?
THE TRIP WAS WORTH IT.
I GOT OVER 30 LEVELS IN A MATTER OF DAYS.
OVER 30?!
SHEESH. YOU MUST HAVE REALLY PUSHED YOURSELF, KID.
NOT REALLY.

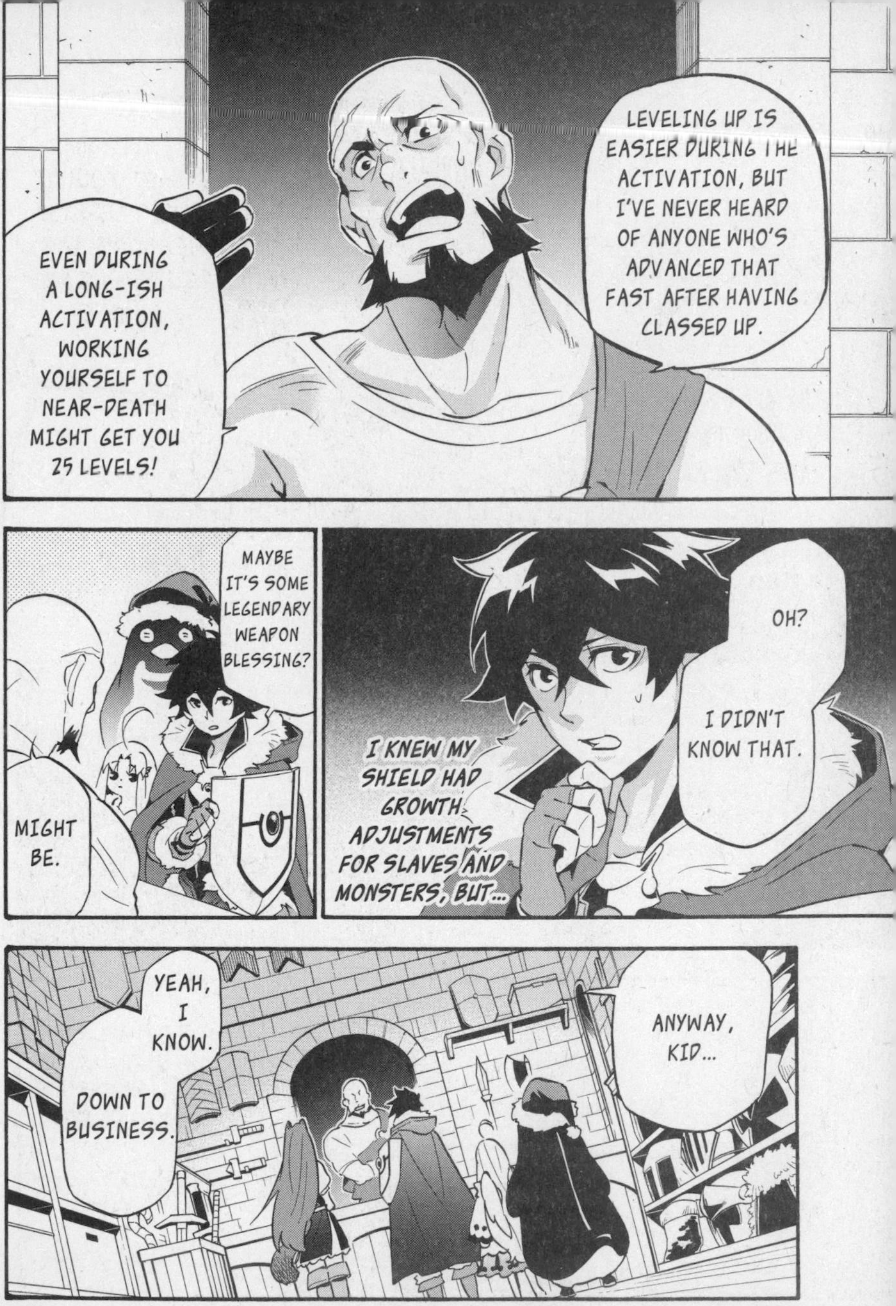
LEVELING UP IS EASIER DURING THE ACTIVATION, BUT I'VE NEVER HEARD OF ANYONE WHO'S ADVANCED THAT FAST AFTER HAVING CLASSED UP.
EVEN DURING A LONG-ISH ACTIVATION, WORKING YOURSELF TO NEAR-DEATH MIGHT GET YOU 25 LEVELS!
OH?
I DIDN'T KNOW THAT.
I KNEW MY SHIELD HAD GROWTH ADJUSTMENTS FOR SLAVES AND MONSTERS, BUT...
MAYBE IT'S SOME LEGENDARY WEAPON BLESSING?
MIGHT BE.
ANYWAY, KID...
YEAH, I KNOW.
DOWN TO BUSINESS.

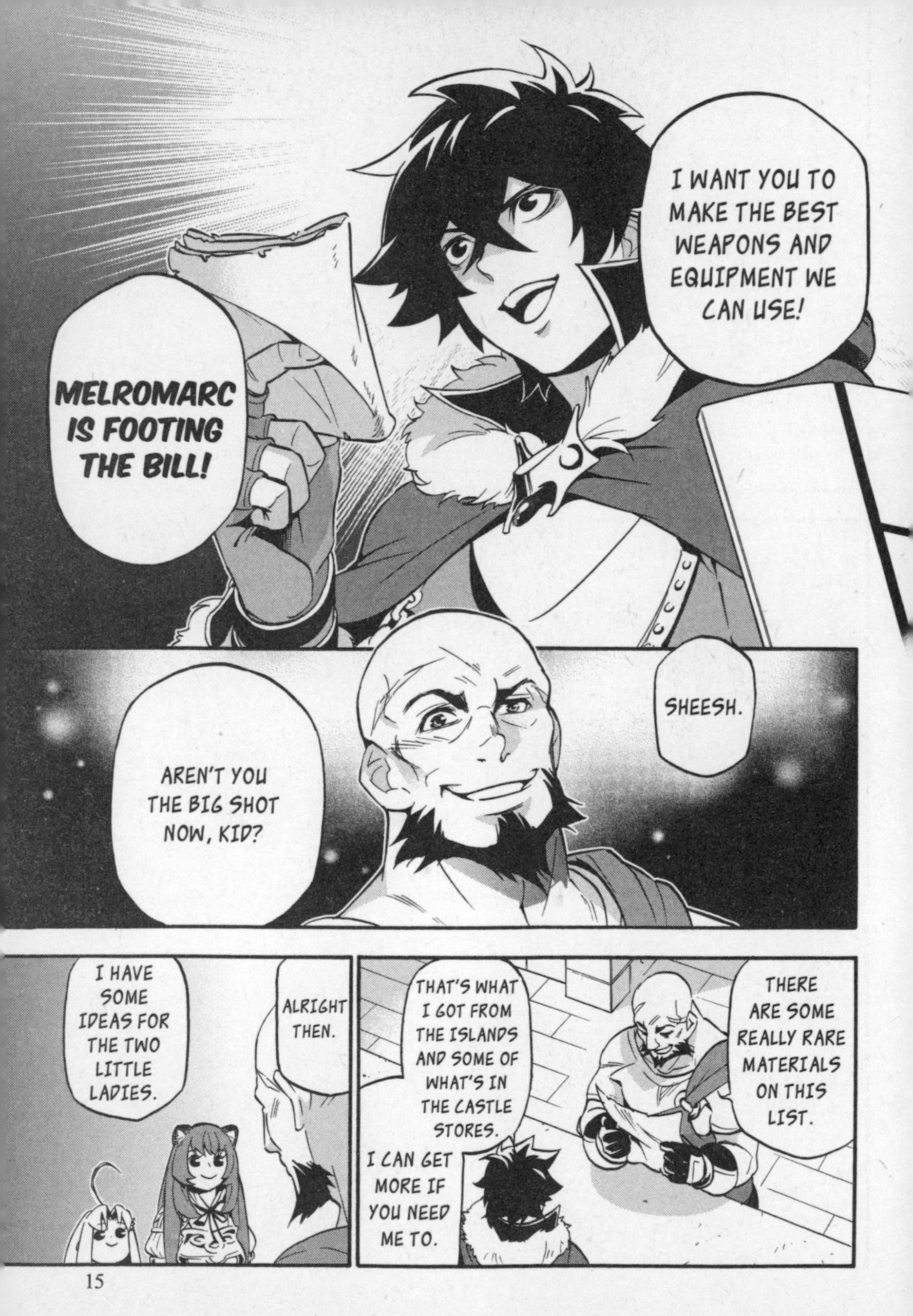
I WANT YOU TO MAKE THE BEST WEAPONS AND EQUIPMENT WE CAN USE!
MELROMARC IS FOOTING THE BILL!
SHEESH.
AREN'T YOU THE BIG SHOT NOW, KID?
THERE ARE SOME REALLY RARE MATERIALS ON THIS LIST.
THAT'S WHAT I GOT FROM THE ISLANDS AND SOME OF WHAT'S IN THE CASTLE STORES.
I CAN GET MORE IF YOU NEED ME TO.
ALRIGHT THEN.
I HAVE SOME IDEAS FOR THE TWO LITTLE LADIES.

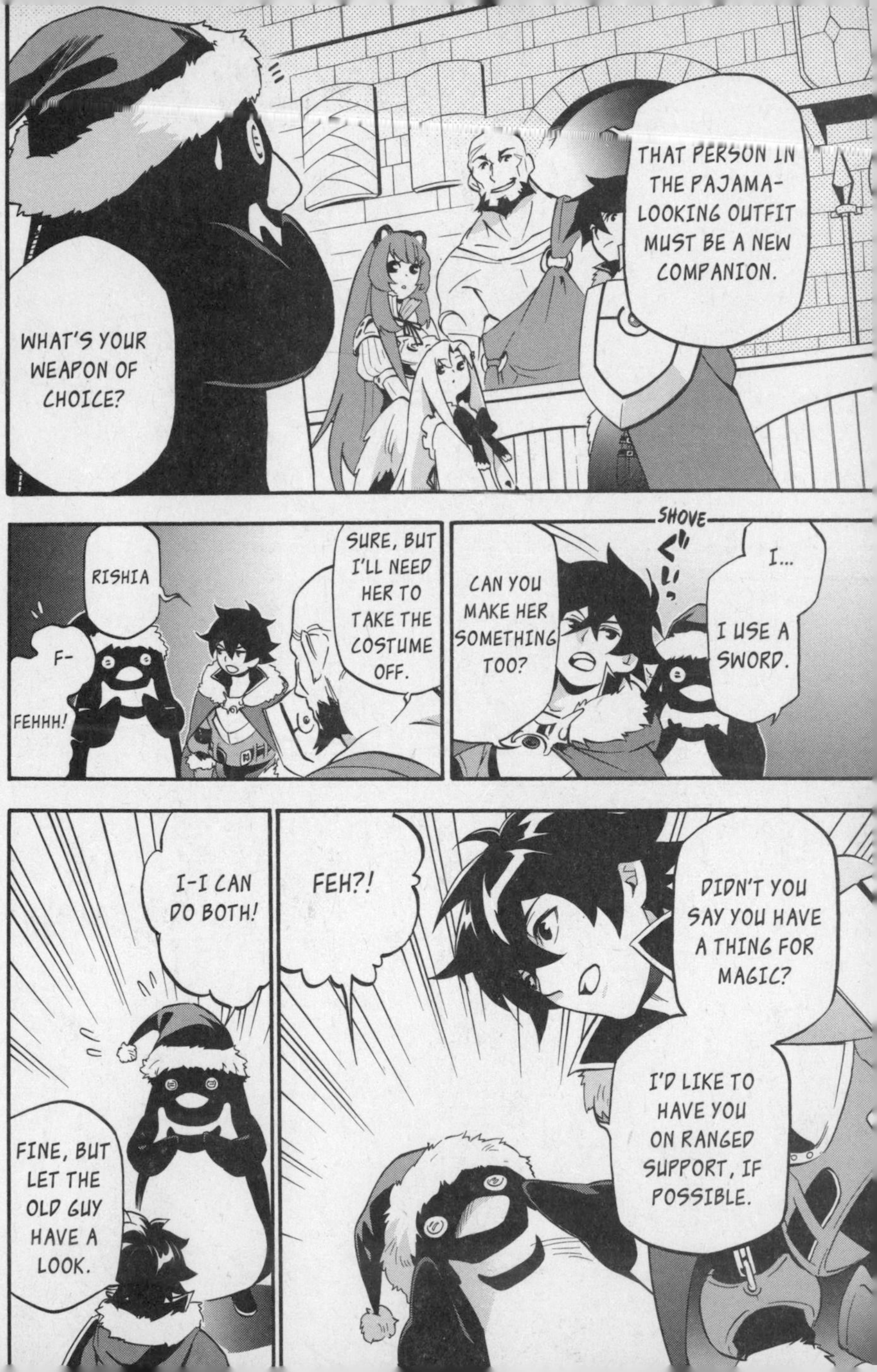

THAT PERSON IN THE PAJAMA-LOOKING OUTFIT MUST BE A NEW COMPANION.
WHAT'S YOUR WEAPON OF CHOICE?
SHOVE
I...
I USE A SWORD.
CAN YOU MAKE HER SOMETHING TOO?
SURE, BUT I'LL NEED HER TO TAKE THE COSTUME OFF.
RISHIA
F-
FEHHH!
DIDN'T YOU SAY YOU HAVE A THING FOR MAGIC?
I'D LIKE TO HAVE YOU ON RANGED SUPPORT, IF POSSIBLE.
FEH?!
I-I CAN DO BOTH!
FINE, BUT LET THE OLD GUY HAVE A LOOK.

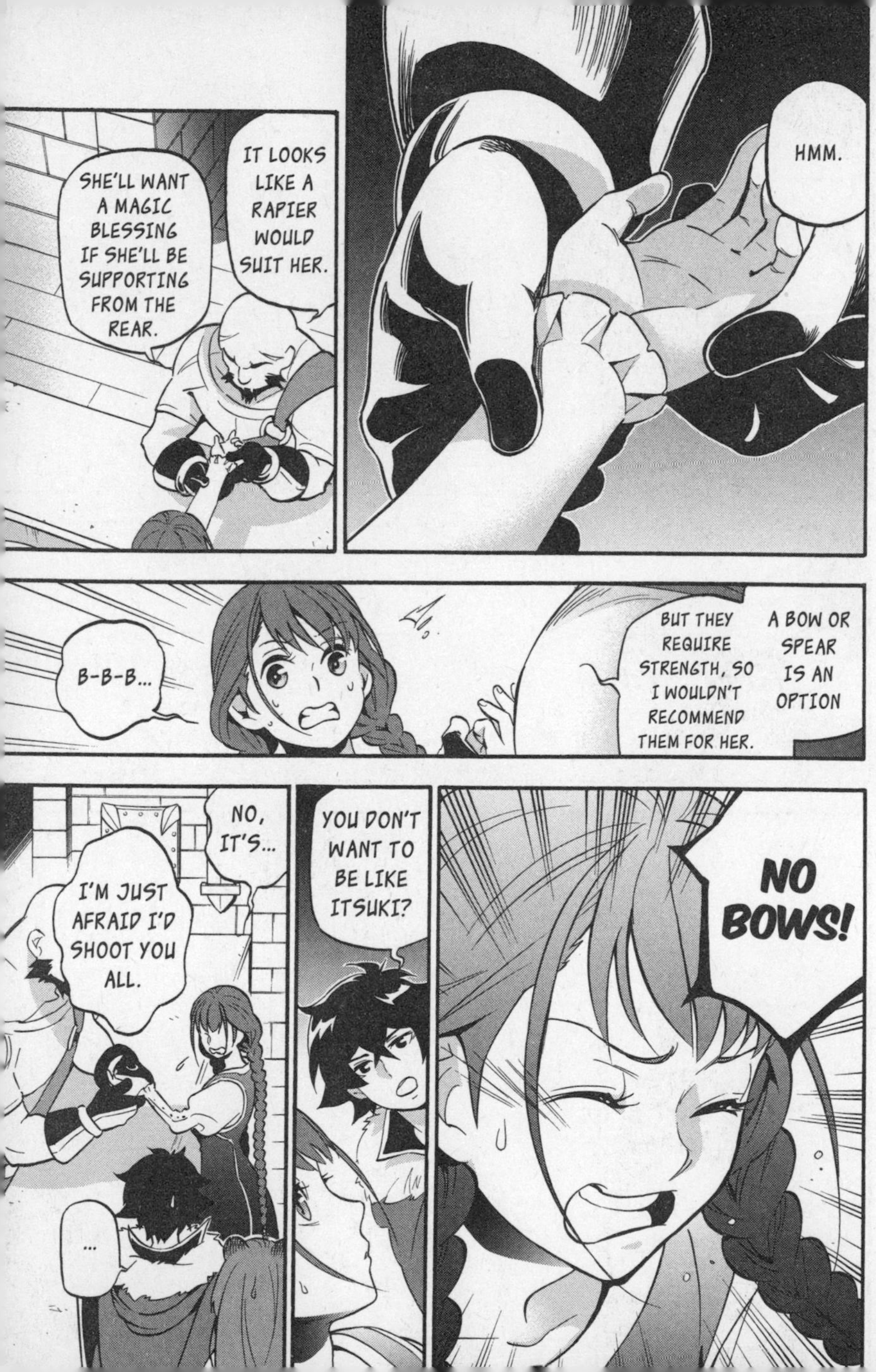
HMM.
IT LOOKS LIKE A RAPIER WOULD SUIT HER.
SHE'LL WANT A MAGIC BLESSING IF SHE'LL BE SUPPORTING FROM THE REAR.
A BOW OR SPEAR IS AN OPTION
BUT THEY REQUIRE STRENGTH, SO I WOULDN'T RECOMMEND THEM FOR HER.
B-B-B...
NO BOWS!
YOU DON'T WANT TO BE LIKE ITSUKI?
NO, IT'S...
I'M JUST AFRAID I'D SHOOT YOU ALL.
...

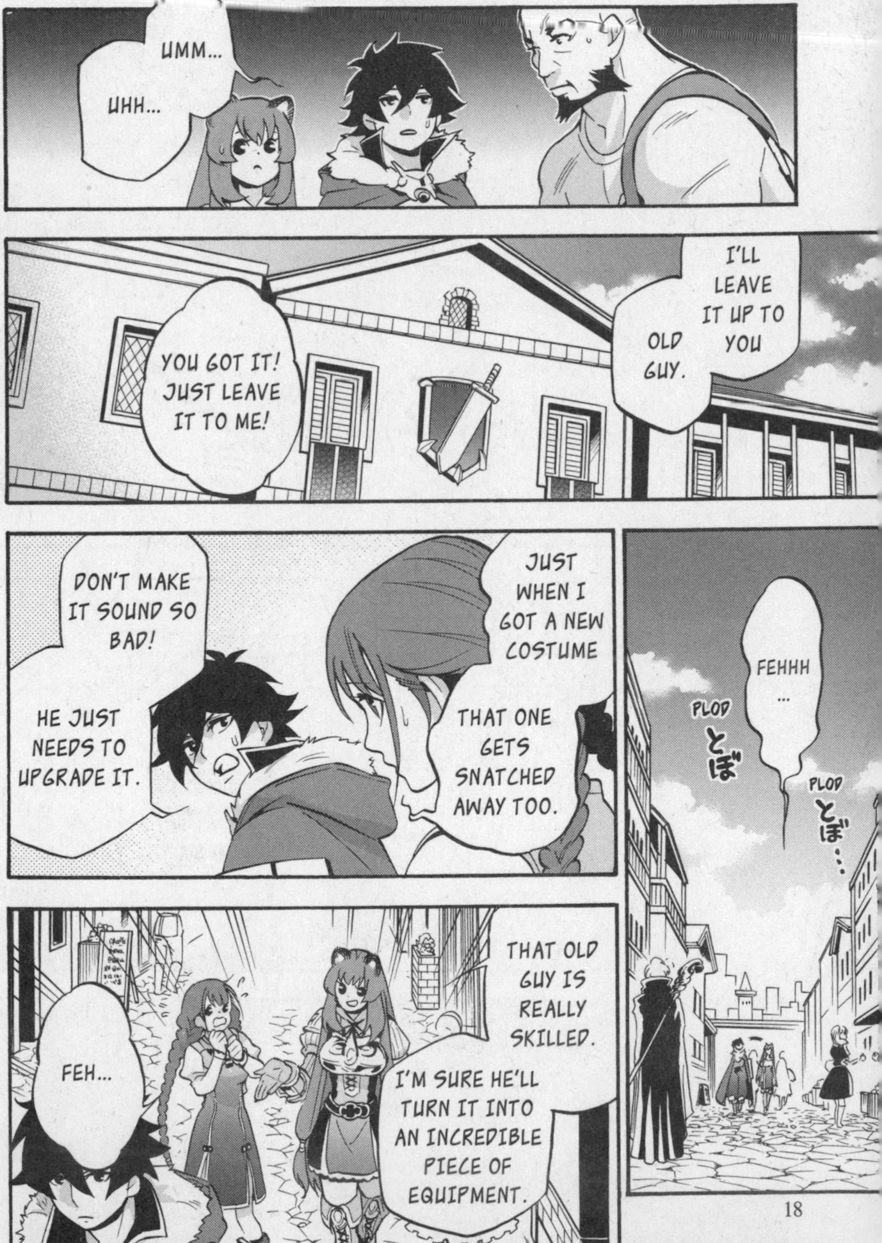
UMM...
UHH...
I'LL LEAVE IT UP TO YOU OLD GUY.
YOU GOT IT! JUST LEAVE IT TO ME!
FEHHH...
PLOD とぼ
PLOD とぼ...
JUST WHEN I GOT A NEW COSTUME
THAT ONE GETS SNATCHED AWAY TOO.
DON'T MAKE IT SOUND SO BAD!
HE JUST NEEDS TO UPGRADE IT.
THAT OLD GUY IS REALLY SKILLED.
I'M SURE HE'LL TURN IT INTO AN INCREDIBLE PIECE OF EQUIPMENT.
FEH...

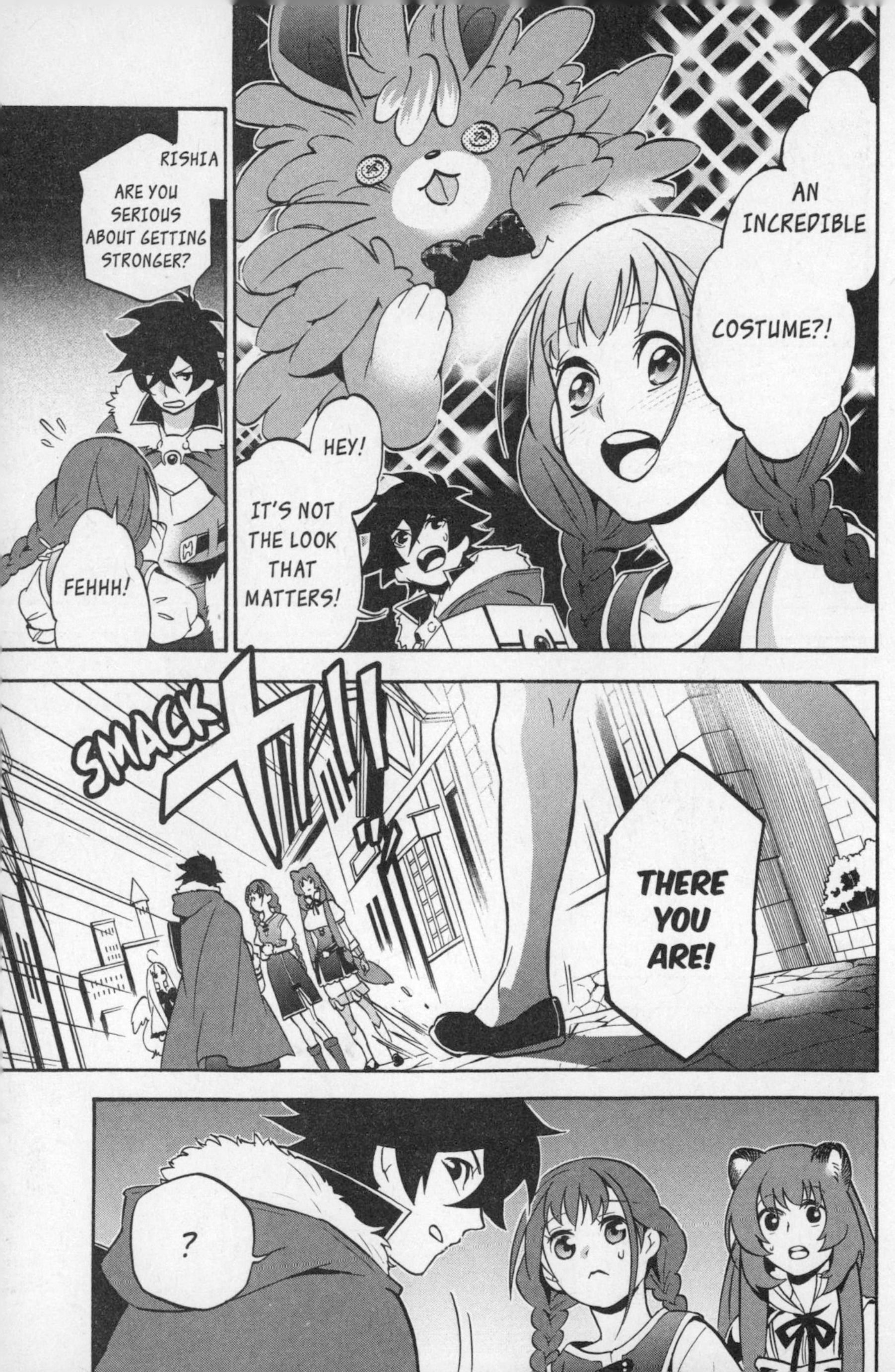
AN INCREDIBLE COSTUME?!
HEY!
IT'S NOT THE LOOK THAT MATTERS!
RISHIA
ARE YOU SERIOUS ABOUT GETTING STRONGER?
FEHHH!
SMACK
THERE YOU ARE!
?

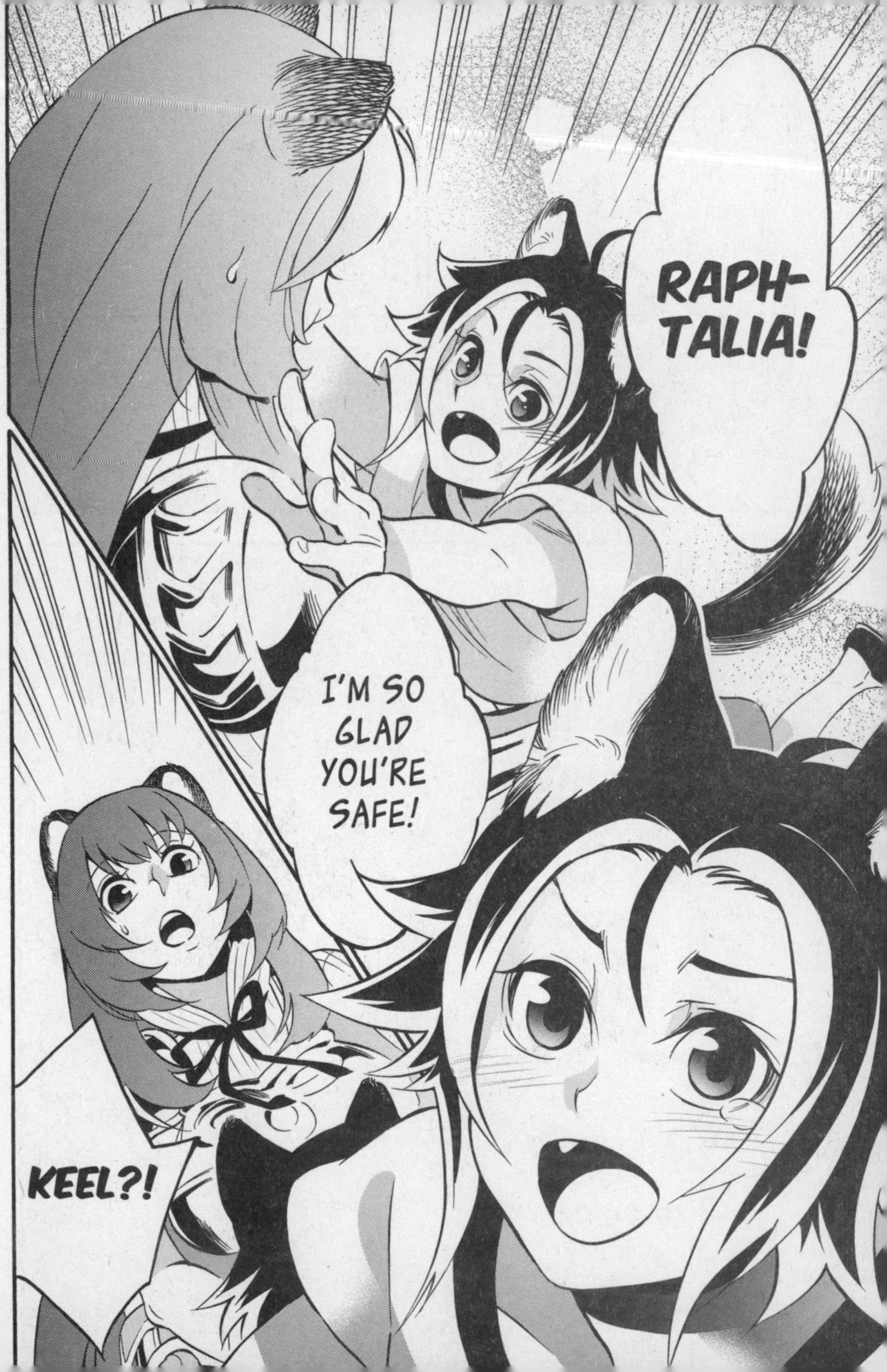
RAPH-TALIA!
I'M SO GLAD YOU'RE SAFE!
KEEL?!

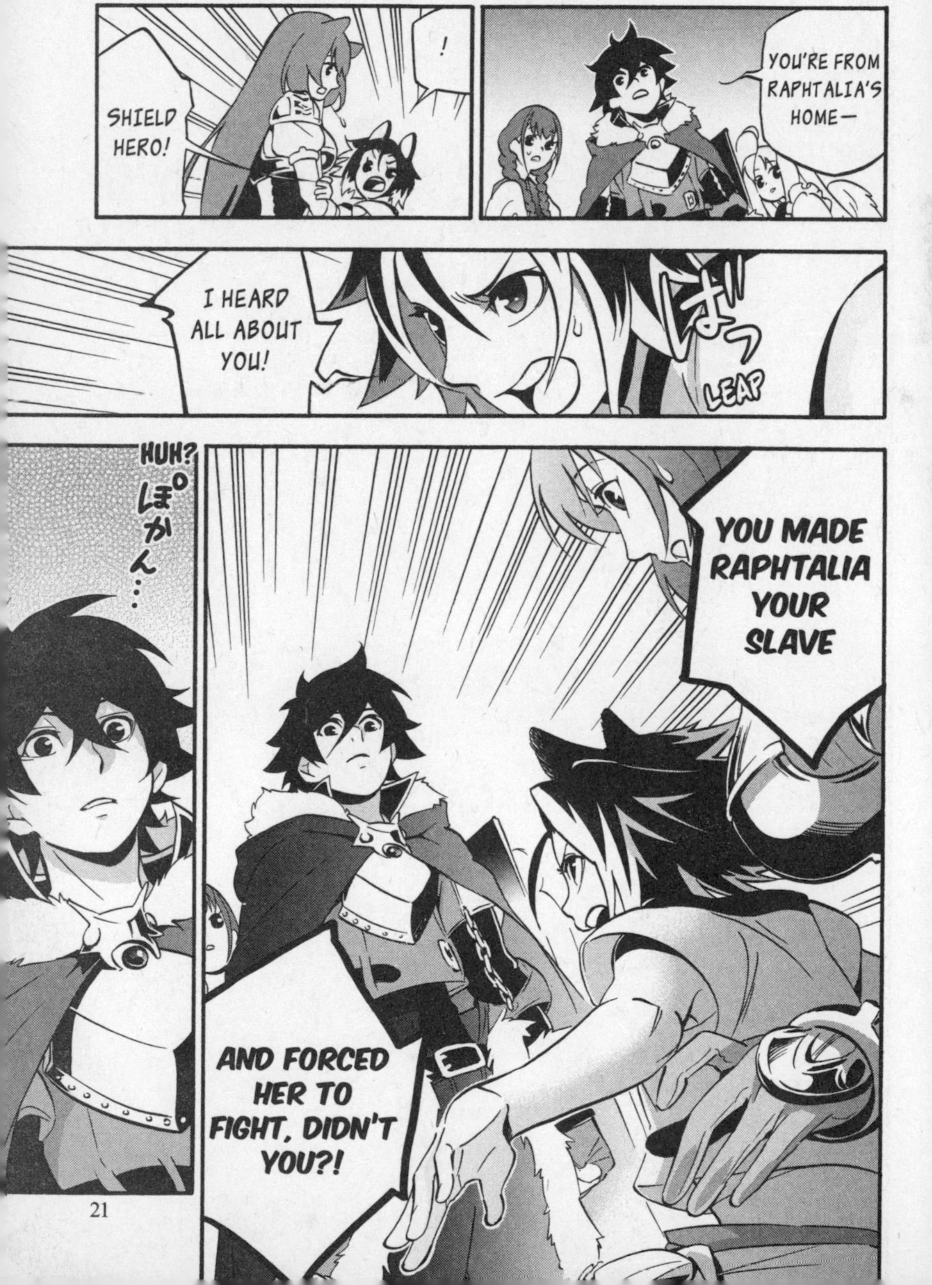
YOU'RE FROM RAPHTALIA'S HOME—
!
SHIELD HERO!
ばっ
LEAP
I HEARD ALL ABOUT YOU!
YOU MADE RAPHTALIA YOUR SLAVE
AND FORCED HER TO FIGHT, DIDN'T YOU?!
HUH?
ぽかん…

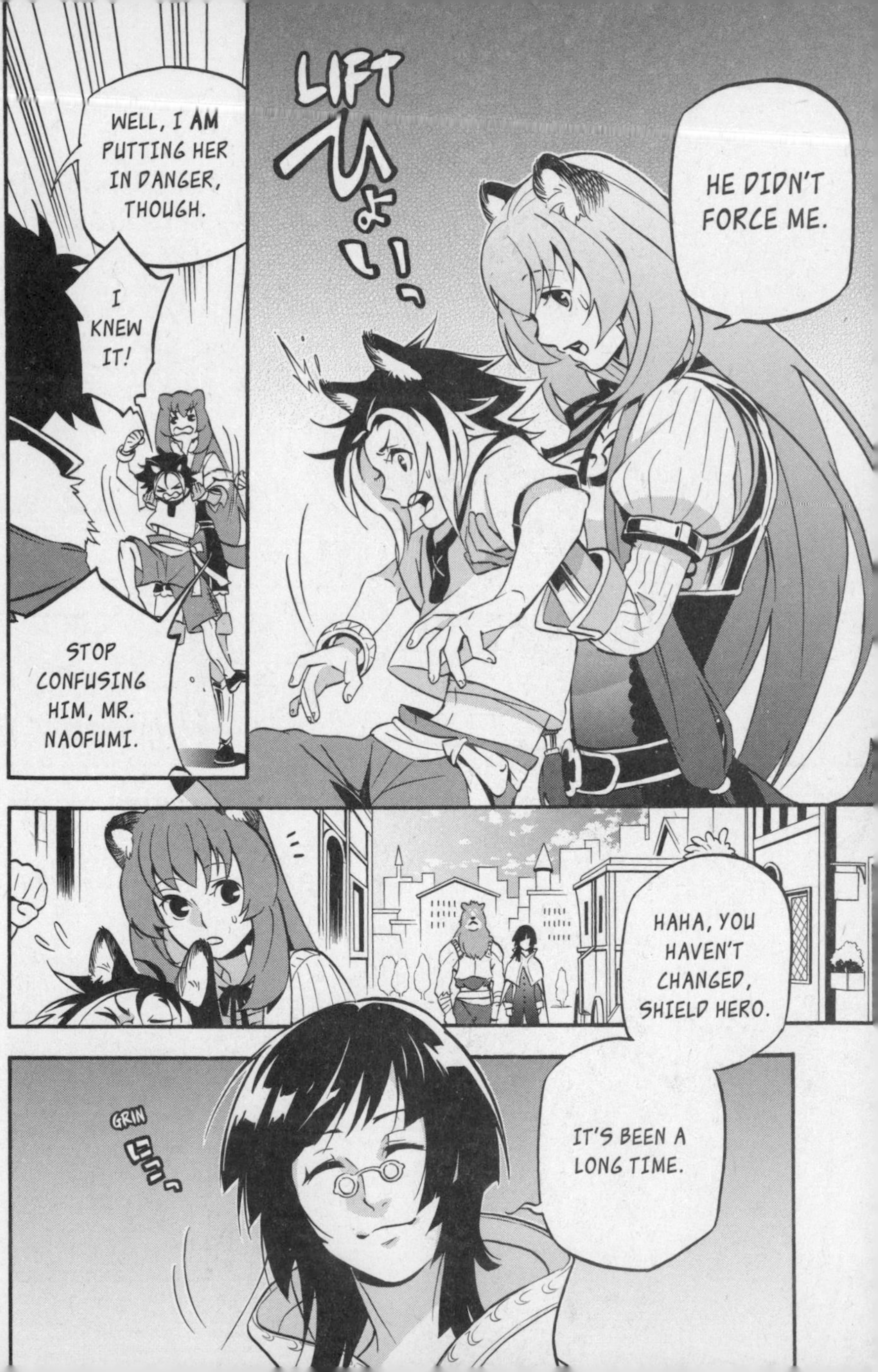
HE DIDN'T FORCE ME.
LIFT
ひょいー
WELL, I AM PUTTING HER IN DANGER, THOUGH.
I KNEW IT!
STOP CONFUSING HIM, MR. NAOFUMI.
HAHA, YOU HAVEN'T CHANGED, SHIELD HERO.
GRIN
IT'S BEEN A LONG TIME.

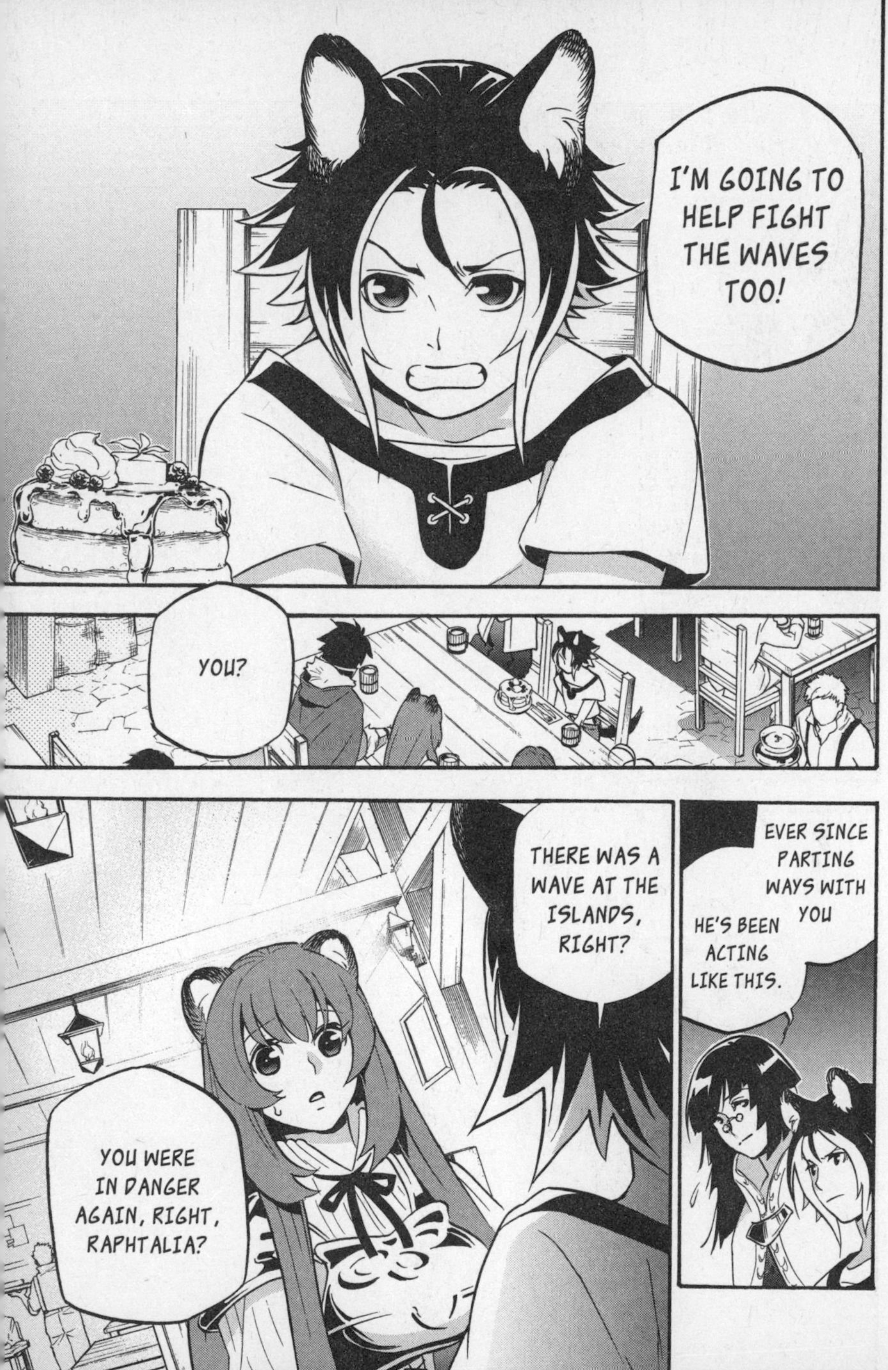
I'M GOING TO HELP FIGHT THE WAVES TOO!
YOU?
EVER SINCE PARTING WAYS WITH YOU
HE'S BEEN ACTING LIKE THIS.
THERE WAS A WAVE AT THE ISLANDS, RIGHT?
YOU WERE IN DANGER AGAIN, RIGHT, RAPHTALIA?

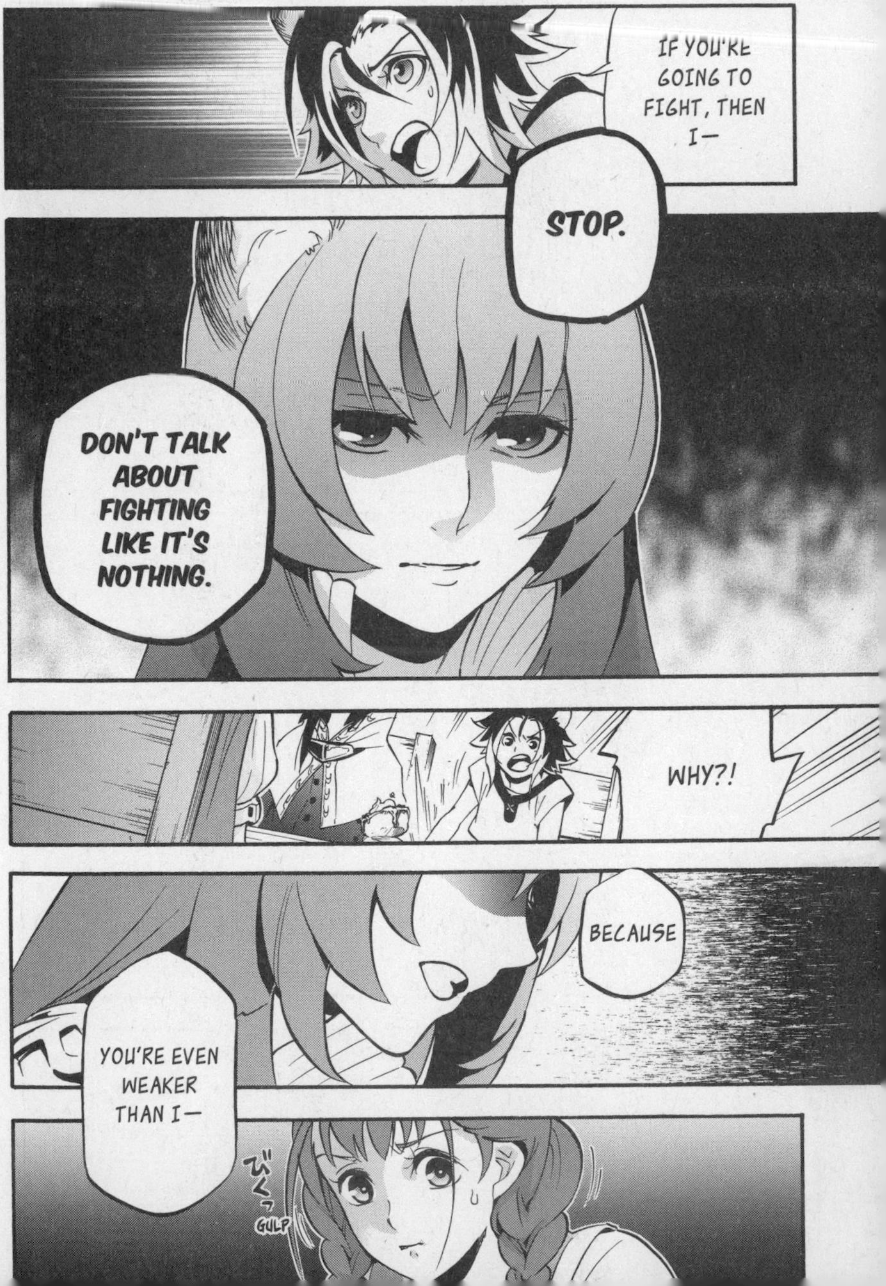
IF YOU'RE GOING TO FIGHT, THEN I—
STOP.
DON'T TALK ABOUT FIGHTING LIKE IT'S NOTHING.
WHY?!
BECAUSE
YOU'RE EVEN WEAKER THAN I—
びくっ
GULP

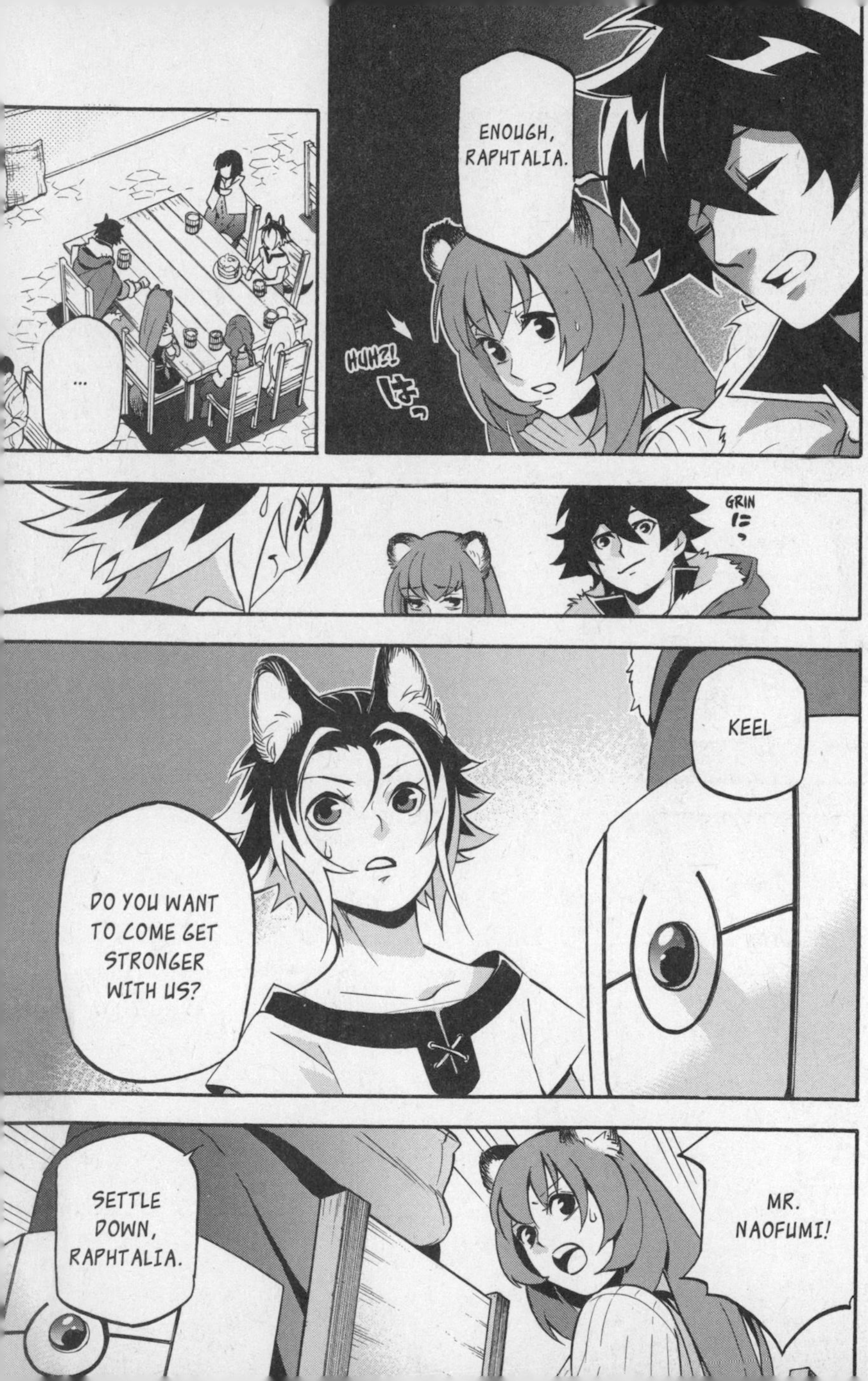
ENOUGH, RAPHTALIA.
HUH?!
はっ
...
GRIN
にっ
KEEL
DO YOU WANT TO COME GET STRONGER WITH US?
MR. NAOFUMI!
SETTLE DOWN, RAPHTALIA.

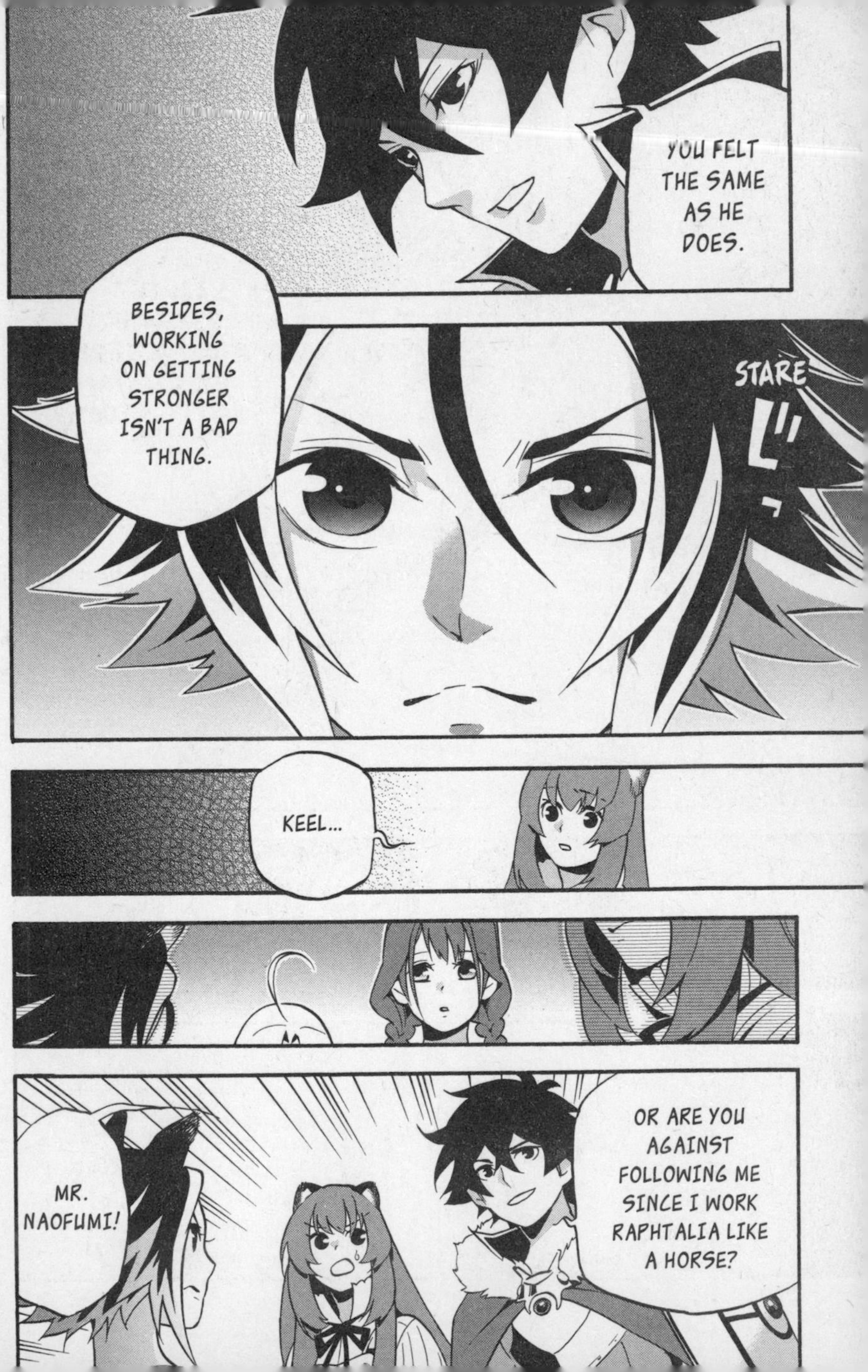
YOU FELT THE SAME AS HE DOES.
BESIDES, WORKING ON GETTING STRONGER ISN'T A BAD THING.
STARE
KEEL...
OR ARE YOU AGAINST FOLLOWING ME SINCE I WORK RAPHTALIA LIKE A HORSE?
MR. NAOFUMI!

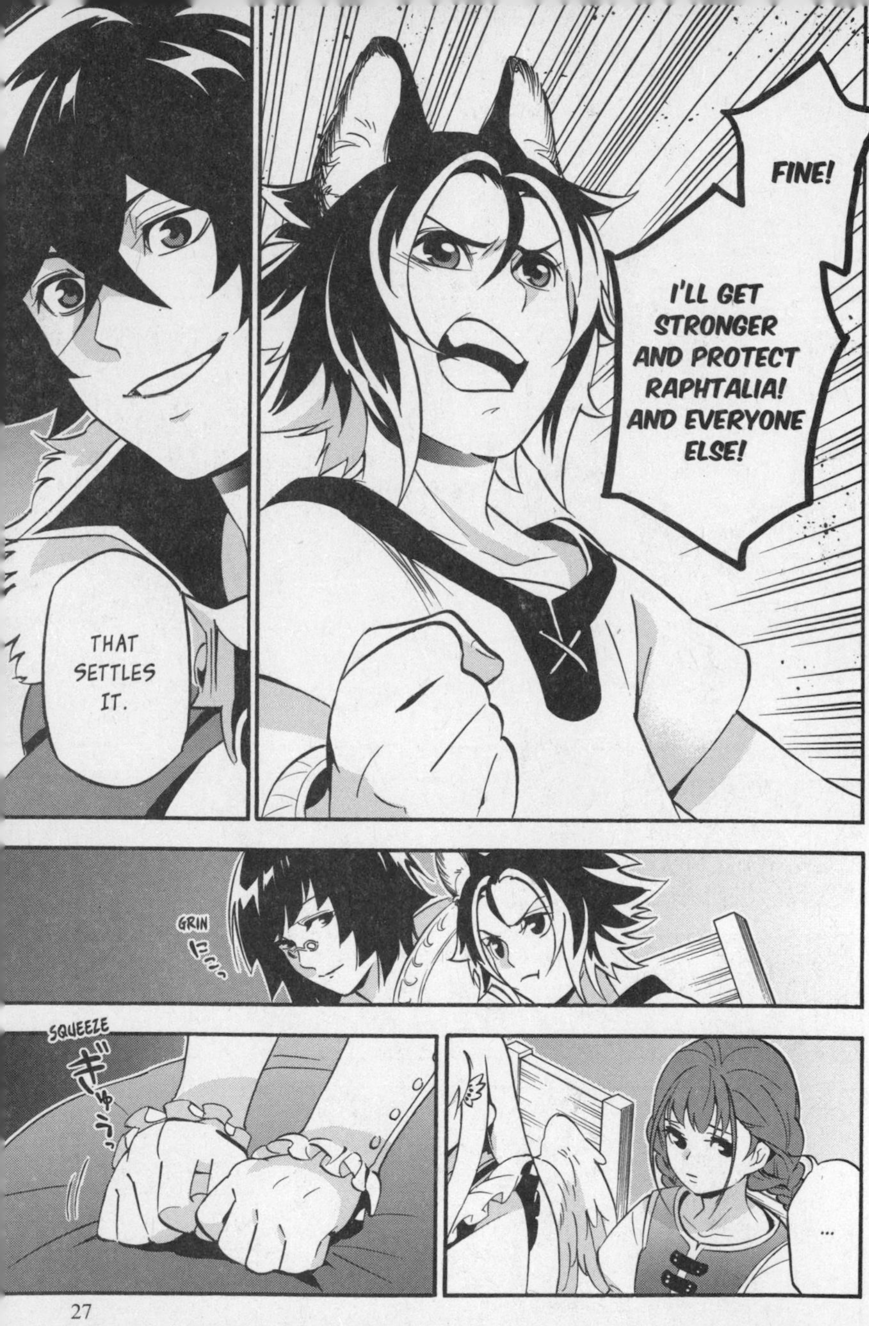
FINE!
I'LL GET STRONGER AND PROTECT RAPHTALIA! AND EVERYONE ELSE!
THAT SETTLES IT.
GRIN
...
SQUEEZE

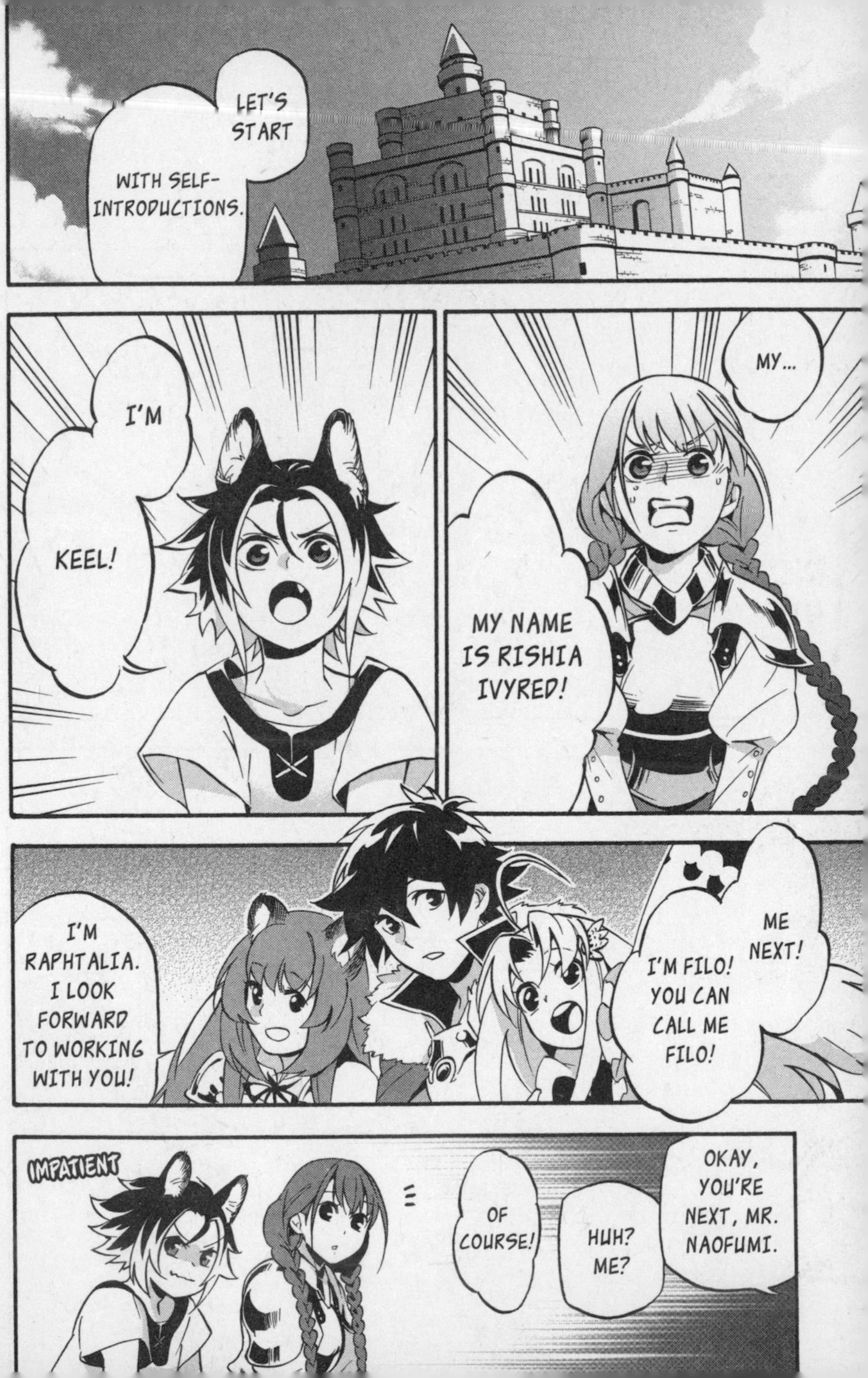
LET'S START WITH SELF-INTRODUCTIONS.
MY...
MY NAME IS RISHIA IVYRED!
I'M KEEL!
ME NEXT!
I'M FILO! YOU CAN CALL ME FILO!
I'M RAPHTALIA. I LOOK FORWARD TO WORKING WITH YOU!
OKAY, YOU'RE NEXT, MR. NAOFUMI.
HUH? ME?
OF COURSE!
IMPATIENT

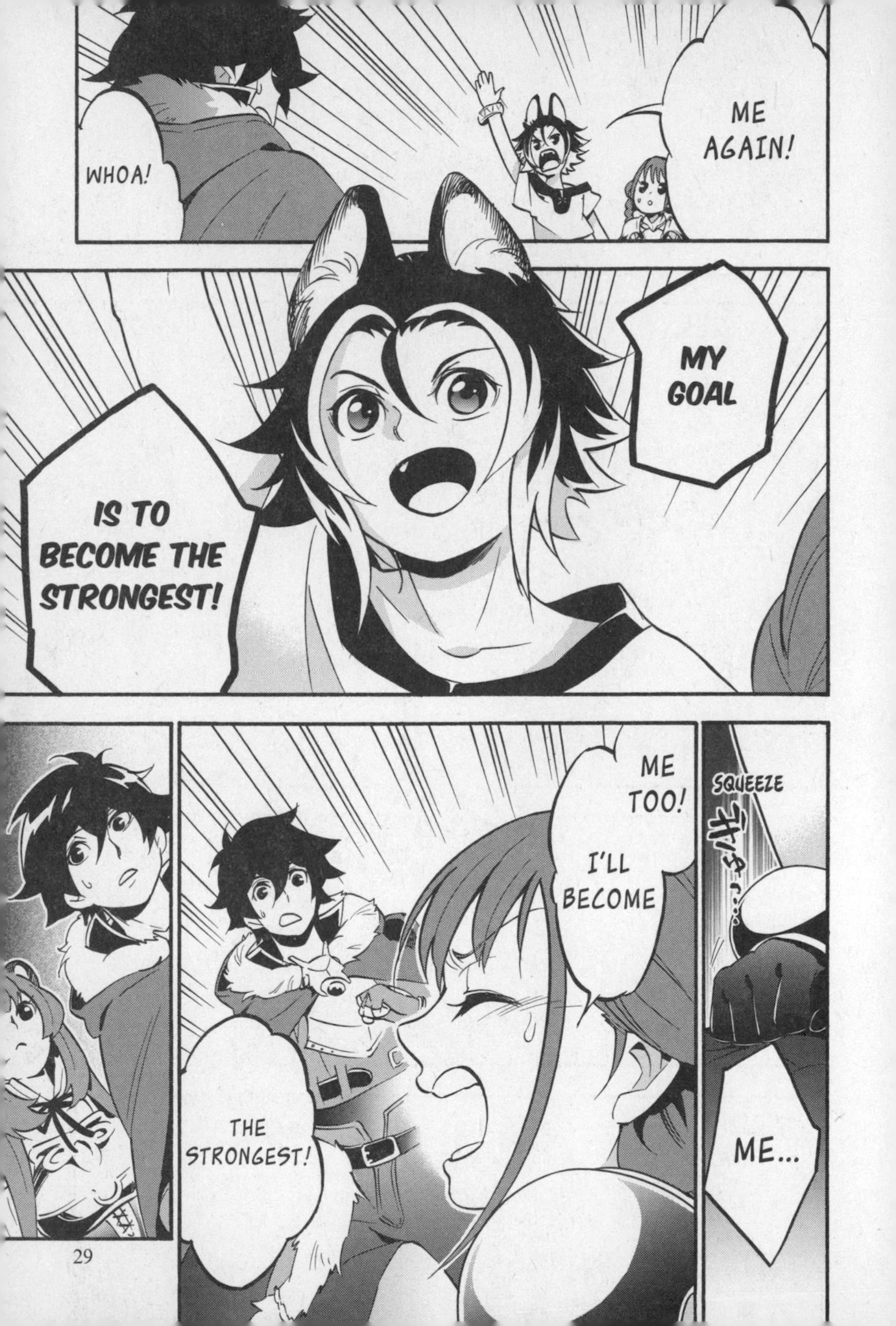
ME AGAIN!
WHOA!
MY GOAL
IS TO BECOME THE STRONGEST!
SQUEEZE
ME...
ME TOO!
I'LL BECOME
THE STRONGEST!

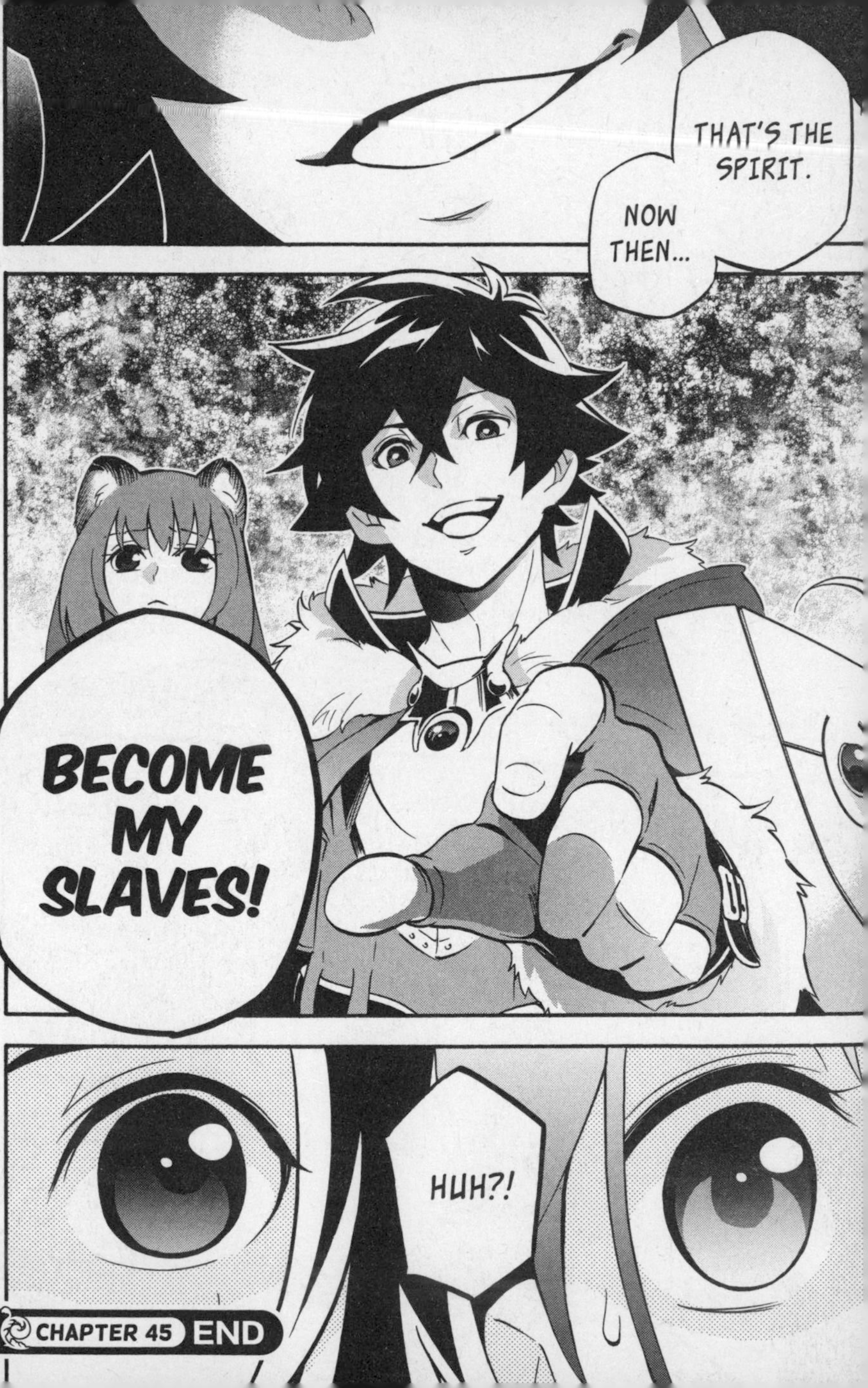
THAT'S THE SPIRIT.
NOW THEN...
BECOME MY SLAVES!
HUH?!
CHAPTER 45 END

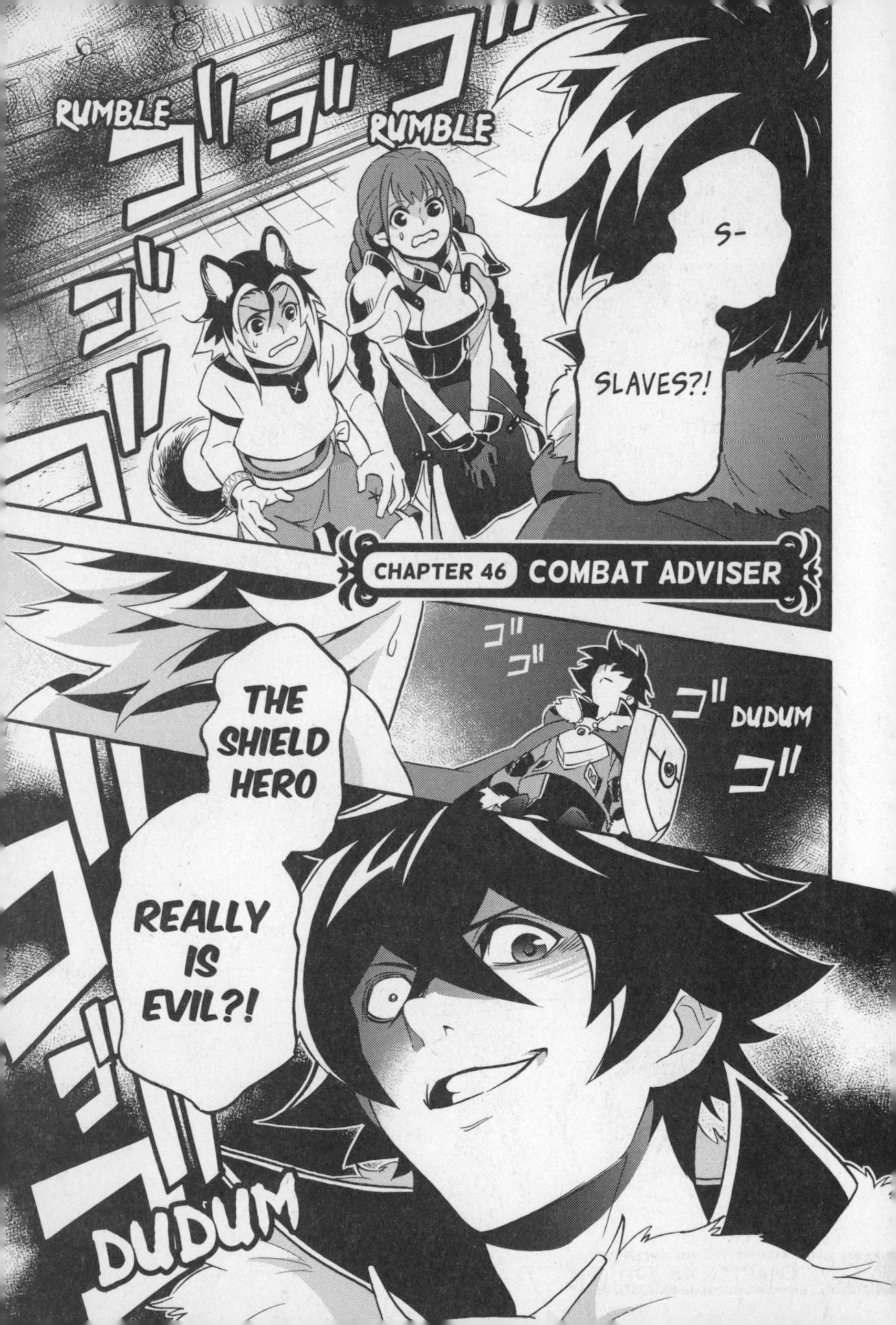
S-
SLAVES?!
RUMBLE
RUMBLE
CHAPTER 46 COMBAT ADVISER
DUDUM
THE SHIELD HERO
REALLY IS EVIL?!
DUDUM

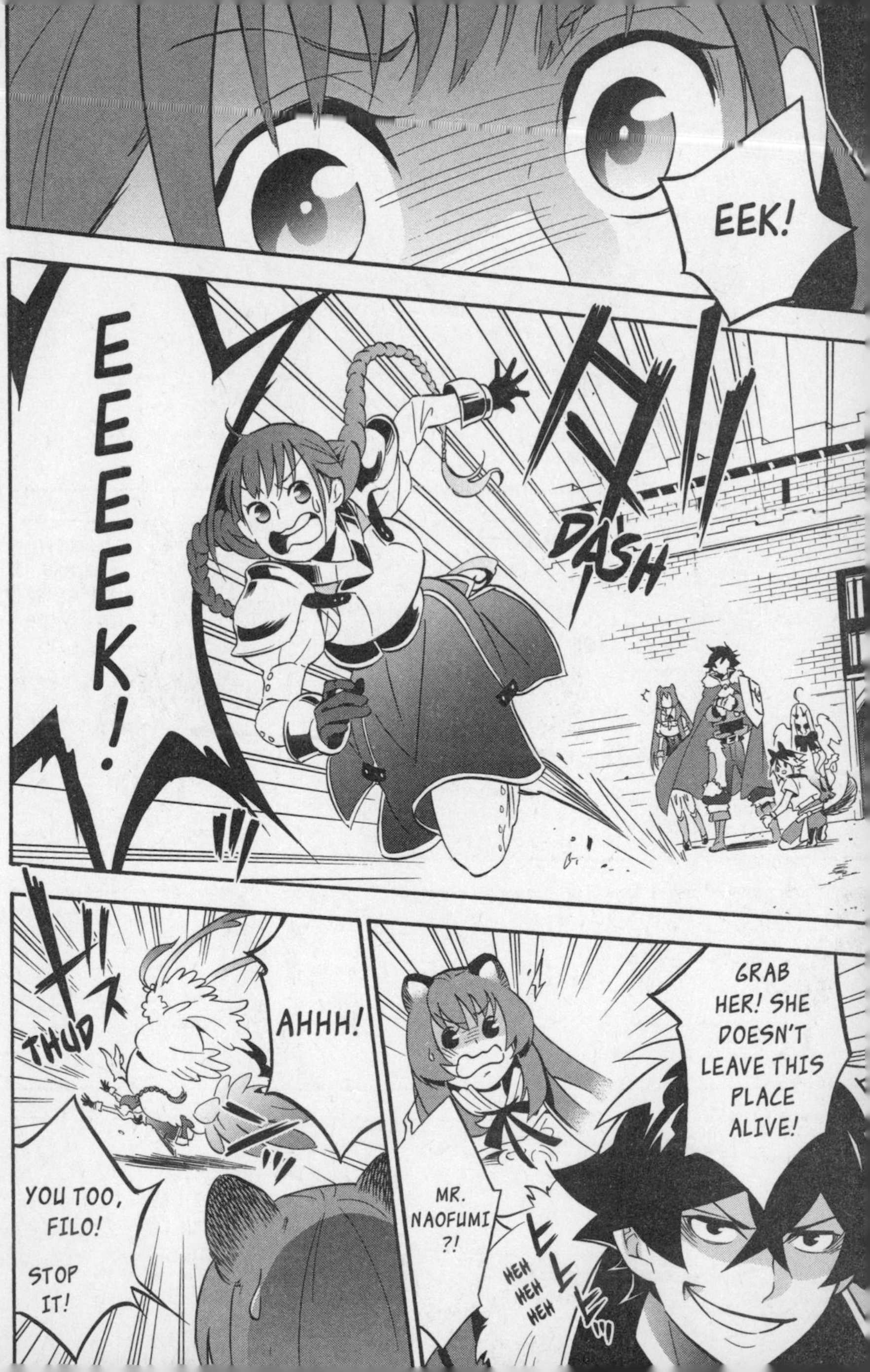
EEK!
DASH
EEEEK!
GRAB HER! SHE DOESN'T LEAVE THIS PLACE ALIVE!
MR. NAOFUMI ?!
HEH HEH HEH
AHHH!
THUD
YOU TOO, FILO!
STOP IT!

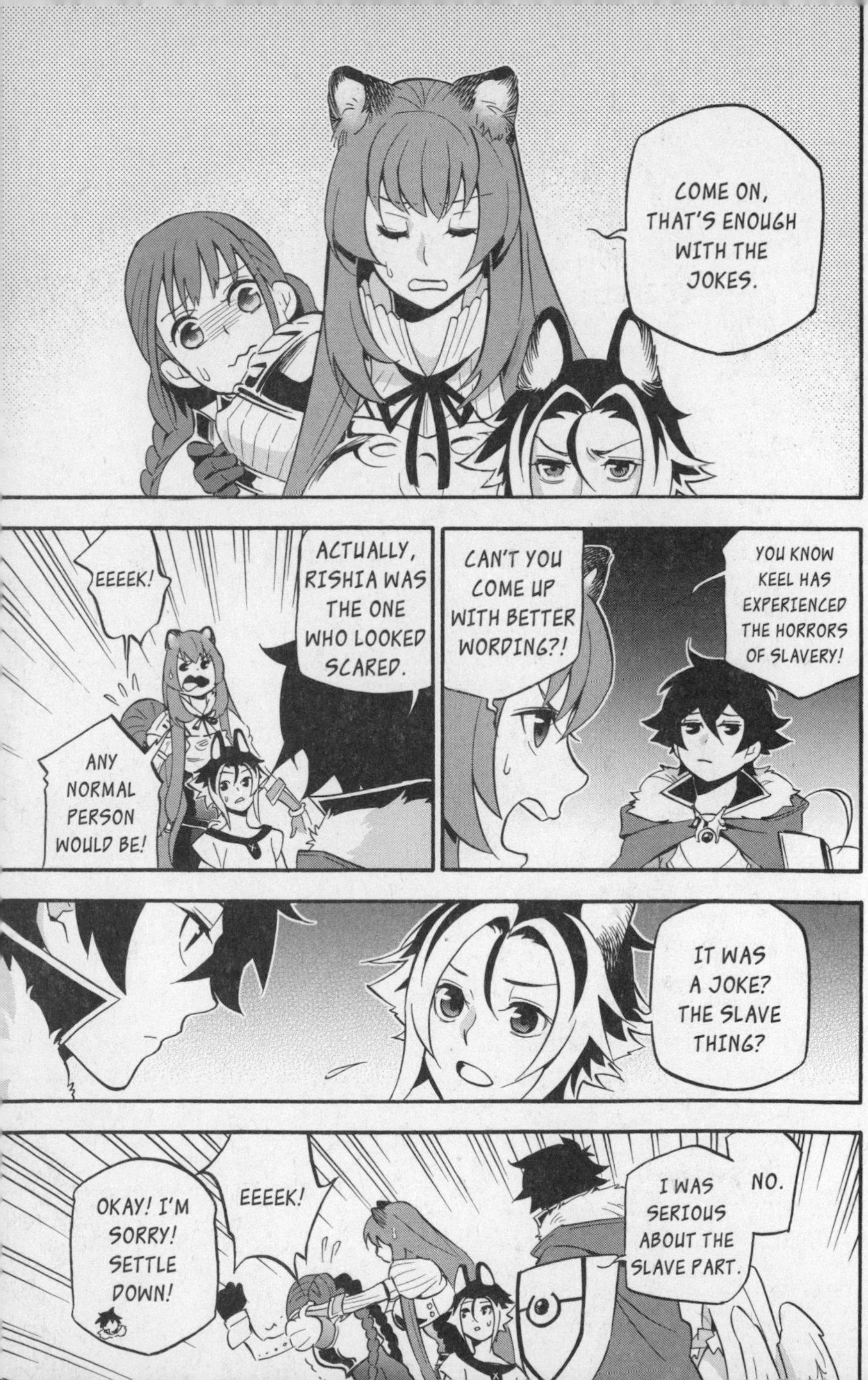
COME ON, THAT'S ENOUGH WITH THE JOKES.
YOU KNOW KEEL HAS EXPERIENCED THE HORRORS OF SLAVERY!
CAN'T YOU COME UP WITH BETTER WORDING?!
ACTUALLY, RISHIA WAS THE ONE WHO LOOKED SCARED.
EEEEK!
ANY NORMAL PERSON WOULD BE!
IT WAS A JOKE? THE SLAVE THING?
NO.
I WAS SERIOUS ABOUT THE SLAVE PART.
EEEEK!
OKAY! I'M SORRY! SETTLE DOWN!

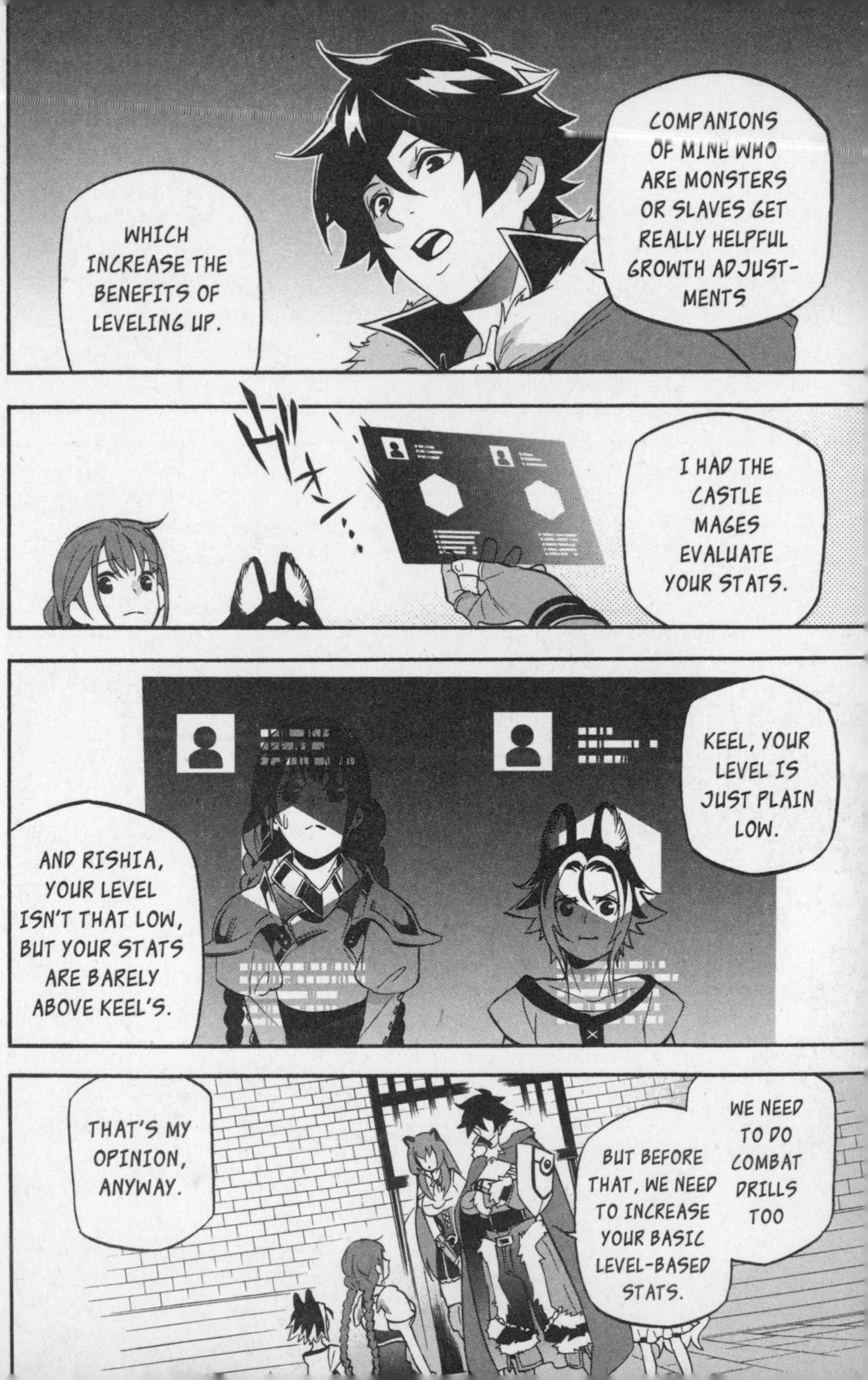
COMPANIONS OF MINE WHO ARE MONSTERS OR SLAVES GET REALLY HELPFUL GROWTH ADJUST-MENTS
WHICH INCREASE THE BENEFITS OF LEVELING UP.
I HAD THE CASTLE MAGES EVALUATE YOUR STATS.
KEEL, YOUR LEVEL IS JUST PLAIN LOW.
AND RISHIA, YOUR LEVEL ISN'T THAT LOW, BUT YOUR STATS ARE BARELY ABOVE KEEL'S.
WE NEED TO DO COMBAT DRILLS TOO
BUT BEFORE THAT, WE NEED TO INCREASE YOUR BASIC LEVEL-BASED STATS.
THAT'S MY OPINION, ANYWAY.

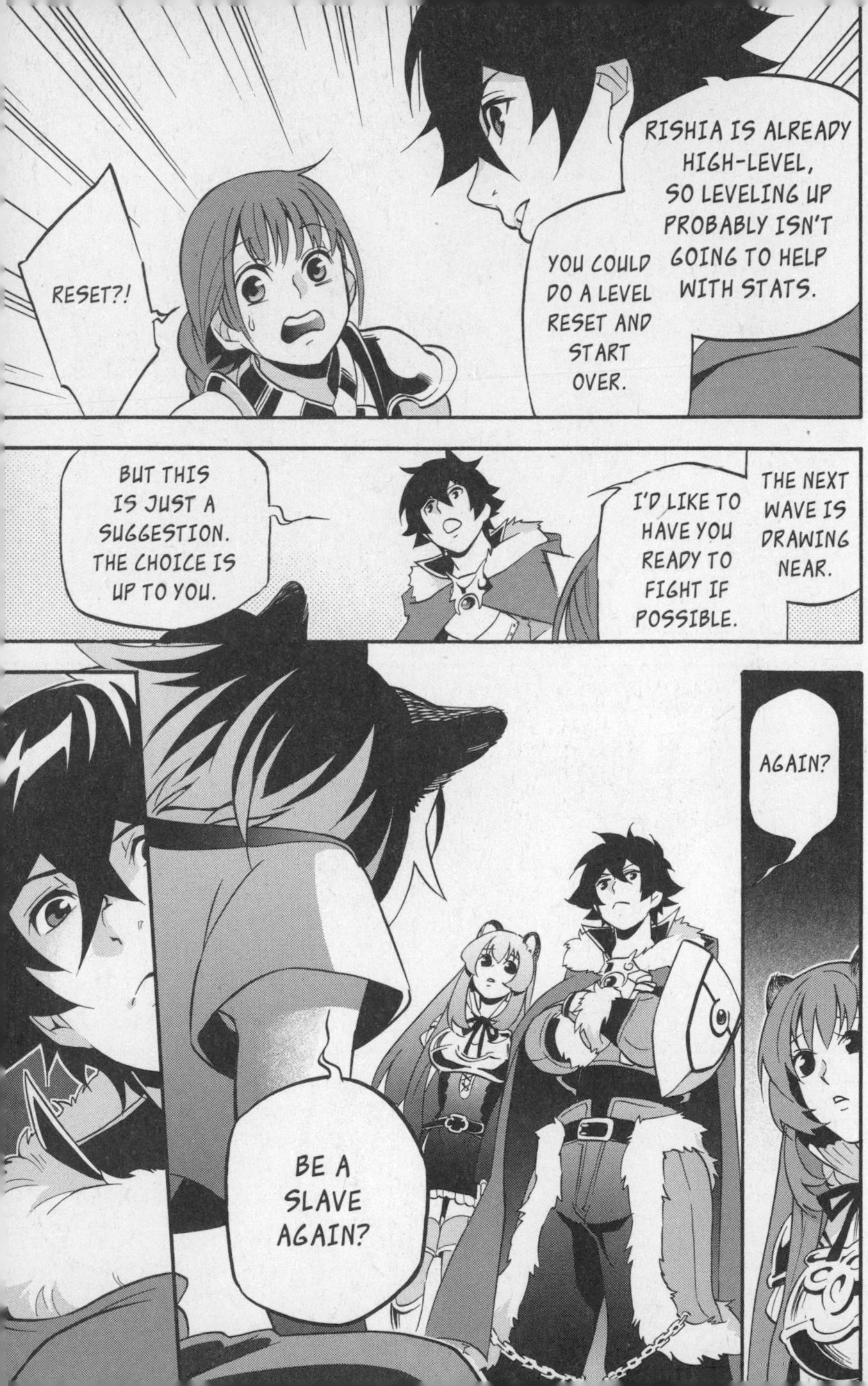
RISHIA IS ALREADY HIGH-LEVEL, SO LEVELING UP PROBABLY ISN'T GOING TO HELP WITH STATS.
YOU COULD DO A LEVEL RESET AND START OVER.
RESET?!
THE NEXT WAVE IS DRAWING NEAR.
I'D LIKE TO HAVE YOU READY TO FIGHT IF POSSIBLE.
BUT THIS IS JUST A SUGGESTION. THE CHOICE IS UP TO YOU.
AGAIN?
BE A SLAVE AGAIN?

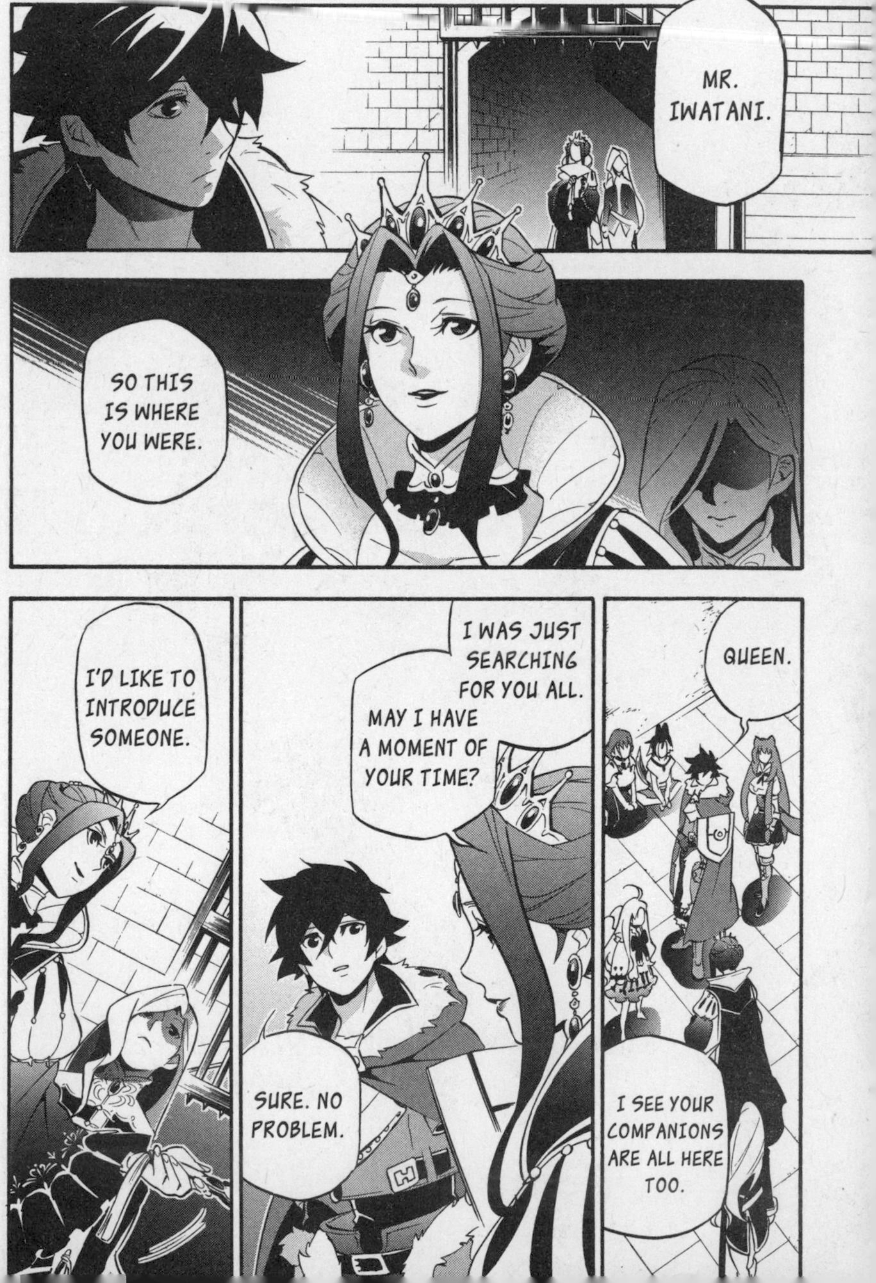
MR. IWATANI.
SO THIS IS WHERE YOU WERE.
QUEEN.
I SEE YOUR COMPANIONS ARE ALL HERE TOO.
I WAS JUST SEARCHING FOR YOU ALL.
MAY I HAVE A MOMENT OF YOUR TIME?
SURE. NO PROBLEM.
I'D LIKE TO INTRODUCE SOMEONE.

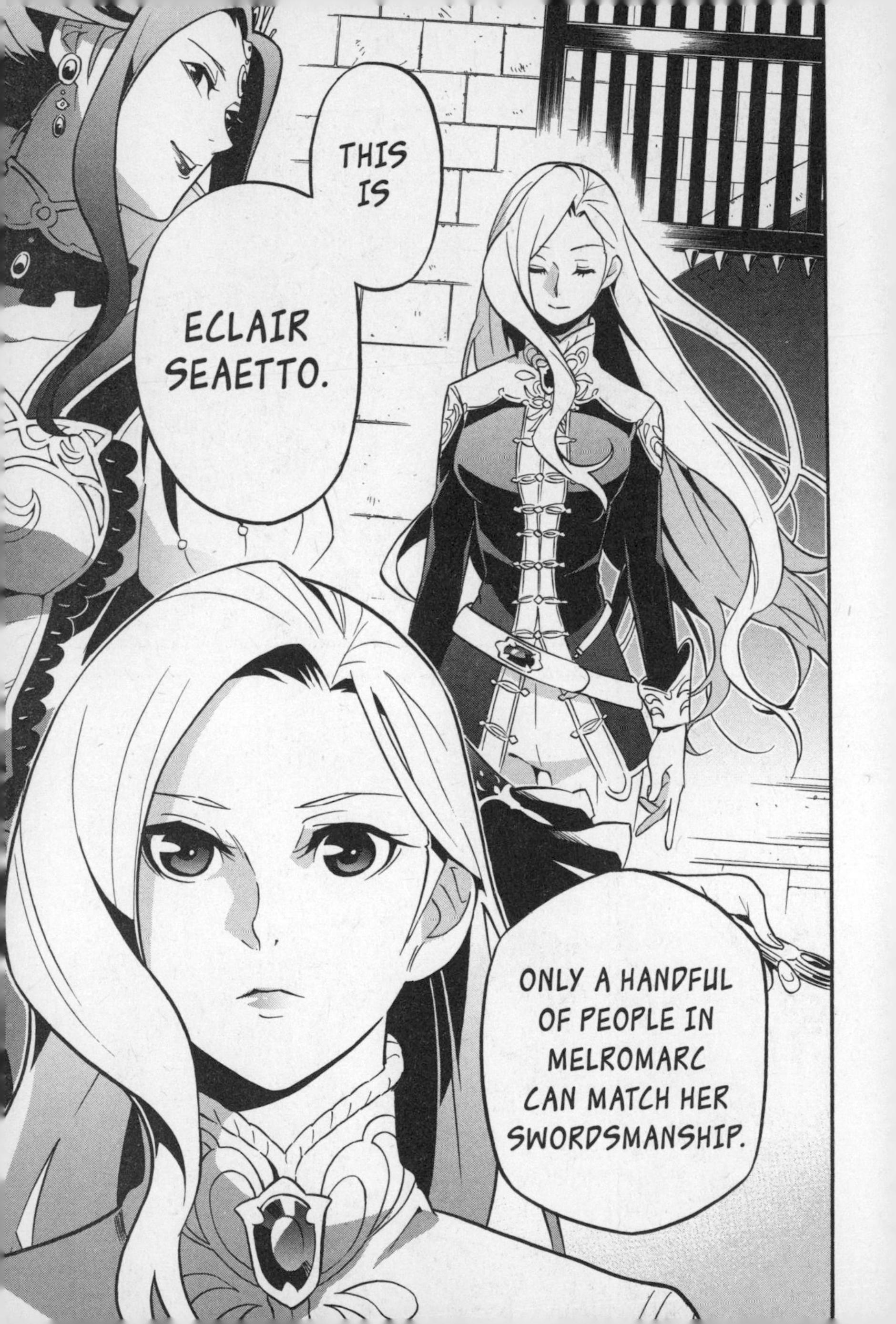
THIS IS ECLAIR SEAETTO.
ONLY A HANDFUL OF PEOPLE IN MELROMARC CAN MATCH HER SWORDSMANSHIP.

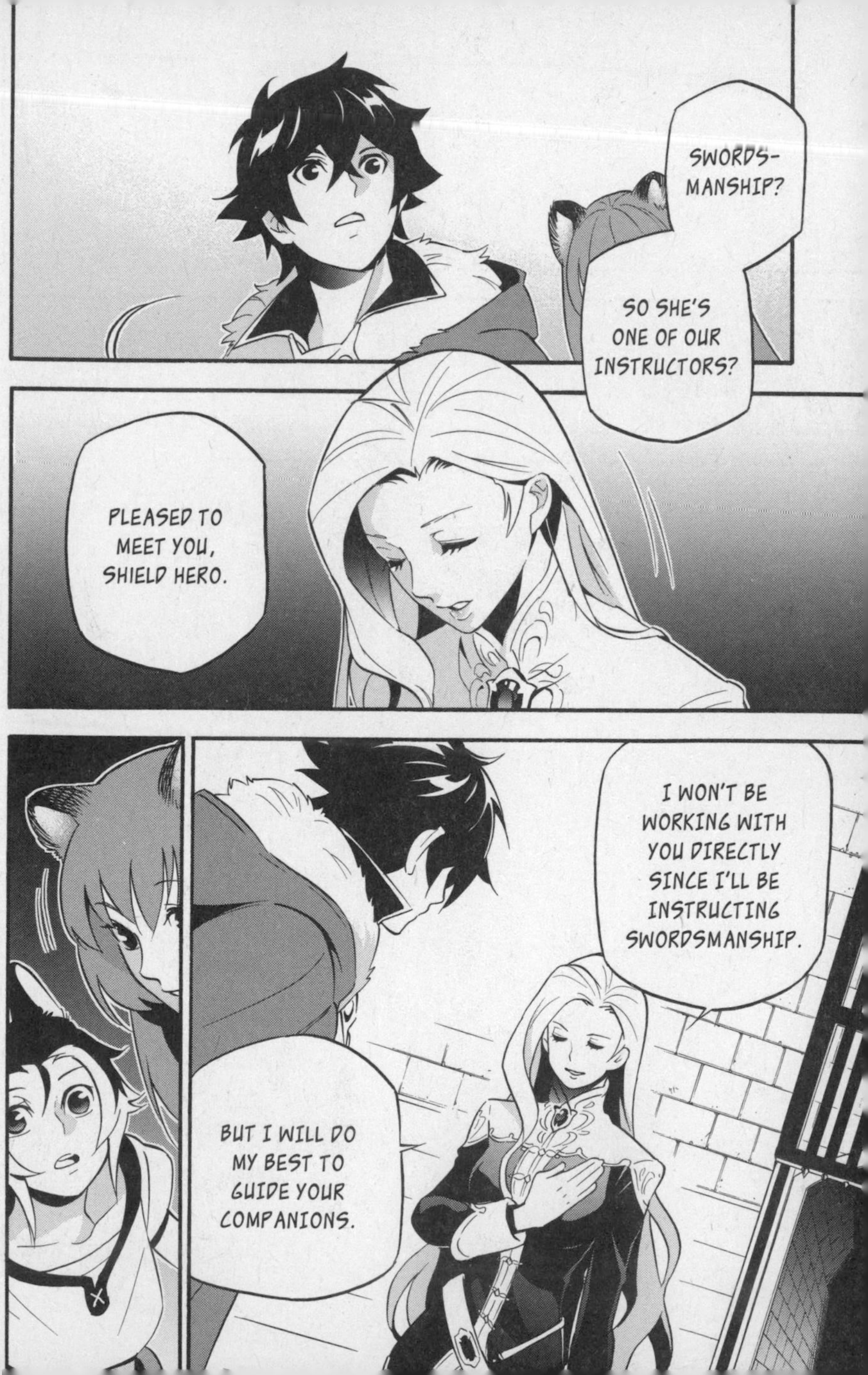
SWORDS-
MANSHIP?
SO SHE'S ONE OF OUR INSTRUCTORS?
PLEASED TO MEET YOU, SHIELD HERO.
I WON'T BE WORKING WITH YOU DIRECTLY SINCE I'LL BE INSTRUCTING SWORDSMANSHIP.
BUT I WILL DO MY BEST TO GUIDE YOUR COMPANIONS.

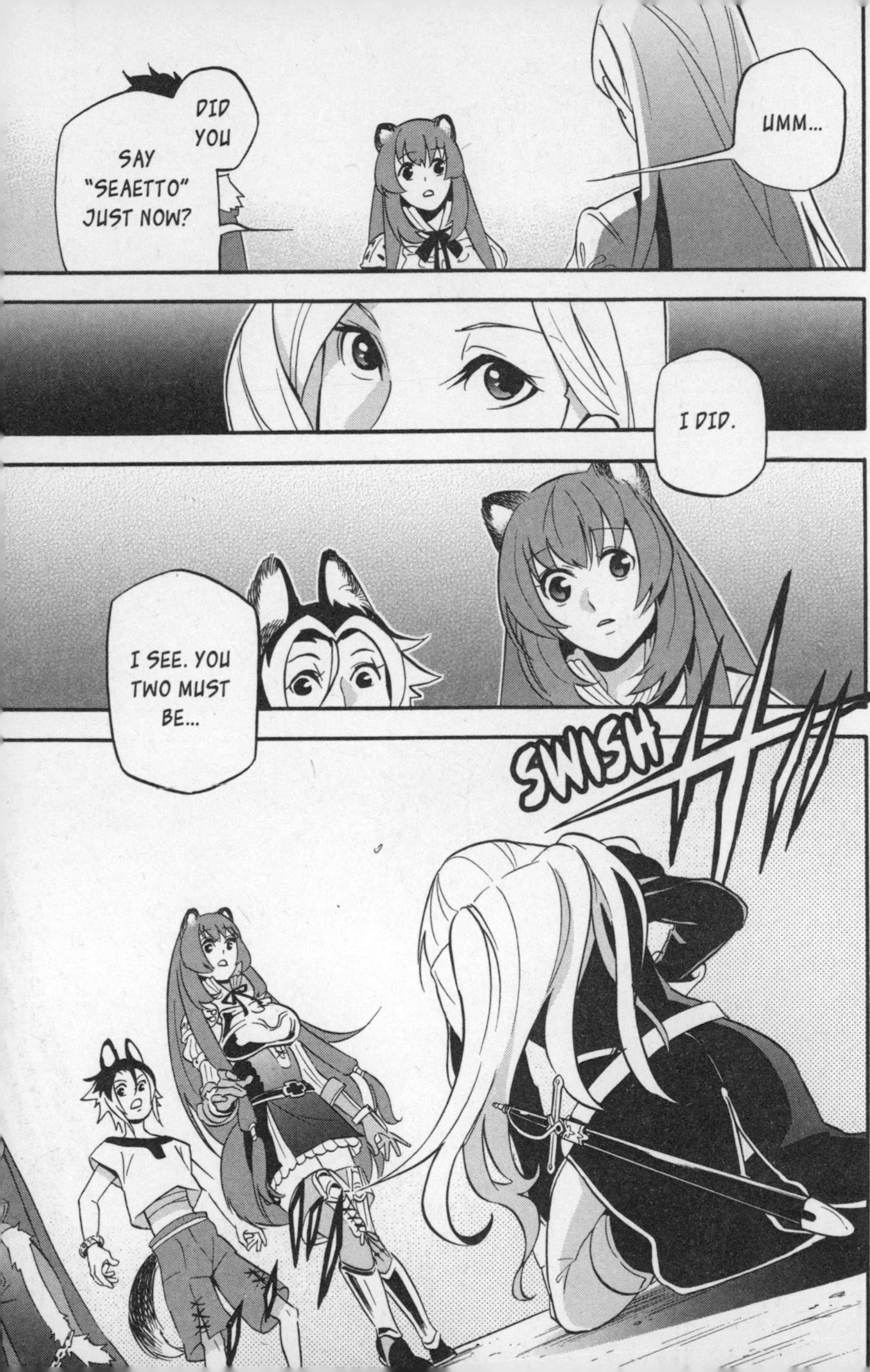
UMM...
DID YOU SAY "SEAETTO" JUST NOW?
I DID.
I SEE. YOU TWO MUST BE...
SWISH

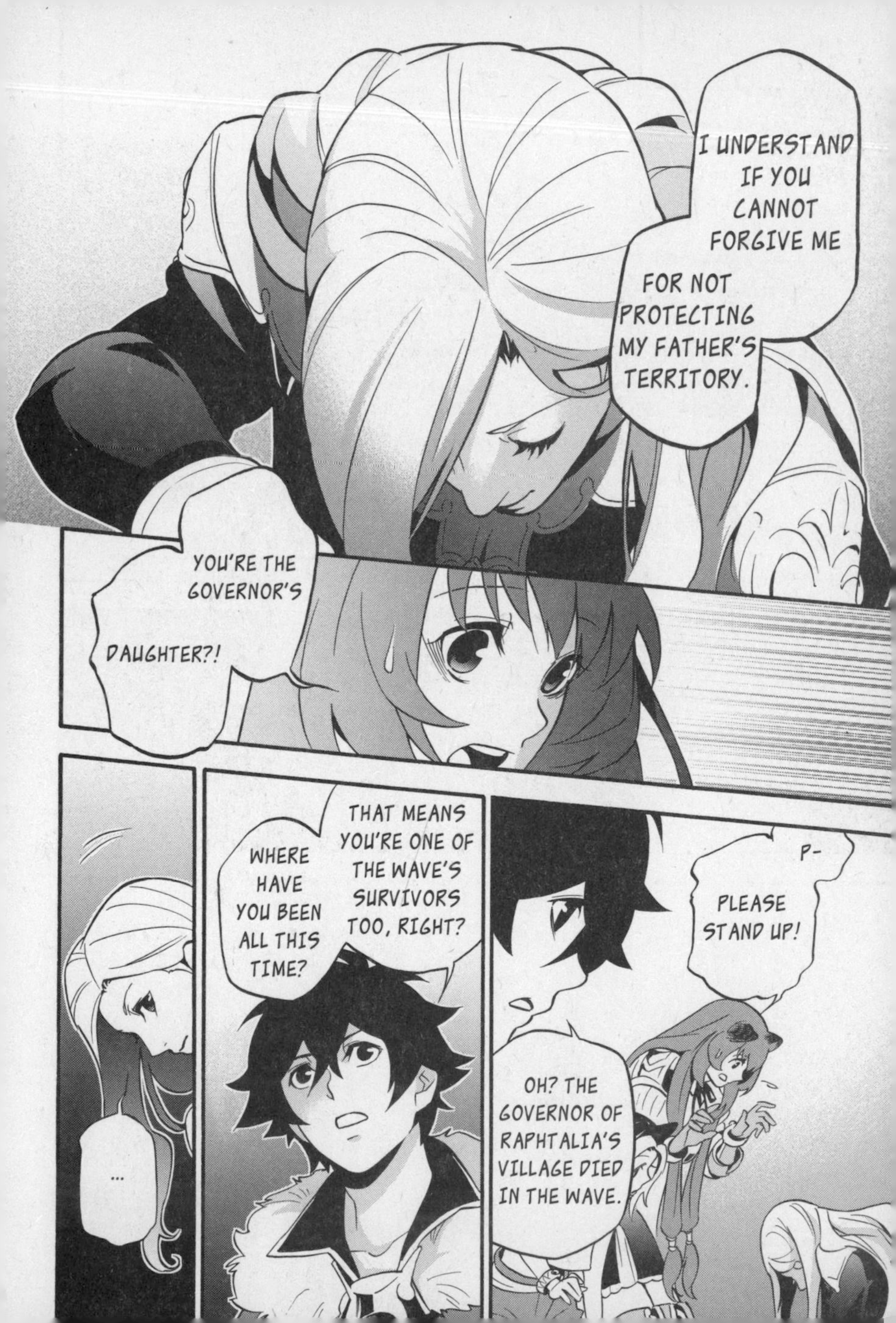
I UNDERSTAND IF YOU CANNOT FORGIVE ME
FOR NOT PROTECTING MY FATHER'S TERRITORY.
YOU'RE THE GOVERNOR'S
DAUGHTER?!
P-
PLEASE STAND UP!
OH? THE GOVERNOR OF RAPHTALIA'S VILLAGE DIED IN THE WAVE.
THAT MEANS YOU'RE ONE OF THE WAVE'S SURVIVORS TOO, RIGHT?
WHERE HAVE YOU BEEN ALL THIS TIME?
...

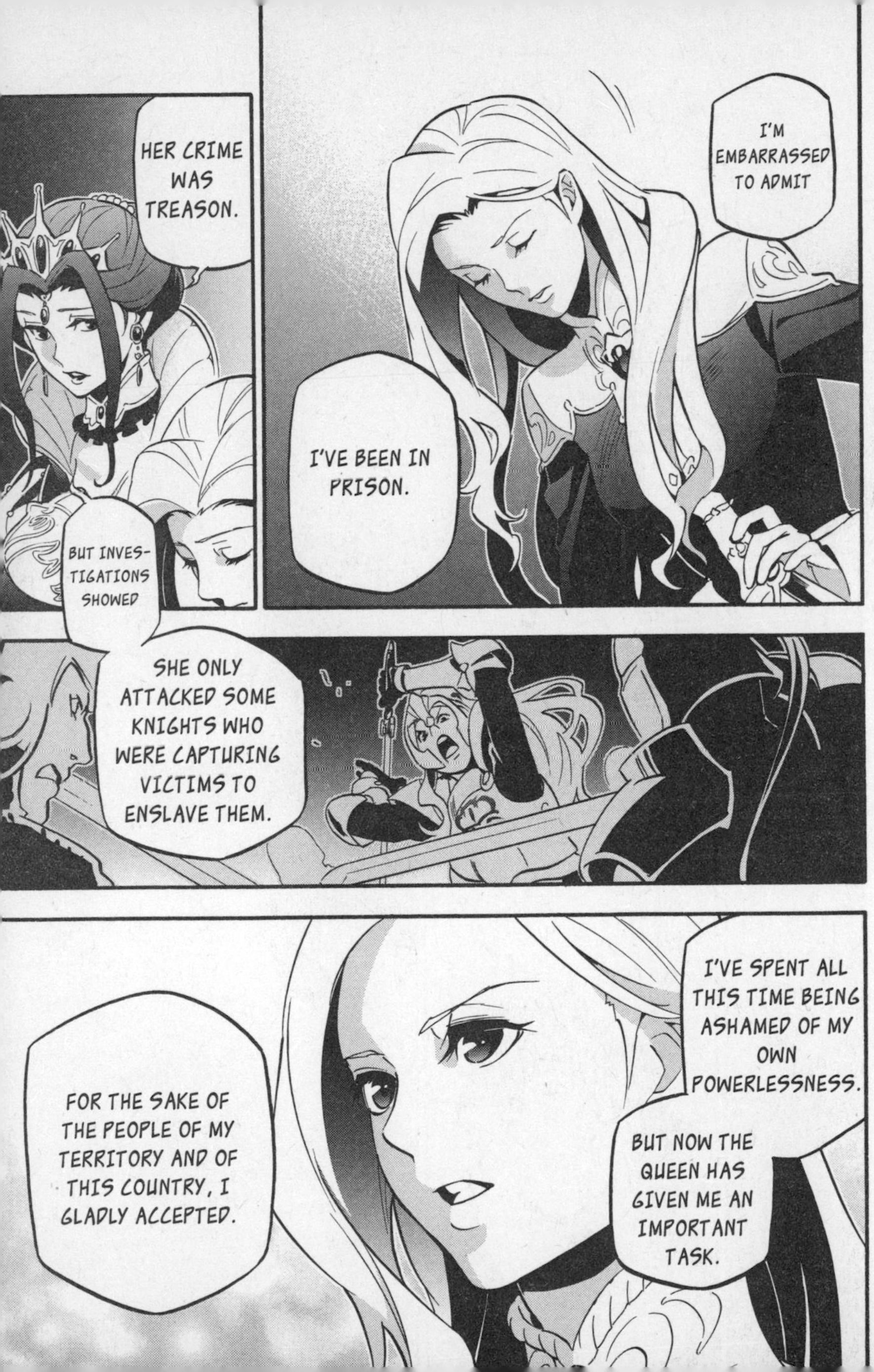
I'M EMBARRASSED TO ADMIT
I'VE BEEN IN PRISON.
HER CRIME WAS TREASON.
BUT INVES-TIGATIONS SHOWED
SHE ONLY ATTACKED SOME KNIGHTS WHO WERE CAPTURING VICTIMS TO ENSLAVE THEM.
I'VE SPENT ALL THIS TIME BEING ASHAMED OF MY OWN POWERLESSNESS.
BUT NOW THE QUEEN HAS GIVEN ME AN IMPORTANT TASK.
FOR THE SAKE OF THE PEOPLE OF MY TERRITORY AND OF THIS COUNTRY, I GLADLY ACCEPTED.

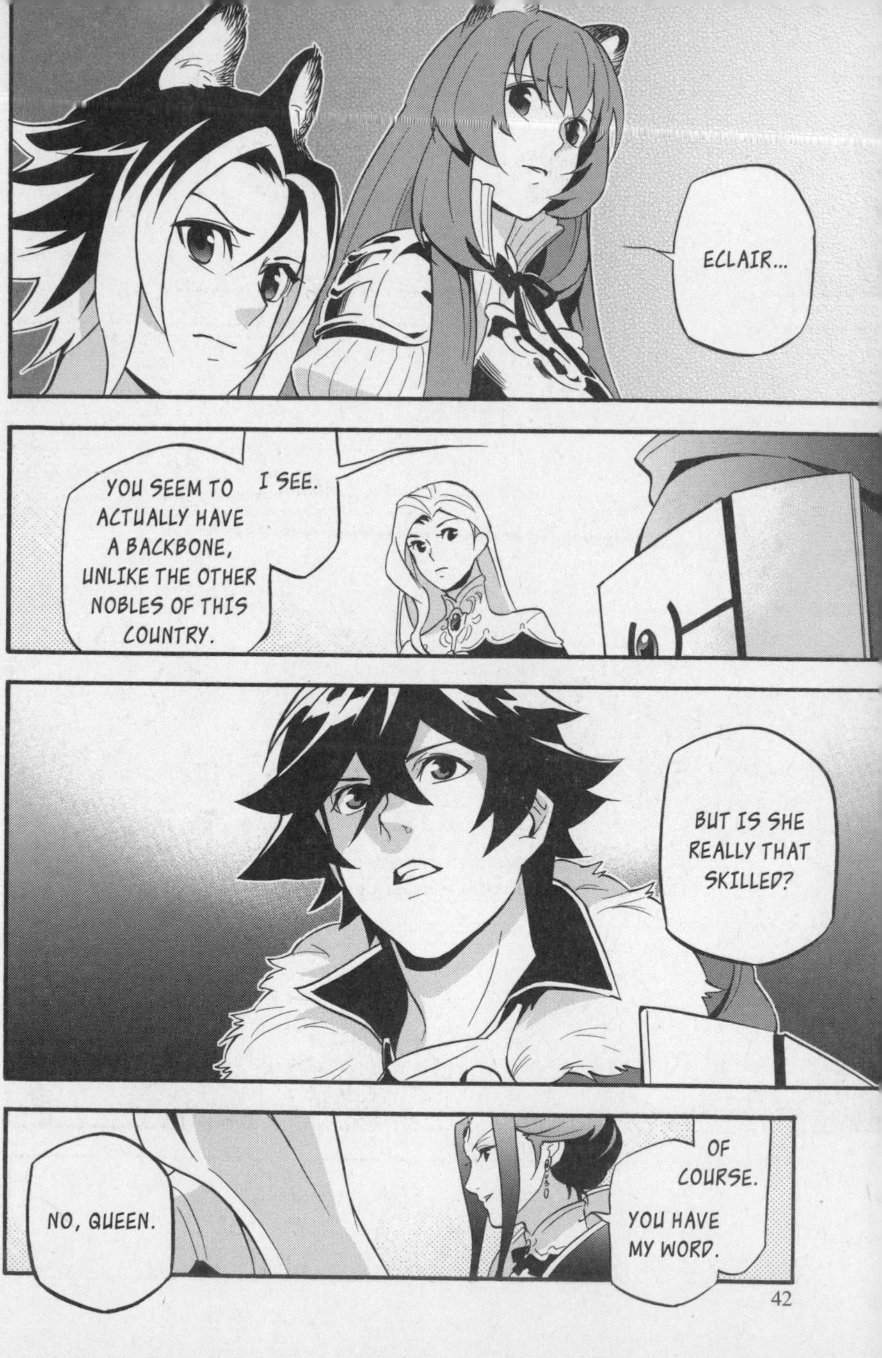
ECLAIR...
I SEE.
YOU SEEM TO ACTUALLY HAVE A BACKBONE, UNLIKE THE OTHER NOBLES OF THIS COUNTRY.
BUT IS SHE REALLY THAT SKILLED?
OF COURSE.
YOU HAVE MY WORD.
NO, QUEEN.

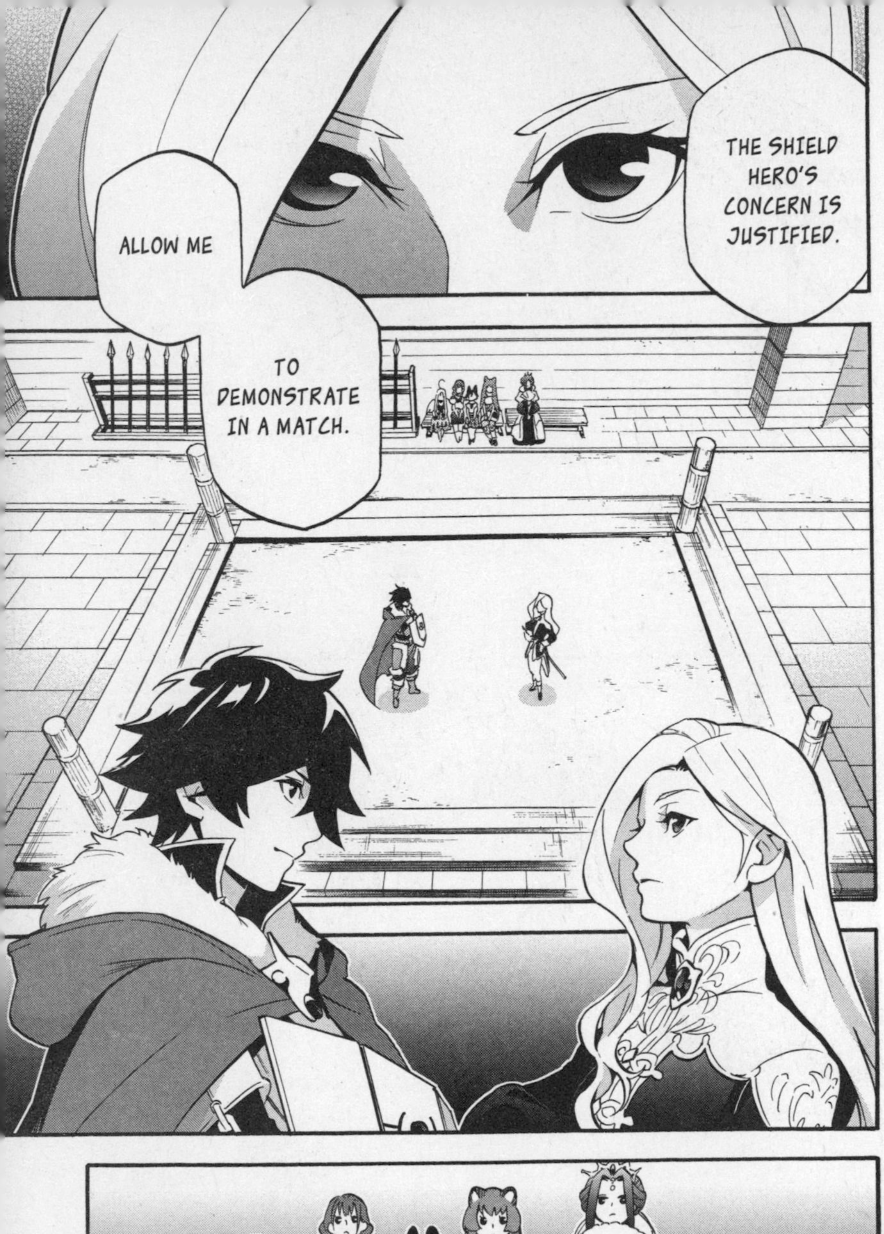
THE SHIELD HERO'S CONCERN IS JUSTIFIED.
ALLOW ME
TO DEMONSTRATE IN A MATCH.

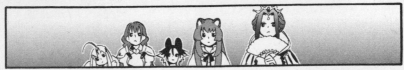

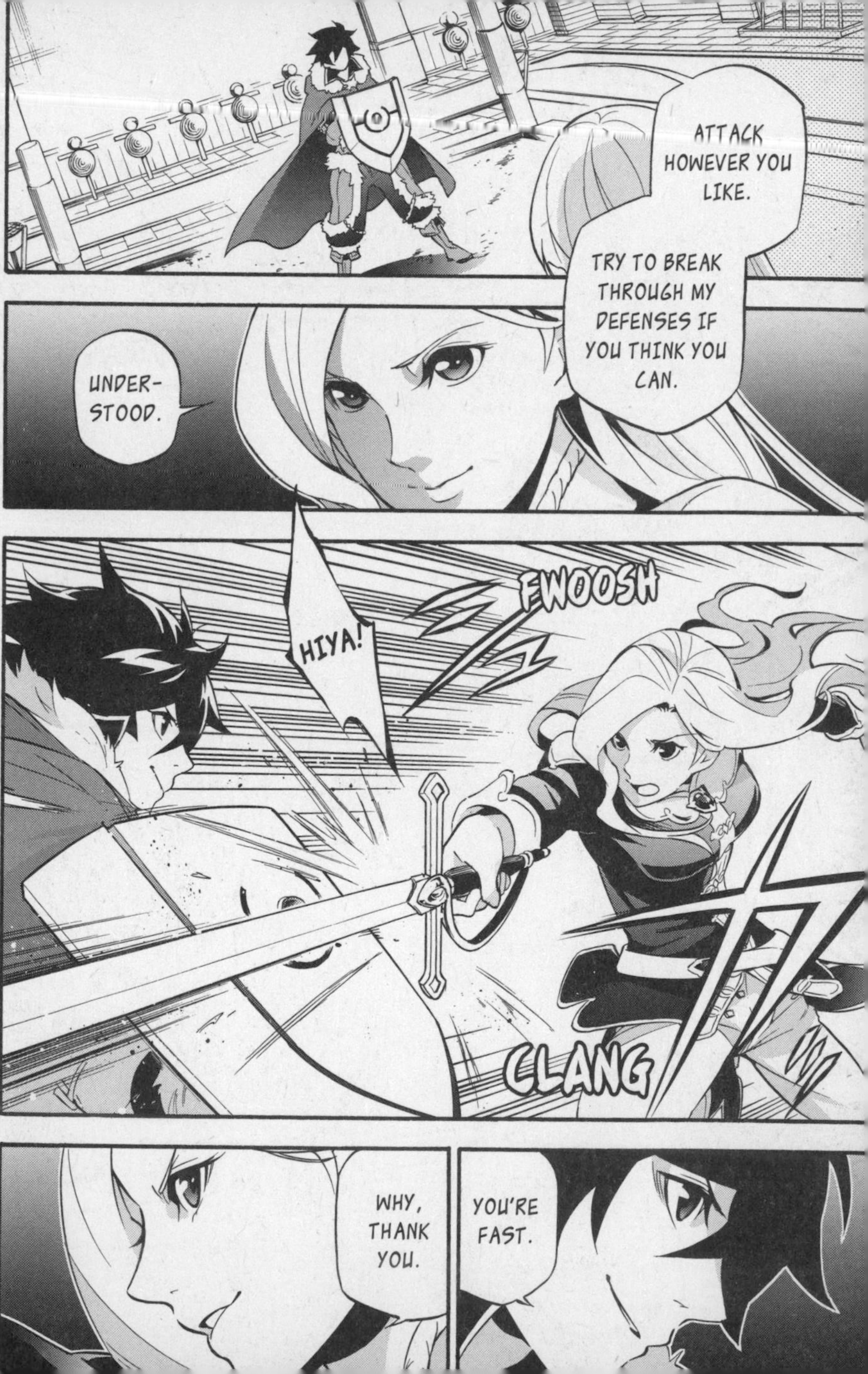
ATTACK HOWEVER YOU LIKE.
TRY TO BREAK THROUGH MY DEFENSES IF YOU THINK YOU CAN.
UNDER-STOOD.
FWOOSH
HIYA!
CLANG
YOU'RE FAST.
WHY, THANK YOU.

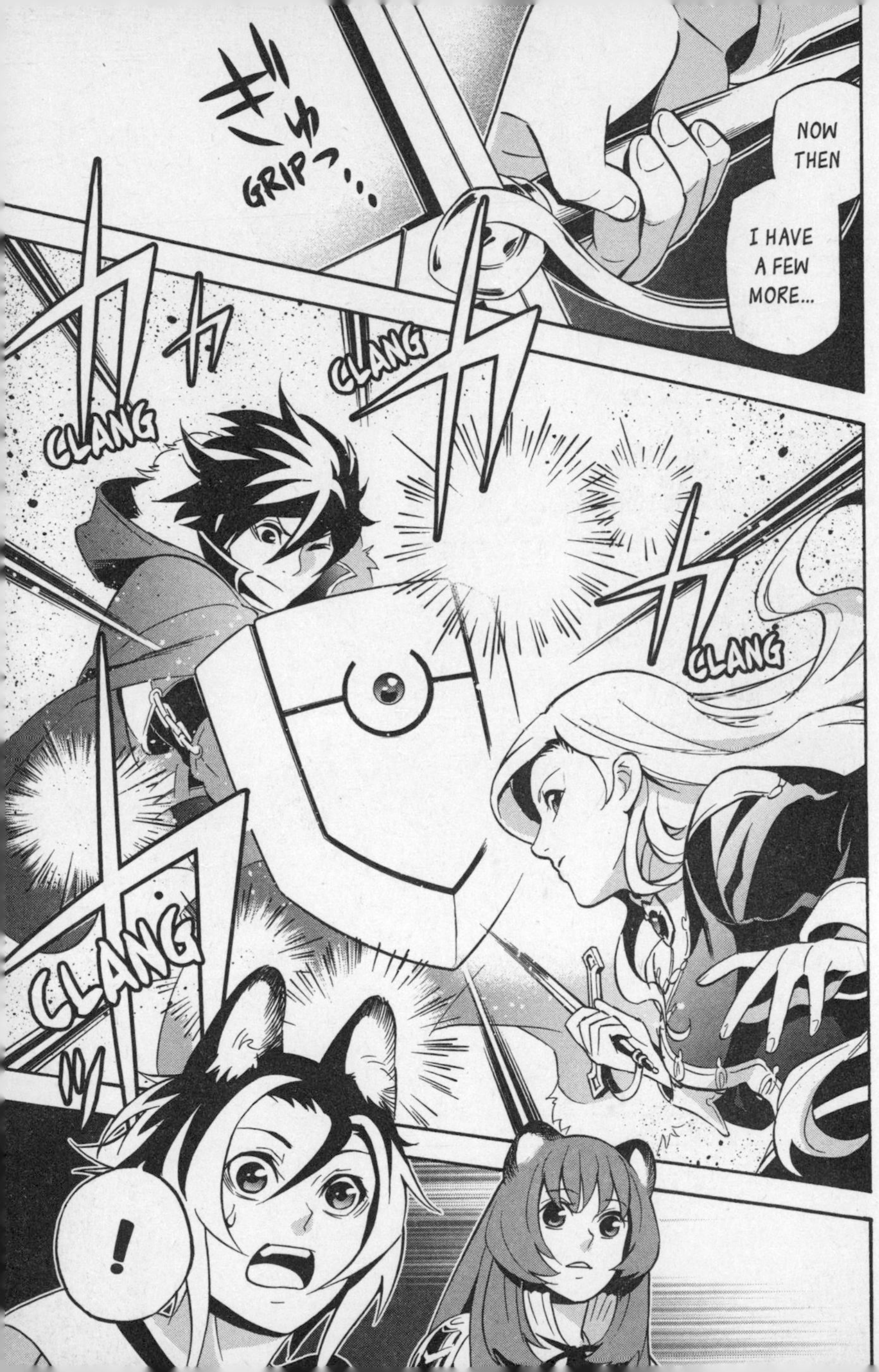
NOW THEN
I HAVE A FEW MORE...
GRIP...
CLANG
CLANG
CLANG
CLANG
!

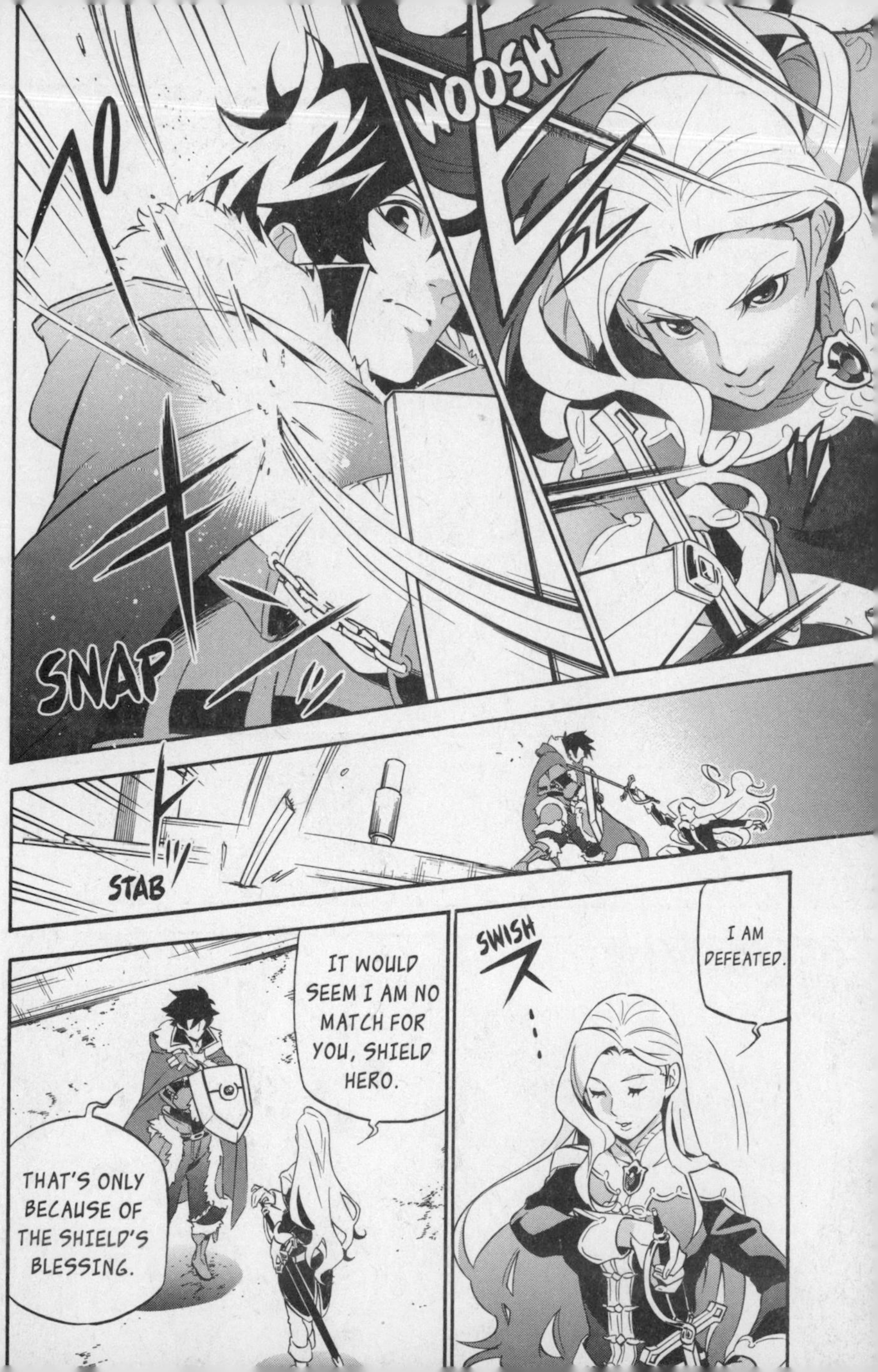
WOOSH
SNAP
STAB
SWISH
...
I AM DEFEATED.
IT WOULD SEEM I AM NO MATCH FOR YOU, SHIELD HERO.
THAT'S ONLY BECAUSE OF THE SHIELD'S BLESSING.

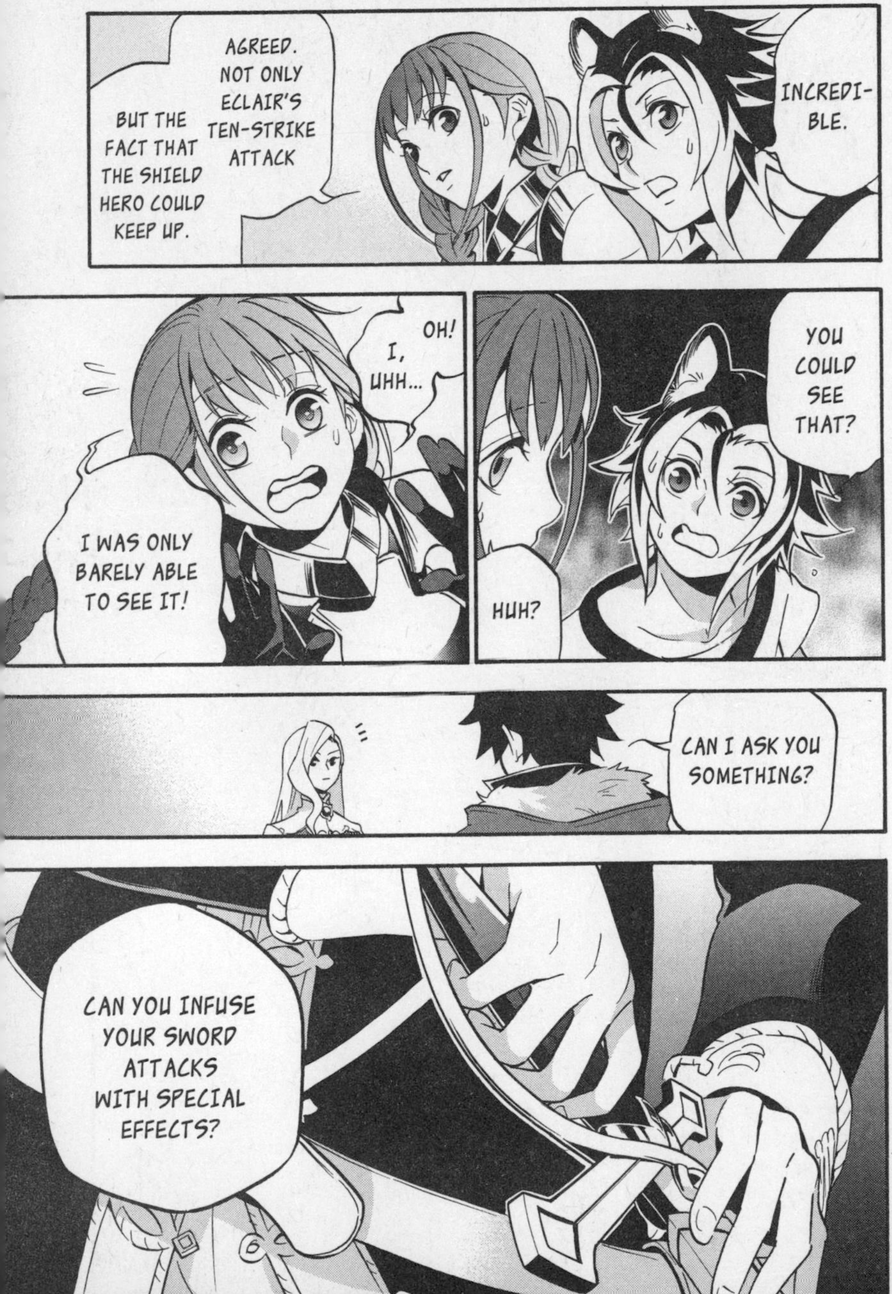
INCREDI-
BLE.
AGREED. NOT ONLY ECLAIR'S TEN-STRIKE ATTACK
BUT THE FACT THAT THE SHIELD HERO COULD KEEP UP.
YOU COULD SEE THAT?
HUH?
OH! I, UHH...
I WAS ONLY BARELY ABLE TO SEE IT!
CAN I ASK YOU SOMETHING?
CAN YOU INFUSE YOUR SWORD ATTACKS WITH SPECIAL EFFECTS?

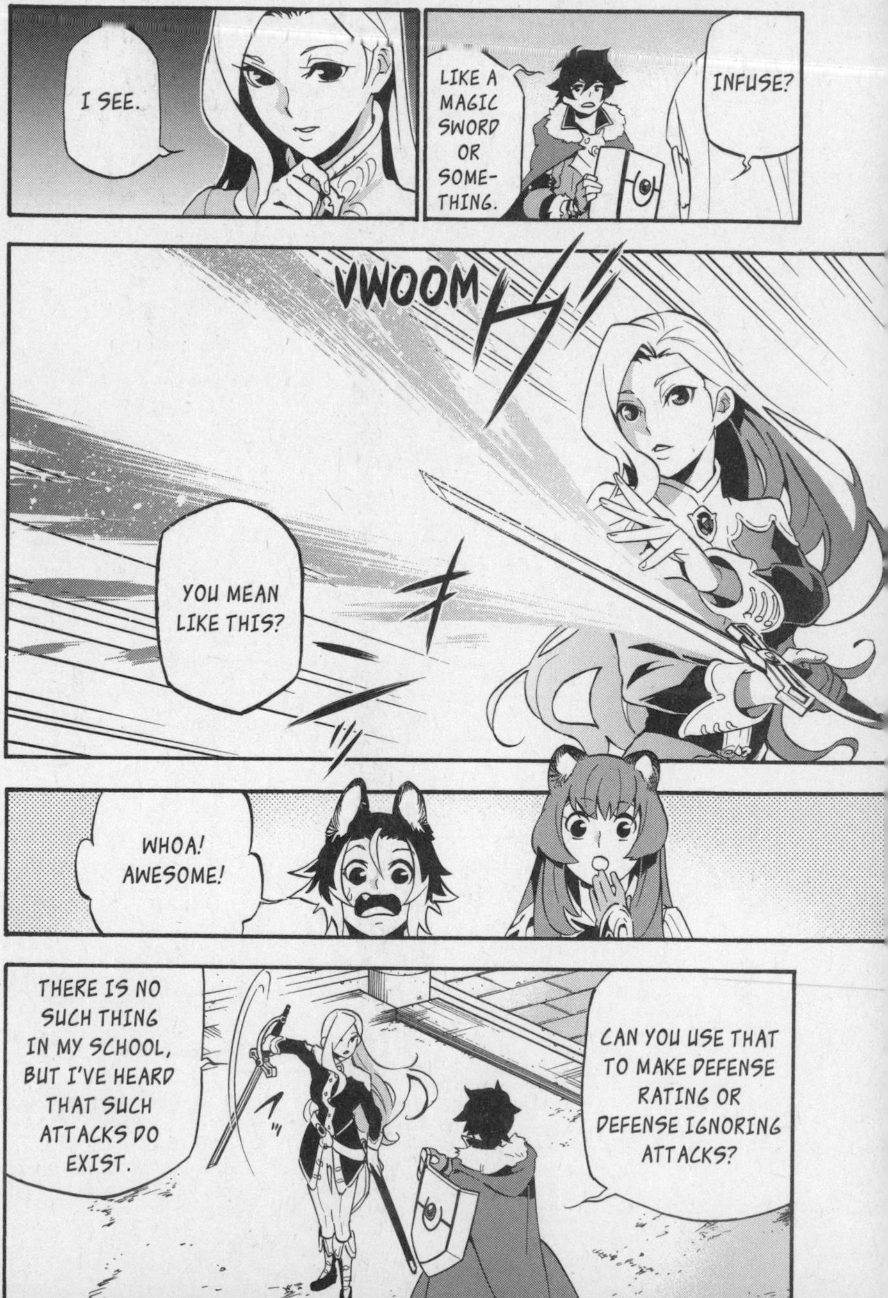
INFUSE?
LIKE A MAGIC SWORD OR SOMETHING.
I SEE.
VWOOM
YOU MEAN LIKE THIS?
WHOA! AWESOME!
CAN YOU USE THAT TO MAKE DEFENSE RATING OR DEFENSE IGNORING ATTACKS?
THERE IS NO SUCH THING IN MY SCHOOL, BUT I'VE HEARD THAT SUCH ATTACKS DO EXIST.

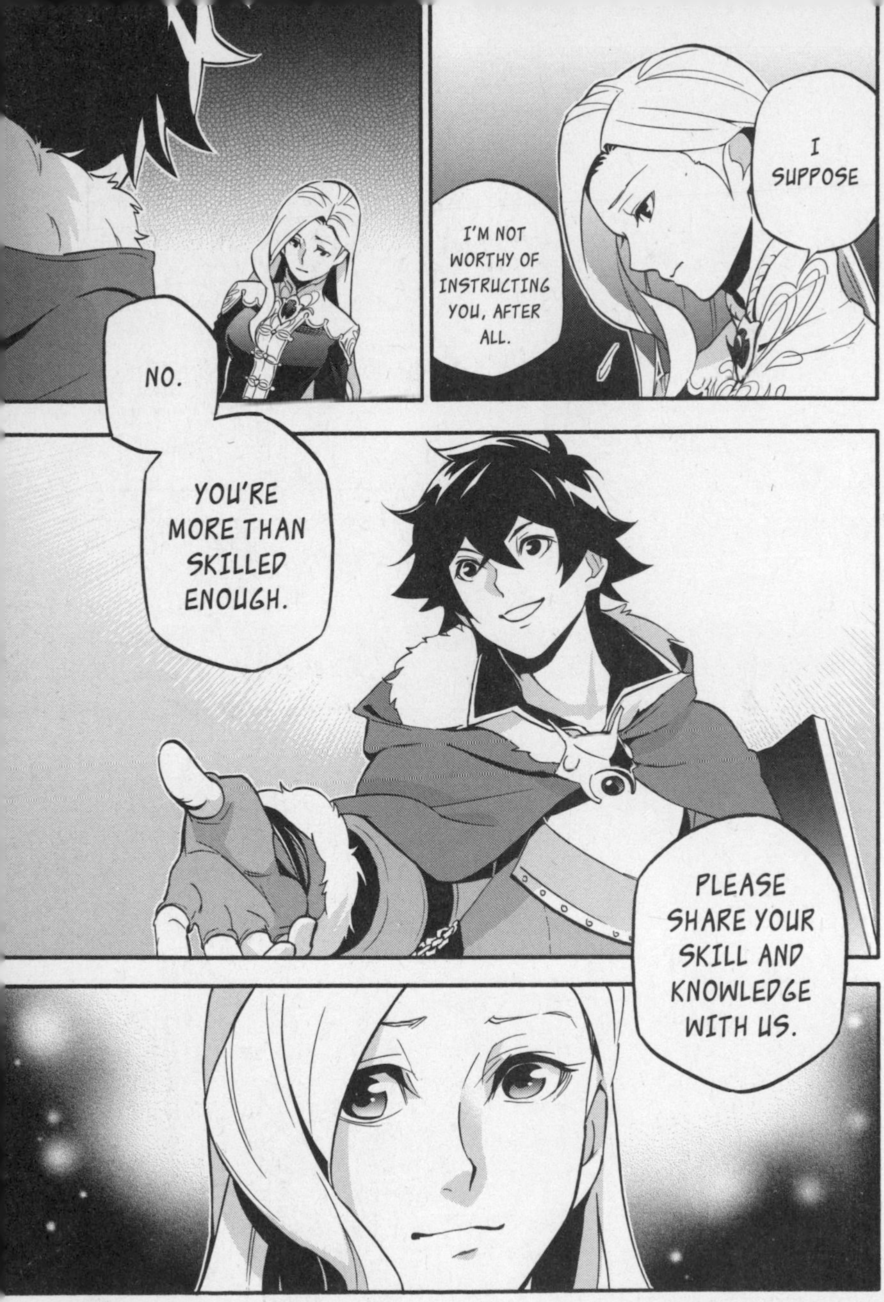
I SUPPOSE
I'M NOT WORTHY OF INSTRUCTING YOU, AFTER ALL.
NO.
YOU'RE MORE THAN SKILLED ENOUGH.
PLEASE SHARE YOUR SKILL AND KNOWLEDGE WITH US.

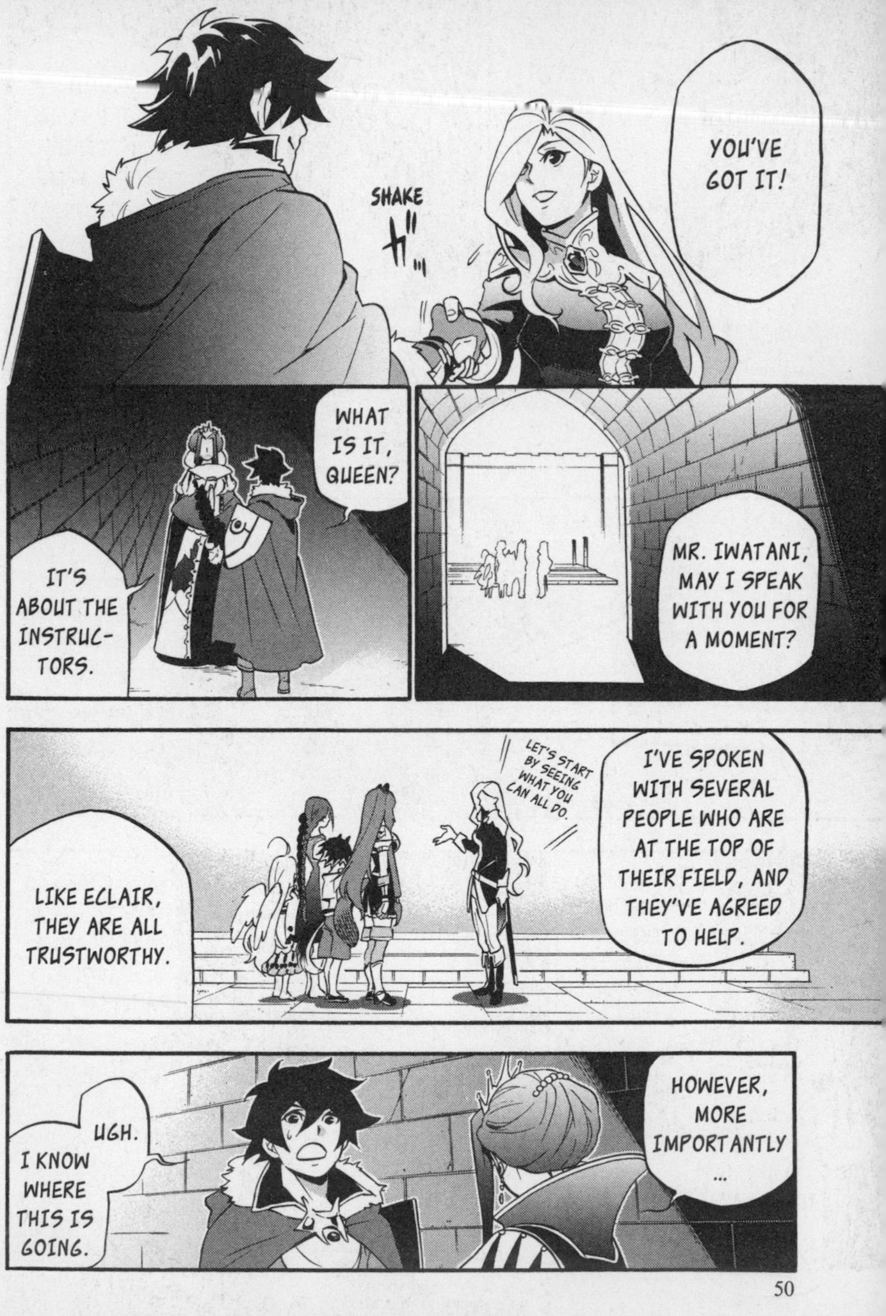
YOU'VE GOT IT!
SHAKE
MR. IWATANI, MAY I SPEAK WITH YOU FOR A MOMENT?
WHAT IS IT, QUEEN?
IT'S ABOUT THE INSTRUC-TORS.
I'VE SPOKEN WITH SEVERAL PEOPLE WHO ARE AT THE TOP OF THEIR FIELD, AND THEY'VE AGREED TO HELP.
LET'S START BY SEEING WHAT YOU CAN ALL DO.
LIKE ECLAIR, THEY ARE ALL TRUSTWORTHY.
HOWEVER, MORE IMPORTANTLY ...
UGH.
I KNOW WHERE THIS IS GOING.

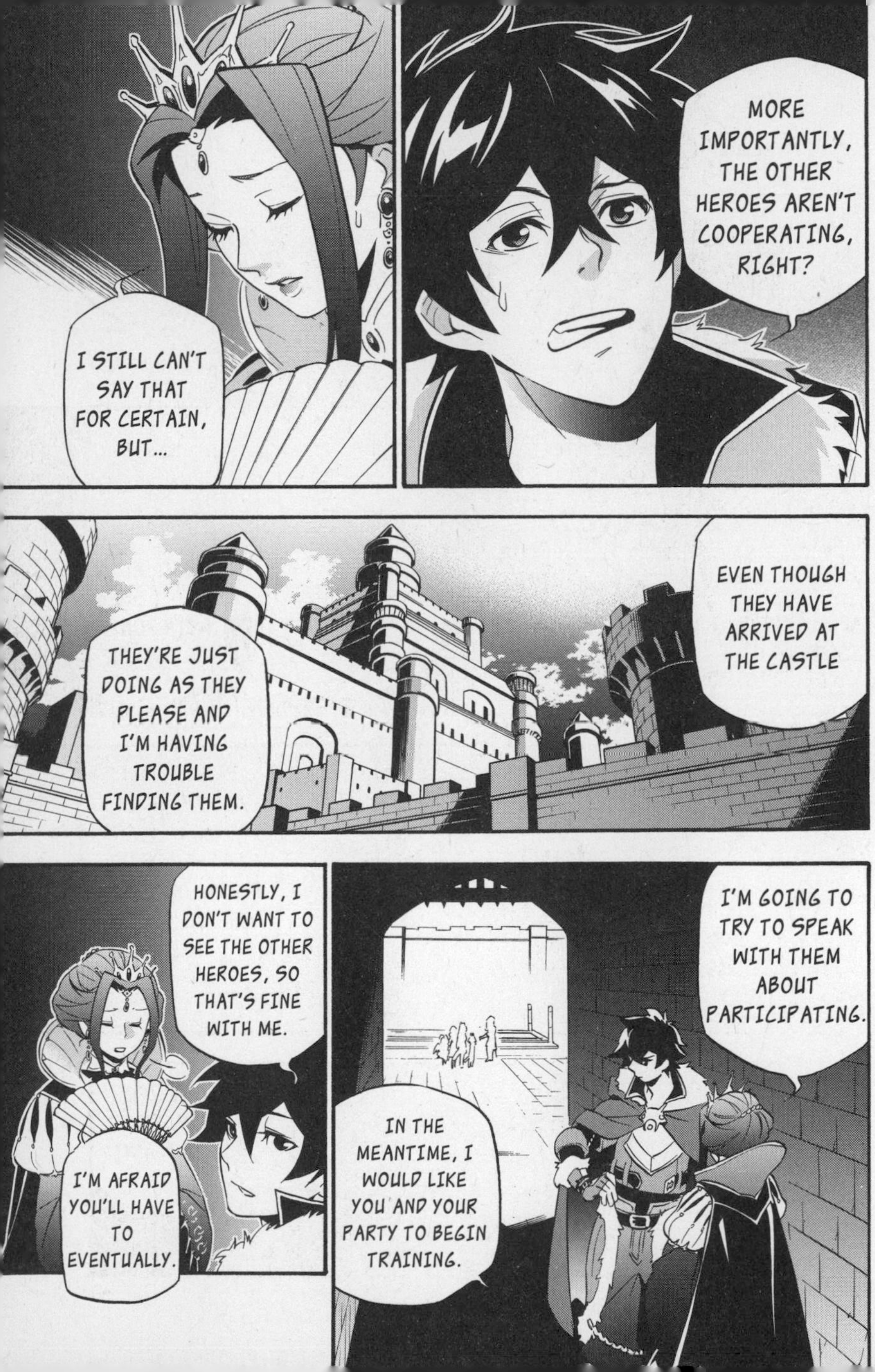
MORE IMPORTANTLY, THE OTHER HEROES AREN'T COOPERATING, RIGHT?
I STILL CAN'T SAY THAT FOR CERTAIN, BUT...
EVEN THOUGH THEY HAVE ARRIVED AT THE CASTLE
THEY'RE JUST DOING AS THEY PLEASE AND I'M HAVING TROUBLE FINDING THEM.
I'M GOING TO TRY TO SPEAK WITH THEM ABOUT PARTICIPATING.
IN THE MEANTIME, I WOULD LIKE YOU AND YOUR PARTY TO BEGIN TRAINING.
HONESTLY, I DON'T WANT TO SEE THE OTHER HEROES, SO THAT'S FINE WITH ME.
I'M AFRAID YOU'LL HAVE TO EVENTUALLY.

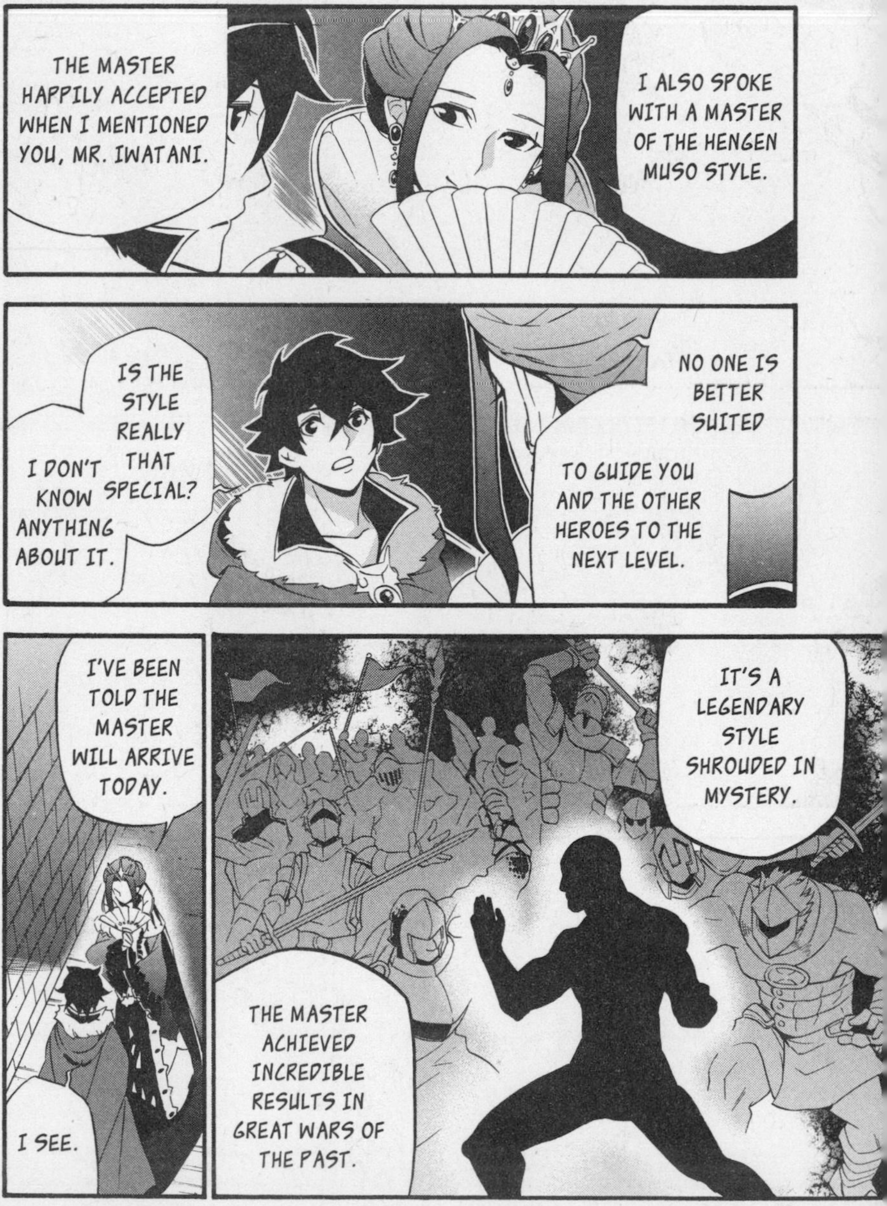
I ALSO SPOKE WITH A MASTER OF THE HENGEN MUSO STYLE.
THE MASTER HAPPILY ACCEPTED WHEN I MENTIONED YOU, MR. IWATANI.
NO ONE IS BETTER SUITED
TO GUIDE YOU AND THE OTHER HEROES TO THE NEXT LEVEL.
IS THE STYLE REALLY THAT SPECIAL?
I DON'T KNOW ANYTHING ABOUT IT.
IT'S A LEGENDARY STYLE SHROUDED IN MYSTERY.
THE MASTER ACHIEVED INCREDIBLE RESULTS IN GREAT WARS OF THE PAST.
I'VE BEEN TOLD THE MASTER WILL ARRIVE TODAY.
I SEE.

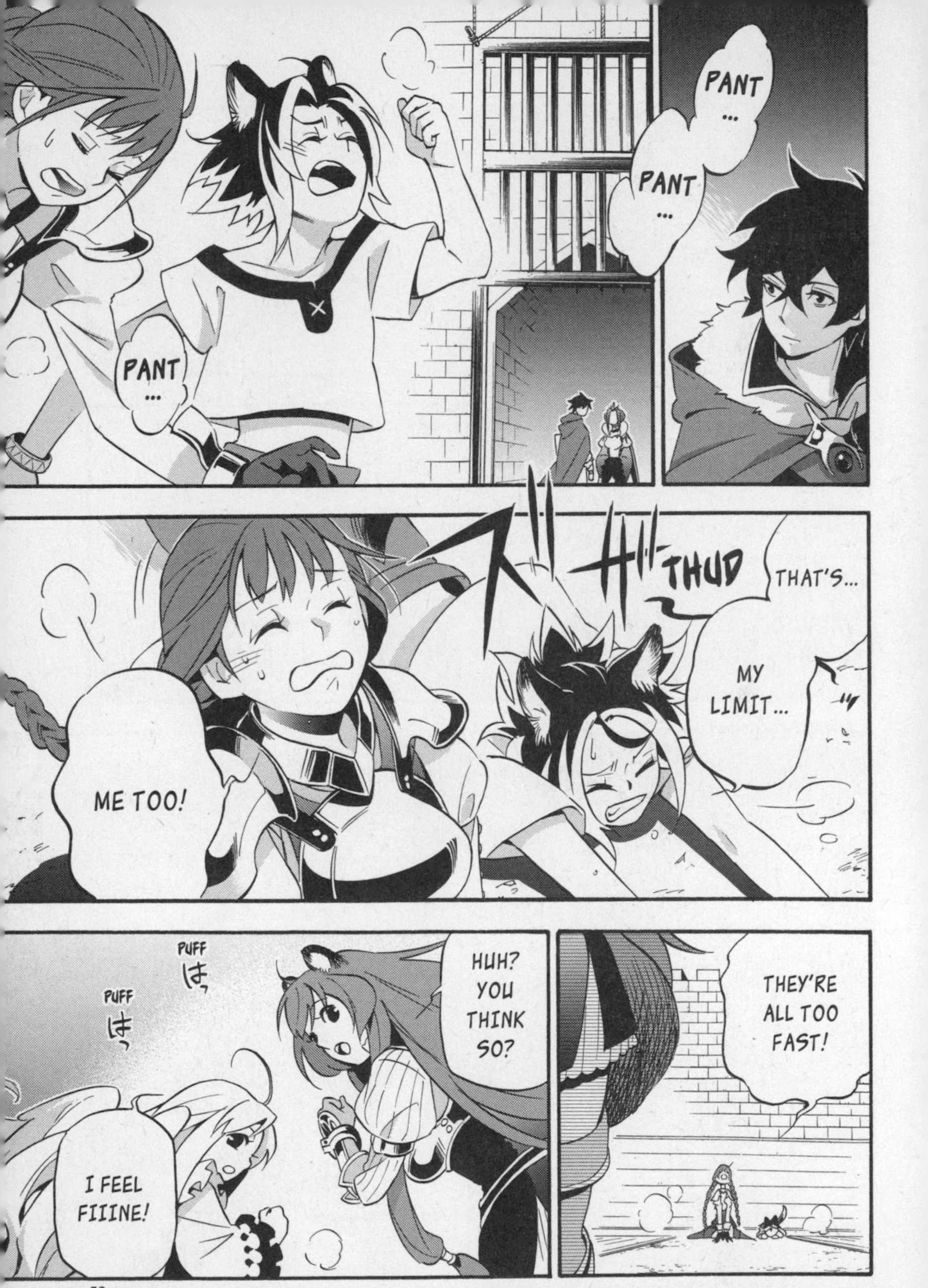

PANT...
PANT...
PANT...
THUD
THAT'S... MY LIMIT...
ME TOO!
THEY'RE ALL TOO FAST!
HUH? YOU THINK SO?
PUFF はっ
PUFF はっ
I FEEL FIIINE!

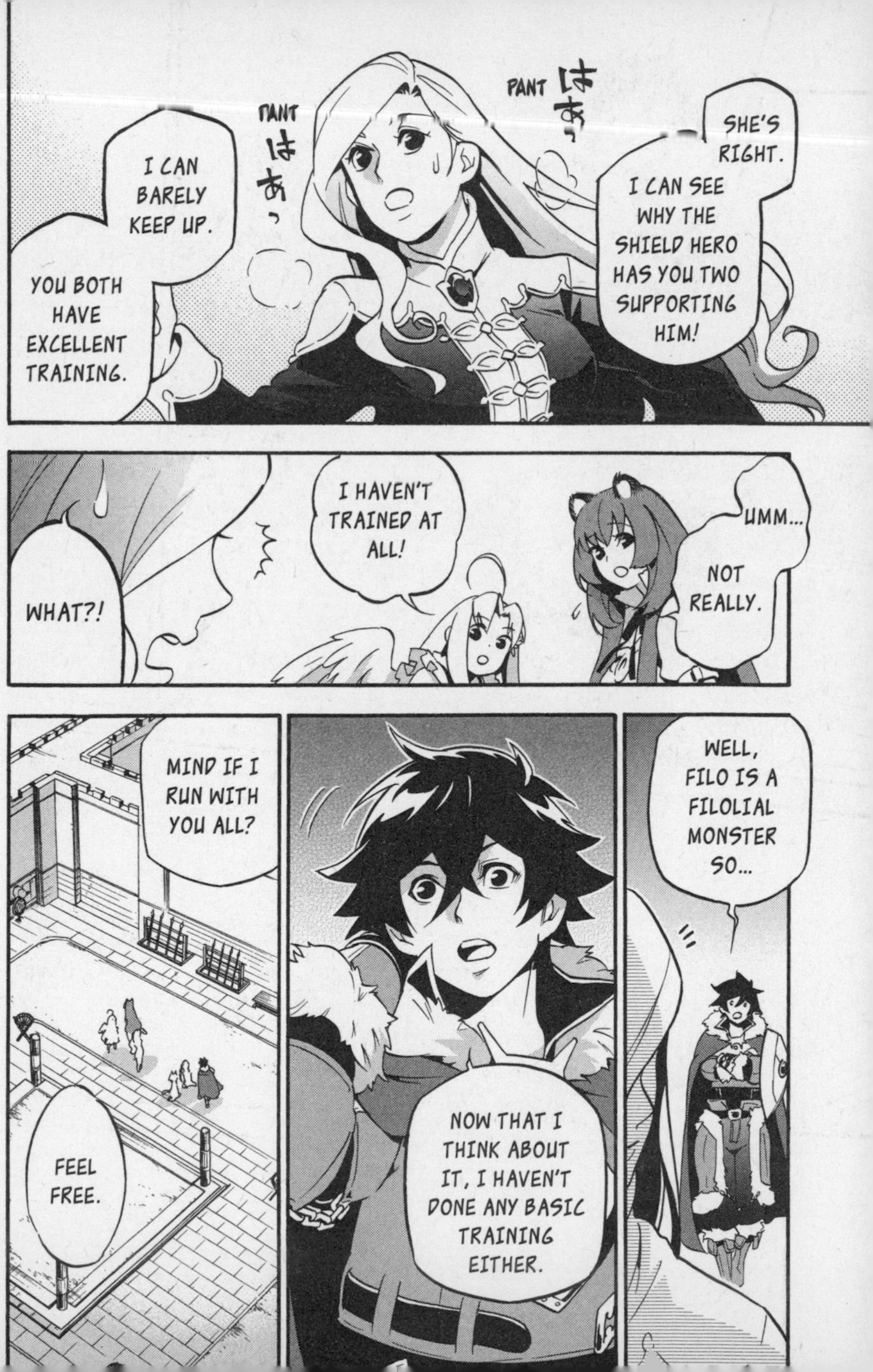
SHE'S RIGHT.
I CAN SEE WHY THE SHIELD HERO HAS YOU TWO SUPPORTING HIM!
PANT はあっ
PANT はあっ
I CAN BARELY KEEP UP.
YOU BOTH HAVE EXCELLENT TRAINING.
UMM... NOT REALLY.
I HAVEN'T TRAINED AT ALL!
WHAT?!
WELL, FILO IS A FILOLIAL MONSTER SO...
NOW THAT I THINK ABOUT IT, I HAVEN'T DONE ANY BASIC TRAINING EITHER.
MIND IF I RUN WITH YOU ALL?
FEEL FREE.

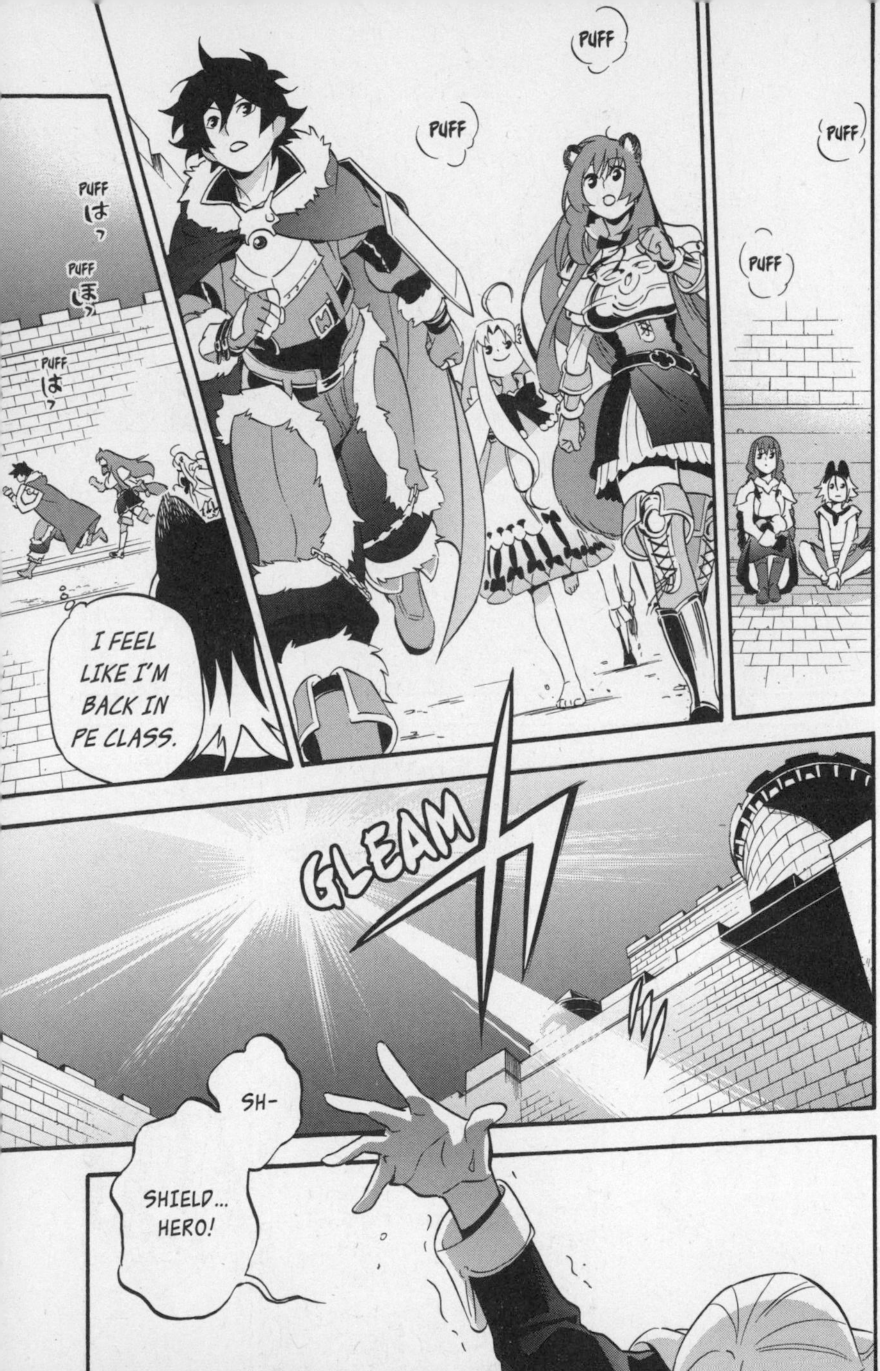
PUFF
PUFF
PUFF
PUFF
PUFF はっ
PUFF ほっ
PUFF はっ
I FEEL LIKE I'M BACK IN PE CLASS.
GLEAM
SH-
SHIELD... HERO!

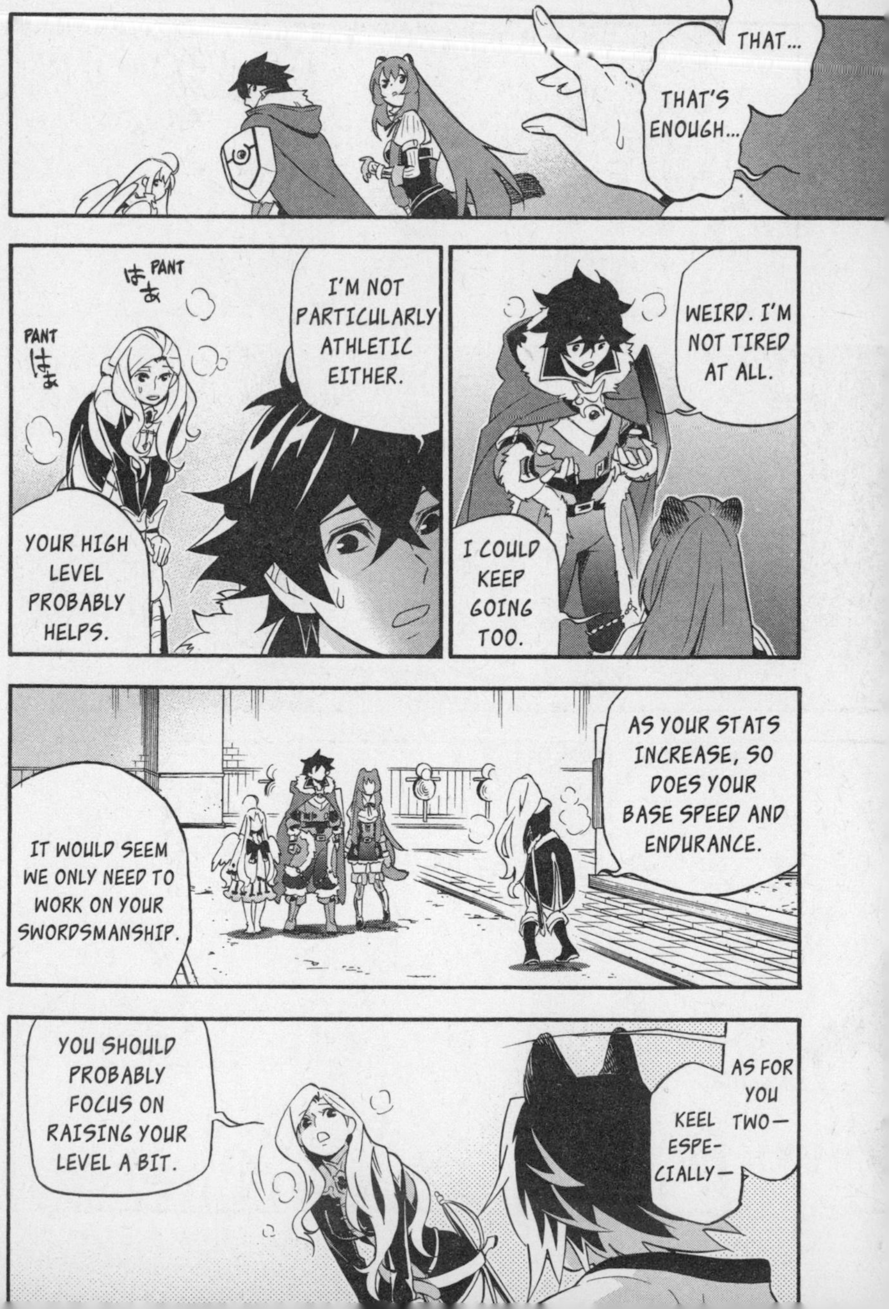
THAT...
THAT'S ENOUGH...
WEIRD. I'M NOT TIRED AT ALL.
I COULD KEEP GOING TOO.
I'M NOT PARTICULARLY ATHLETIC EITHER.
はあ PANT
PANT はあ
YOUR HIGH LEVEL PROBABLY HELPS.
AS YOUR STATS INCREASE, SO DOES YOUR BASE SPEED AND ENDURANCE.
IT WOULD SEEM WE ONLY NEED TO WORK ON YOUR SWORDSMANSHIP.
AS FOR YOU TWO—
KEEL ESPE-CIALLY—
YOU SHOULD PROBABLY FOCUS ON RAISING YOUR LEVEL A BIT.

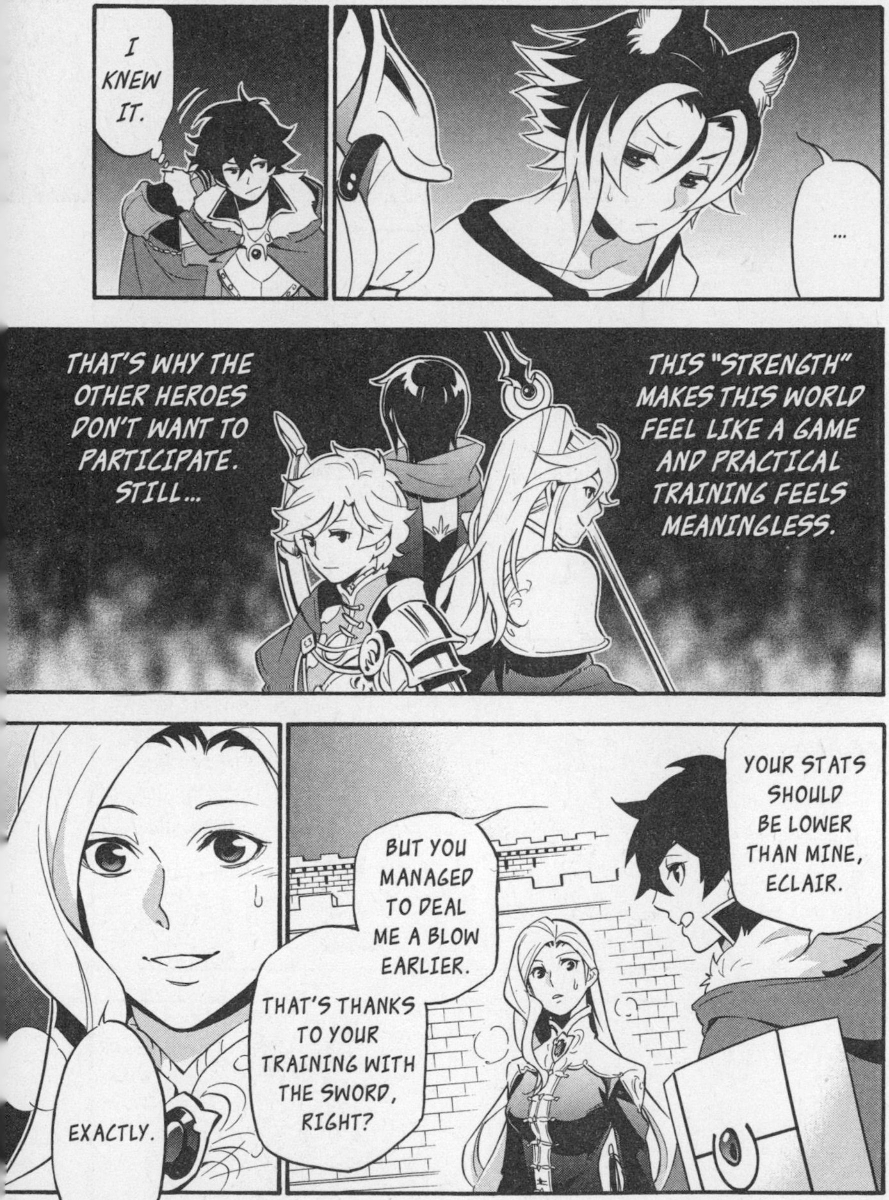
...
I KNEW IT.
THIS "STRENGTH" MAKES THIS WORLD FEEL LIKE A GAME AND PRACTICAL TRAINING FEELS MEANINGLESS.
THAT'S WHY THE OTHER HEROES DON'T WANT TO PARTICIPATE. STILL...
YOUR STATS SHOULD BE LOWER THAN MINE, ECLAIR.
BUT YOU MANAGED TO DEAL ME A BLOW EARLIER.
THAT'S THANKS TO YOUR TRAINING WITH THE SWORD, RIGHT?
EXACTLY.

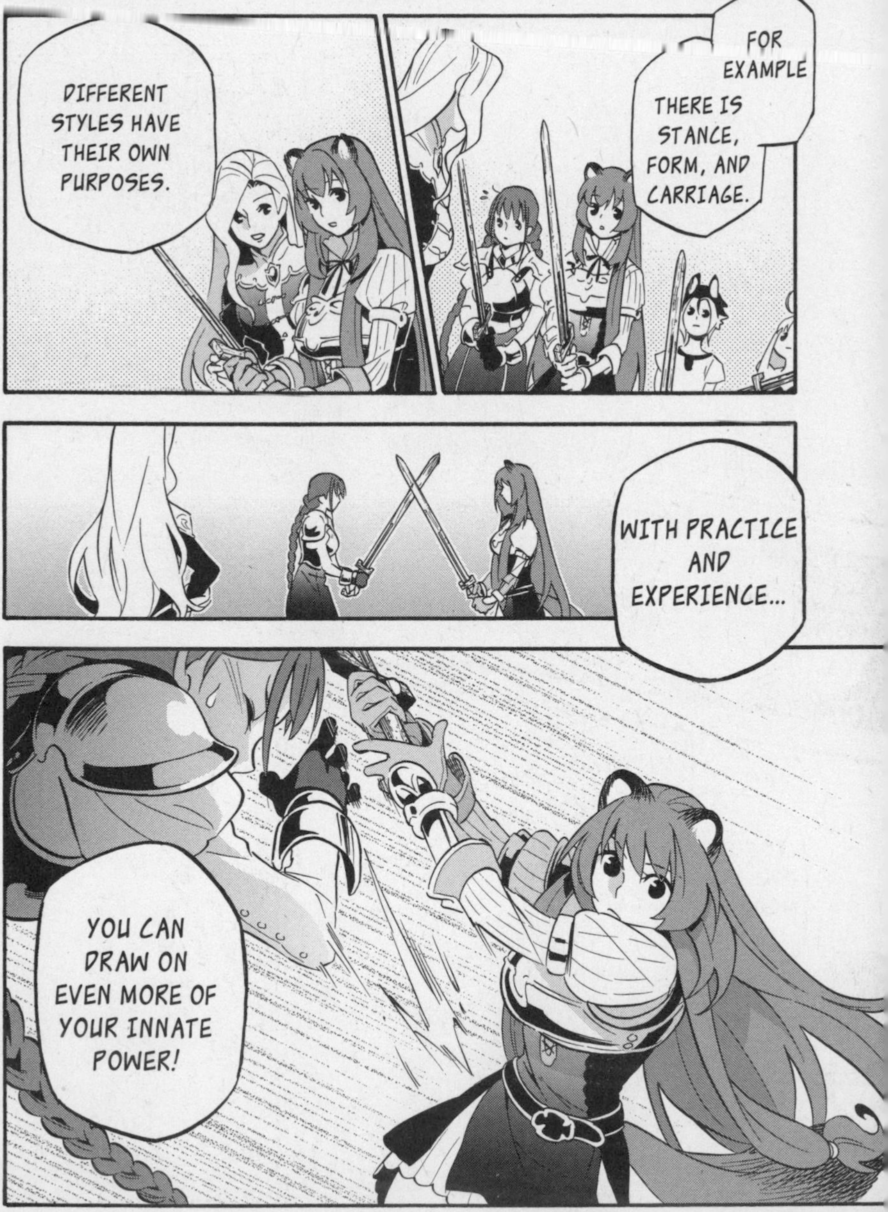
FOR EXAMPLE
THERE IS STANCE, FORM, AND CARRIAGE.
DIFFERENT STYLES HAVE THEIR OWN PURPOSES.
WITH PRACTICE AND EXPERIENCE...
YOU CAN DRAW ON EVEN MORE OF YOUR INNATE POWER!

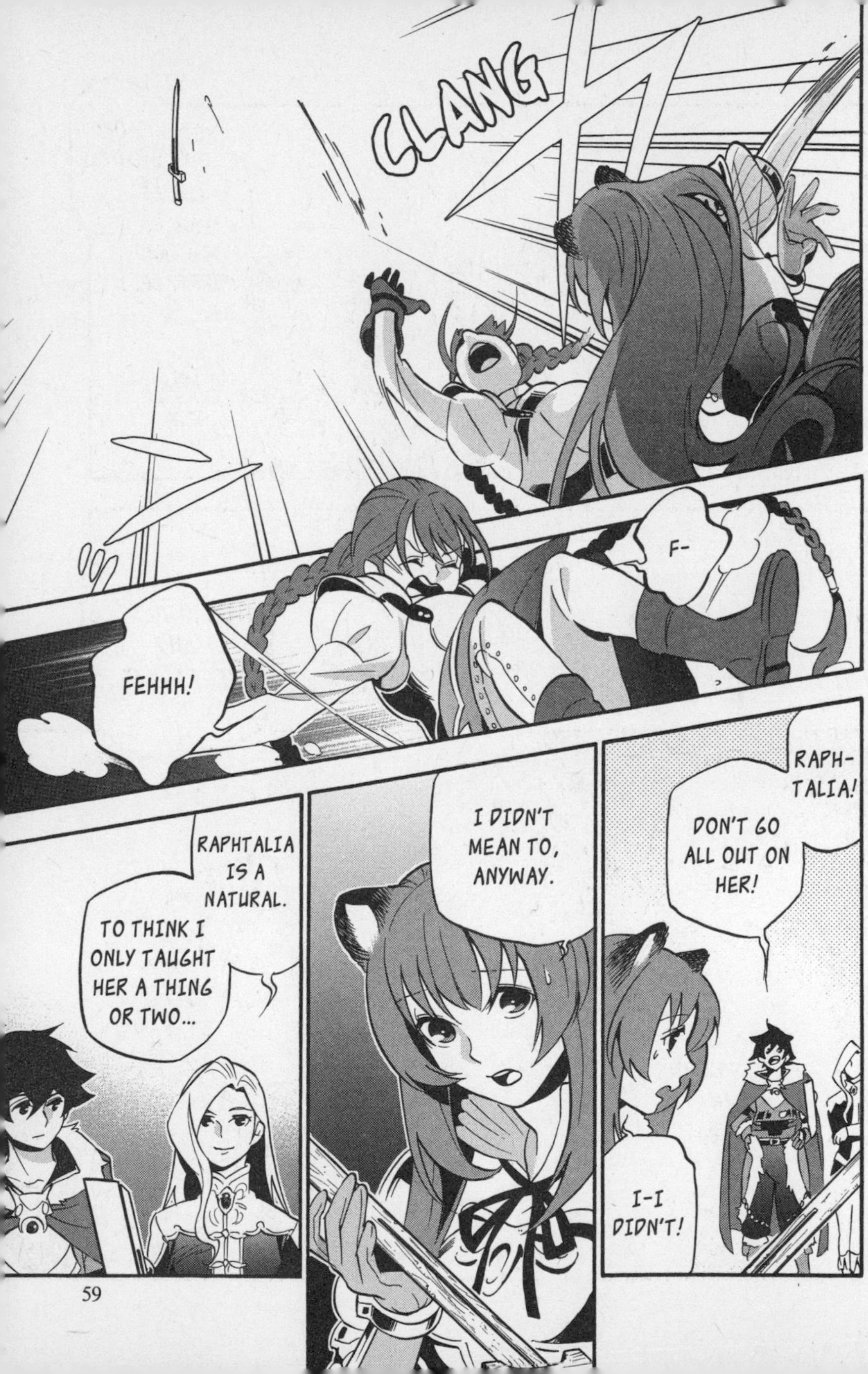
CLANG
F-
FEHHH!
RAPH-TALIA!
DON'T GO ALL OUT ON HER!
I-I DIDN'T!
I DIDN'T MEAN TO, ANYWAY.
RAPHTALIA IS A NATURAL.
TO THINK I ONLY TAUGHT HER A THING OR TWO...

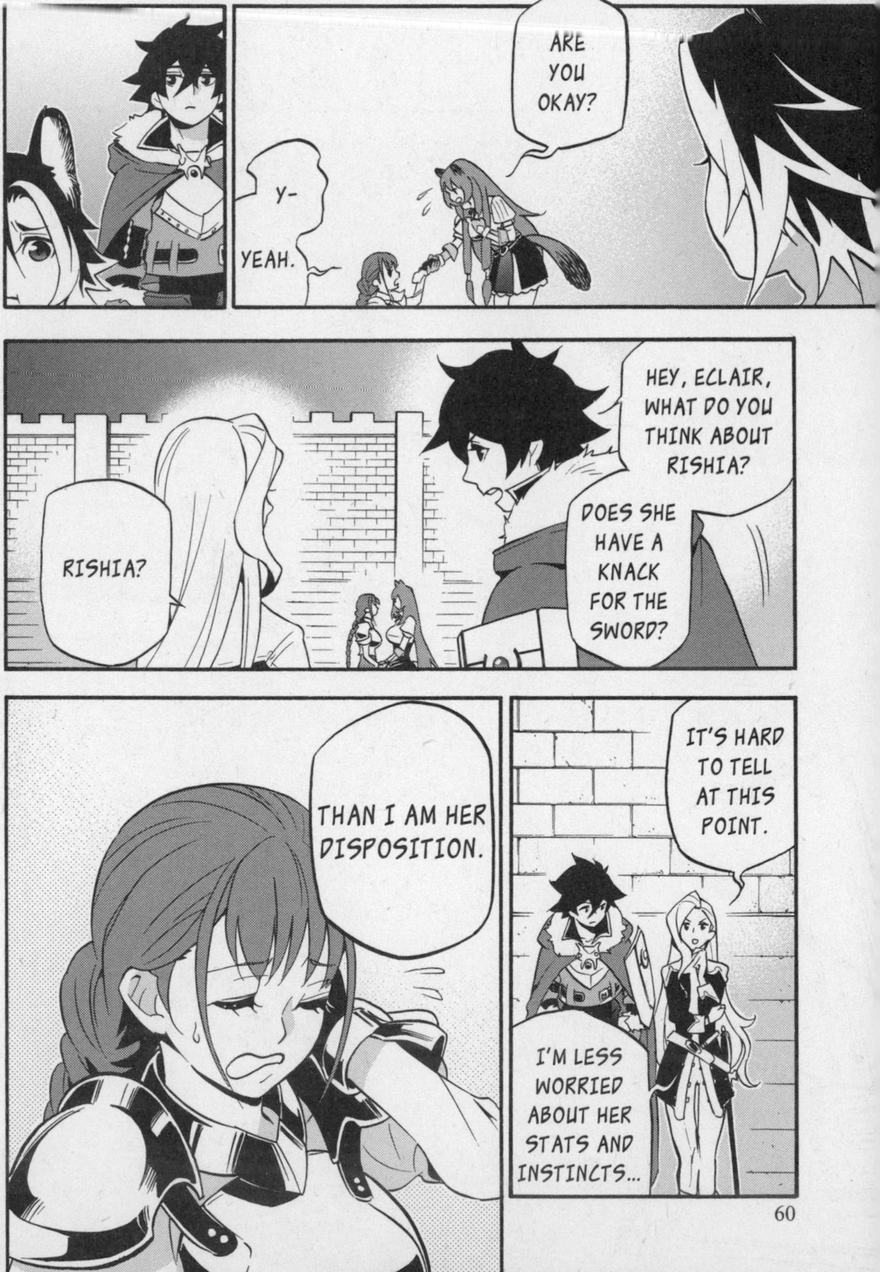
ARE YOU OKAY?
Y- YEAH.
HEY, ECLAIR, WHAT DO YOU THINK ABOUT RISHIA?
DOES SHE HAVE A KNACK FOR THE SWORD?
RISHIA?
IT'S HARD TO TELL AT THIS POINT.
I'M LESS WORRIED ABOUT HER STATS AND INSTINCTS...
THAN I AM HER DISPOSITION.

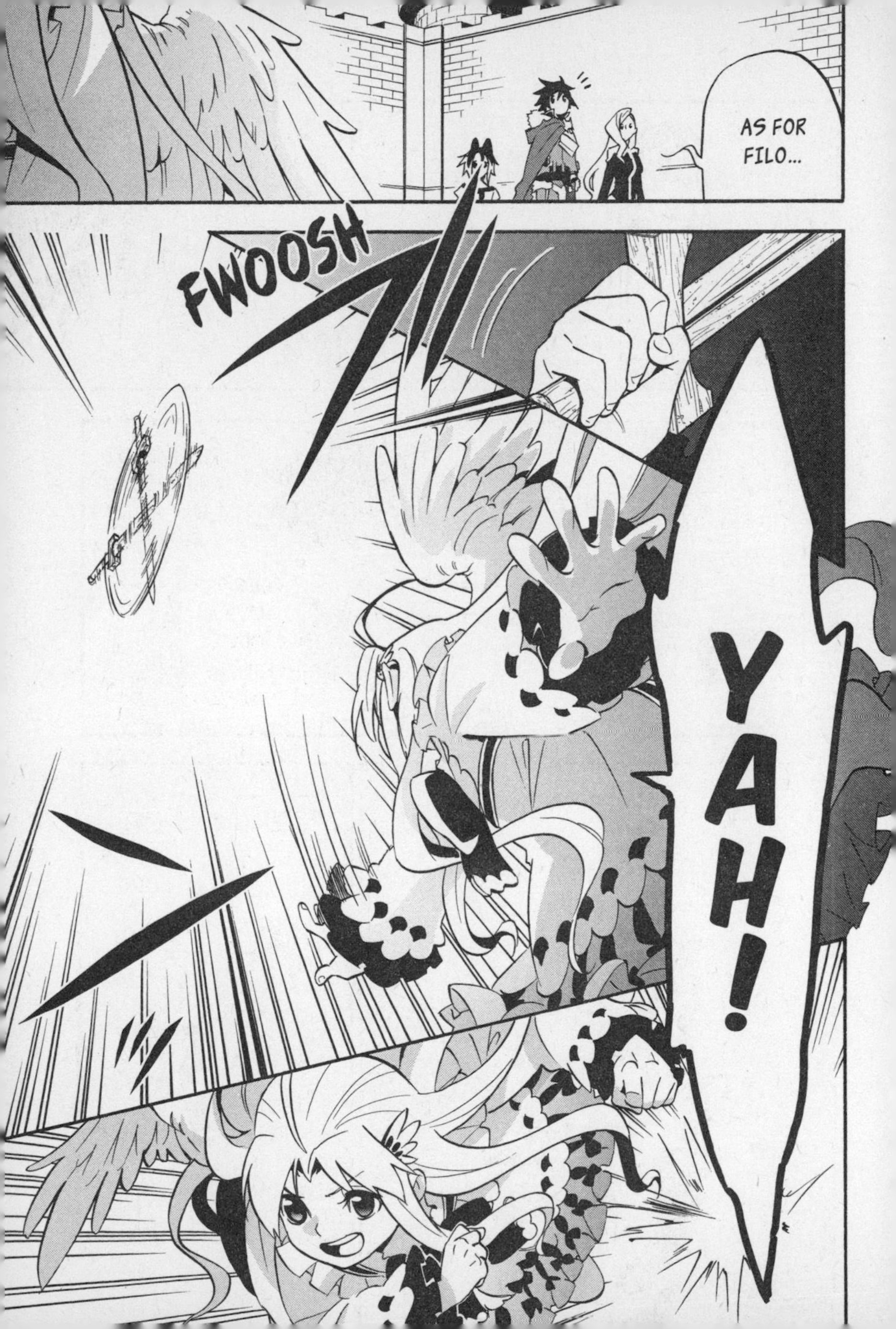
AS FOR FILO...
FWOOSH
YAH!

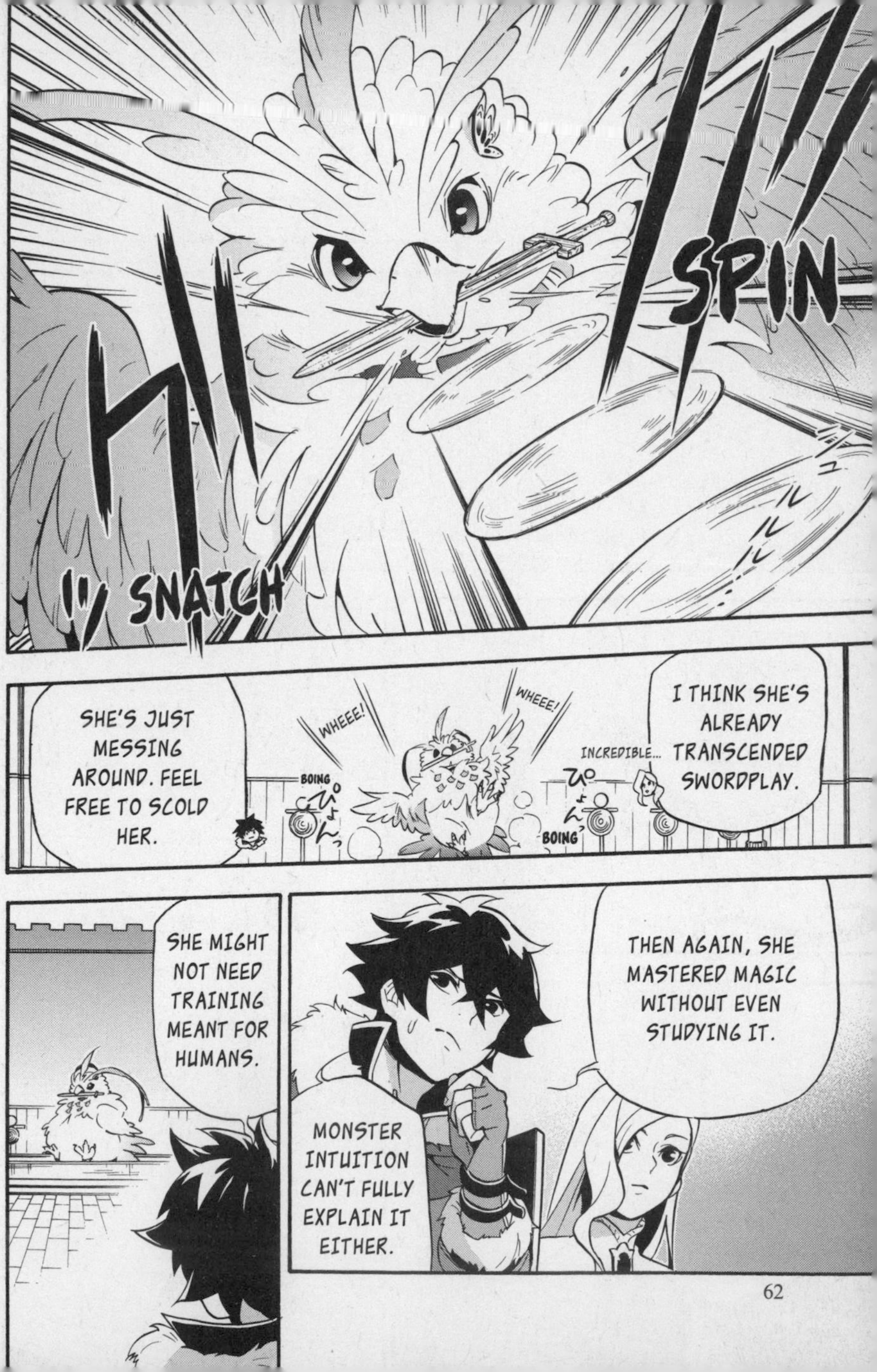
SPIN
SNATCH
I THINK SHE'S ALREADY TRANSCENDED SWORDPLAY.
INCREDIBLE...
WHEEE!
WHEEE!
BOING
BOING
SHE'S JUST MESSING AROUND. FEEL FREE TO SCOLD HER.
THEN AGAIN, SHE MASTERED MAGIC WITHOUT EVEN STUDYING IT.
MONSTER INTUITION CAN'T FULLY EXPLAIN IT EITHER.
SHE MIGHT NOT NEED TRAINING MEANT FOR HUMANS.

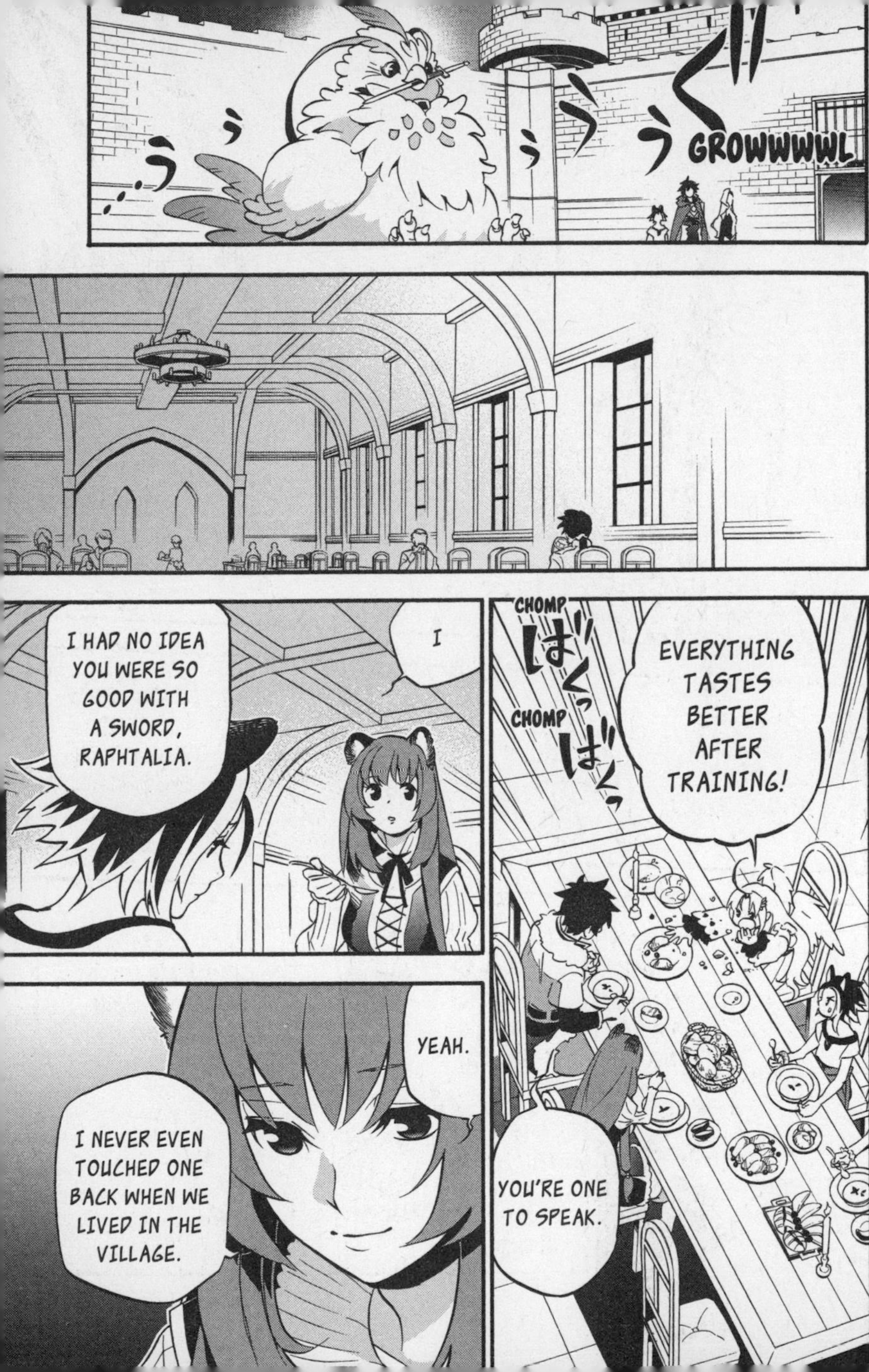
GROWWWWL
CHOMP
CHOMP
EVERYTHING TASTES BETTER AFTER TRAINING!
YOU'RE ONE TO SPEAK.
I
I HAD NO IDEA YOU WERE SO GOOD WITH A SWORD, RAPHTALIA.
YEAH.
I NEVER EVEN TOUCHED ONE BACK WHEN WE LIVED IN THE VILLAGE.

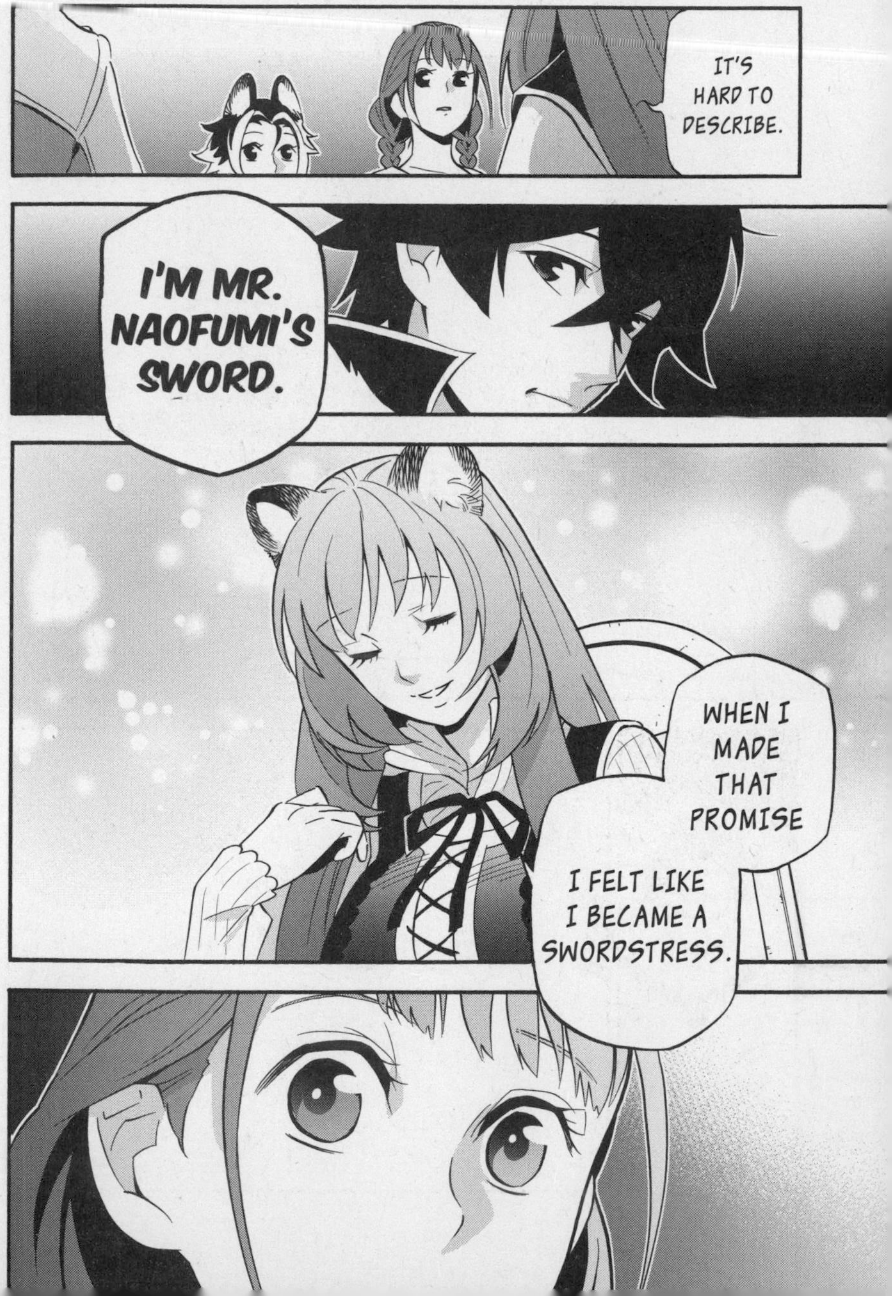
IT'S HARD TO DESCRIBE.
I'M MR. NAOFUMI'S SWORD.
WHEN I MADE THAT PROMISE
I FELT LIKE I BECAME A SWORDSTRESS.

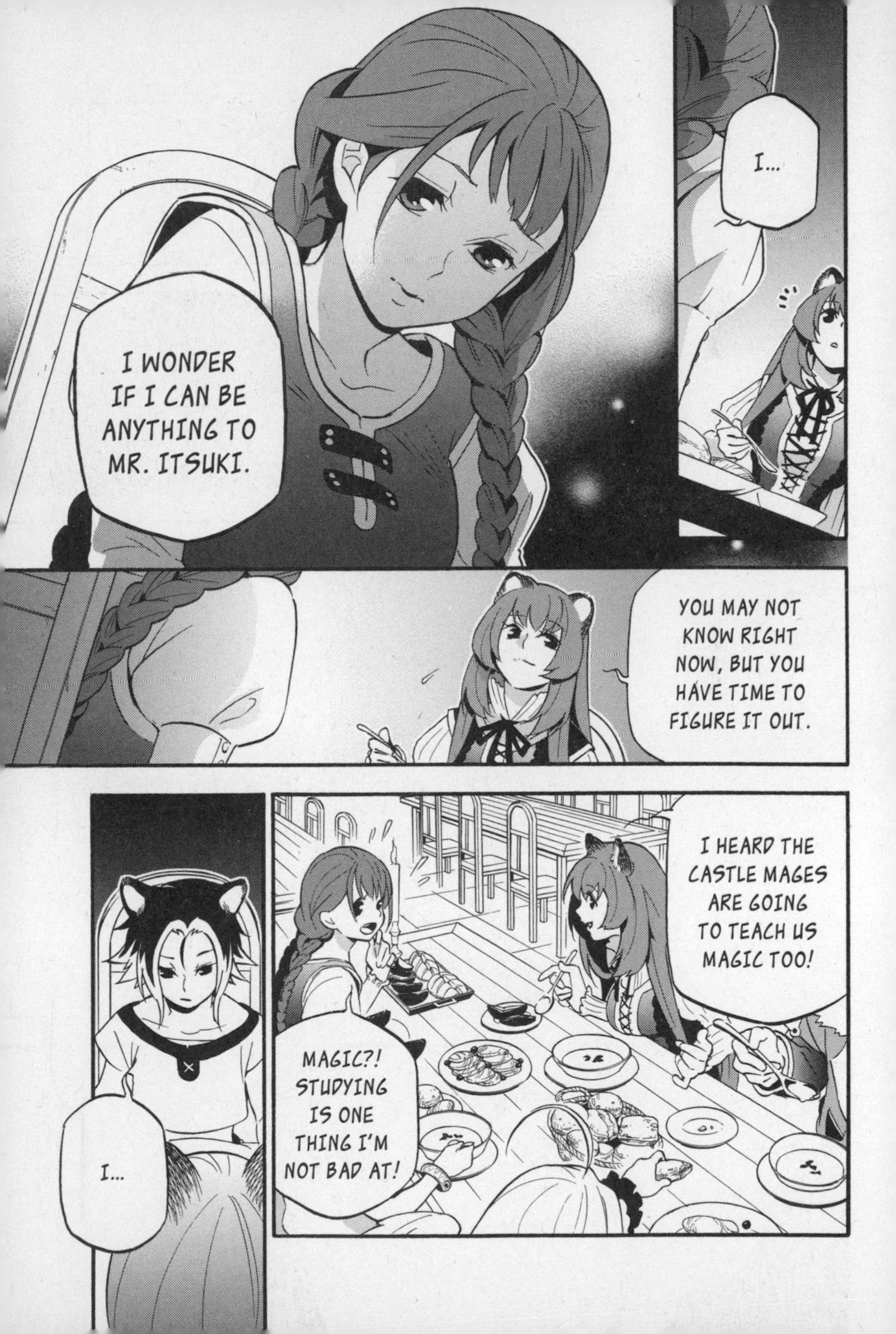
I...
I WONDER IF I CAN BE ANYTHING TO MR. ITSUKI.
YOU MAY NOT KNOW RIGHT NOW, BUT YOU HAVE TIME TO FIGURE IT OUT.
I HEARD THE CASTLE MAGES ARE GOING TO TEACH US MAGIC TOO!
MAGIC?! STUDYING IS ONE THING I'M NOT BAD AT!
I...

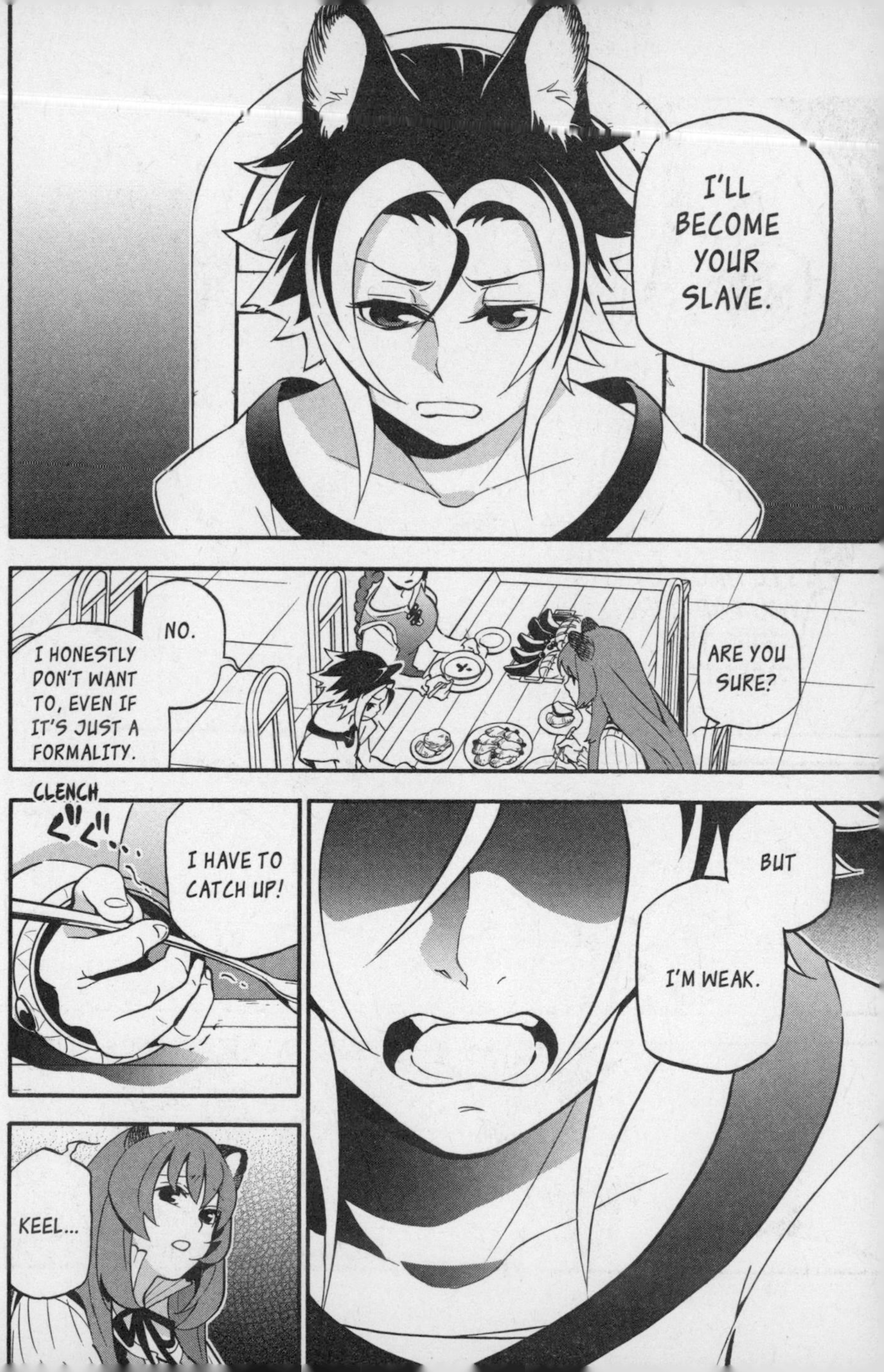
I'LL BECOME YOUR SLAVE.
ARE YOU SURE?
NO.
I HONESTLY DON'T WANT TO, EVEN IF IT'S JUST A FORMALITY.
BUT
I'M WEAK.
CLENCH
I HAVE TO CATCH UP!
KEEL...

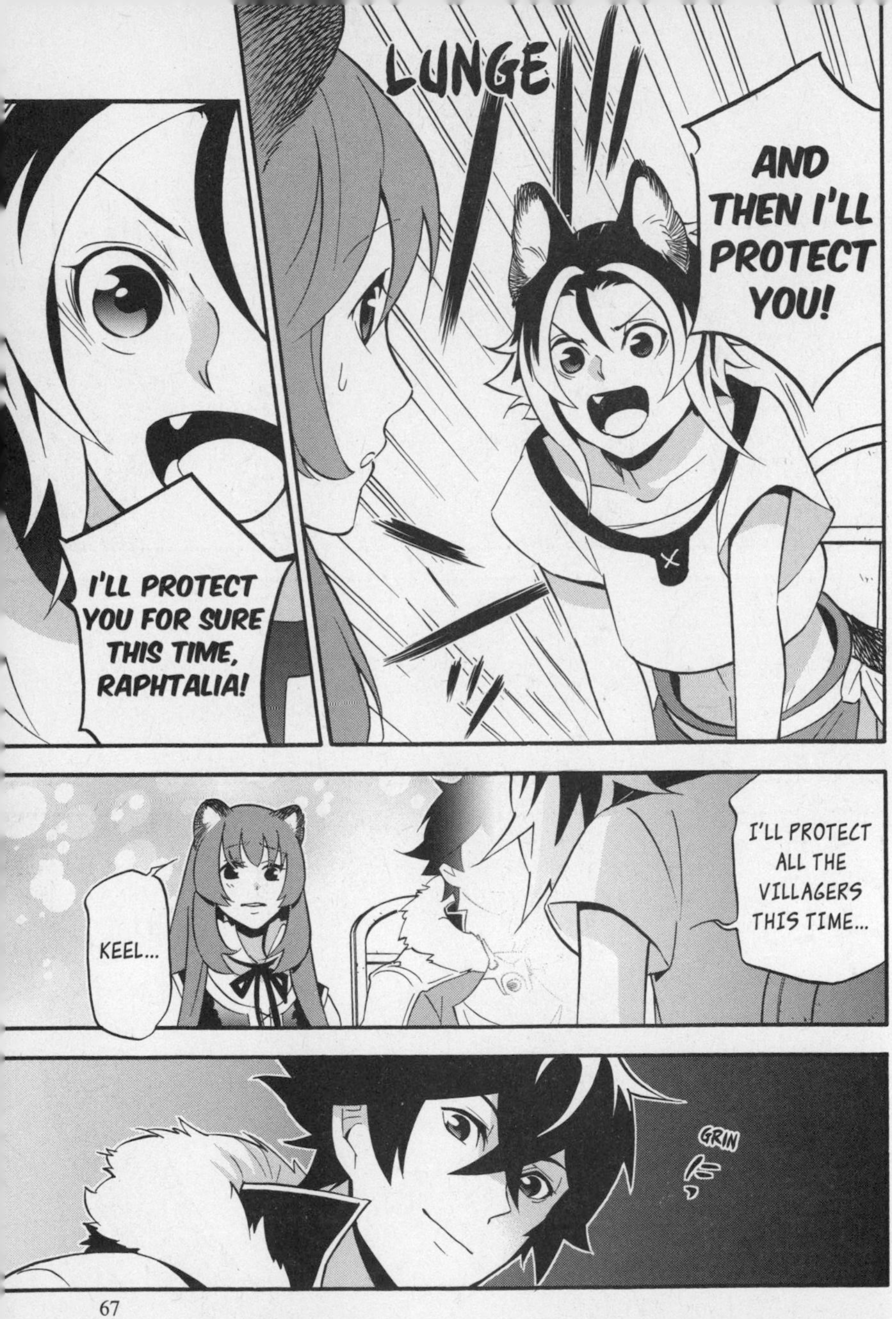
LUNGE
AND THEN I'LL PROTECT YOU!
I'LL PROTECT YOU FOR SURE THIS TIME, RAPHTALIA!
I'LL PROTECT ALL THE VILLAGERS THIS TIME...
KEEL...
GRIN

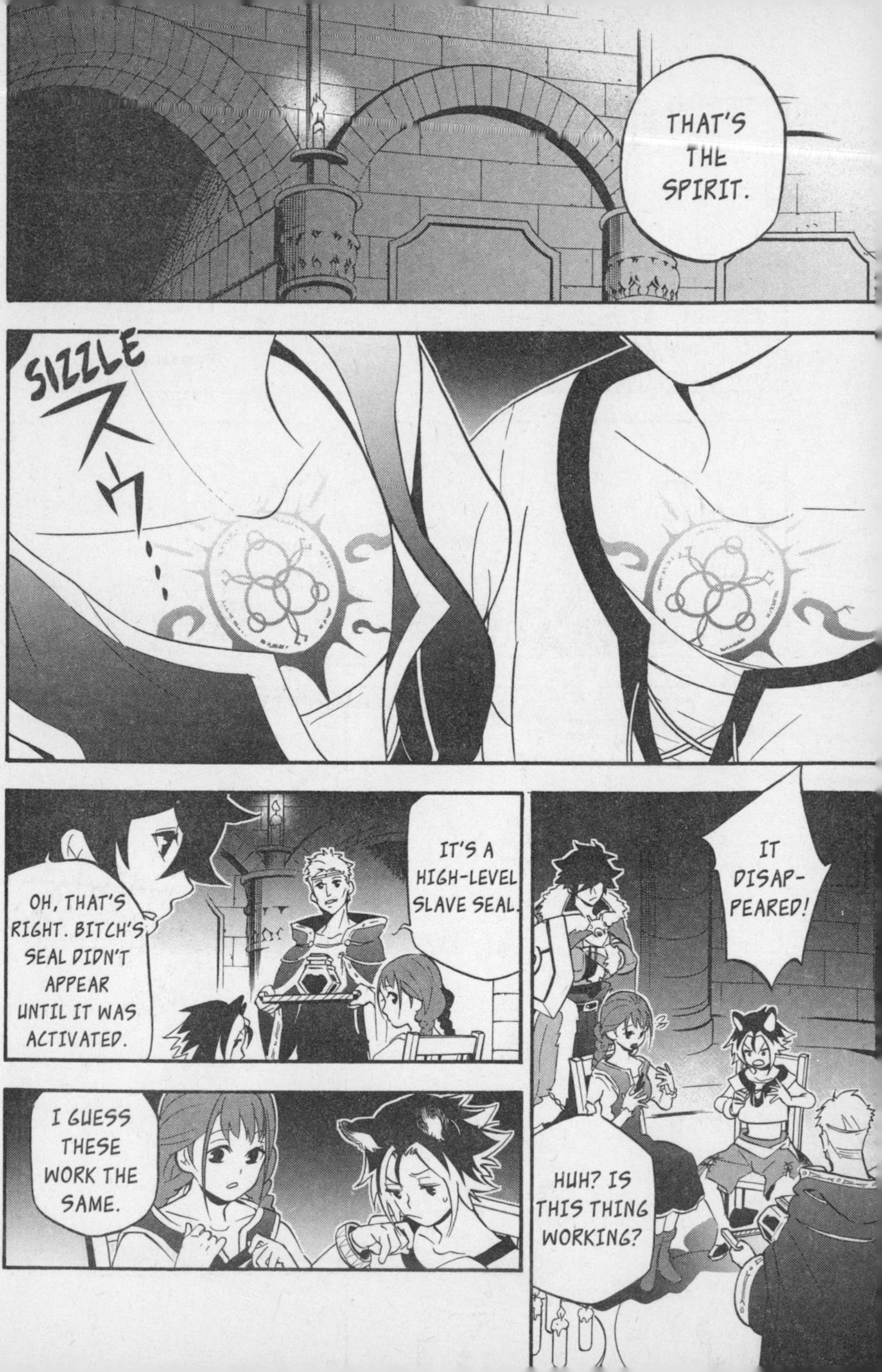
THAT'S THE SPIRIT.
SIZZLE
スゥ…
IT DISAP-PEARED!
HUH? IS THIS THING WORKING?
IT'S A HIGH-LEVEL SLAVE SEAL.
OH, THAT'S RIGHT. BITCH'S SEAL DIDN'T APPEAR UNTIL IT WAS ACTIVATED.
I GUESS THESE WORK THE SAME.

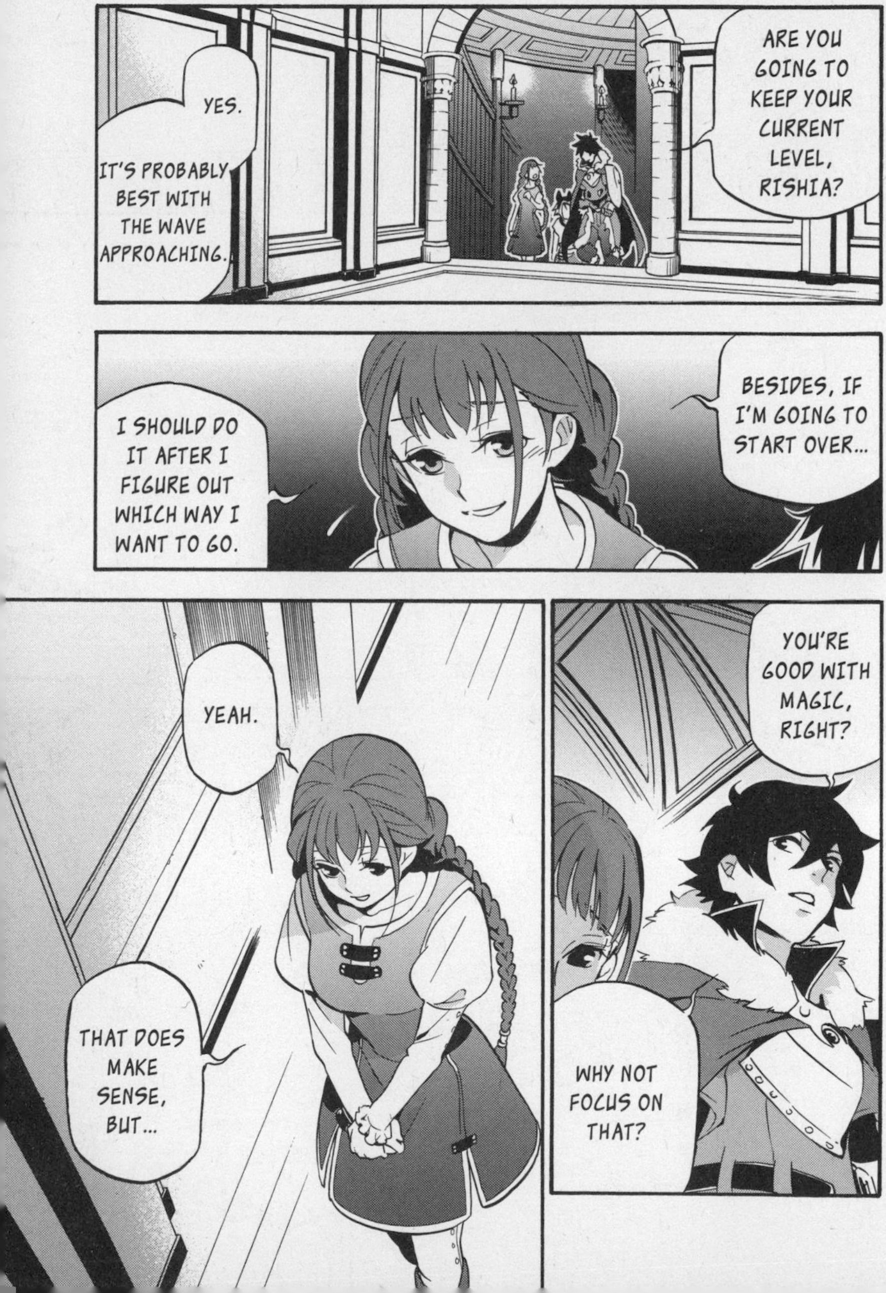
ARE YOU GOING TO KEEP YOUR CURRENT LEVEL, RISHIA?
YES.
IT'S PROBABLY BEST WITH THE WAVE APPROACHING.
BESIDES, IF I'M GOING TO START OVER...
I SHOULD DO IT AFTER I FIGURE OUT WHICH WAY I WANT TO GO.
YOU'RE GOOD WITH MAGIC, RIGHT?
WHY NOT FOCUS ON THAT?
YEAH.
THAT DOES MAKE SENSE, BUT...

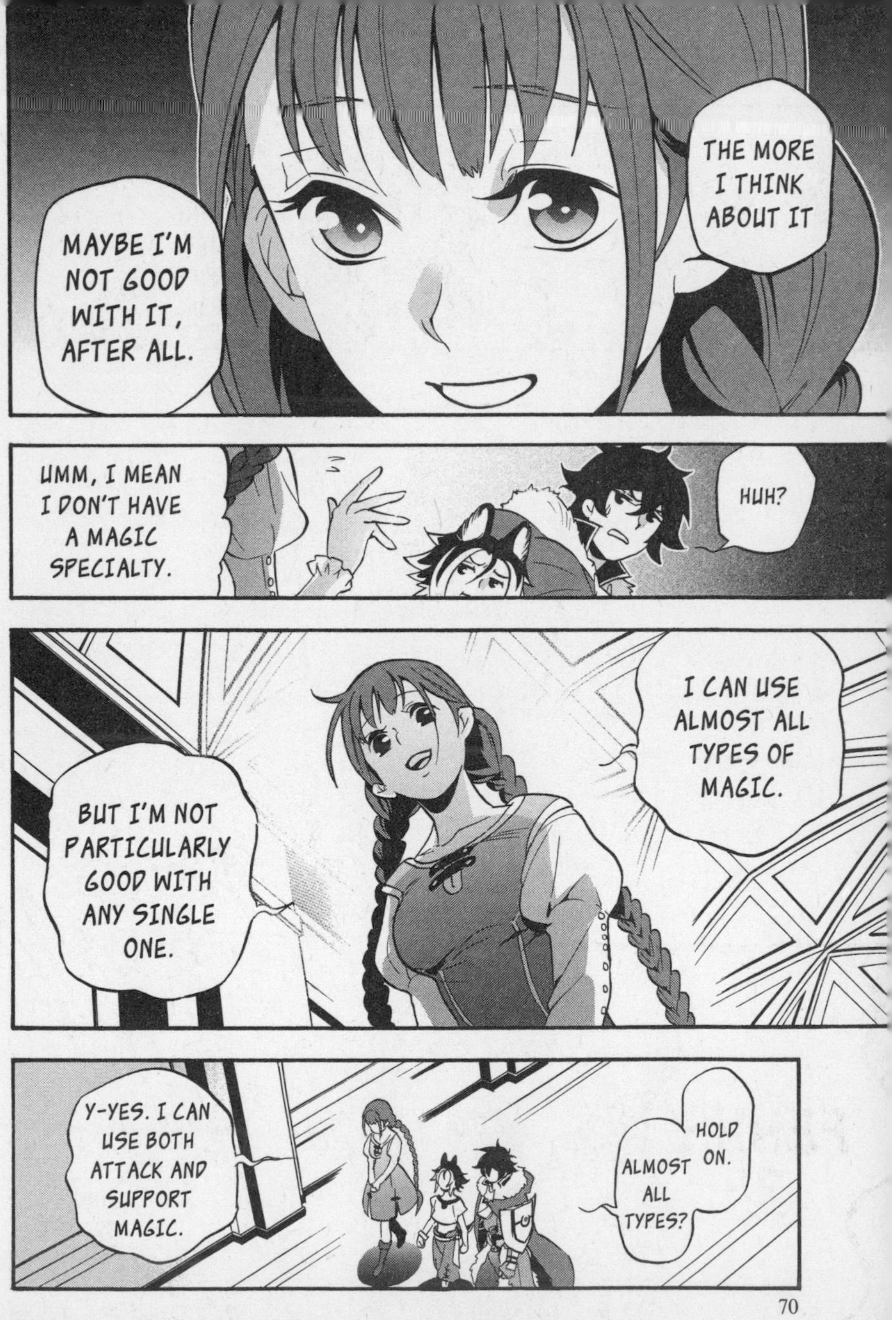
THE MORE I THINK ABOUT IT
MAYBE I'M NOT GOOD WITH IT, AFTER ALL.
HUH?
UMM, I MEAN I DON'T HAVE A MAGIC SPECIALTY.
I CAN USE ALMOST ALL TYPES OF MAGIC.
BUT I'M NOT PARTICULARLY GOOD WITH ANY SINGLE ONE.
HOLD ON.
ALMOST ALL TYPES?
Y-YES. I CAN USE BOTH ATTACK AND SUPPORT MAGIC.

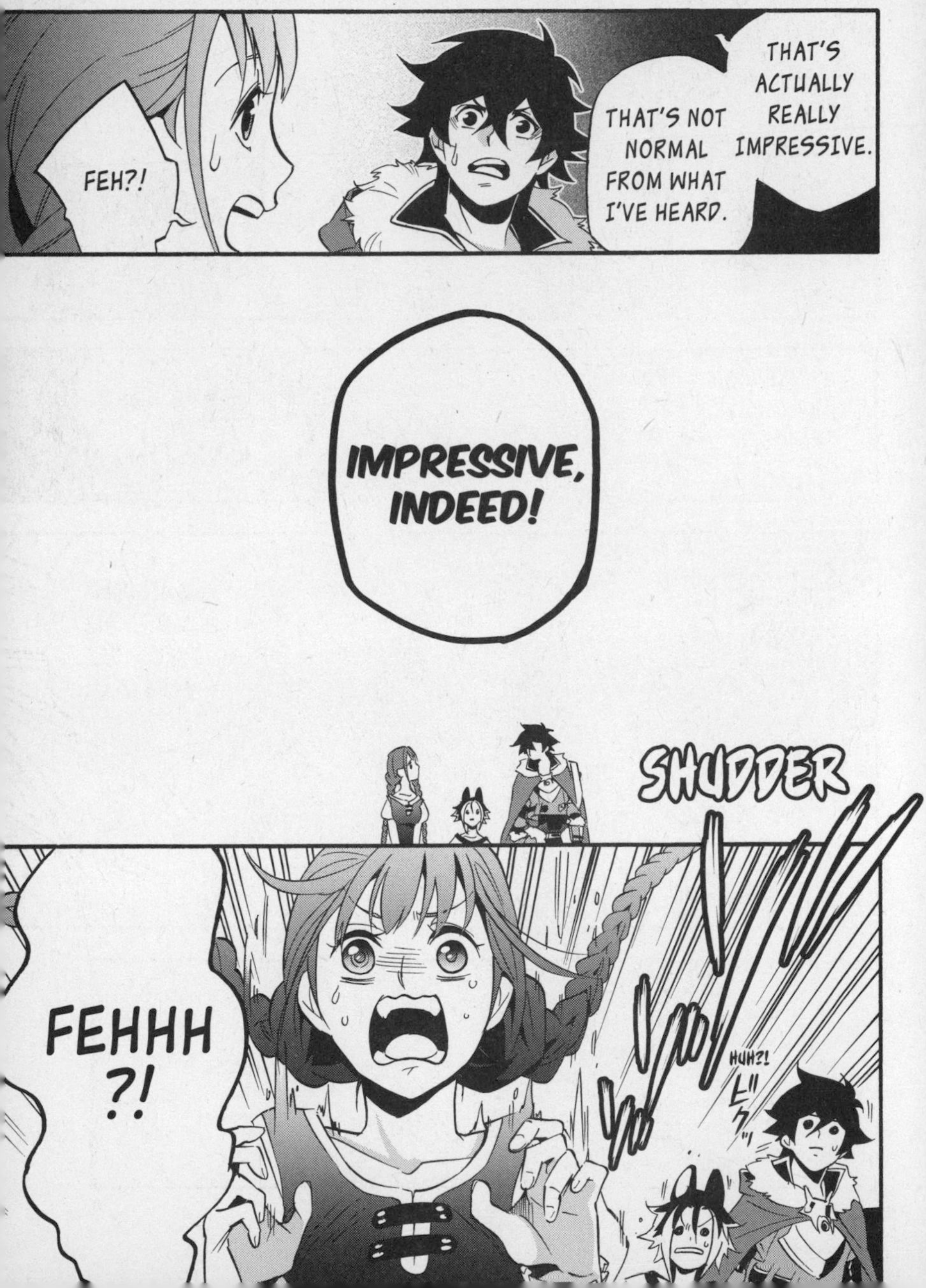
THAT'S ACTUALLY REALLY IMPRESSIVE.
THAT'S NOT NORMAL FROM WHAT I'VE HEARD.
FEH?!
IMPRESSIVE, INDEED!
SHUDDER
HUH?!
FEHHH ?!

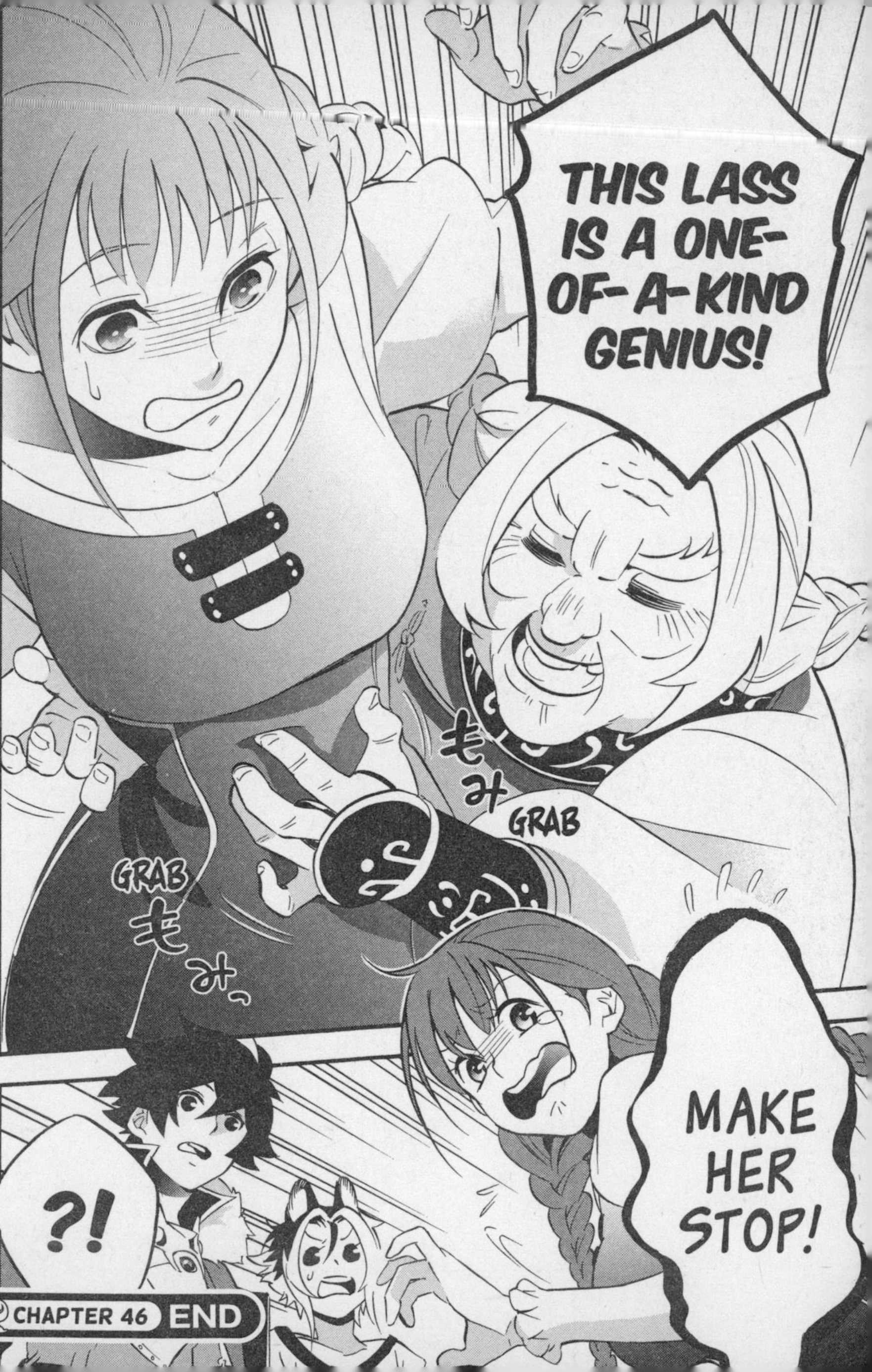
THIS LASS IS A ONE-OF-A-KIND GENIUS!
もみ
GRAB
GRAB
もみっ
MAKE HER STOP!
?!
CHAPTER 46 END

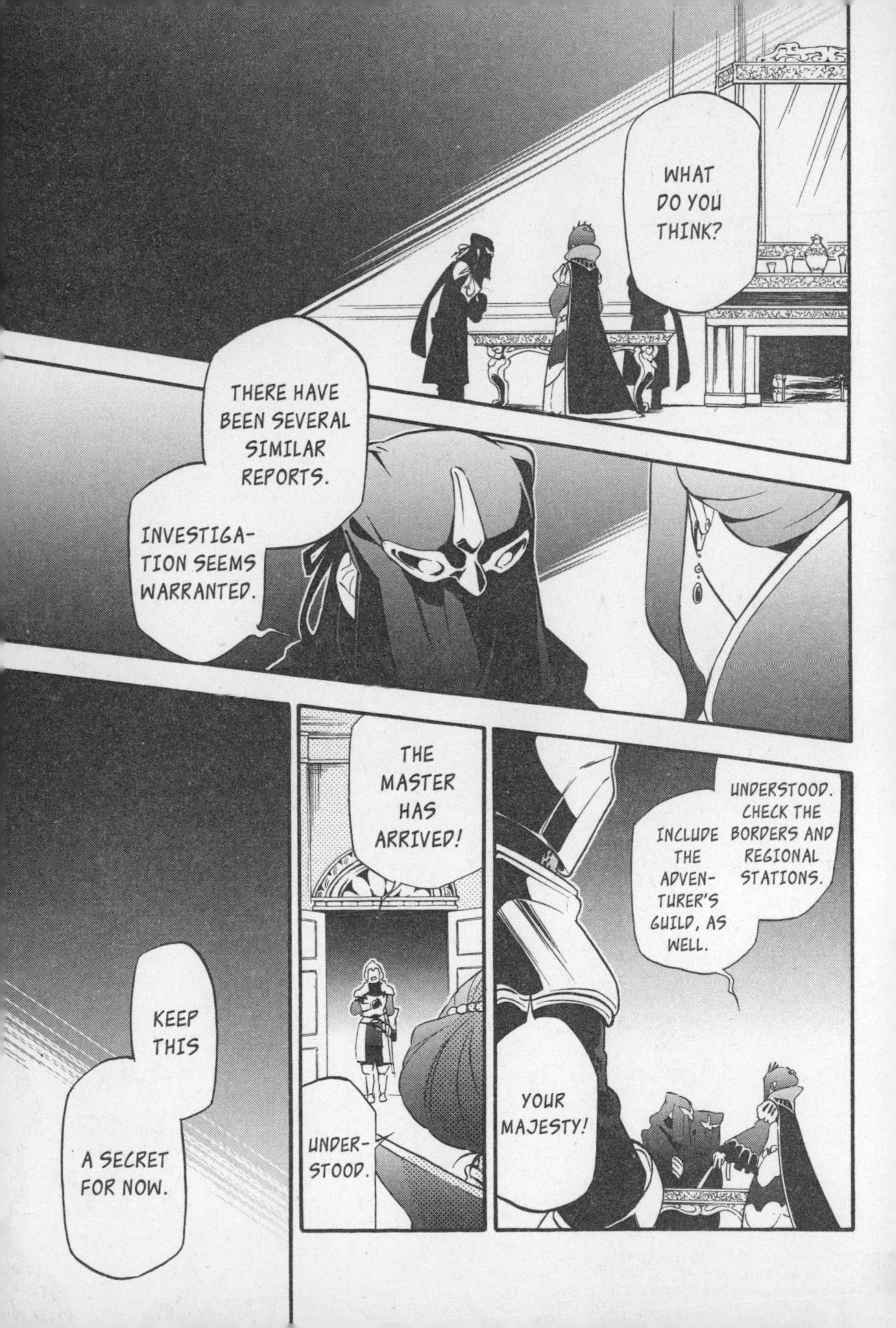
WHAT DO YOU THINK?
THERE HAVE BEEN SEVERAL SIMILAR REPORTS.
INVESTIGATION SEEMS WARRANTED.
UNDERSTOOD. CHECK THE BORDERS AND REGIONAL STATIONS.
INCLUDE THE ADVENTURER'S GUILD, AS WELL.
YOUR MAJESTY!
THE MASTER HAS ARRIVED!
UNDER-STOOD.
KEEP THIS
A SECRET FOR NOW.

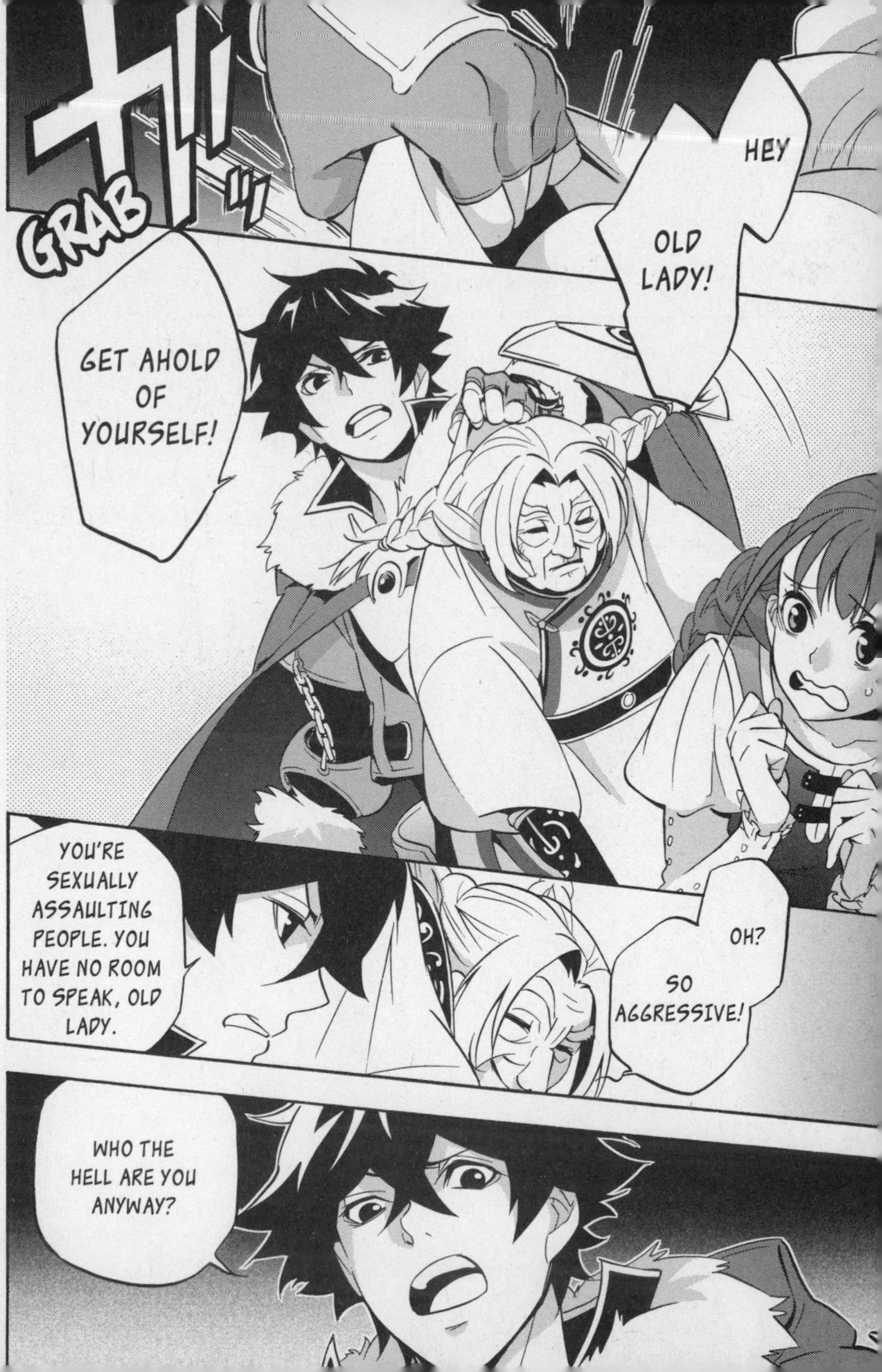
GRAB
HEY OLD LADY!
GET AHOLD OF YOURSELF!
OH? SO AGGRESSIVE!
YOU'RE SEXUALLY ASSAULTING PEOPLE. YOU HAVE NO ROOM TO SPEAK, OLD LADY.
WHO THE HELL ARE YOU ANYWAY?

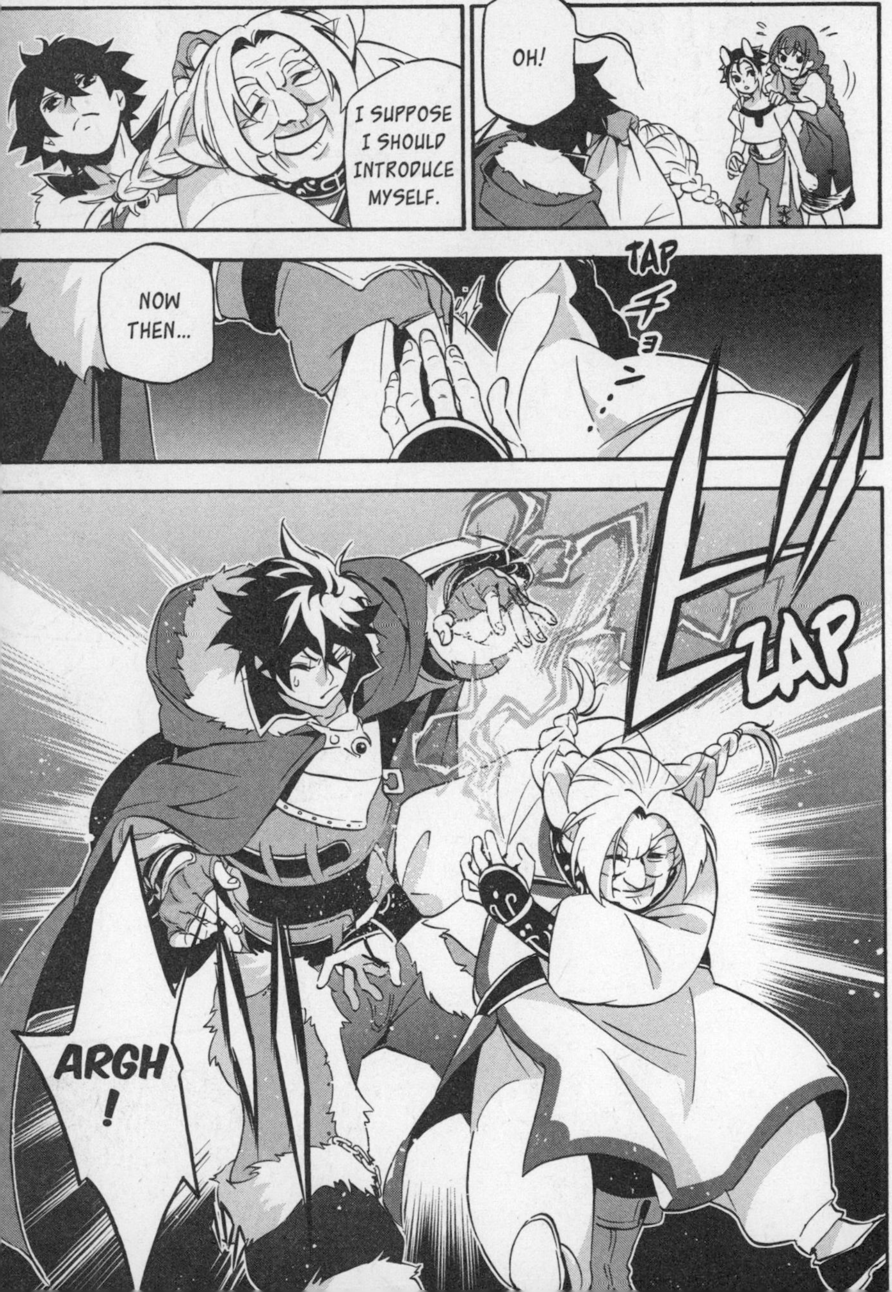
OH!
I SUPPOSE I SHOULD INTRODUCE MYSELF.
TAP
チョン
NOW THEN...
ZAP
ARGH!

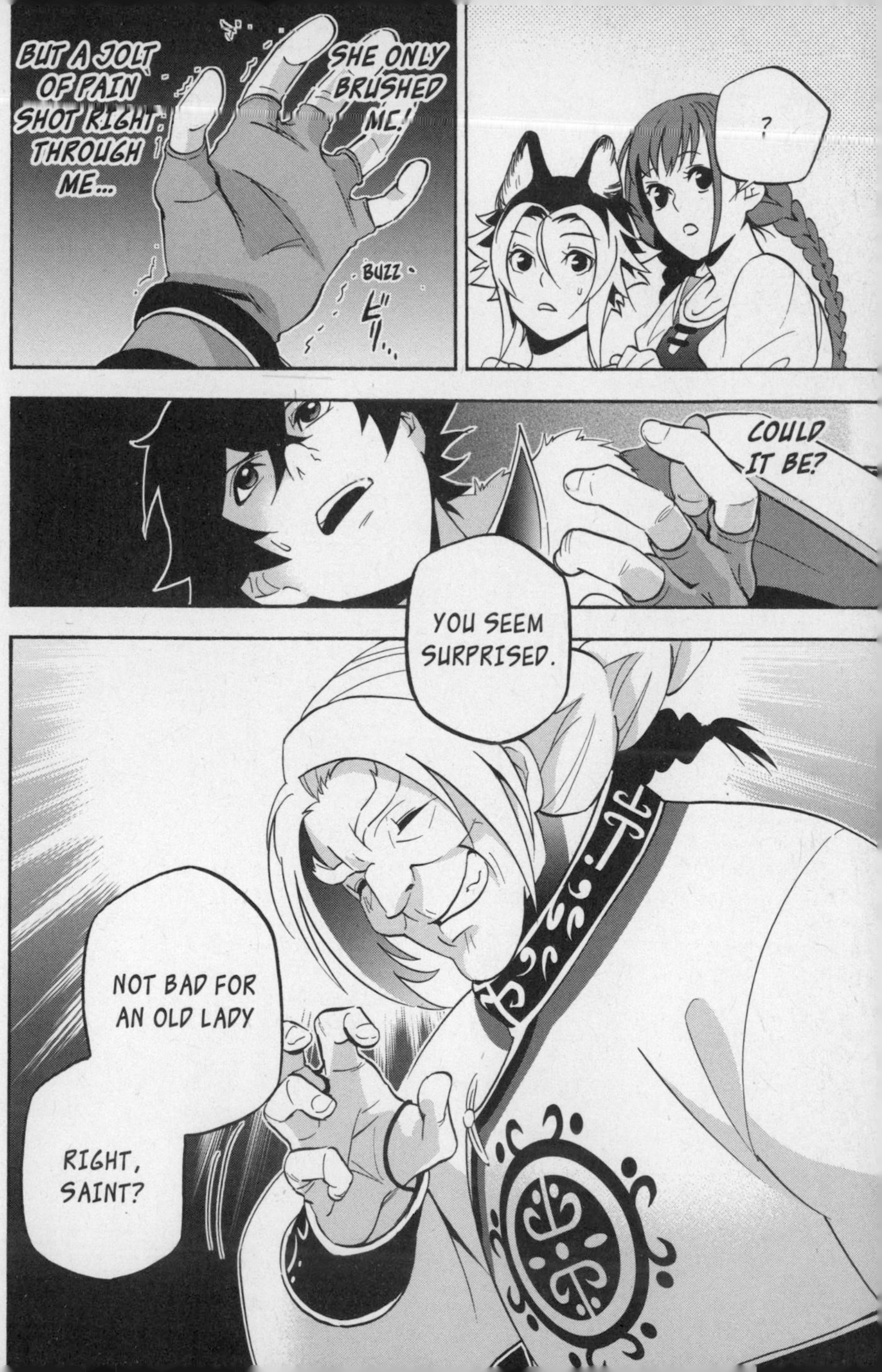
?
SHE ONLY BRUSHED ME!
BUT A JOLT OF PAIN SHOT RIGHT THROUGH ME...
BUZZ
ビリ…
COULD IT BE?
YOU SEEM SURPRISED.
NOT BAD FOR AN OLD LADY
RIGHT, SAINT?

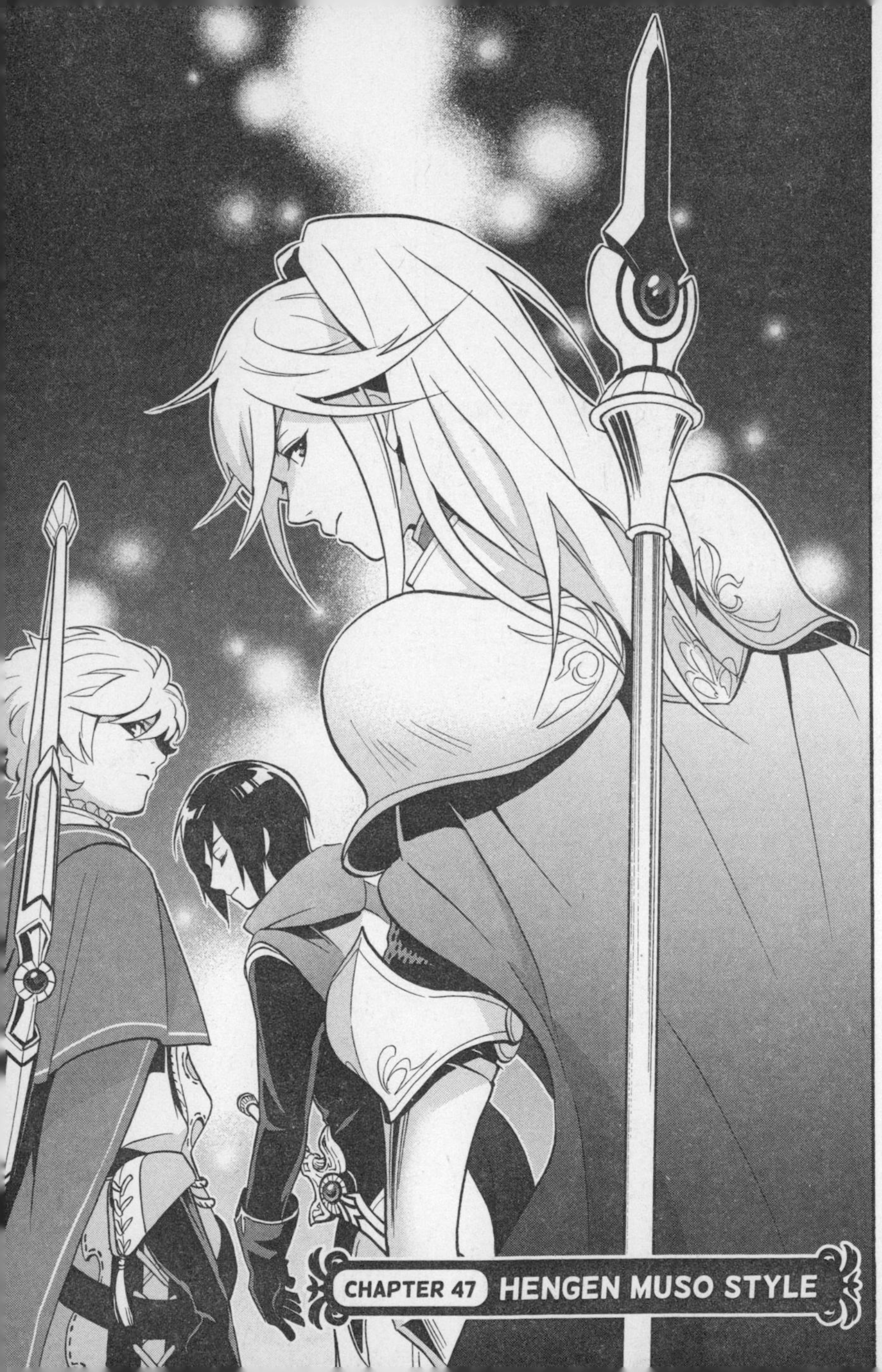
CHAPTER 47 HENGEN MUSO STYLE

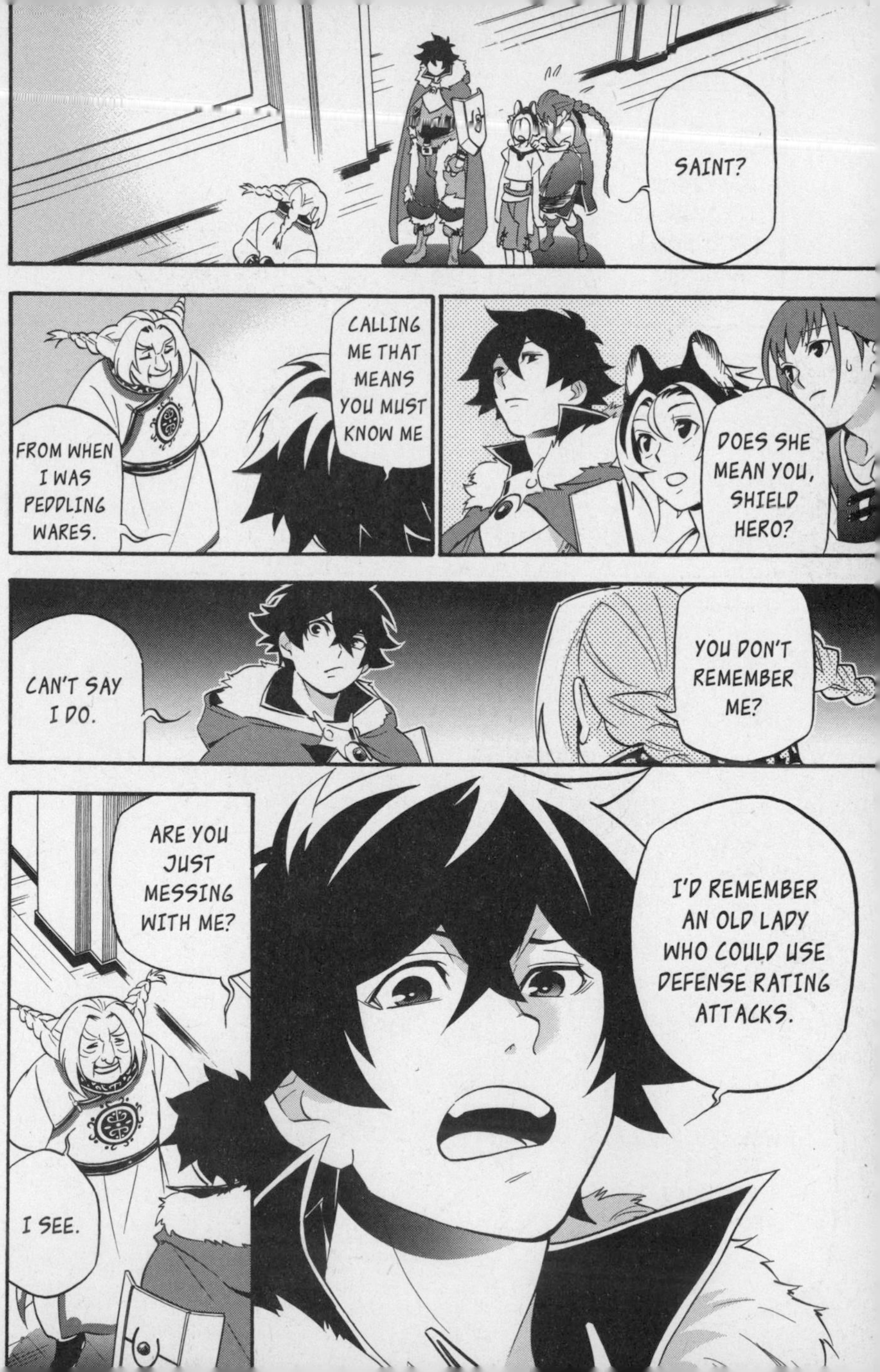
SAINT?
DOES SHE MEAN YOU, SHIELD HERO?
CALLING ME THAT MEANS YOU MUST KNOW ME
FROM WHEN I WAS PEDDLING WARES.
YOU DON'T REMEMBER ME?
CAN'T SAY I DO.
I'D REMEMBER AN OLD LADY WHO COULD USE DEFENSE RATING ATTACKS.
ARE YOU JUST MESSING WITH ME?
I SEE.

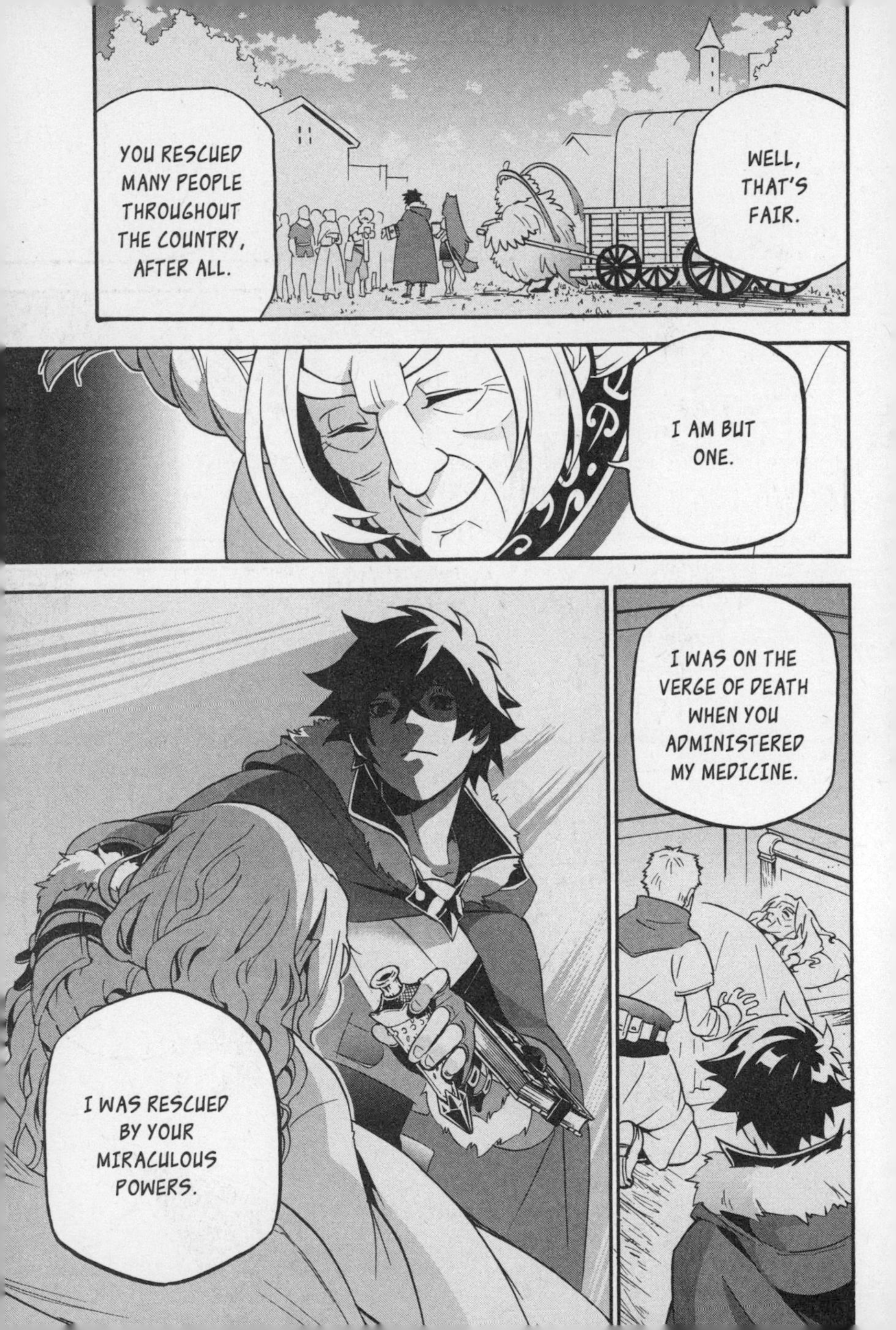
WELL, THAT'S FAIR.
YOU RESCUED MANY PEOPLE THROUGHOUT THE COUNTRY, AFTER ALL.
I AM BUT ONE.
I WAS ON THE VERGE OF DEATH WHEN YOU ADMINISTERED MY MEDICINE.
I WAS RESCUED BY YOUR MIRACULOUS POWERS.

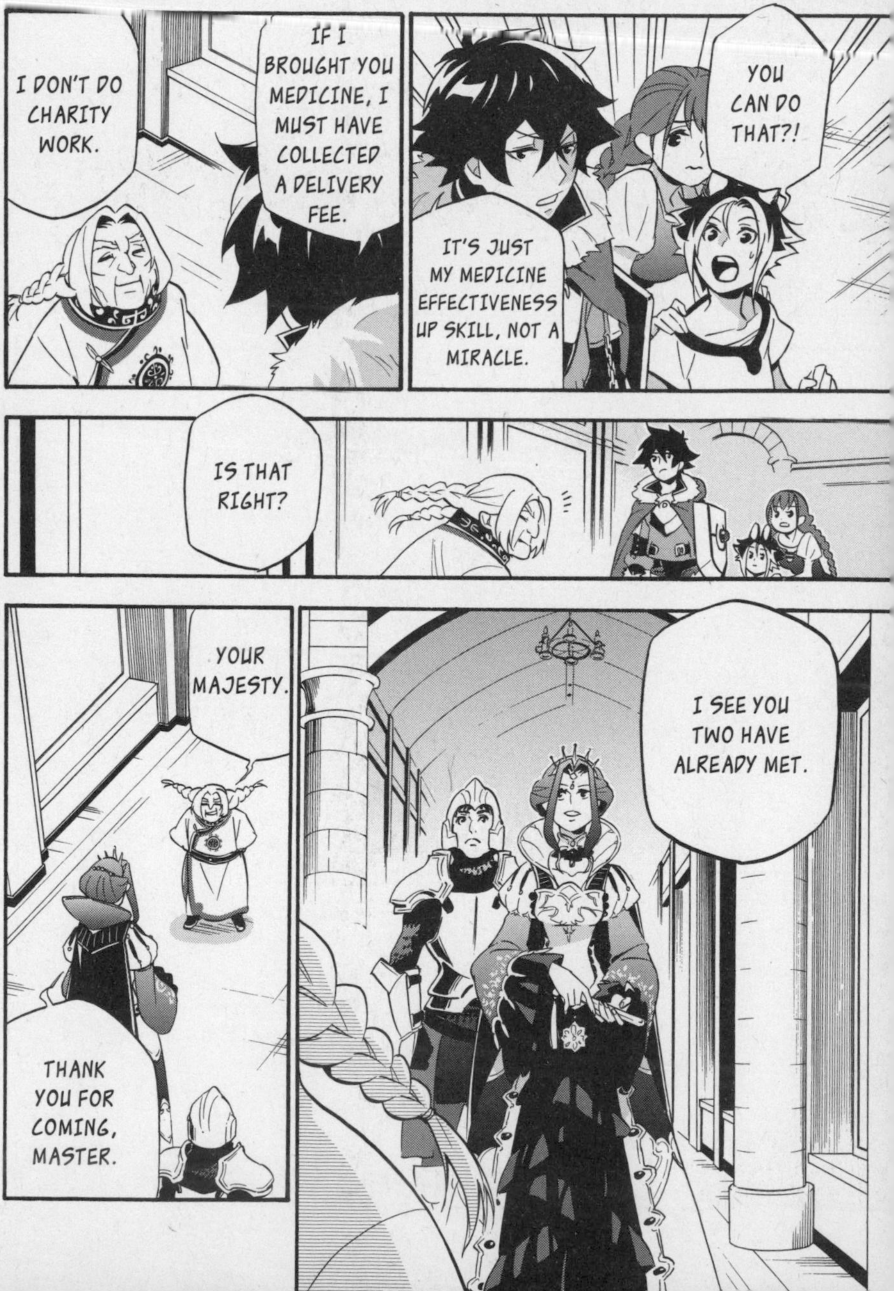
YOU CAN DO THAT?!
IT'S JUST MY MEDICINE EFFECTIVENESS UP SKILL, NOT A MIRACLE.
IF I BROUGHT YOU MEDICINE, I MUST HAVE COLLECTED A DELIVERY FEE.
I DON'T DO CHARITY WORK.
IS THAT RIGHT?
I SEE YOU TWO HAVE ALREADY MET.
YOUR MAJESTY.
THANK YOU FOR COMING, MASTER.

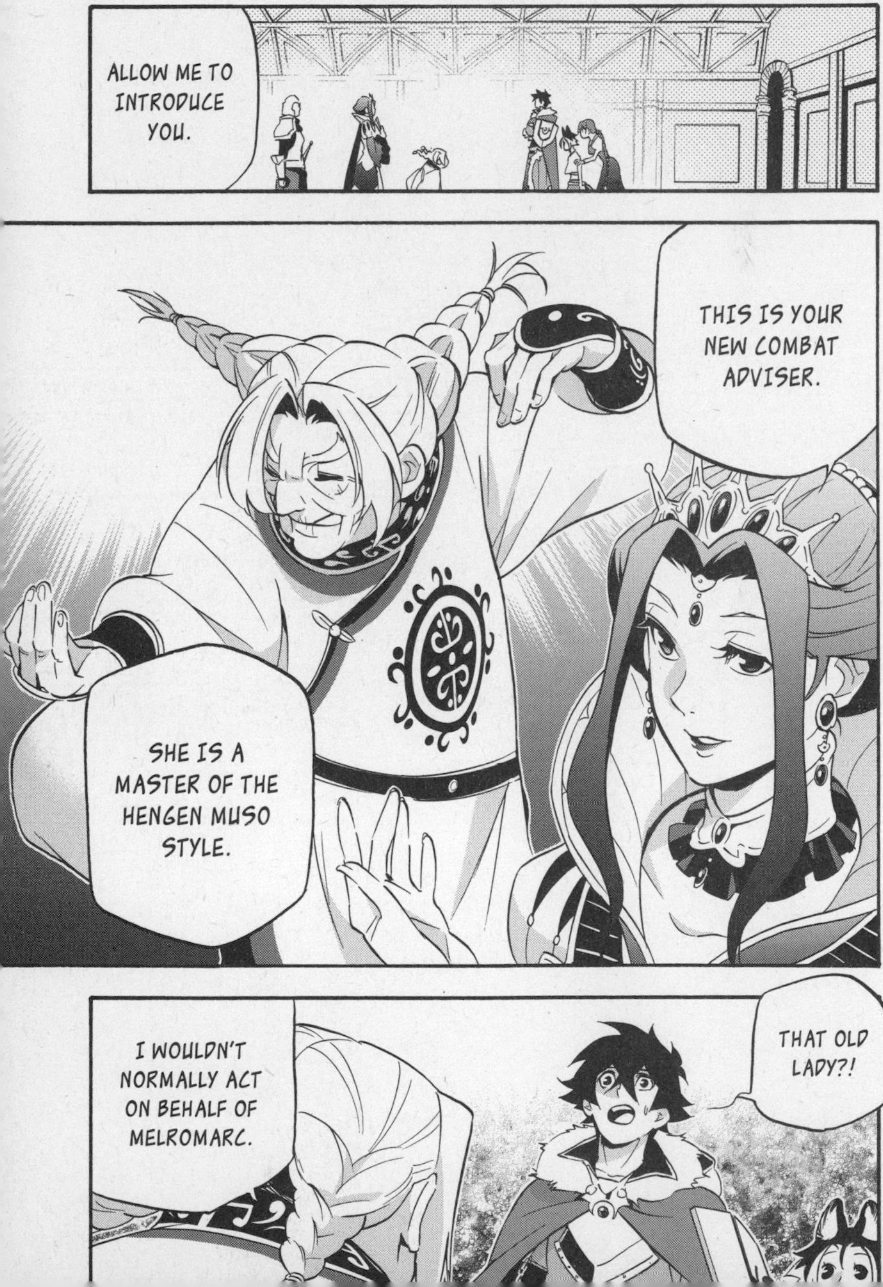
ALLOW ME TO INTRODUCE YOU.
THIS IS YOUR NEW COMBAT ADVISER.
SHE IS A MASTER OF THE HENGEN MUSO STYLE.
THAT OLD LADY?!
I WOULDN'T NORMALLY ACT ON BEHALF OF MELROMARC.

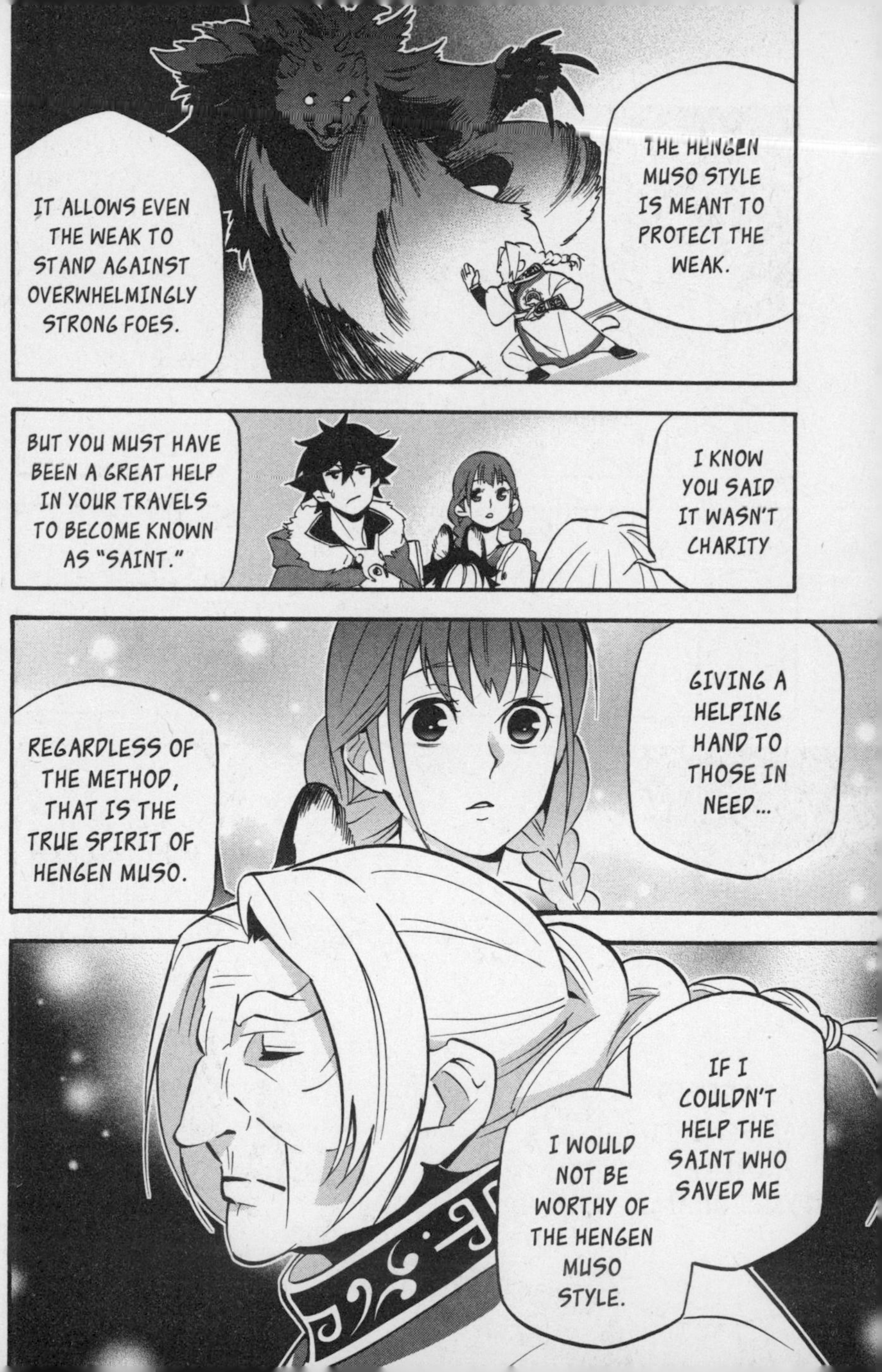
THE HENGEN MUSO STYLE IS MEANT TO PROTECT THE WEAK.
IT ALLOWS EVEN THE WEAK TO STAND AGAINST OVERWHELMINGLY STRONG FOES.
I KNOW YOU SAID IT WASN'T CHARITY
BUT YOU MUST HAVE BEEN A GREAT HELP IN YOUR TRAVELS TO BECOME KNOWN AS "SAINT."
GIVING A HELPING HAND TO THOSE IN NEED...
REGARDLESS OF THE METHOD, THAT IS THE TRUE SPIRIT OF HENGEN MUSO.
IF I COULDN'T HELP THE SAINT WHO SAVED ME
I WOULD NOT BE WORTHY OF THE HENGEN MUSO STYLE.

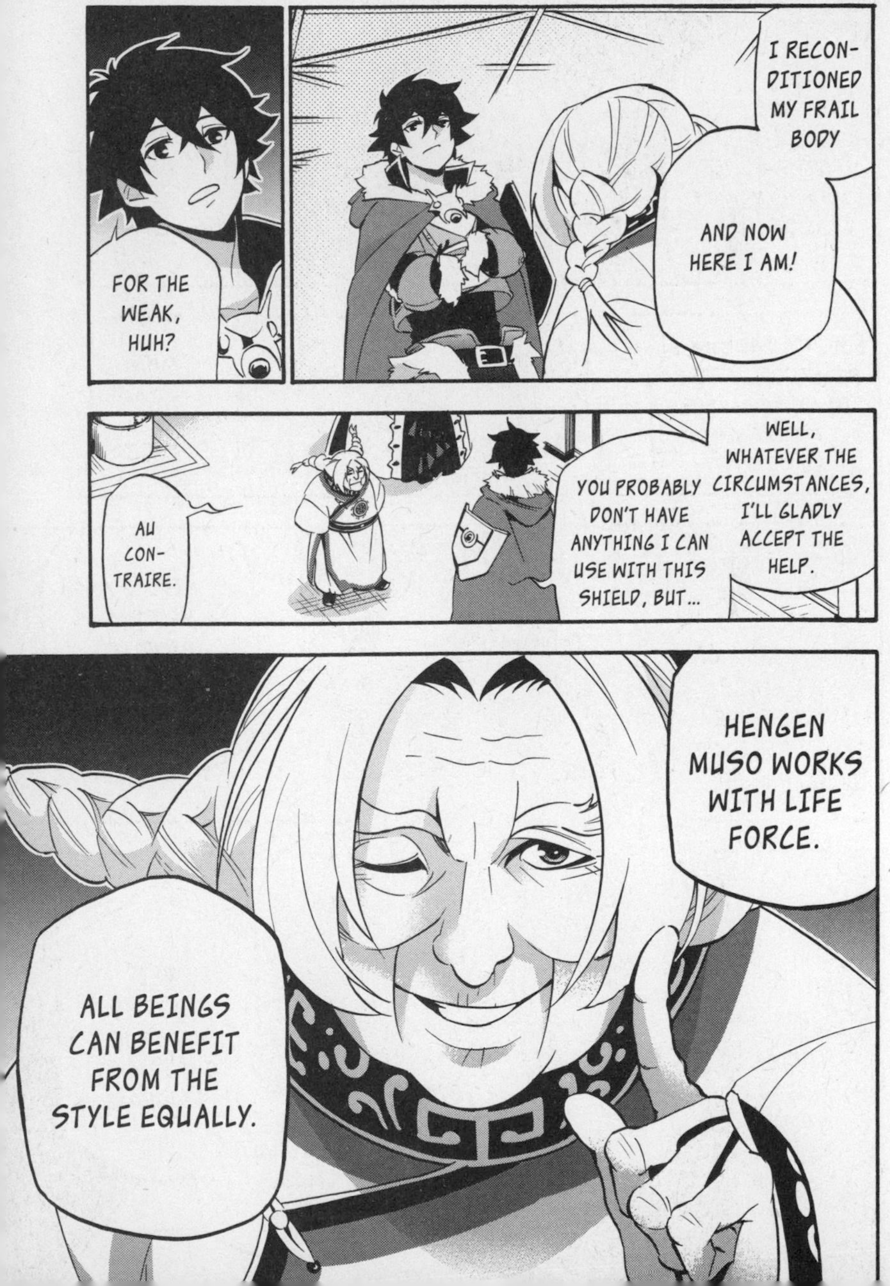
I RECONDITIONED MY FRAIL BODY
AND NOW HERE I AM!
FOR THE WEAK, HUH?
WELL, WHATEVER THE CIRCUMSTANCES, I'LL GLADLY ACCEPT THE HELP.
YOU PROBABLY DON'T HAVE ANYTHING I CAN USE WITH THIS SHIELD, BUT...
AU CONTRAIRE.
HENGEN MUSO WORKS WITH LIFE FORCE.
ALL BEINGS CAN BENEFIT FROM THE STYLE EQUALLY.

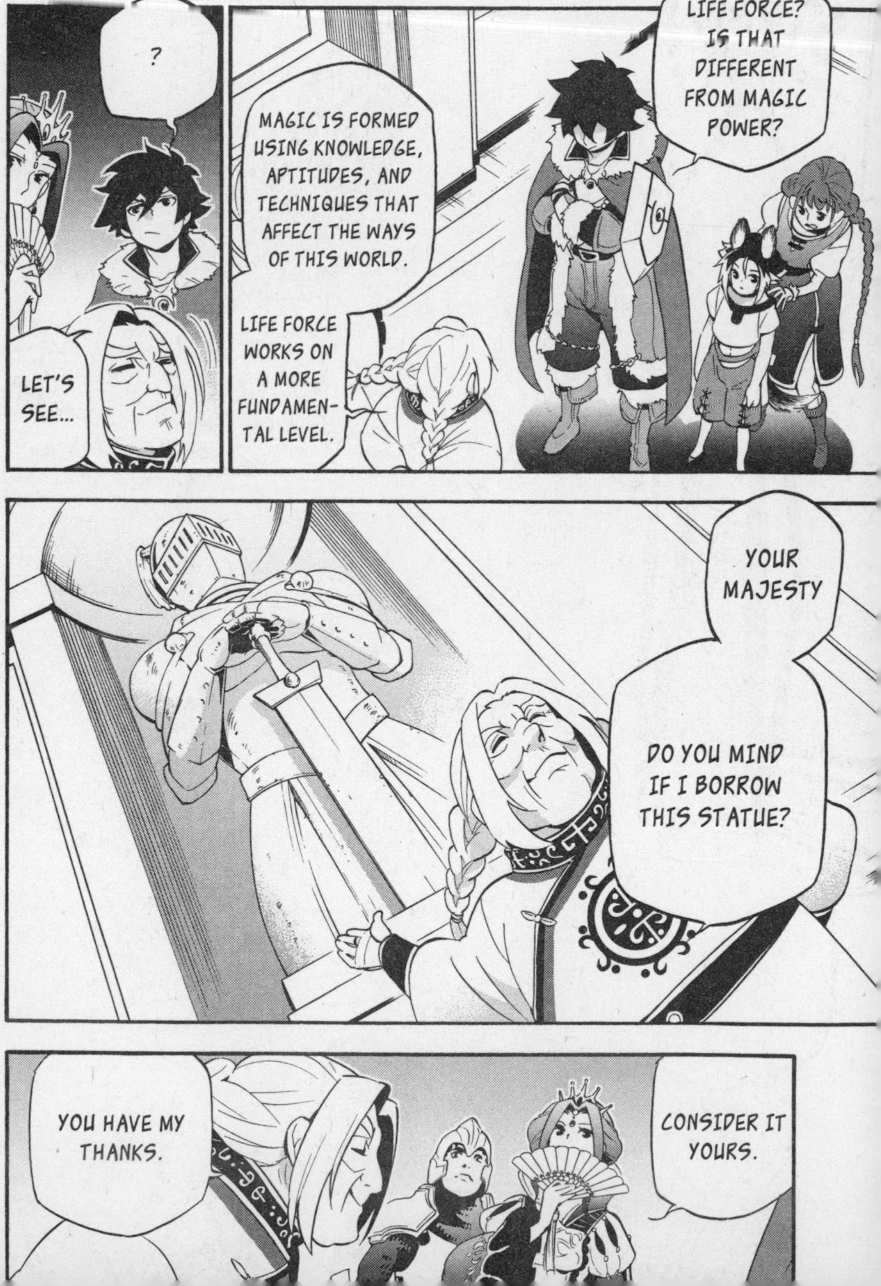
LIFE FORCE? IS THAT DIFFERENT FROM MAGIC POWER?
MAGIC IS FORMED USING KNOWLEDGE, APTITUDES, AND TECHNIQUES THAT AFFECT THE WAYS OF THIS WORLD.
LIFE FORCE WORKS ON A MORE FUNDAMEN-TAL LEVEL.
?
LET'S SEE...
YOUR MAJESTY
DO YOU MIND IF I BORROW THIS STATUE?
CONSIDER IT YOURS.
YOU HAVE MY THANKS.

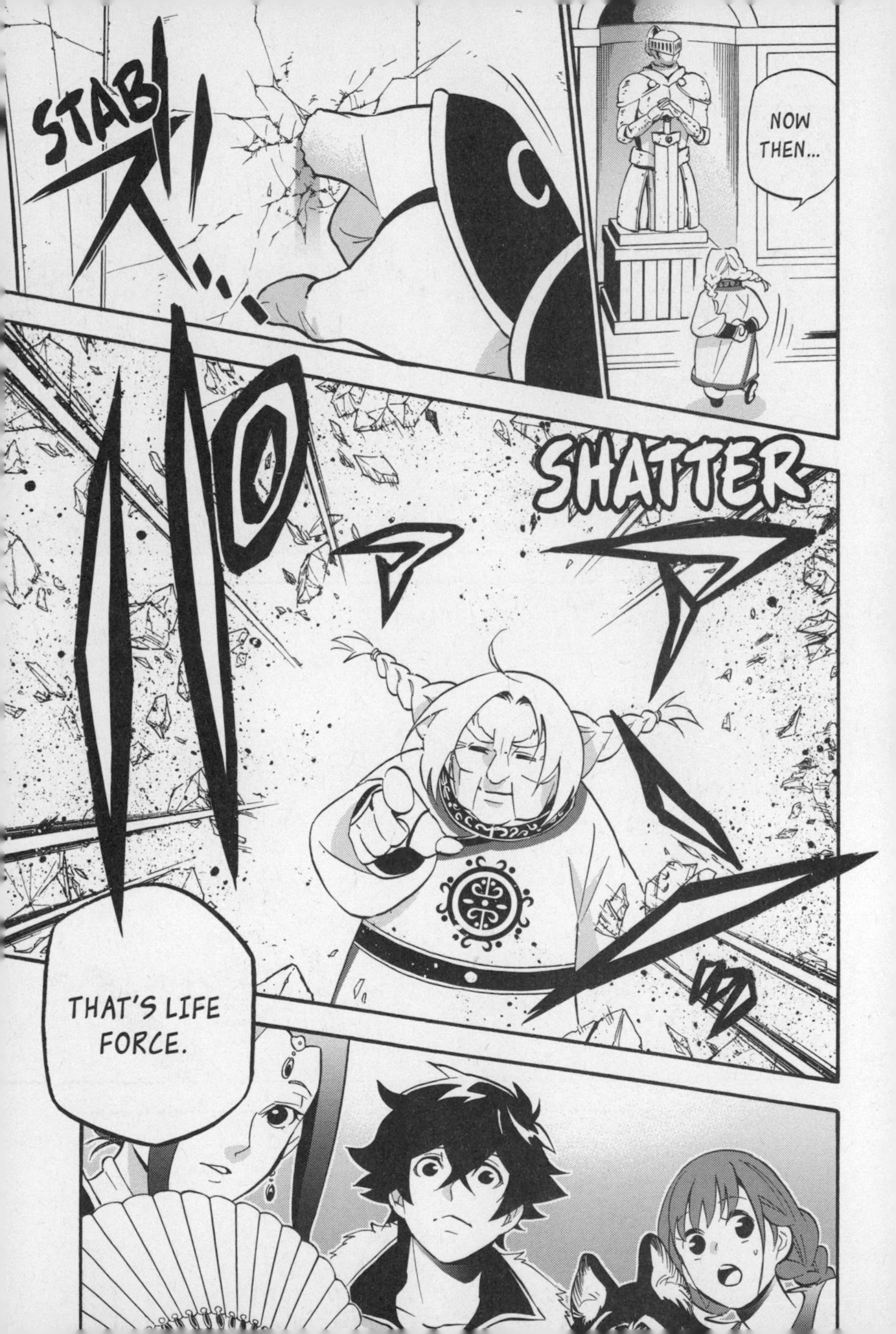
NOW THEN...
STAB
SHATTER
THAT'S LIFE FORCE.

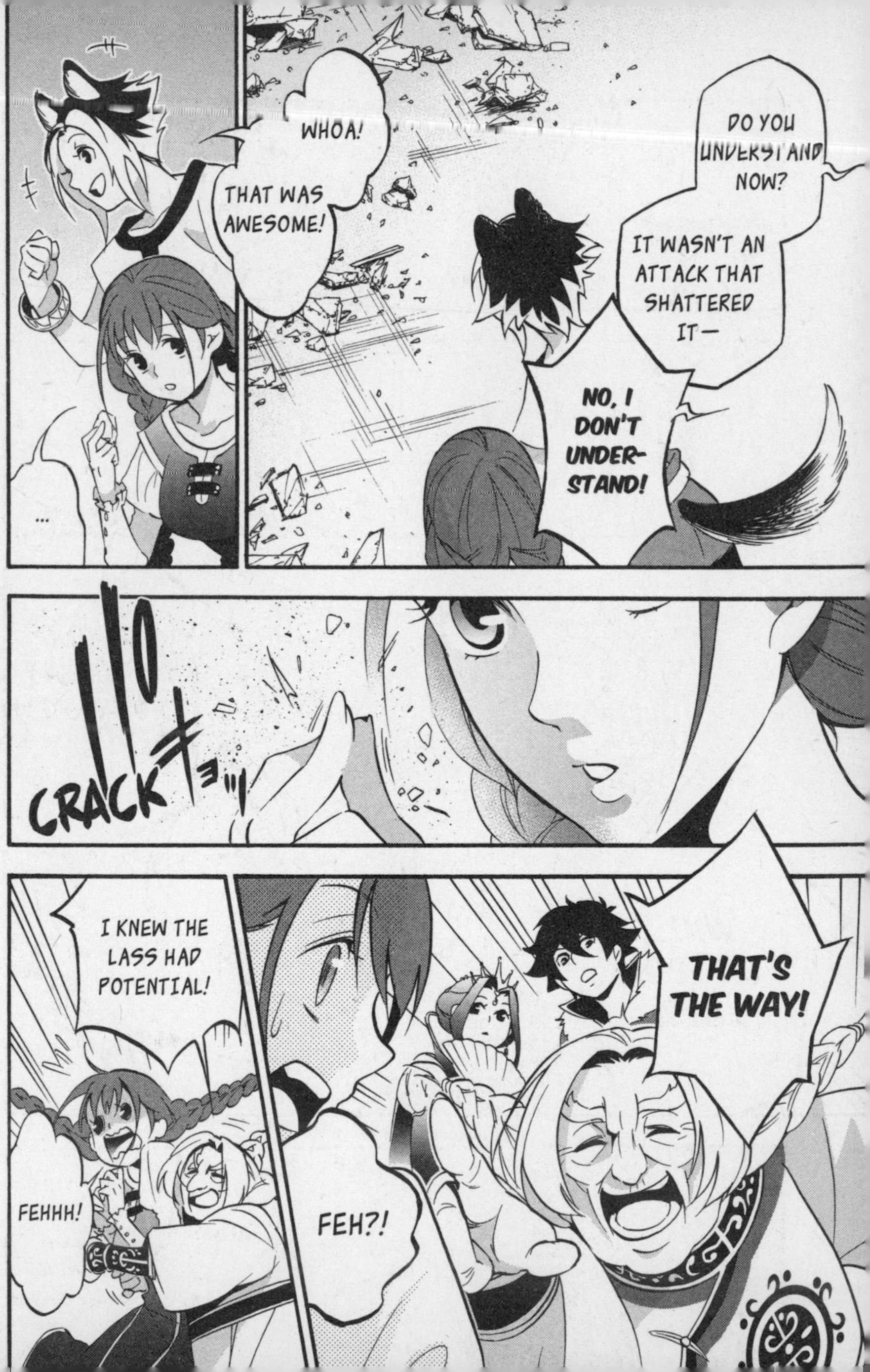

DO YOU UNDERSTAND NOW?
IT WASN'T AN ATTACK THAT SHATTERED IT—
NO, I DON'T UNDER-STAND!
WHOA!
THAT WAS AWESOME!
...
CRACK
THAT'S THE WAY!
FEH?!
I KNEW THE LASS HAD POTENTIAL!
FEHHH!

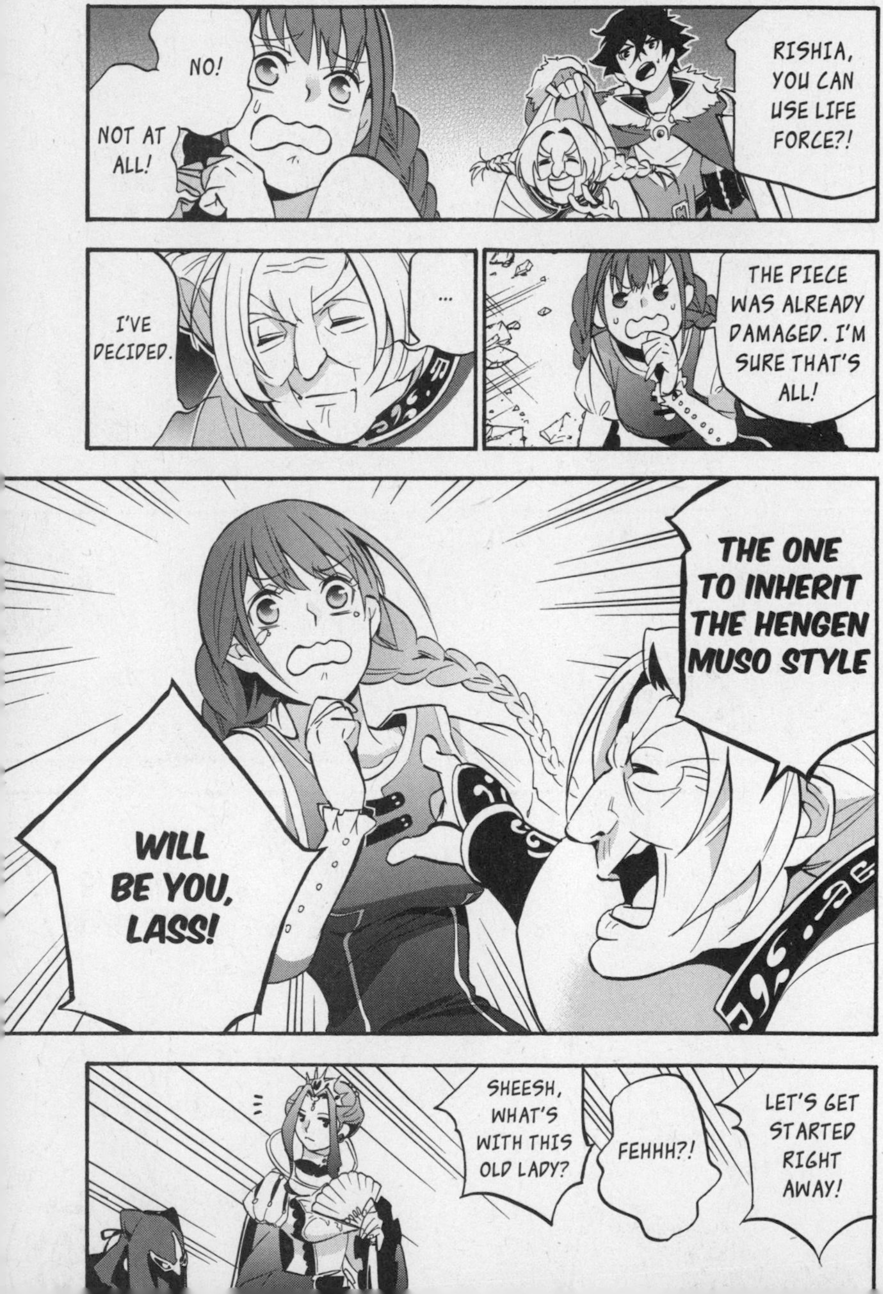
RISHIA, YOU CAN USE LIFE FORCE?!
NO!
NOT AT ALL!
THE PIECE WAS ALREADY DAMAGED. I'M SURE THAT'S ALL!
...
I'VE DECIDED.
THE ONE TO INHERIT THE HENGEN MUSO STYLE
WILL BE YOU, LASS!
LET'S GET STARTED RIGHT AWAY!
FEHHH?!
SHEESH, WHAT'S WITH THIS OLD LADY?

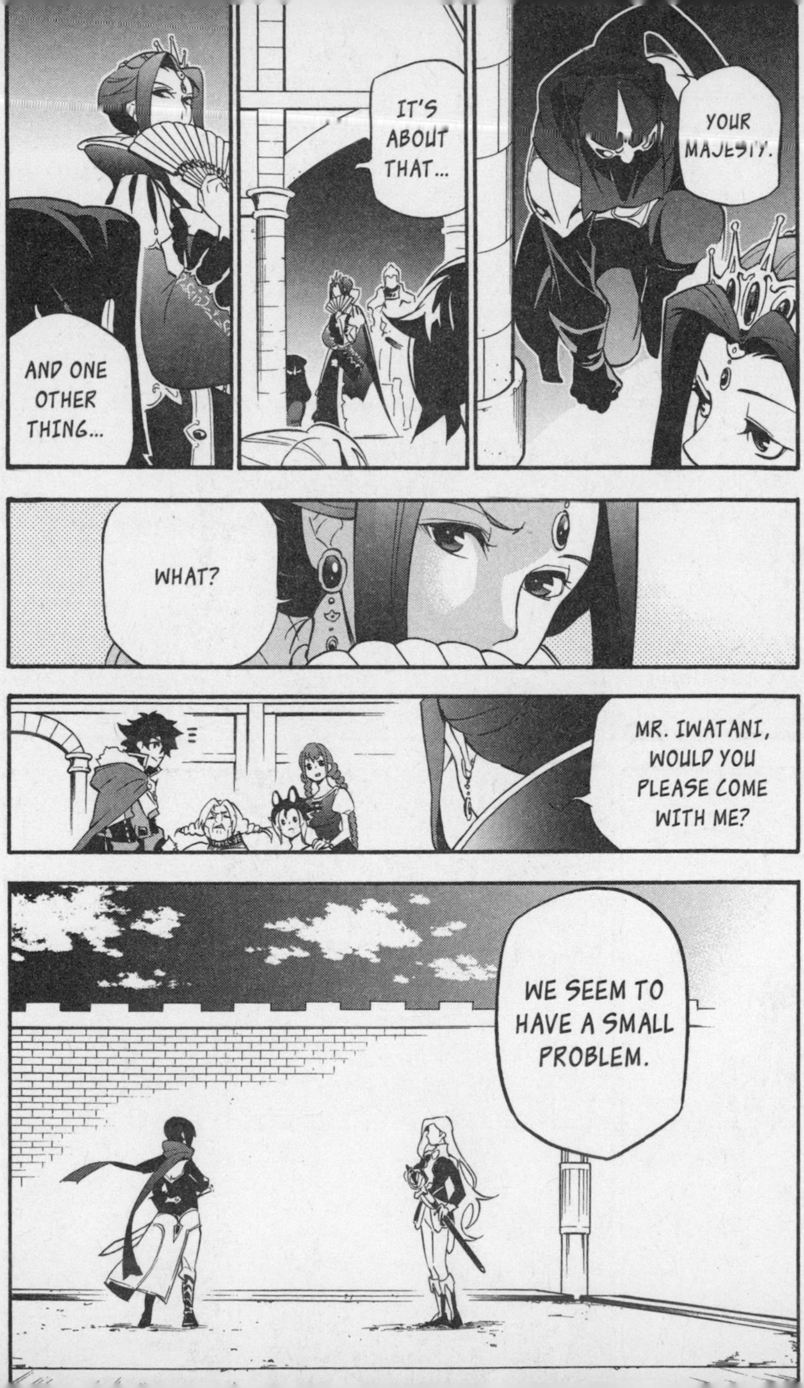
YOUR MAJESTY.
IT'S ABOUT THAT...
AND ONE OTHER THING...
WHAT?
MR. IWATANI, WOULD YOU PLEASE COME WITH ME?
WE SEEM TO HAVE A SMALL PROBLEM.

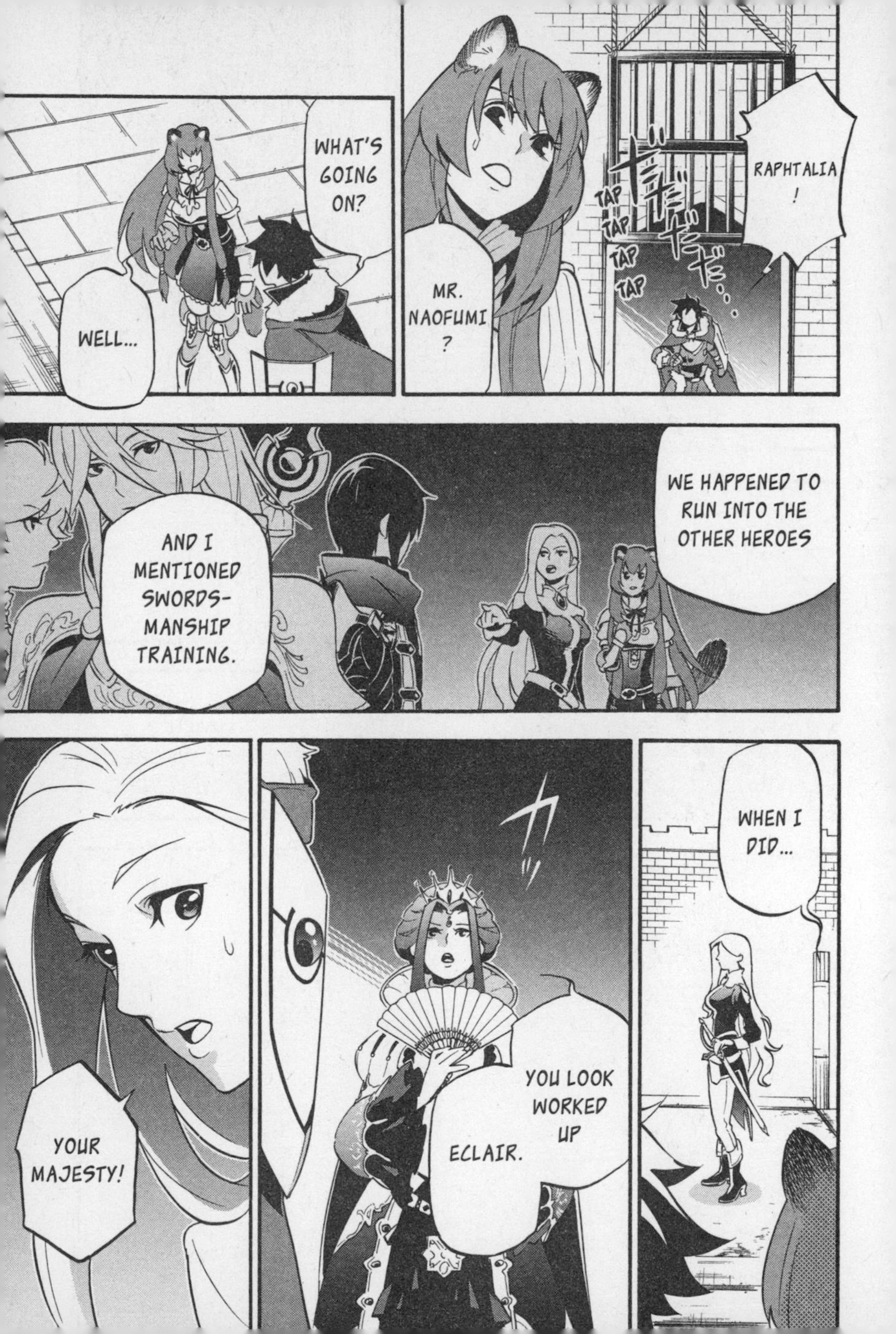
RAPHTALIA!
TAP TAP TAP TAP
MR. NAOFUMI?
WHAT'S GOING ON?
WELL...
WE HAPPENED TO RUN INTO THE OTHER HEROES
AND I MENTIONED SWORDS-MANSHIP TRAINING.
WHEN I DID...
YOU LOOK WORKED UP
ECLAIR.
YOUR MAJESTY!

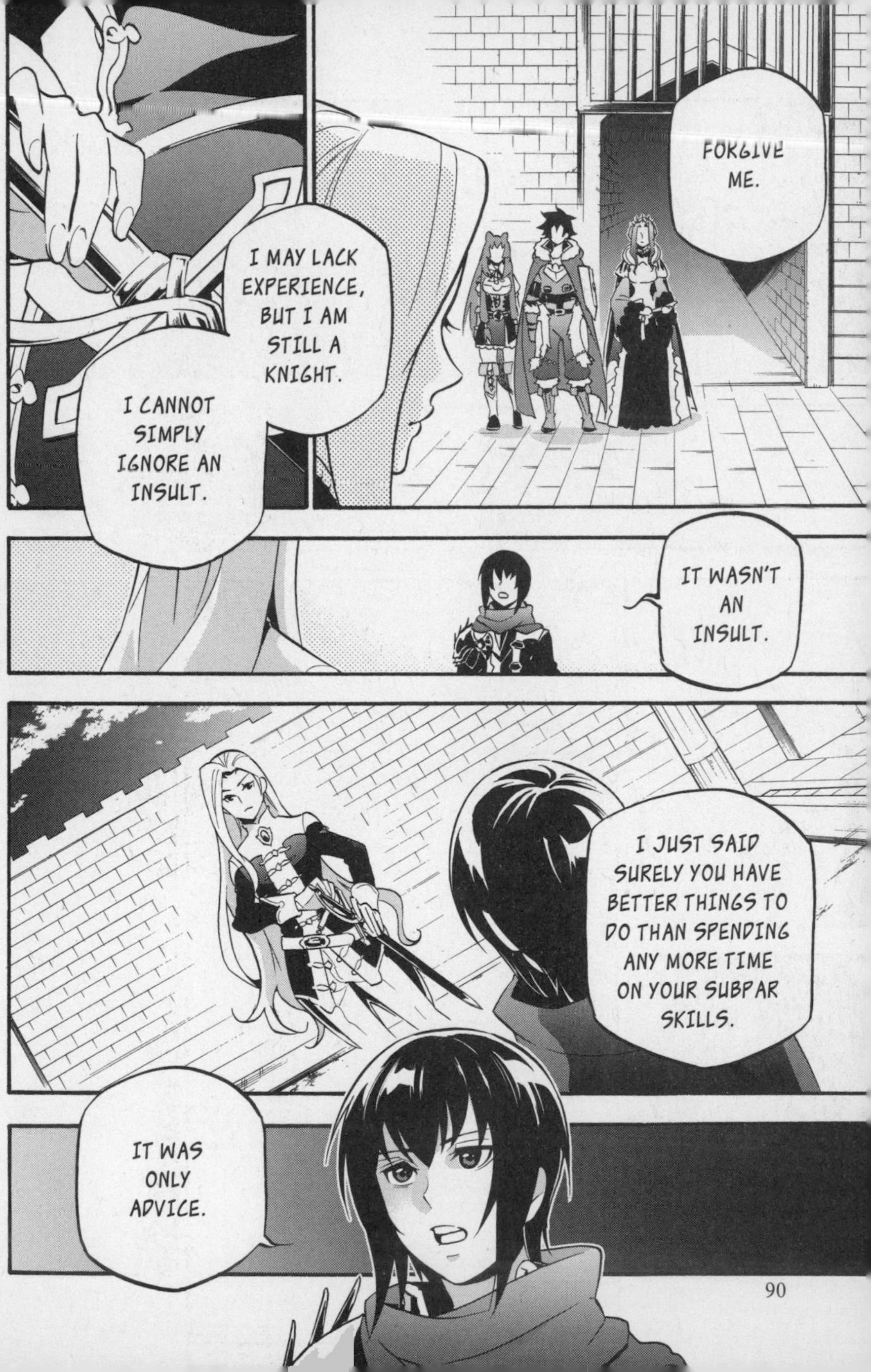
FORGIVE ME.
I MAY LACK EXPERIENCE, BUT I AM STILL A KNIGHT.
I CANNOT SIMPLY IGNORE AN INSULT.
IT WASN'T AN INSULT.
I JUST SAID SURELY YOU HAVE BETTER THINGS TO DO THAN SPENDING ANY MORE TIME ON YOUR SUBPAR SKILLS.
IT WAS ONLY ADVICE.

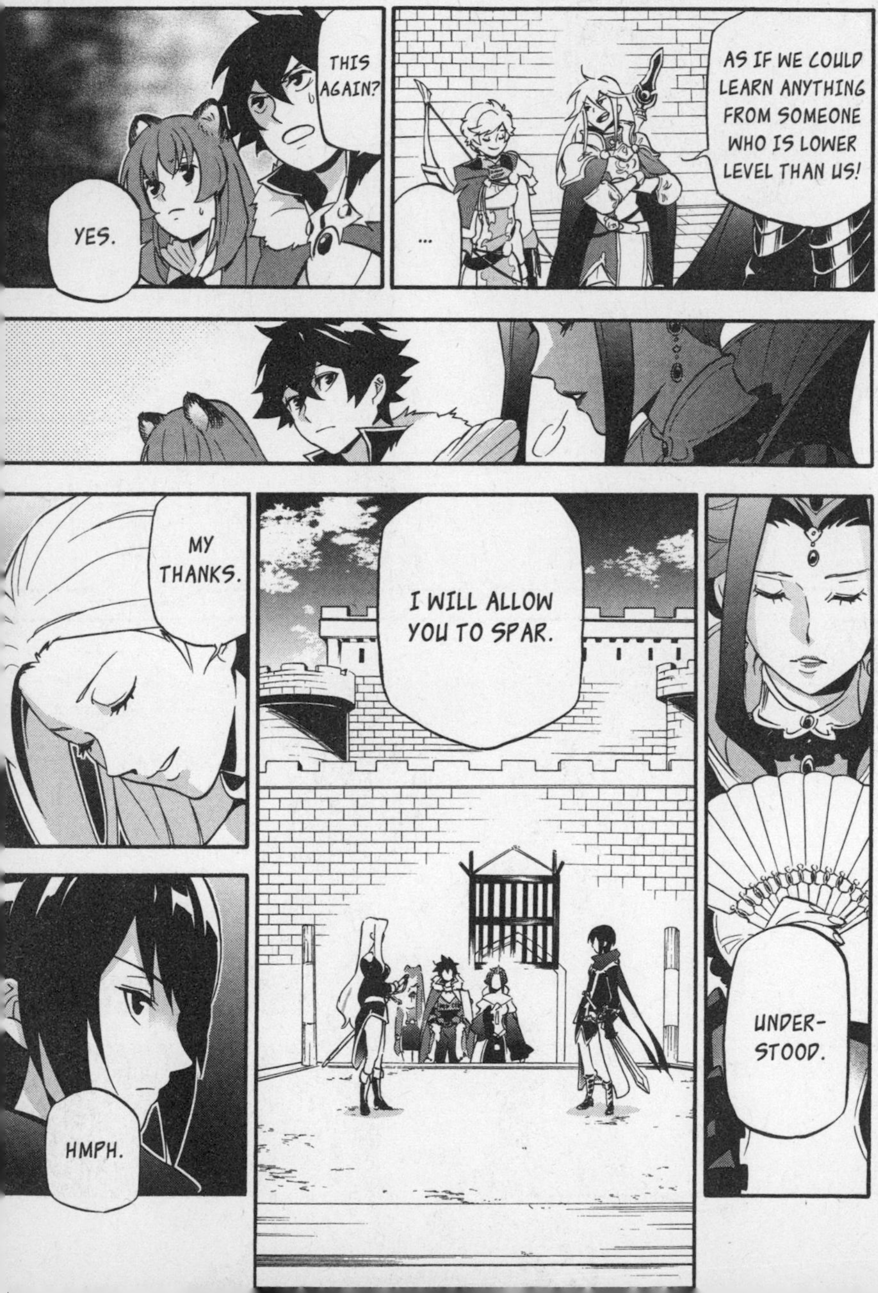
AS IF WE COULD LEARN ANYTHING FROM SOMEONE WHO IS LOWER LEVEL THAN US!
...
THIS AGAIN?
YES.
UNDER-STOOD.
I WILL ALLOW YOU TO SPAR.
MY THANKS.
HMPH.

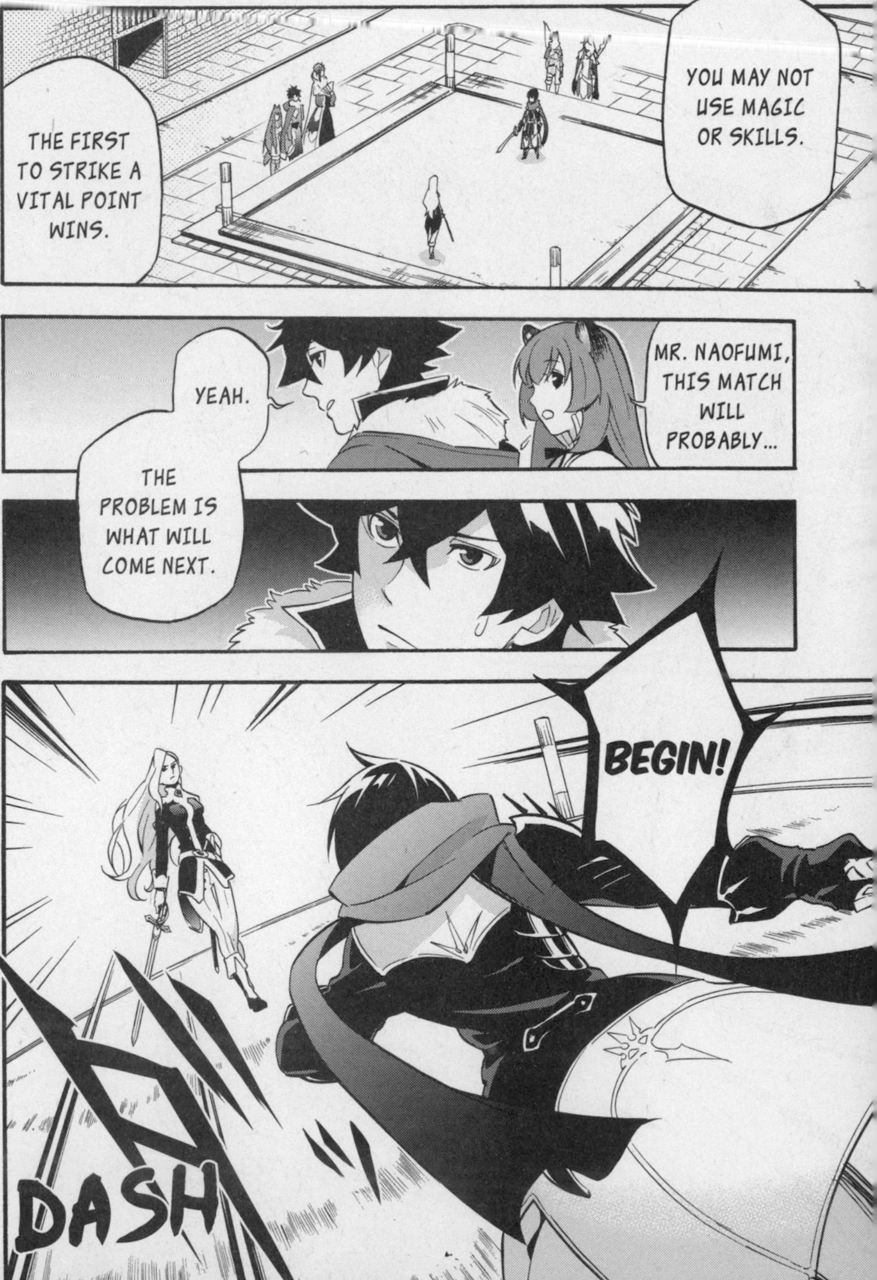
YOU MAY NOT USE MAGIC OR SKILLS.
THE FIRST TO STRIKE A VITAL POINT WINS.
MR. NAOFUMI, THIS MATCH WILL PROBABLY...
YEAH.
THE PROBLEM IS WHAT WILL COME NEXT.
BEGIN!
DASH

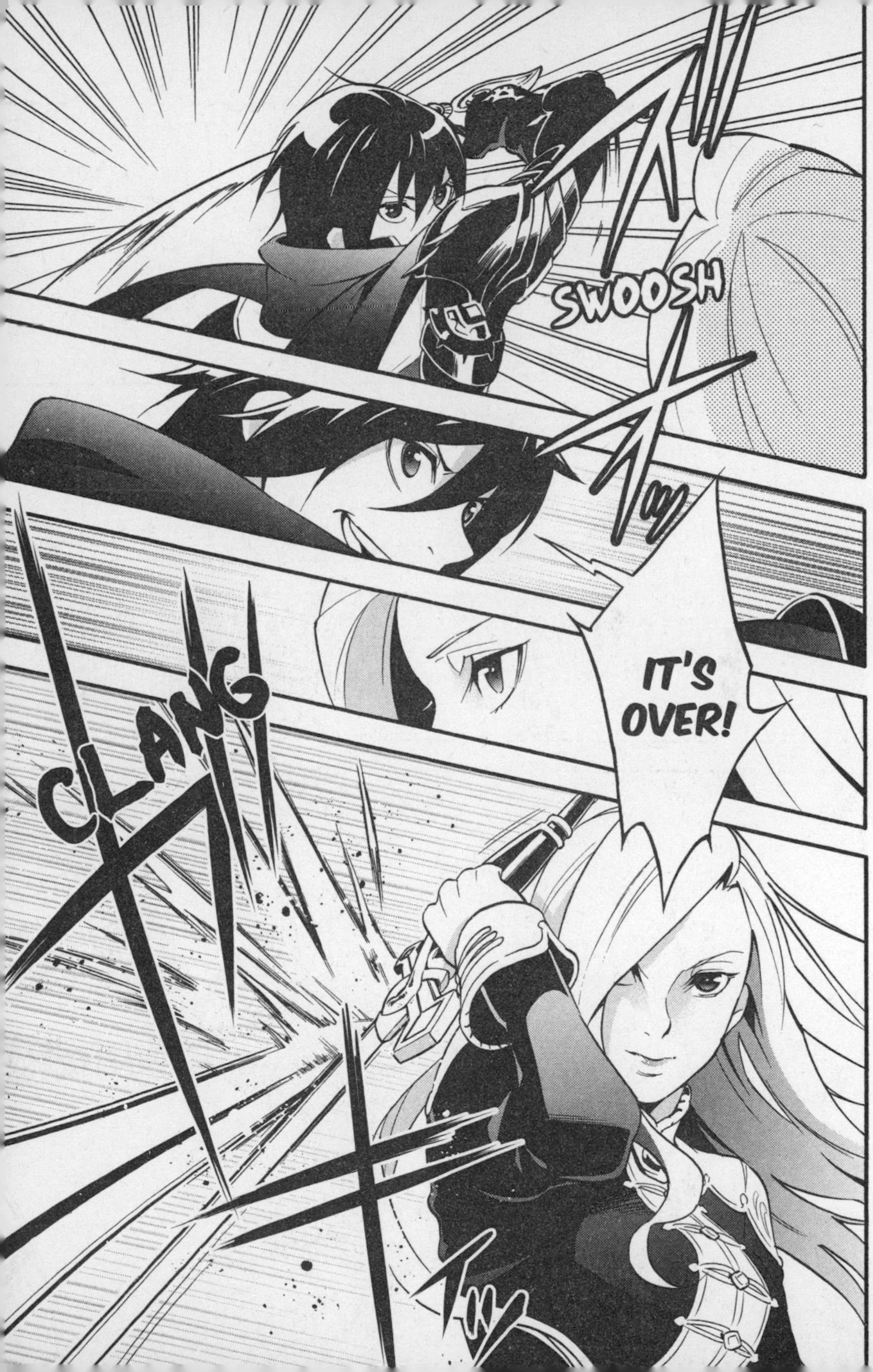
SWOOSH
IT'S OVER!
CLANG

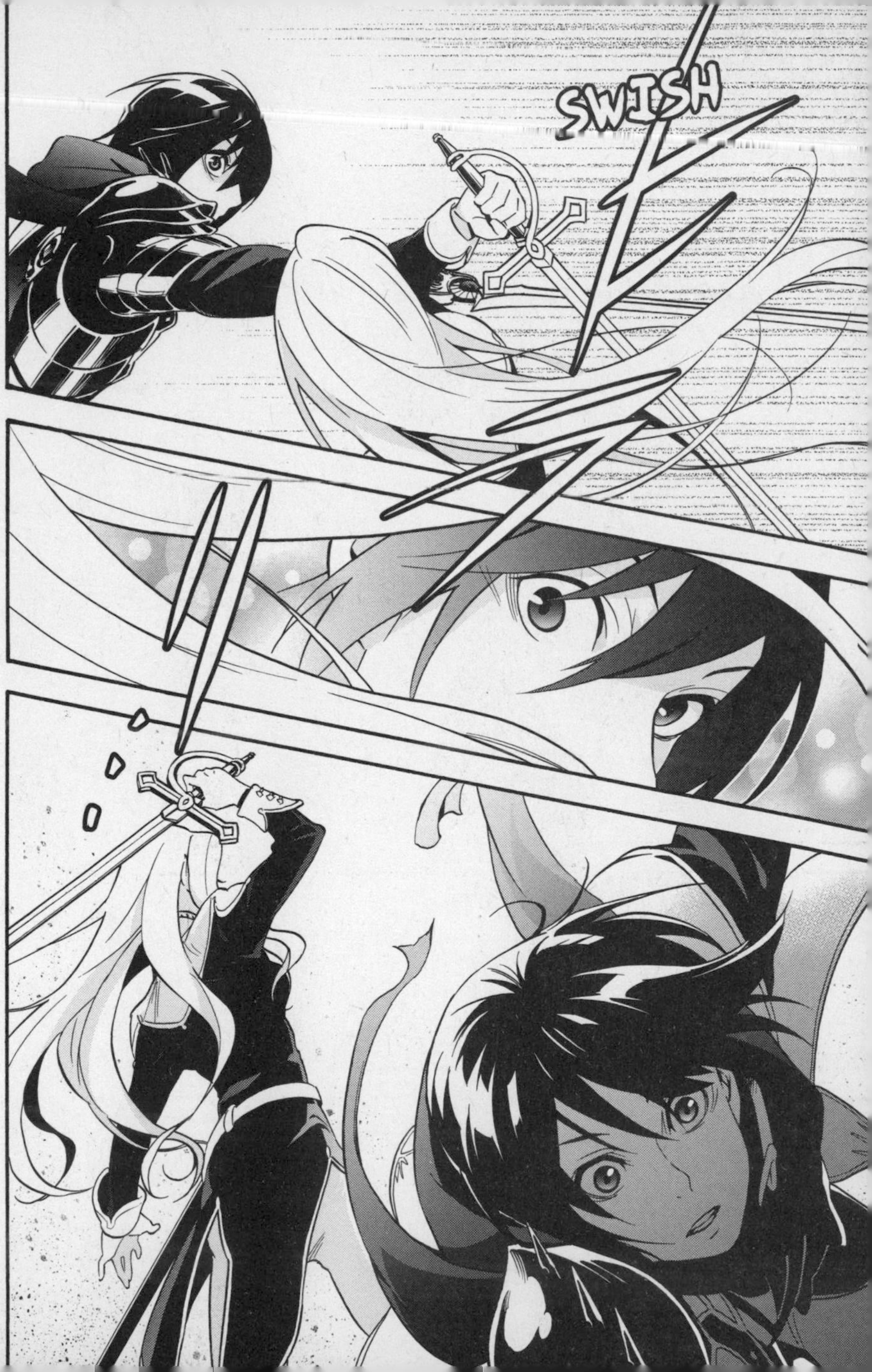
SWISH

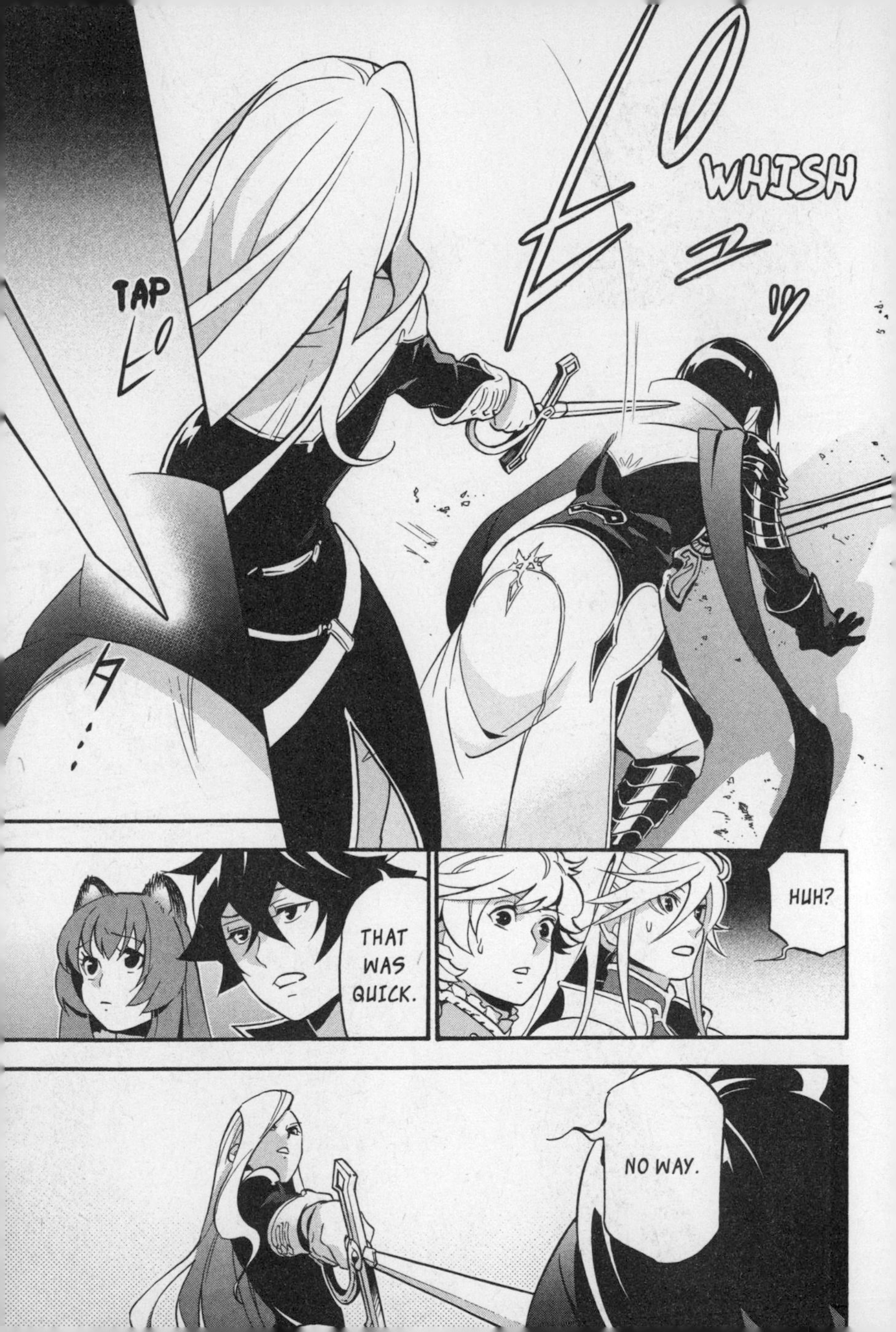
WHISH
TAP
HUH?
THAT WAS QUICK.
NO WAY.

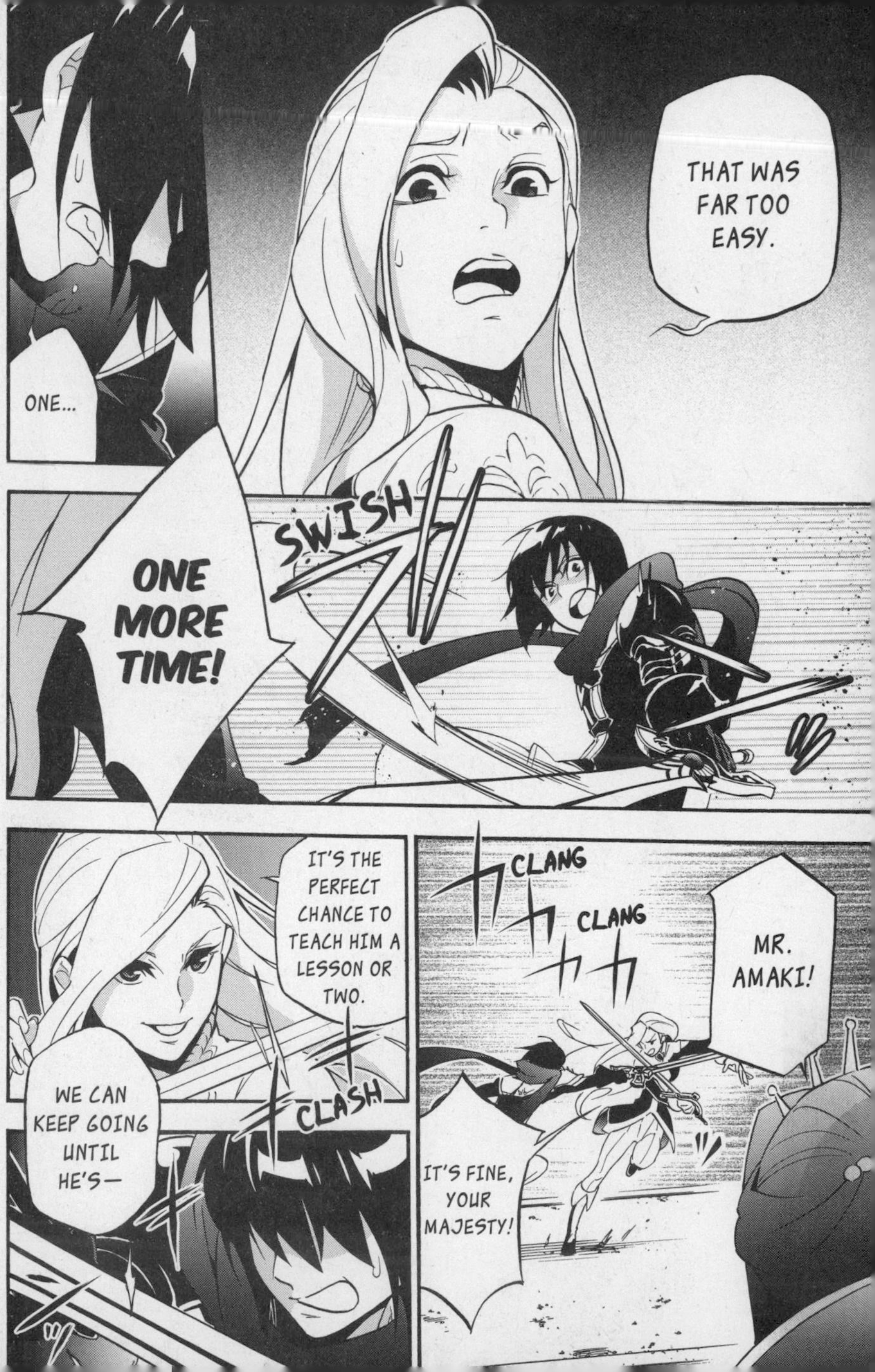
THAT WAS FAR TOO EASY.
ONE...
SWISH
ONE MORE TIME!
CLANG
CLANG
MR. AMAKI!
IT'S FINE, YOUR MAJESTY!
IT'S THE PERFECT CHANCE TO TEACH HIM A LESSON OR TWO.
CLASH
WE CAN KEEP GOING UNTIL HE'S—

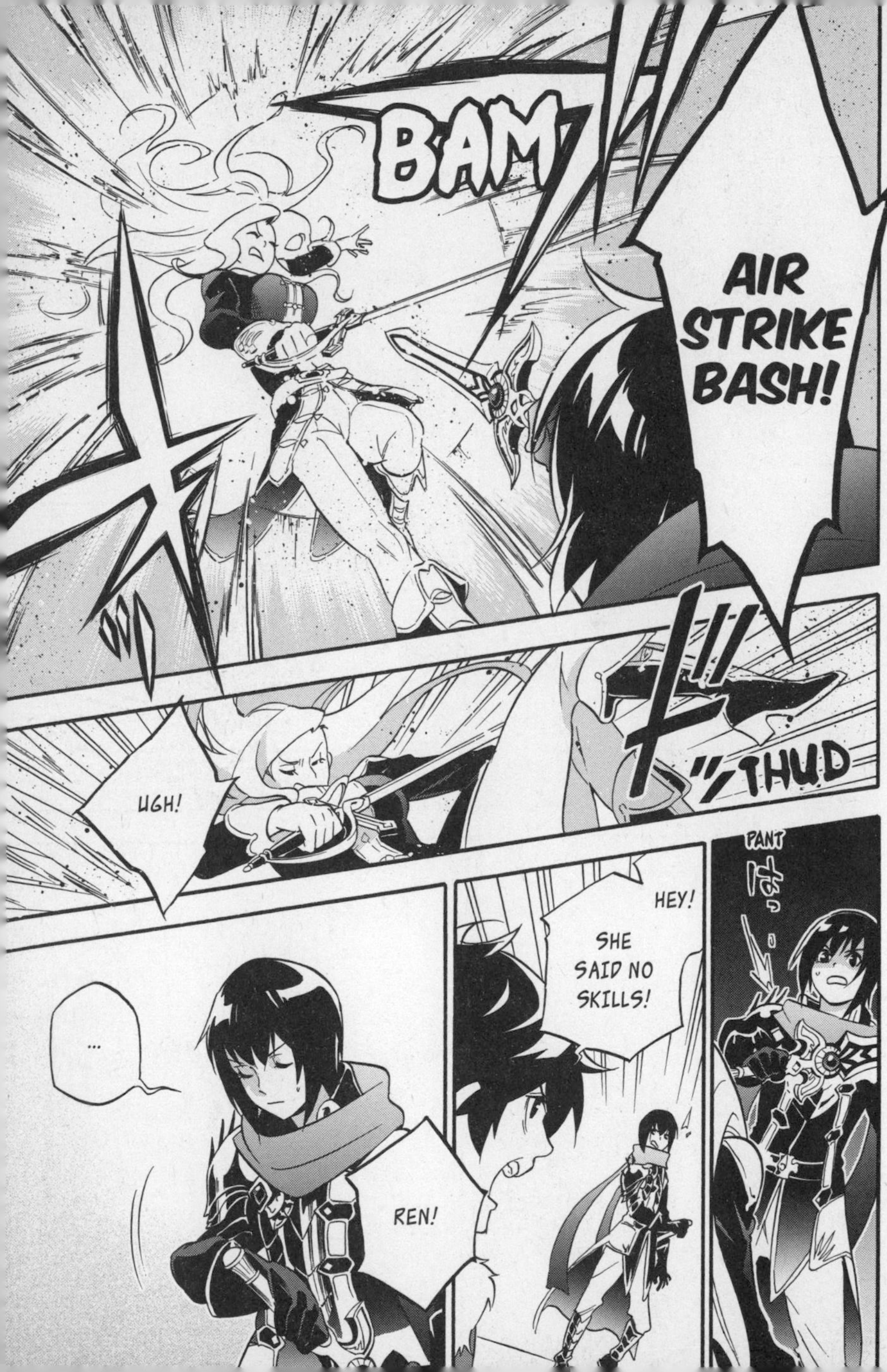
AIR STRIKE BASH!
BAM
THUD
UGH!
PANT
はっ
HEY!
SHE SAID NO SKILLS!
REN!
...

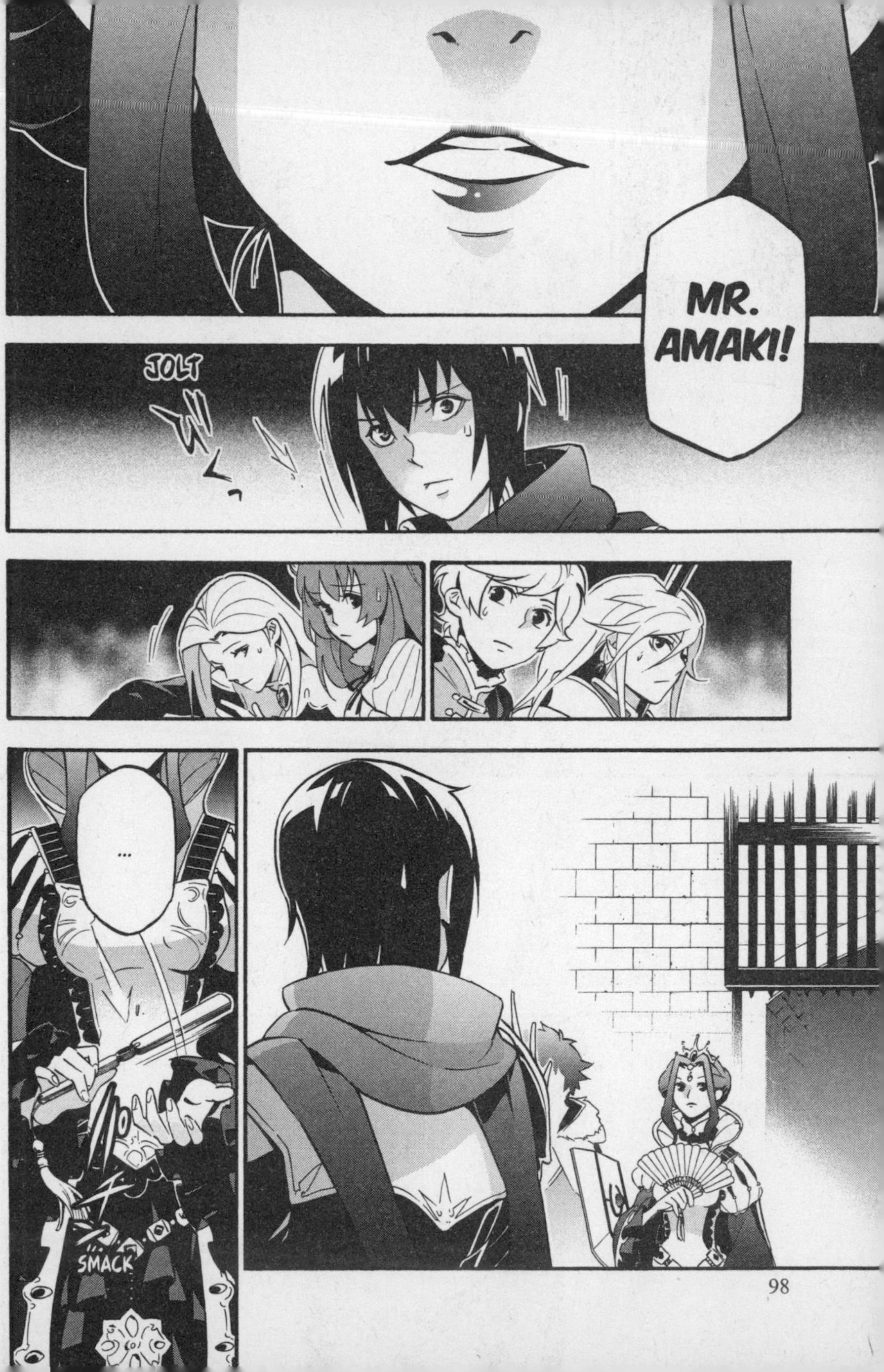
MR. AMAKI!
JOLT
...
SMACK

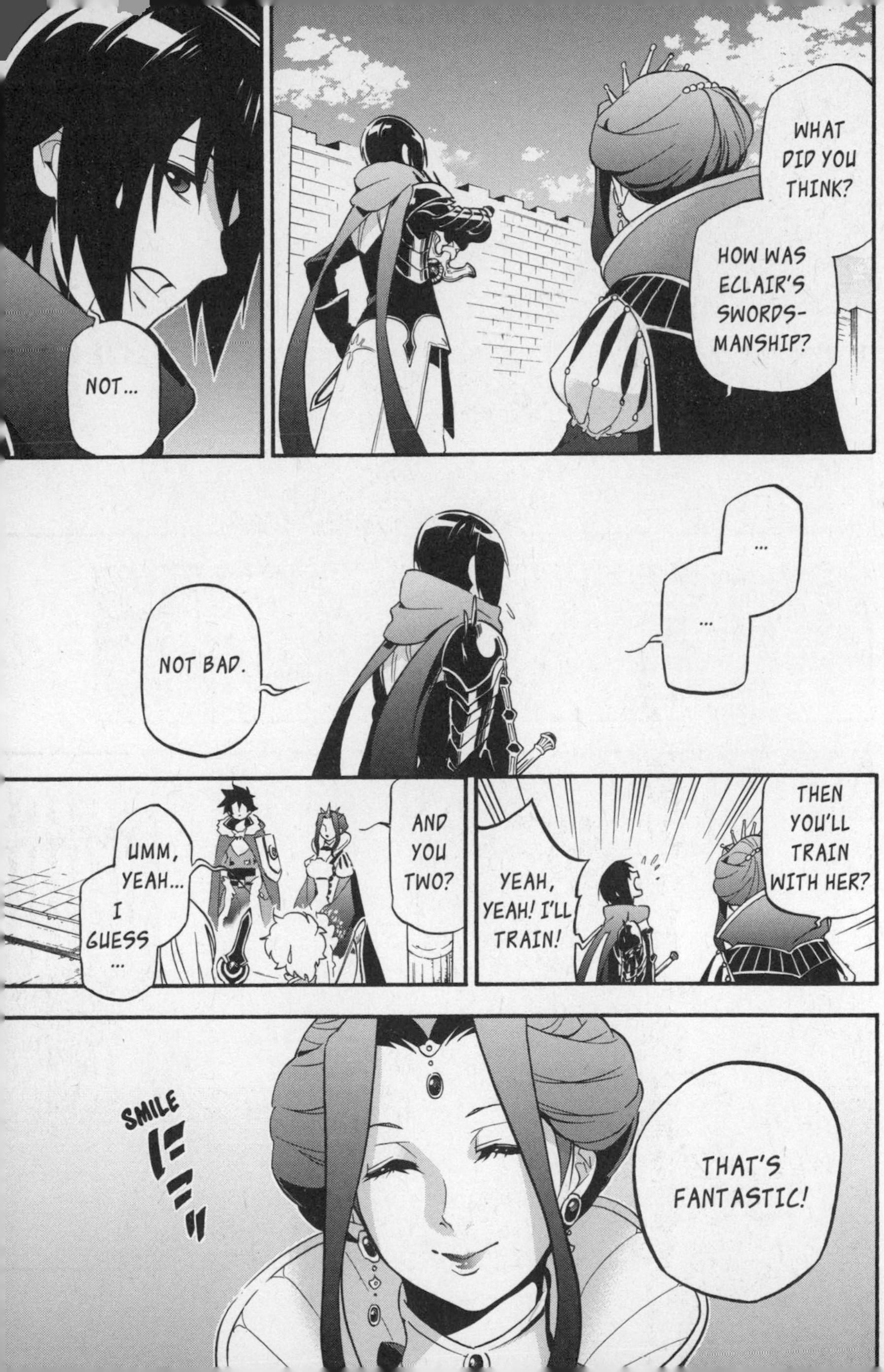
WHAT DID YOU THINK?
HOW WAS ECLAIR'S SWORDS-MANSHIP?
NOT...
...
...
NOT BAD.
THEN YOU'LL TRAIN WITH HER?
YEAH, YEAH! I'LL TRAIN!
AND YOU TWO?
UMM, YEAH... I GUESS...
THAT'S FANTASTIC!
SMILE

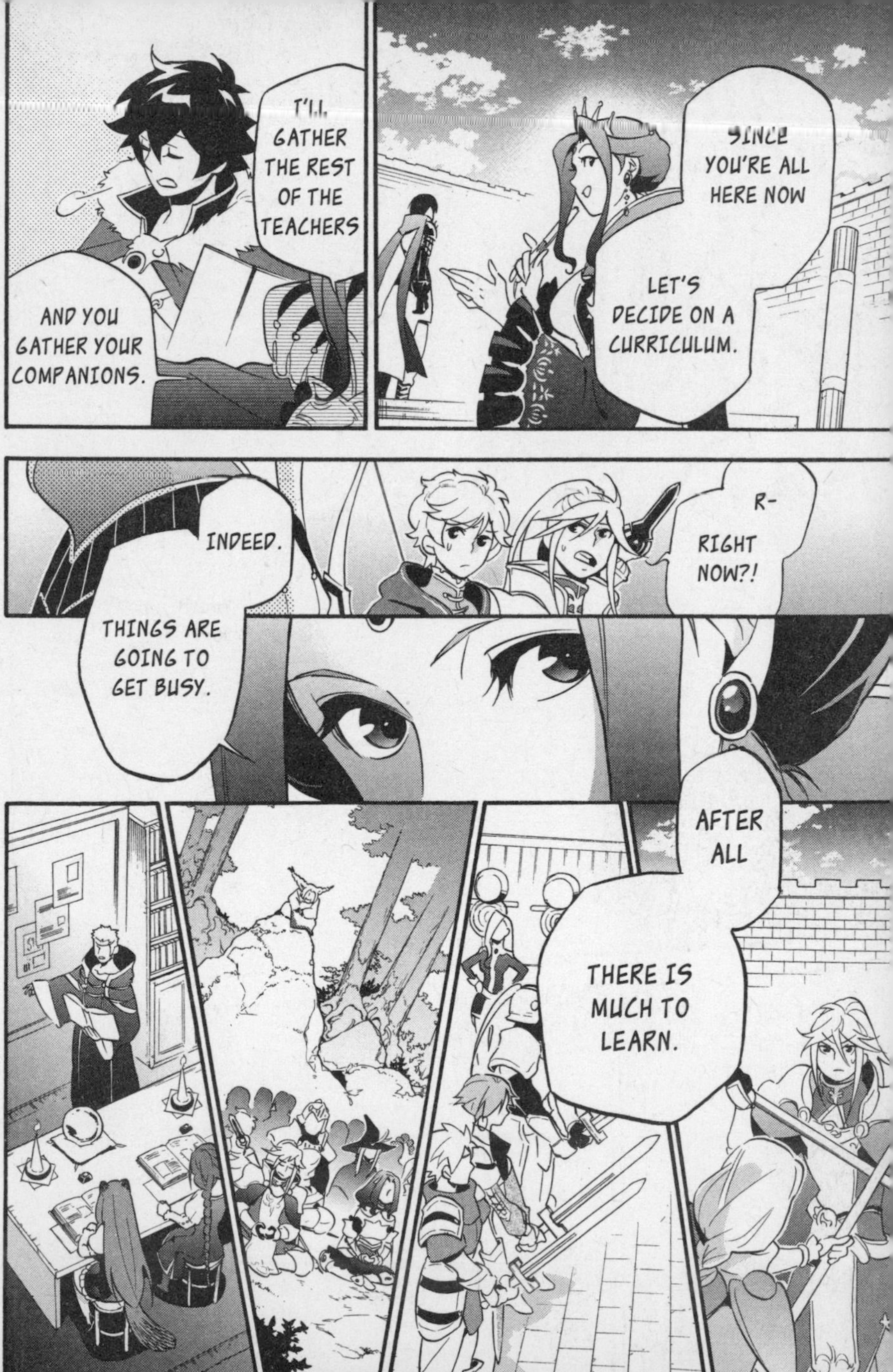
SINCE YOU'RE ALL HERE NOW
LET'S DECIDE ON A CURRICULUM.
I'LL GATHER THE REST OF THE TEACHERS
AND YOU GATHER YOUR COMPANIONS.
R- RIGHT NOW?!
INDEED.
THINGS ARE GOING TO GET BUSY.
AFTER ALL
THERE IS MUCH TO LEARN.

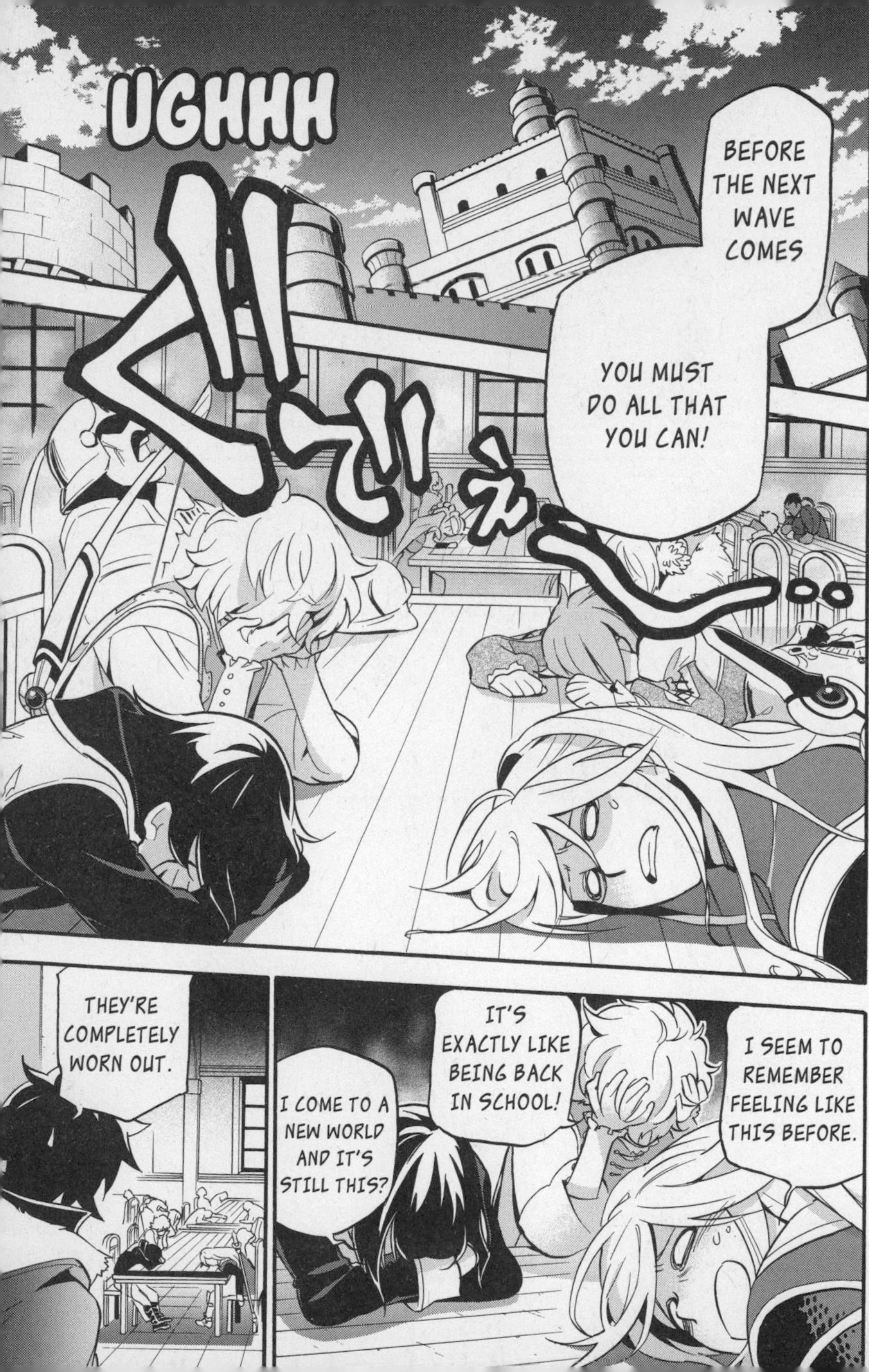
BEFORE THE NEXT WAVE COMES
YOU MUST DO ALL THAT YOU CAN!
UGHHH
I SEEM TO REMEMBER FEELING LIKE THIS BEFORE.
IT'S EXACTLY LIKE BEING BACK IN SCHOOL!
I COME TO A NEW WORLD AND IT'S STILL THIS?
THEY'RE COMPLETELY WORN OUT.

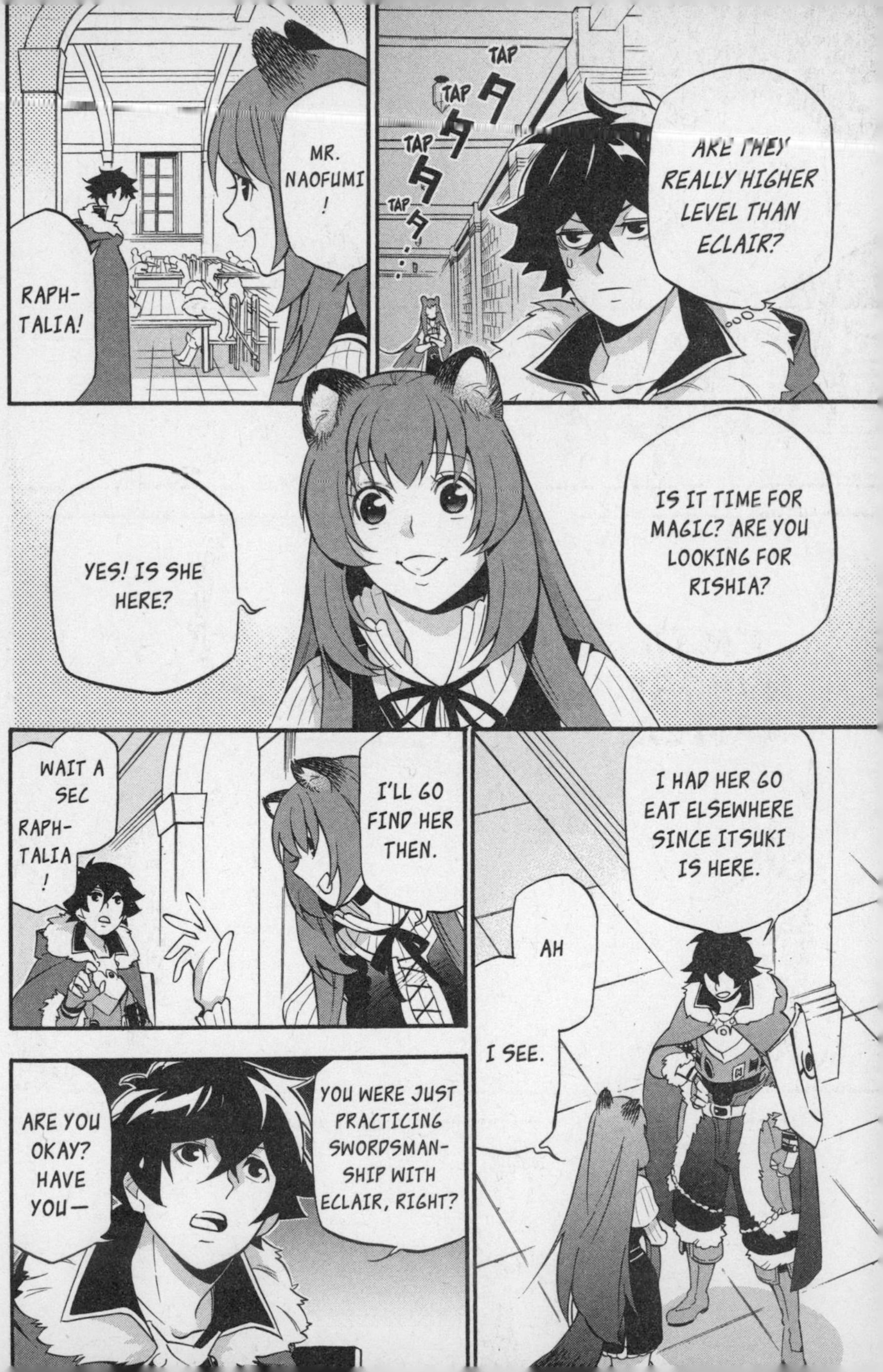
ARE THEY REALLY HIGHER LEVEL THAN ECLAIR?
TAP
TAP
TAP
TAP
MR. NAOFUMI!
RAPH-TALIA!
IS IT TIME FOR MAGIC? ARE YOU LOOKING FOR RISHIA?
YES! IS SHE HERE?
I HAD HER GO EAT ELSEWHERE SINCE ITSUKI IS HERE.
AH
I SEE.
I'LL GO FIND HER THEN.
WAIT A SEC RAPH-TALIA!
YOU WERE JUST PRACTICING SWORDSMAN-SHIP WITH ECLAIR, RIGHT?
ARE YOU OKAY? HAVE YOU—

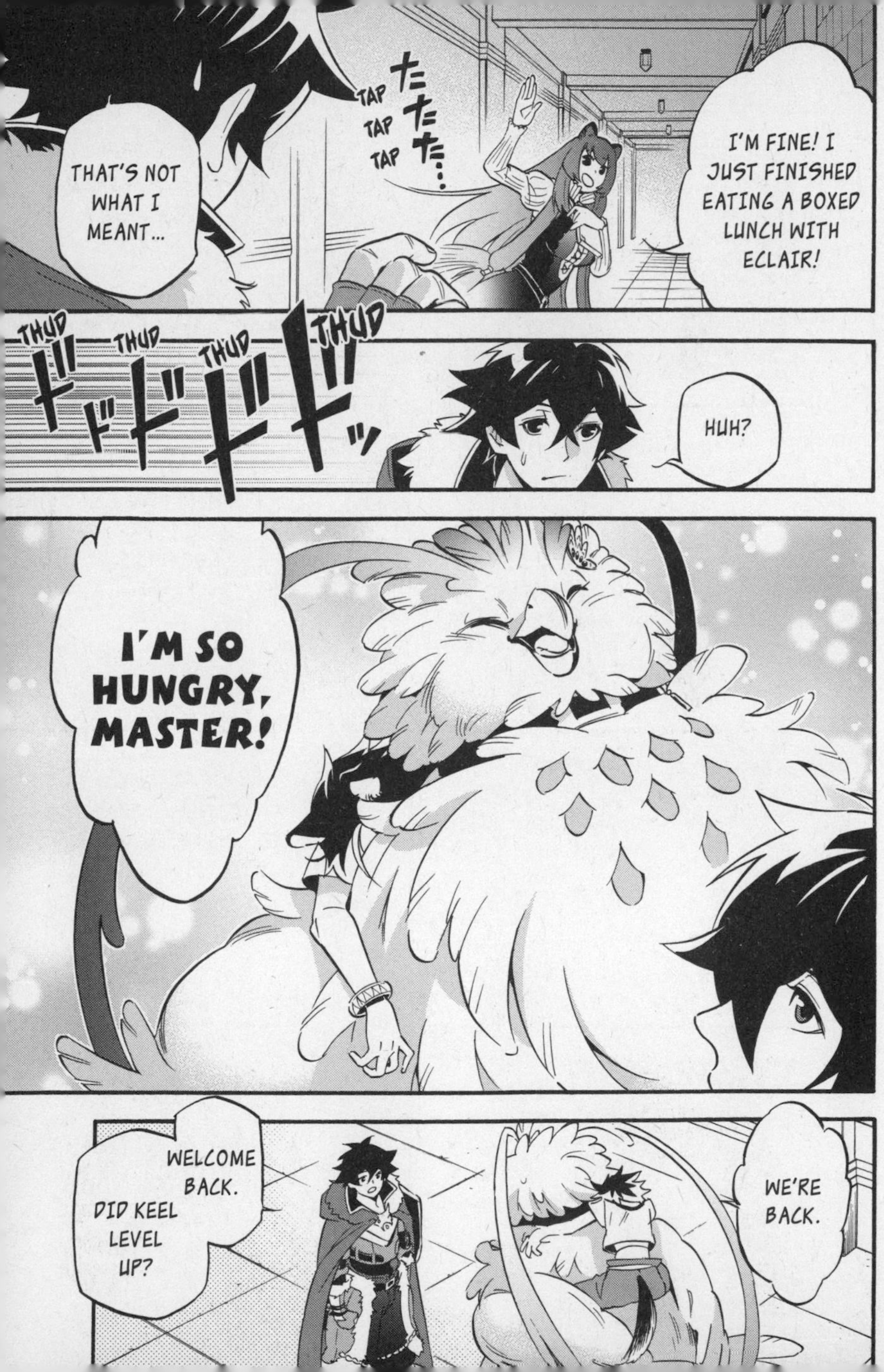
I'M FINE! I JUST FINISHED EATING A BOXED LUNCH WITH ECLAIR!
TAP TAP TAP
たたた…
THAT'S NOT WHAT I MEANT...
HUH?
THUD THUD THUD THUD
ドドドドッ
I'M SO HUNGRY, MASTER!
WE'RE BACK.
WELCOME BACK.
DID KEEL LEVEL UP?

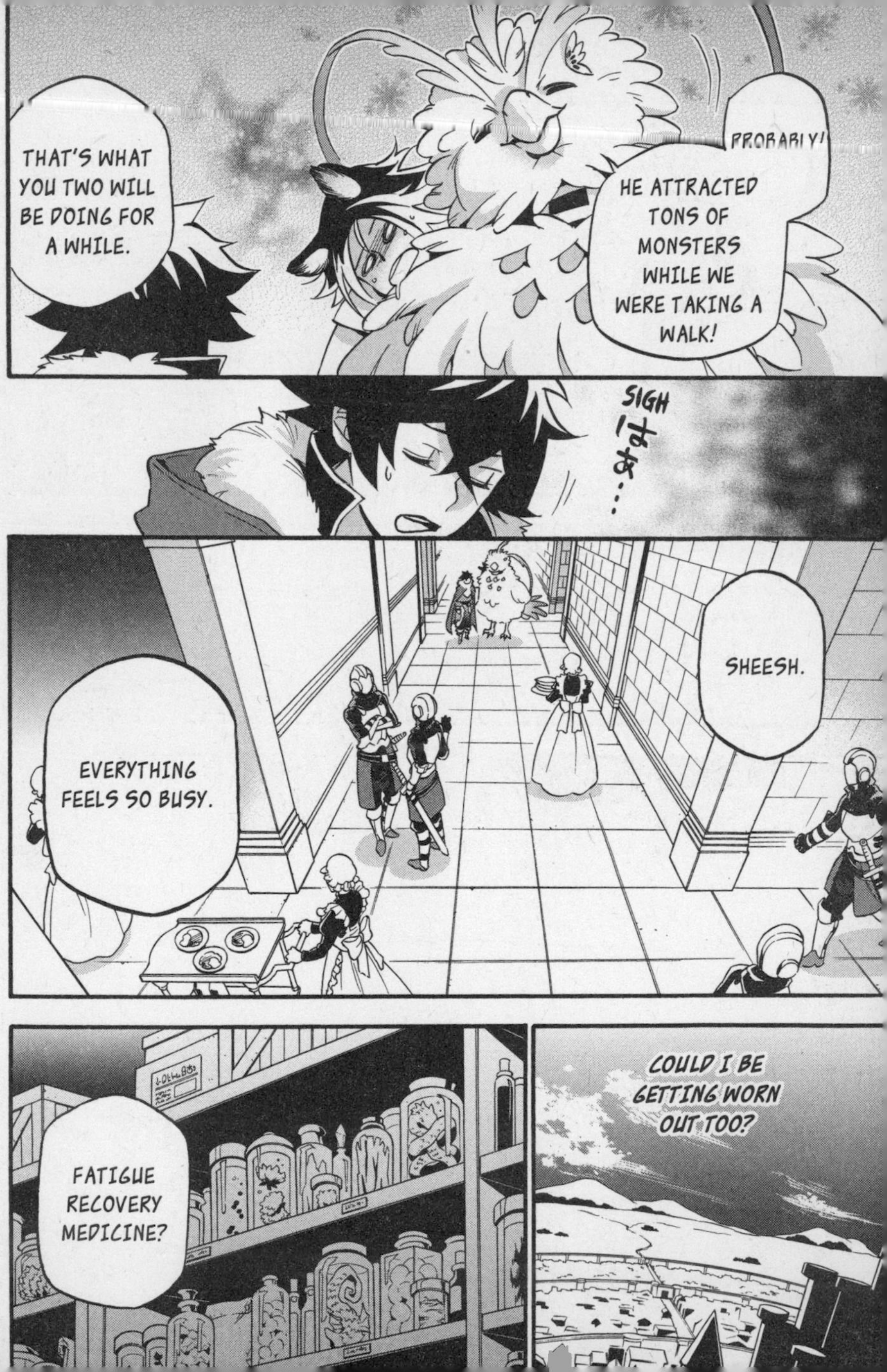
PROBABLY!
HE ATTRACTED TONS OF MONSTERS WHILE WE WERE TAKING A WALK!
THAT'S WHAT YOU TWO WILL BE DOING FOR A WHILE.
SIGH はぁ...
SHEESH.
EVERYTHING FEELS SO BUSY.
COULD I BE GETTING WORN OUT TOO?
FATIGUE RECOVERY MEDICINE?

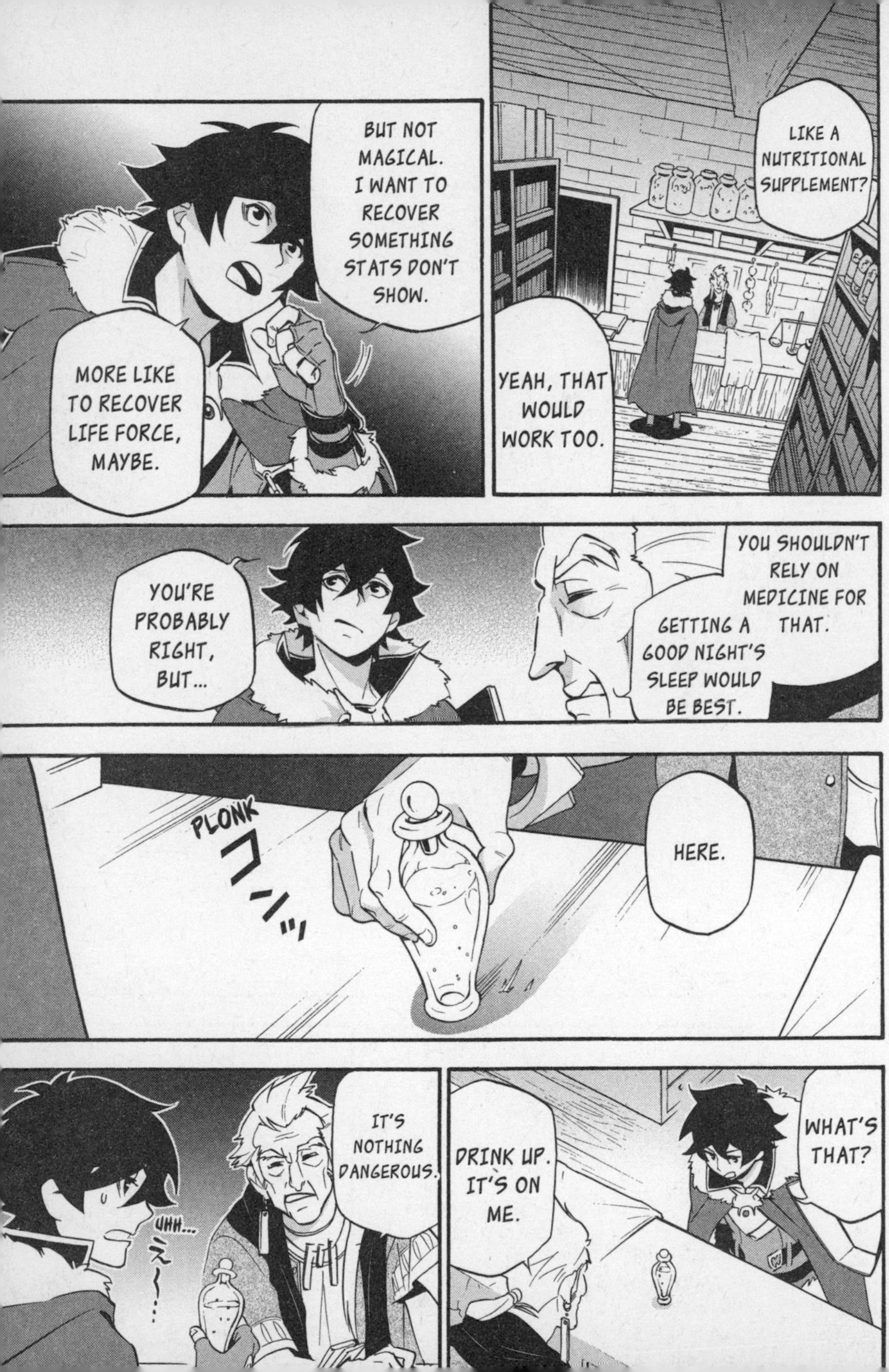
LIKE A NUTRITIONAL SUPPLEMENT?
YEAH, THAT WOULD WORK TOO.
BUT NOT MAGICAL. I WANT TO RECOVER SOMETHING STATS DON'T SHOW.
MORE LIKE TO RECOVER LIFE FORCE, MAYBE.
YOU SHOULDN'T RELY ON MEDICINE FOR THAT.
GETTING A GOOD NIGHT'S SLEEP WOULD BE BEST.
YOU'RE PROBABLY RIGHT, BUT...
HERE.
PLONK
コンッ
WHAT'S THAT?
DRINK UP. IT'S ON ME.
IT'S NOTHING DANGEROUS.
UHH...
えー…

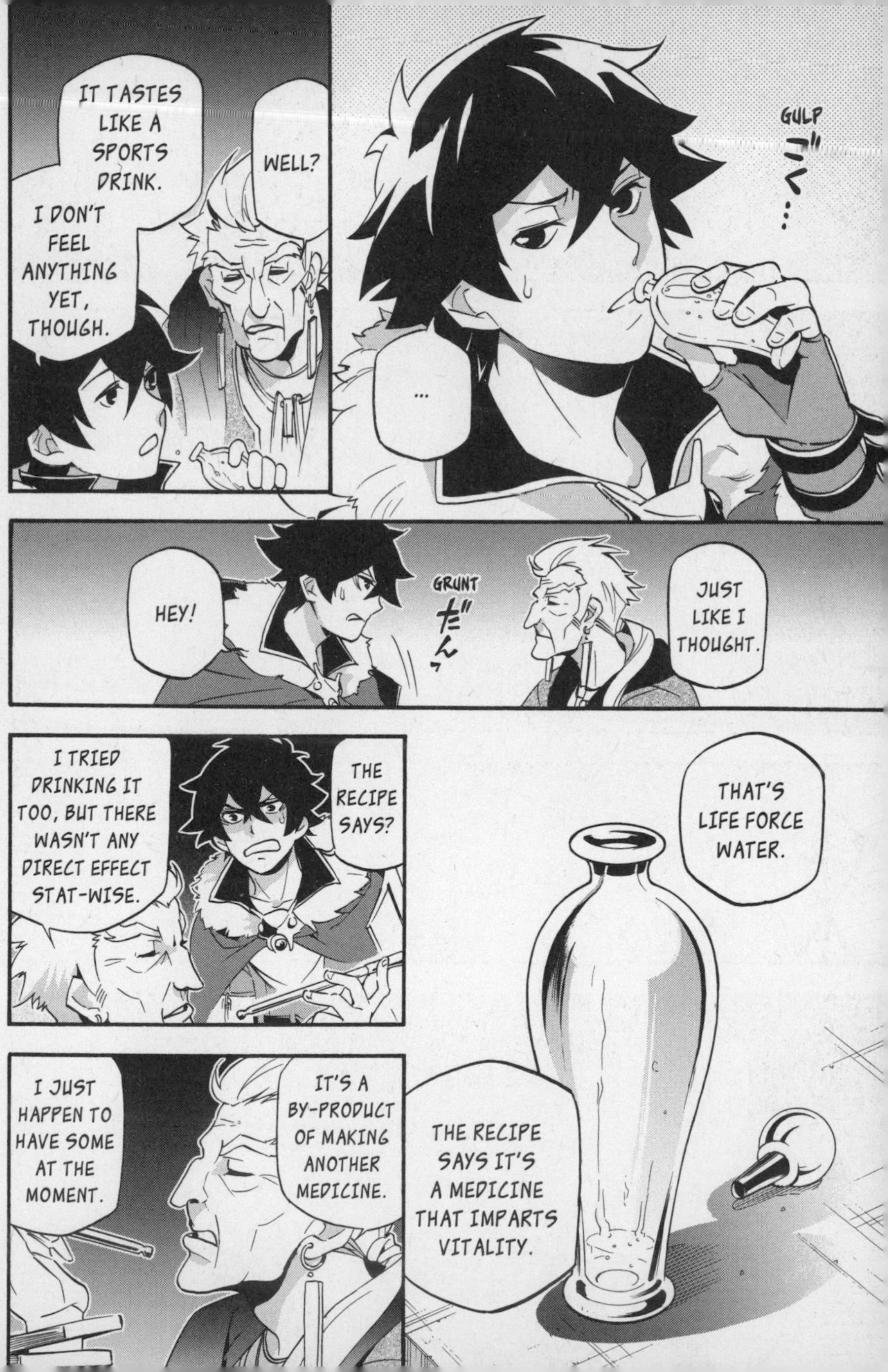
GULP
ごく…
...
WELL?
IT TASTES LIKE A SPORTS DRINK.
I DON'T FEEL ANYTHING YET, THOUGH.
JUST LIKE I THOUGHT.
GRUNT
だん
HEY!
THAT'S LIFE FORCE WATER.
THE RECIPE SAYS IT'S A MEDICINE THAT IMPARTS VITALITY.
THE RECIPE SAYS?
I TRIED DRINKING IT TOO, BUT THERE WASN'T ANY DIRECT EFFECT STAT-WISE.
IT'S A BY-PRODUCT OF MAKING ANOTHER MEDICINE.
I JUST HAPPEN TO HAVE SOME AT THE MOMENT.

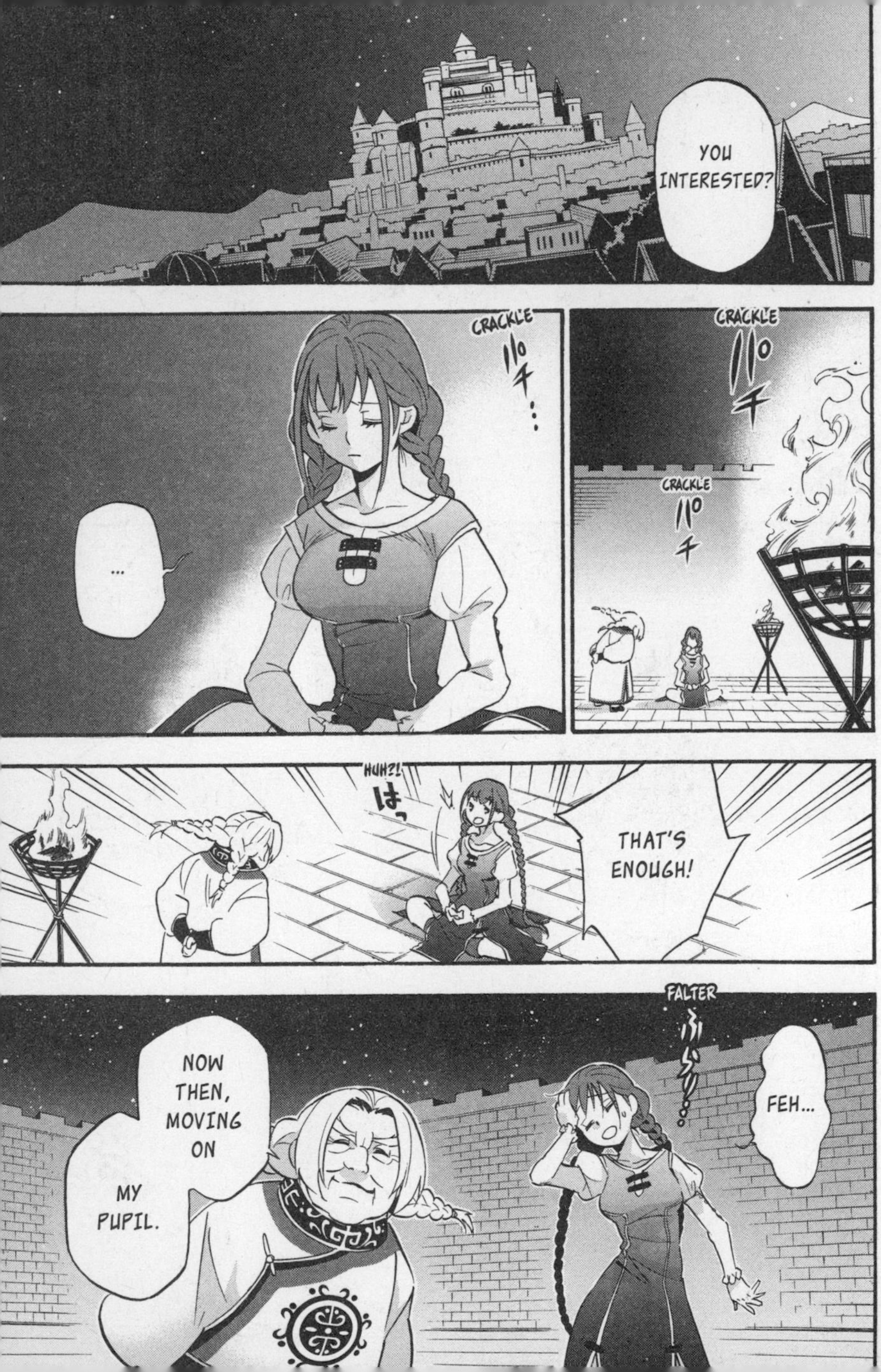
YOU INTERESTED?
CRACKLE
パチ
CRACKLE
パチ
CRACKLE
パチ…
...
HUH?!
はっ
THAT'S ENOUGH!
FALTER
ふらり
FEH...
NOW THEN, MOVING ON
MY PUPIL.

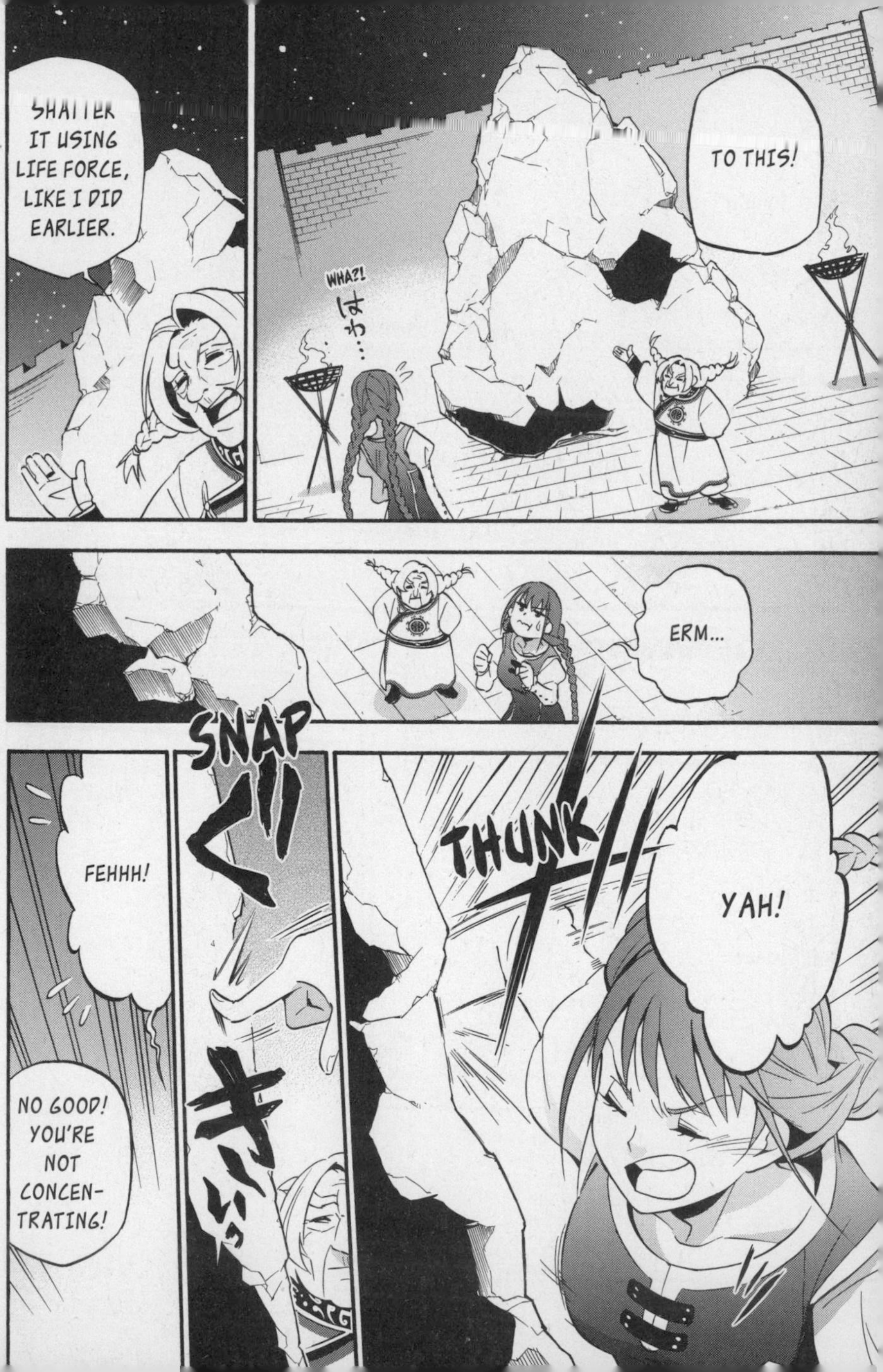
TO THIS!
WHA?!
はわ…
SHATTER IT USING LIFE FORCE, LIKE I DID EARLIER.
ERM...
YAH!
THUNK
SNAP
くり
FEHHH!
NO GOOD! YOU'RE NOT CONCEN-TRATING!

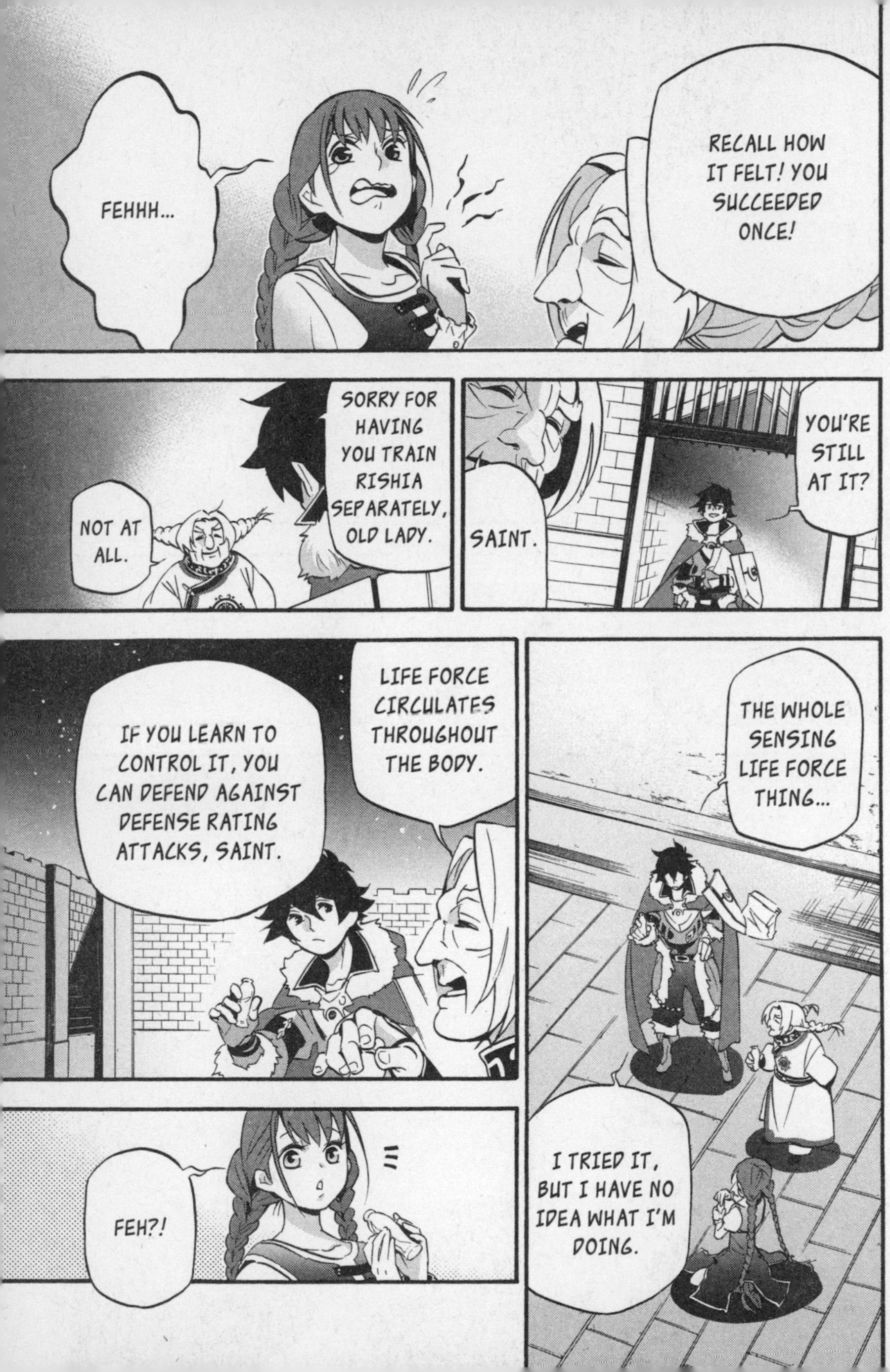
RECALL HOW IT FELT! YOU SUCCEEDED ONCE!
FEHHH...
YOU'RE STILL AT IT?
SAINT.
SORRY FOR HAVING YOU TRAIN RISHIA SEPARATELY, OLD LADY.
NOT AT ALL.
THE WHOLE SENSING LIFE FORCE THING...
I TRIED IT, BUT I HAVE NO IDEA WHAT I'M DOING.
LIFE FORCE CIRCULATES THROUGHOUT THE BODY.
IF YOU LEARN TO CONTROL IT, YOU CAN DEFEND AGAINST DEFENSE RATING ATTACKS, SAINT.
FEH?!

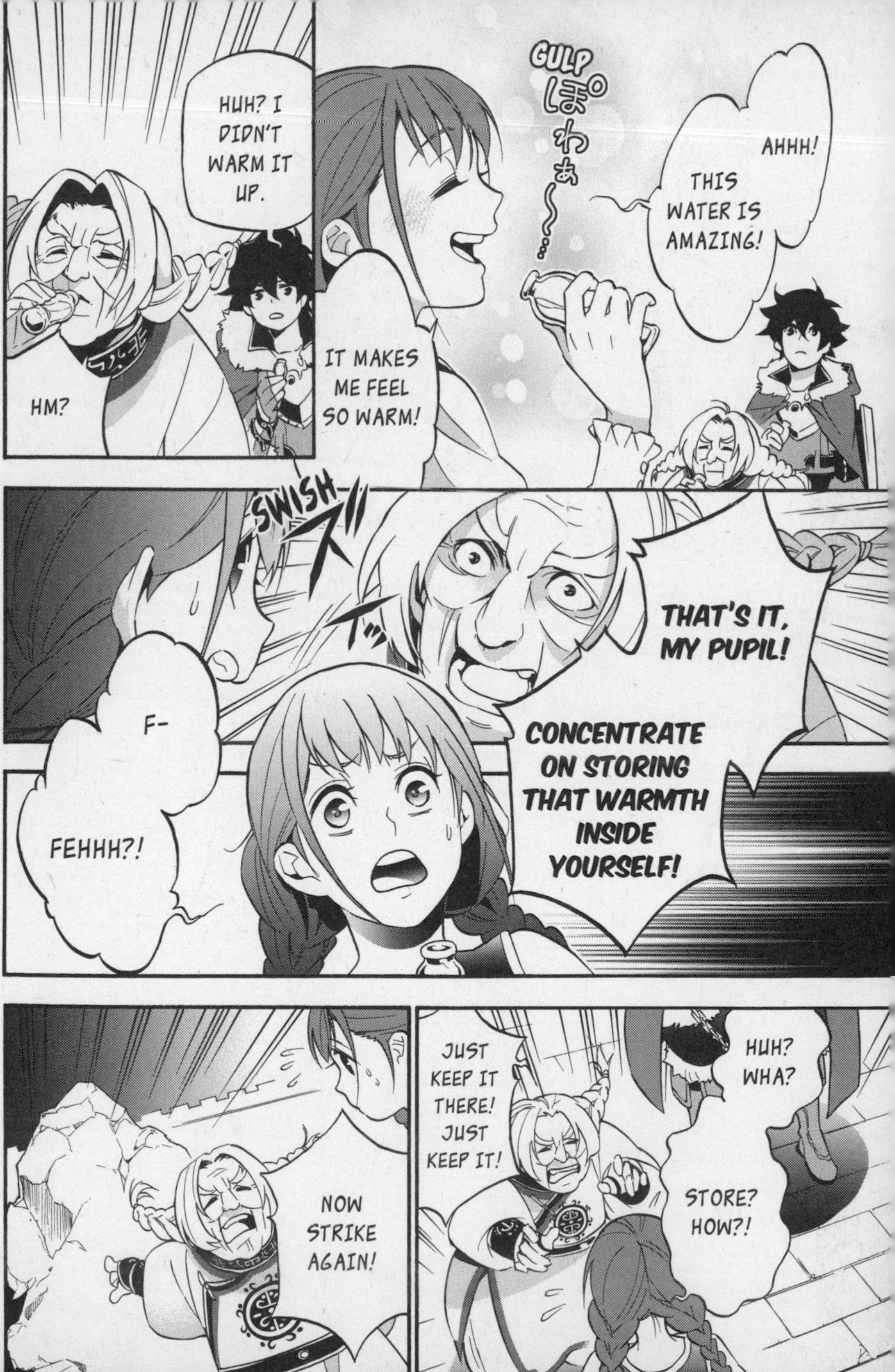
GULP
ぽわぁ～…
AHHH!
THIS WATER IS AMAZING!
IT MAKES ME FEEL SO WARM!
HUH? I DIDN'T WARM IT UP.
HM?
SWISH
THAT'S IT, MY PUPIL!
CONCENTRATE ON STORING THAT WARMTH INSIDE YOURSELF!
F-
FEHHH?!
HUH? WHA?
JUST KEEP IT THERE! JUST KEEP IT!
STORE? HOW?!
NOW STRIKE AGAIN!

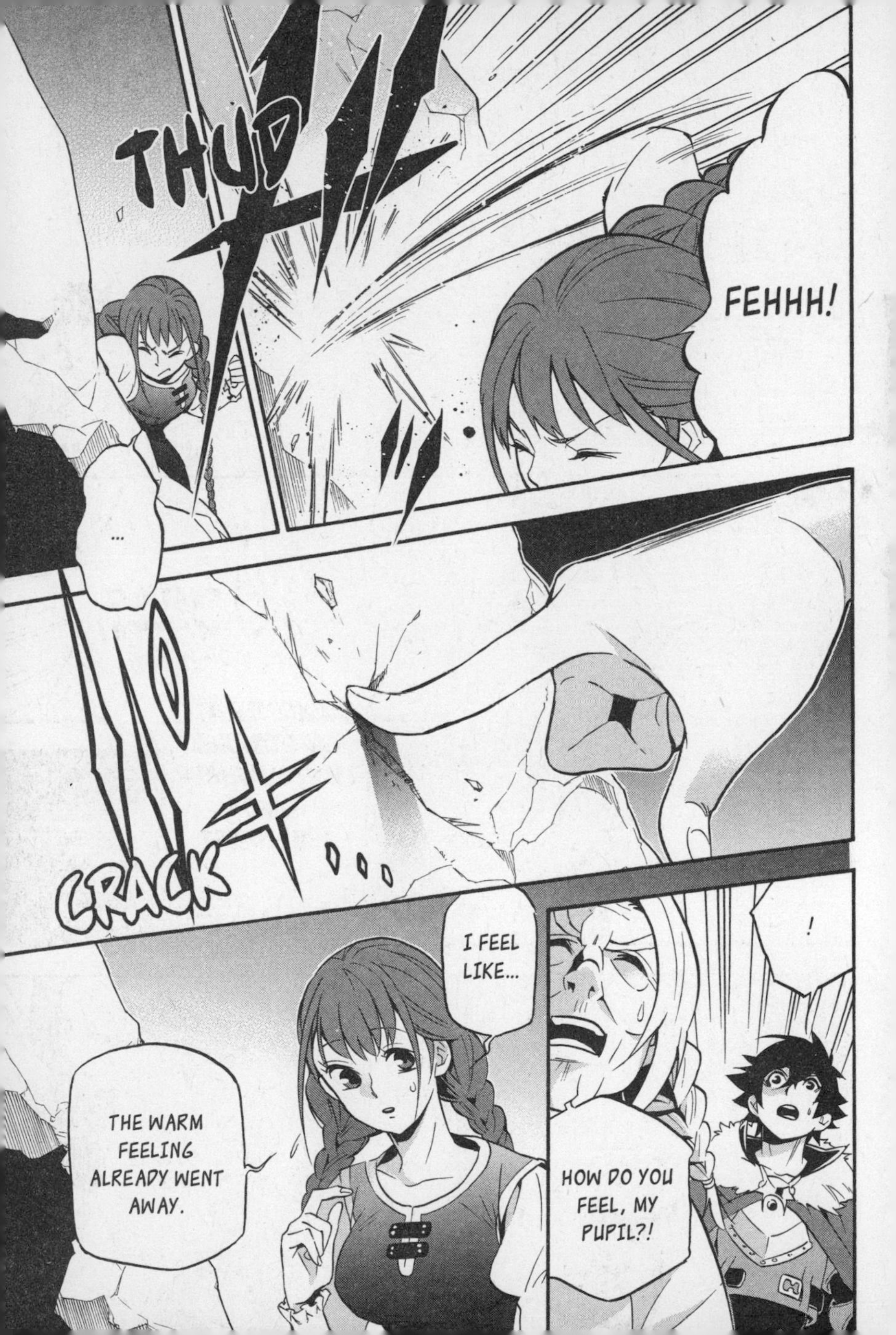
FEHHH!
THUD
...
CRACK
!
HOW DO YOU FEEL, MY PUPIL?!
I FEEL LIKE...
THE WARM FEELING ALREADY WENT AWAY.

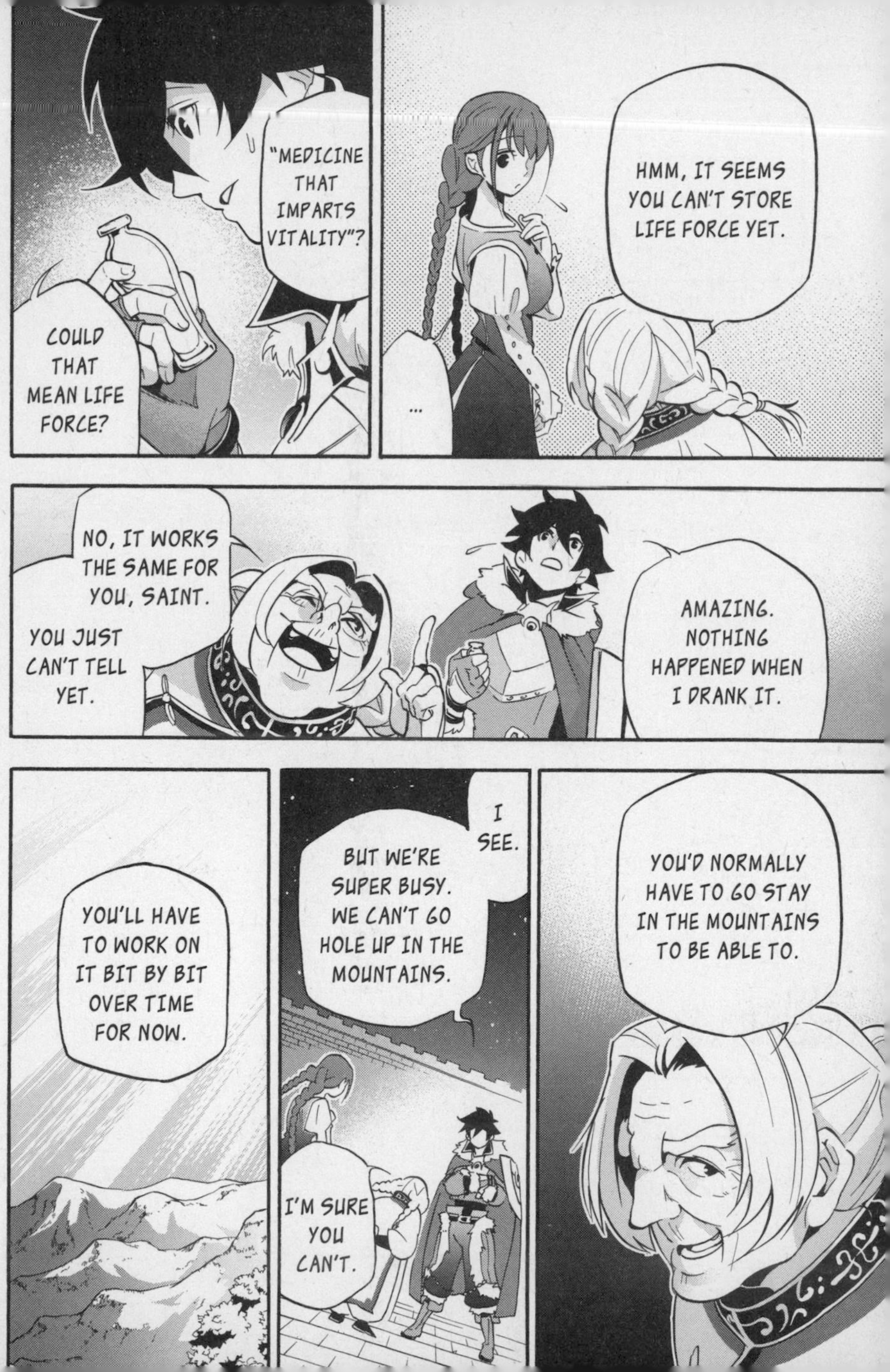
HMM, IT SEEMS YOU CAN'T STORE LIFE FORCE YET.
...
"MEDICINE THAT IMPARTS VITALITY"?
COULD THAT MEAN LIFE FORCE?
AMAZING. NOTHING HAPPENED WHEN I DRANK IT.
NO, IT WORKS THE SAME FOR YOU, SAINT.
YOU JUST CAN'T TELL YET.
YOU'D NORMALLY HAVE TO GO STAY IN THE MOUNTAINS TO BE ABLE TO.
I SEE.
BUT WE'RE SUPER BUSY. WE CAN'T GO HOLE UP IN THE MOUNTAINS.
I'M SURE YOU CAN'T.
YOU'LL HAVE TO WORK ON IT BIT BY BIT OVER TIME FOR NOW.

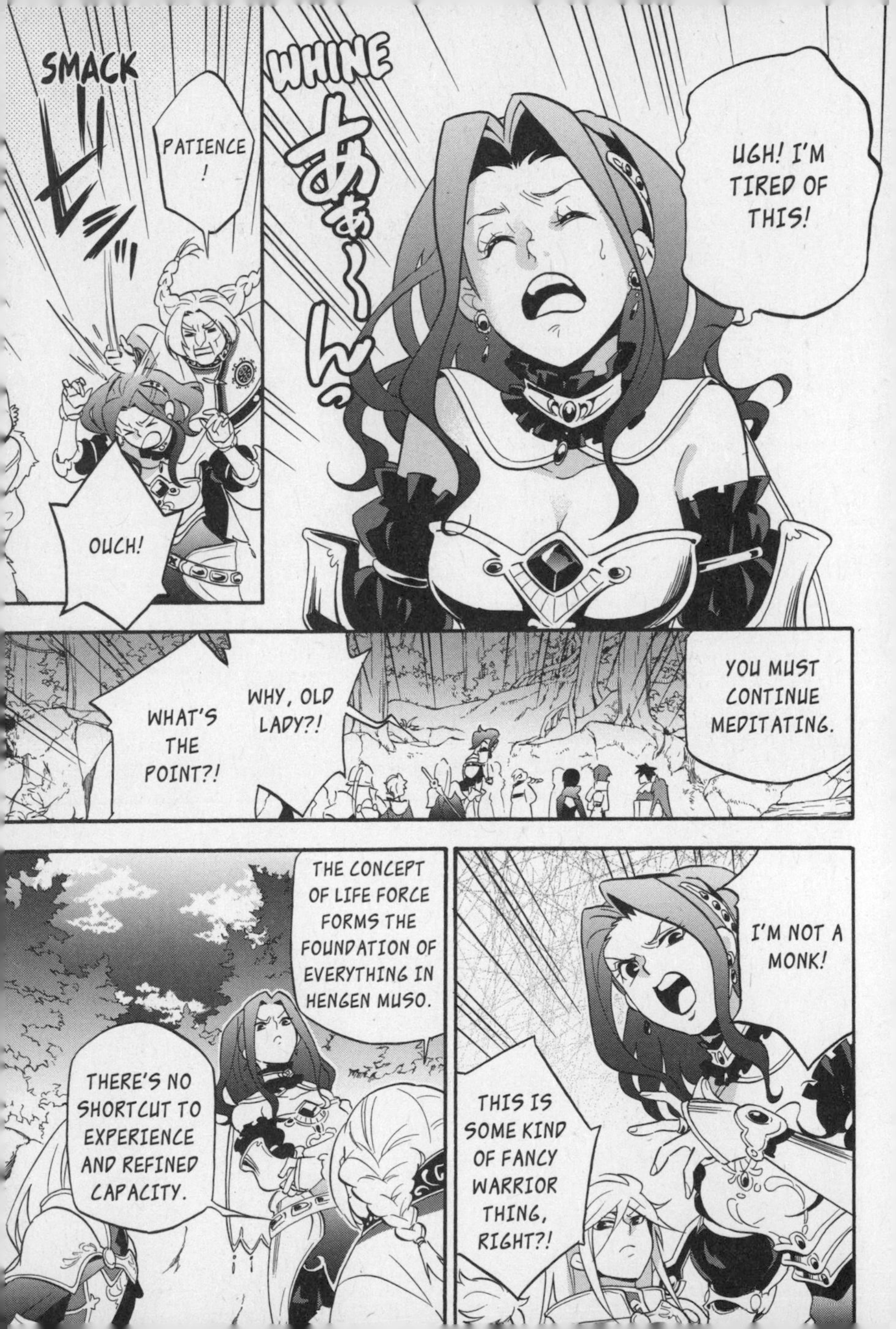
UGH! I'M TIRED OF THIS!
WHINE
あぁ〜んっ
PATIENCE!
SMACK
OUCH!
YOU MUST CONTINUE MEDITATING.
WHY, OLD LADY?!
WHAT'S THE POINT?!
I'M NOT A MONK!
THIS IS SOME KIND OF FANCY WARRIOR THING, RIGHT?!
THE CONCEPT OF LIFE FORCE FORMS THE FOUNDATION OF EVERYTHING IN HENGEN MUSO.
THERE'S NO SHORTCUT TO EXPERIENCE AND REFINED CAPACITY.

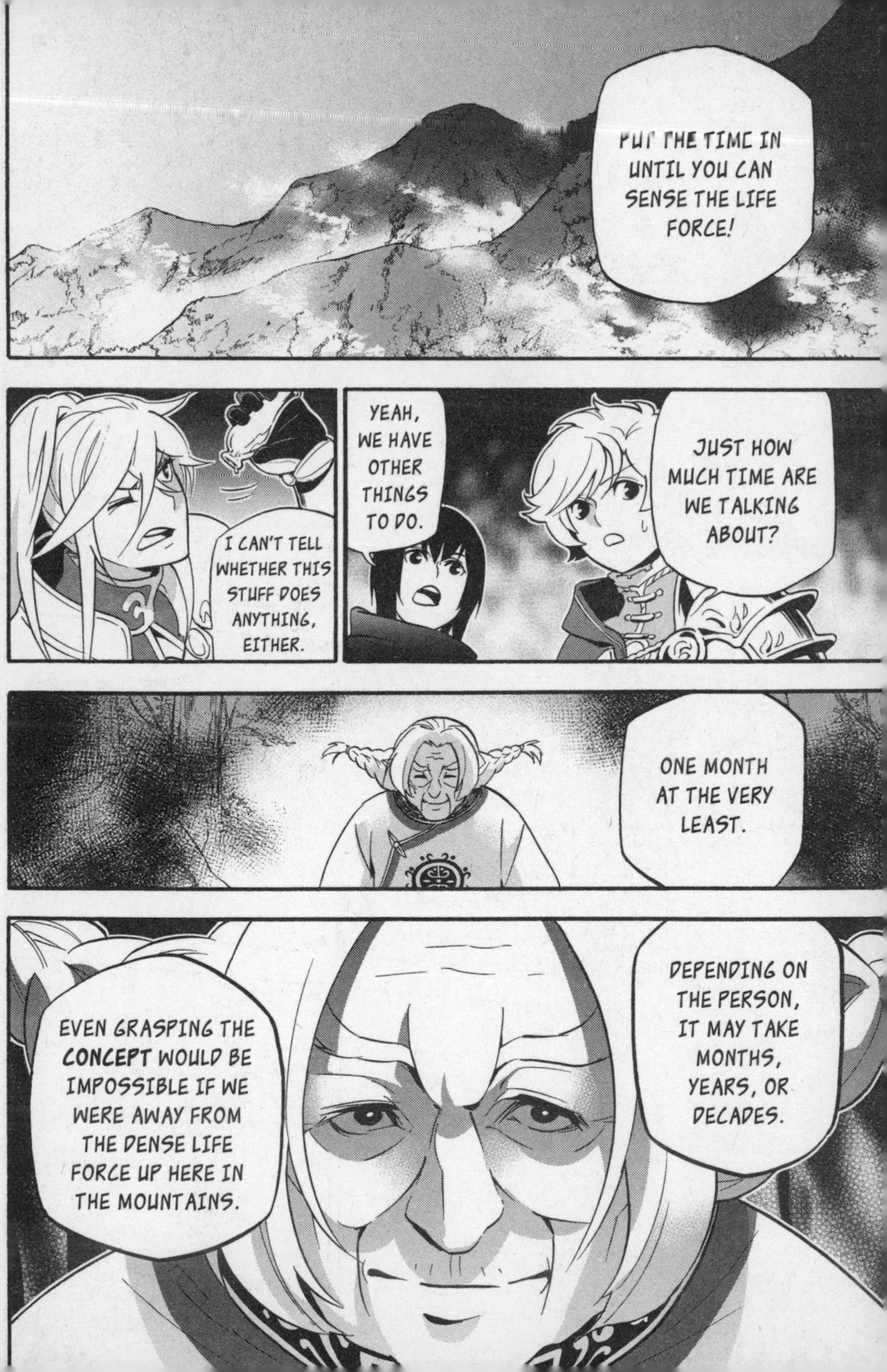
PUT THE TIME IN UNTIL YOU CAN SENSE THE LIFE FORCE!
JUST HOW MUCH TIME ARE WE TALKING ABOUT?
YEAH, WE HAVE OTHER THINGS TO DO.
I CAN'T TELL WHETHER THIS STUFF DOES ANYTHING, EITHER.
ONE MONTH AT THE VERY LEAST.
DEPENDING ON THE PERSON, IT MAY TAKE MONTHS, YEARS, OR DECADES.
EVEN GRASPING THE **CONCEPT** WOULD BE IMPOSSIBLE IF WE WERE AWAY FROM THE DENSE LIFE FORCE UP HERE IN THE MOUNTAINS.

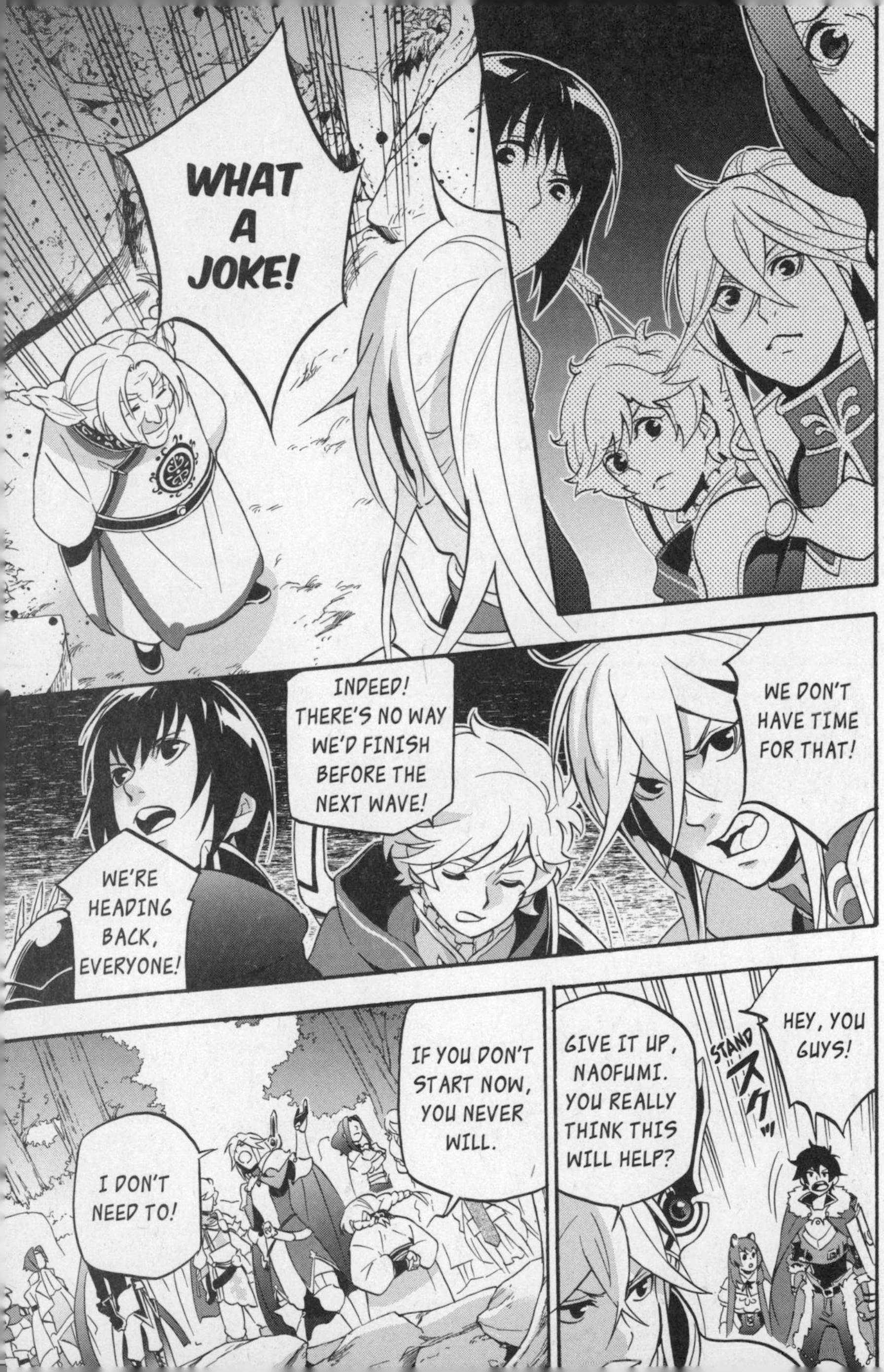
WHAT A JOKE!
WE DON'T HAVE TIME FOR THAT!
INDEED! THERE'S NO WAY WE'D FINISH BEFORE THE NEXT WAVE!
WE'RE HEADING BACK, EVERYONE!
HEY, YOU GUYS!
STAND
スクッ
GIVE IT UP, NAOFUMI. YOU REALLY THINK THIS WILL HELP?
IF YOU DON'T START NOW, YOU NEVER WILL.
I DON'T NEED TO!

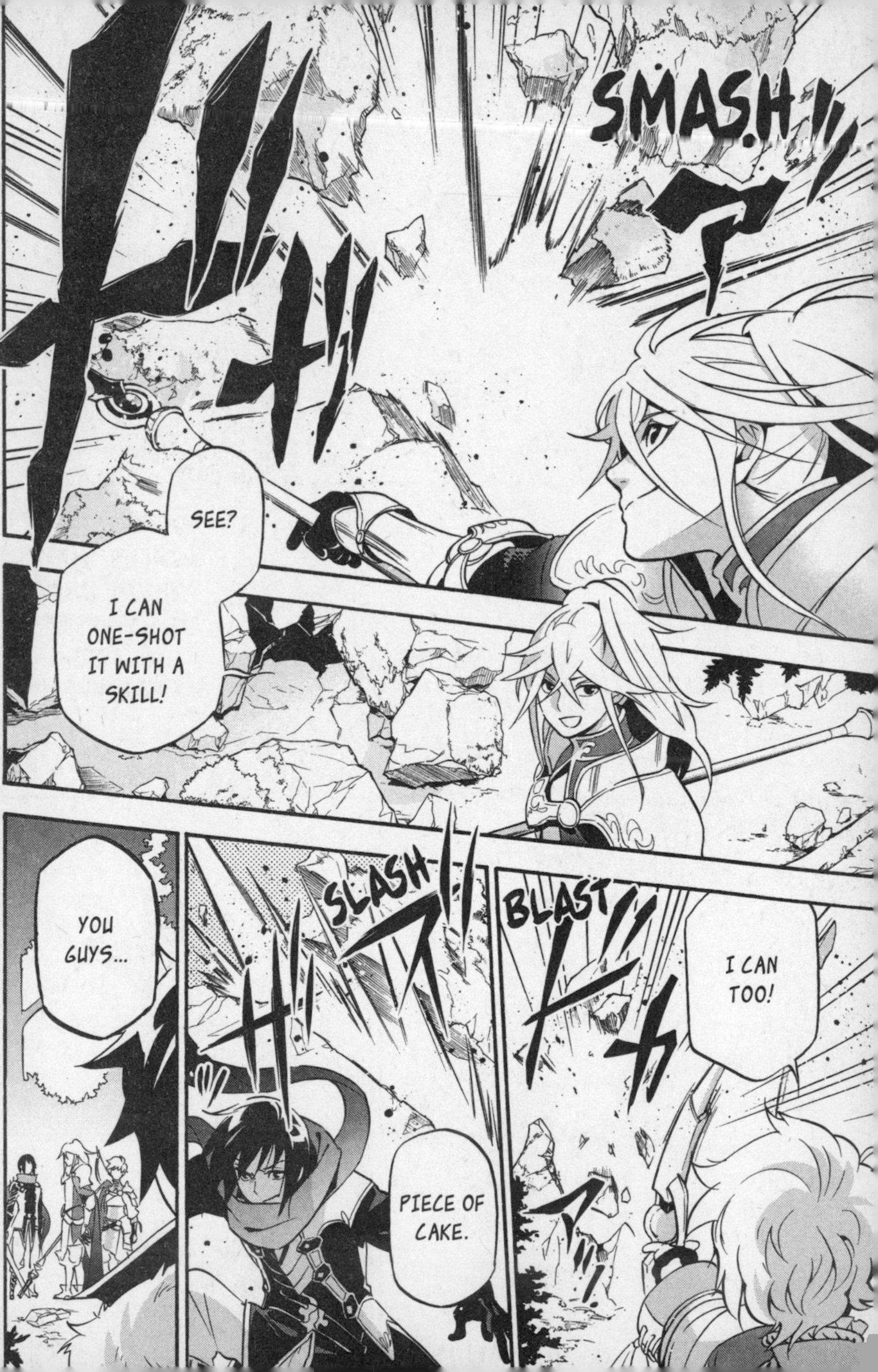
SMASH
SEE?
I CAN ONE-SHOT IT WITH A SKILL!
BLAST
I CAN TOO!
SLASH
PIECE OF CAKE.
YOU GUYS...

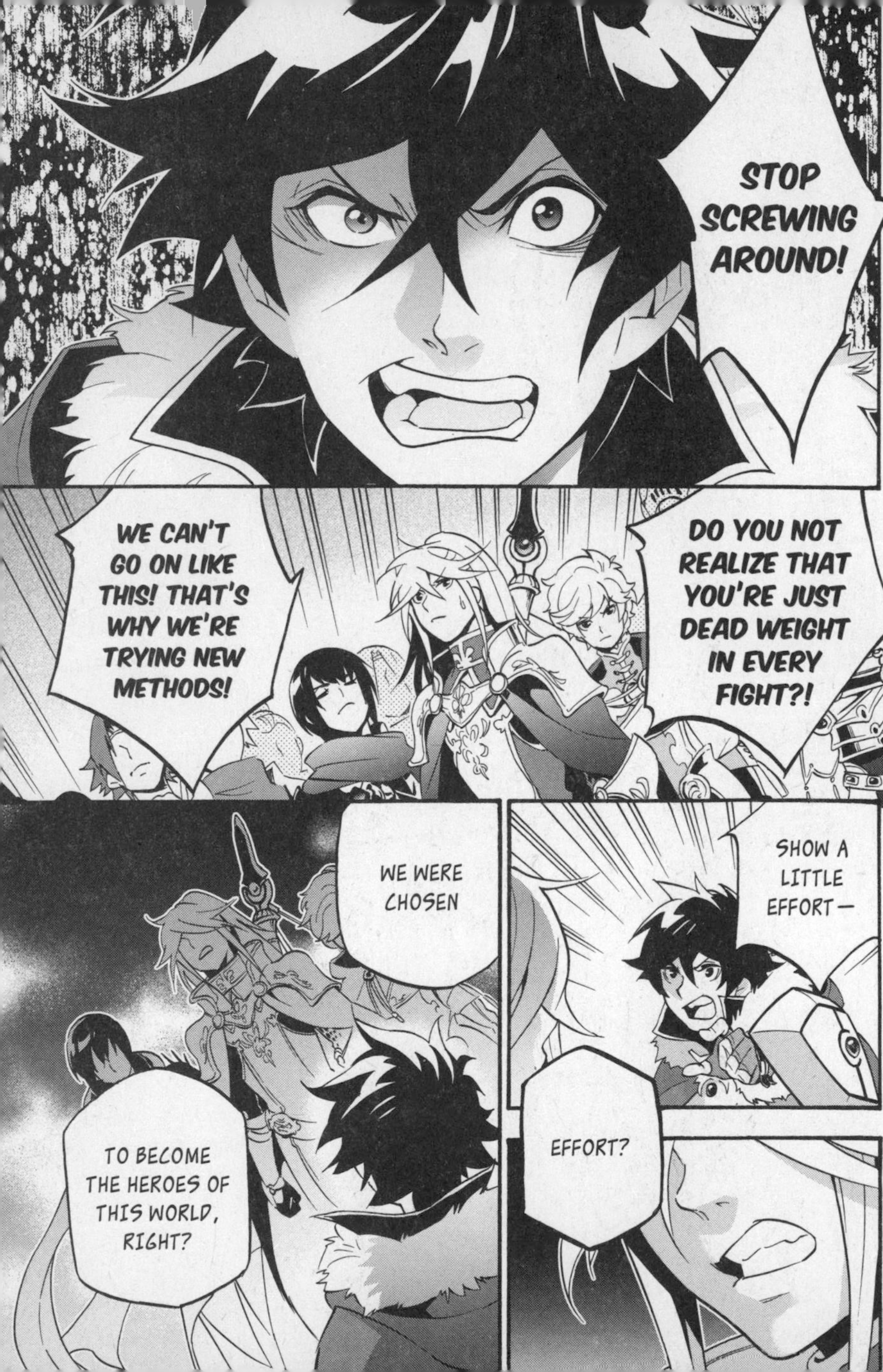
STOP SCREWING AROUND!
DO YOU NOT REALIZE THAT YOU'RE JUST DEAD WEIGHT IN EVERY FIGHT?!
WE CAN'T GO ON LIKE THIS! THAT'S WHY WE'RE TRYING NEW METHODS!
SHOW A LITTLE EFFORT—
EFFORT?
WE WERE CHOSEN
TO BECOME THE HEROES OF THIS WORLD, RIGHT?

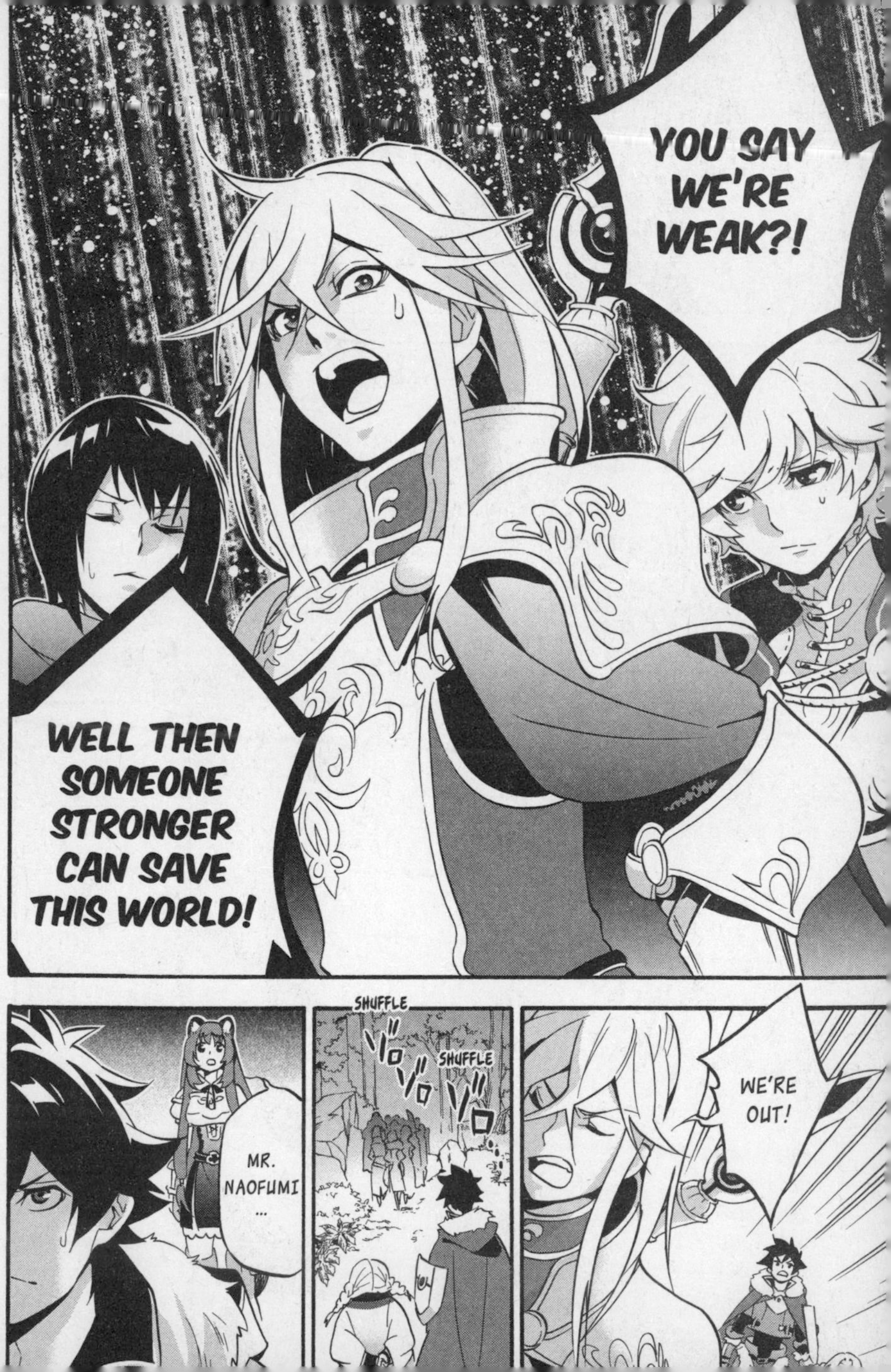
YOU SAY WE'RE WEAK?!
WELL THEN SOMEONE STRONGER CAN SAVE THIS WORLD!
WE'RE OUT!
SHUFFLE
SHUFFLE
MR. NAOFUMI ...

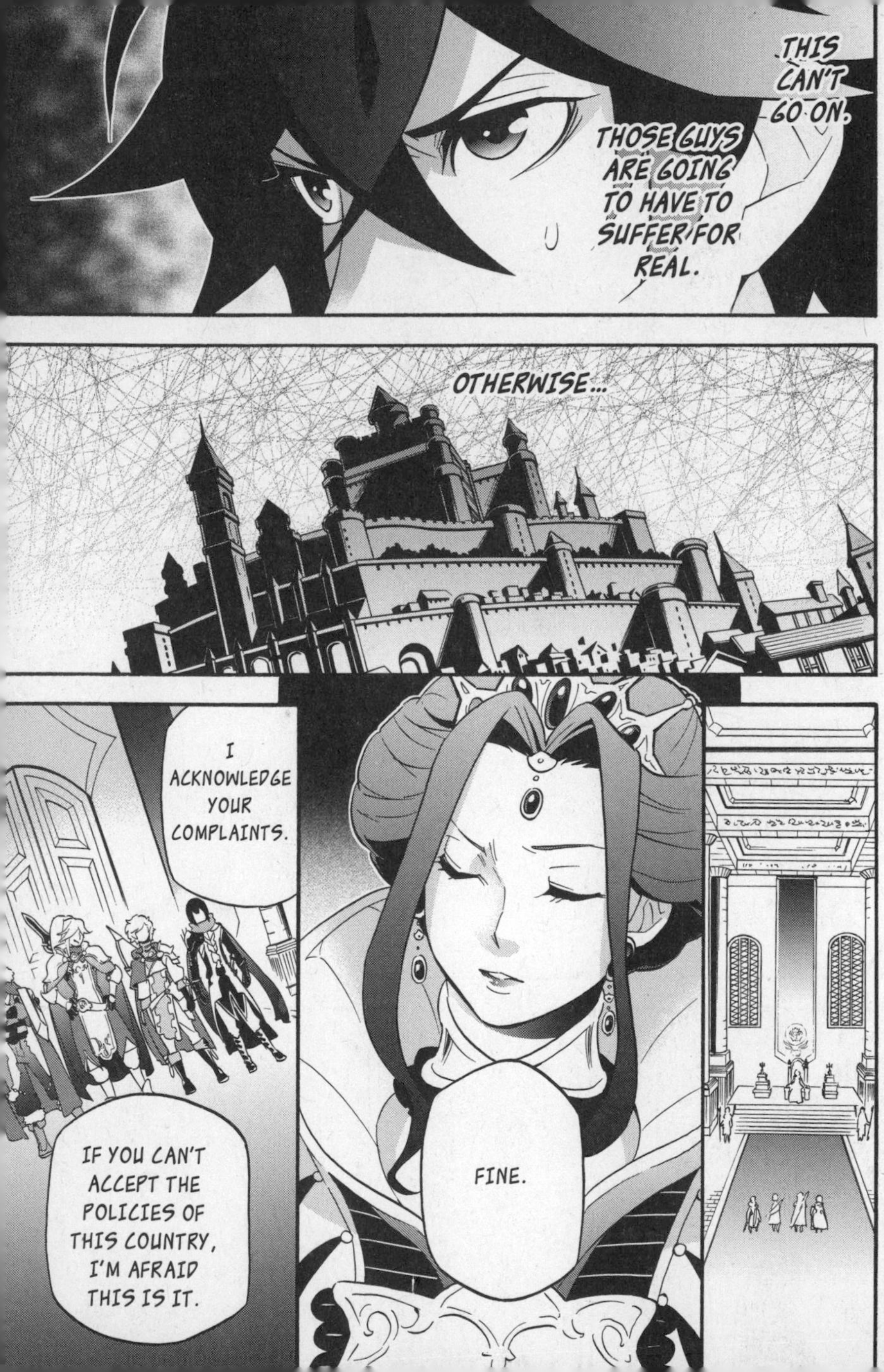
THIS CAN'T GO ON.
THOSE GUYS ARE GOING TO HAVE TO SUFFER FOR REAL.
OTHERWISE...
FINE.
I ACKNOWLEDGE YOUR COMPLAINTS.
IF YOU CAN'T ACCEPT THE POLICIES OF THIS COUNTRY, I'M AFRAID THIS IS IT.

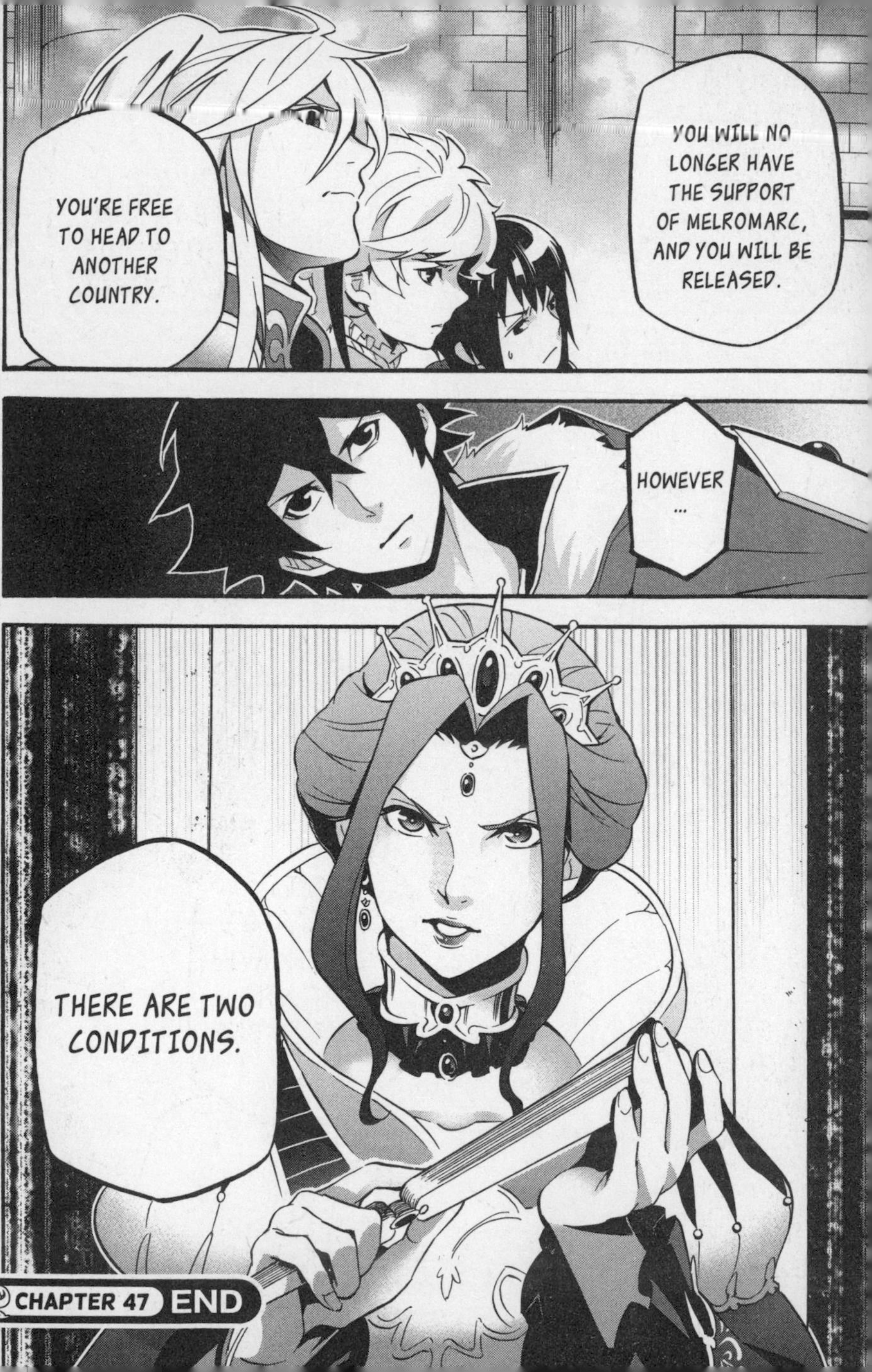
YOU WILL NO LONGER HAVE THE SUPPORT OF MELROMARC, AND YOU WILL BE RELEASED.
YOU'RE FREE TO HEAD TO ANOTHER COUNTRY.
HOWEVER ...
THERE ARE TWO CONDITIONS.
CHAPTER 47 END

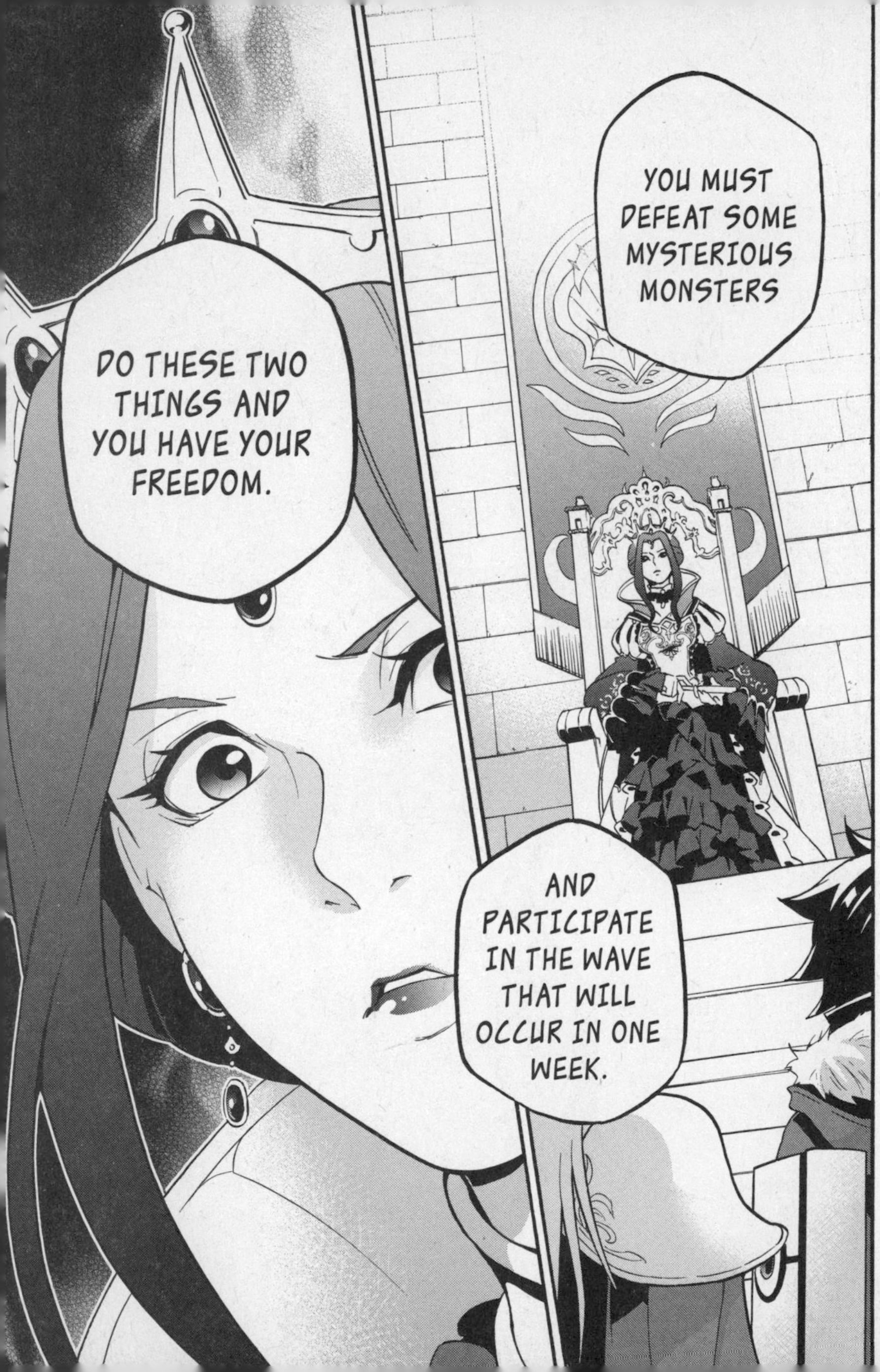
YOU MUST DEFEAT SOME MYSTERIOUS MONSTERS
AND PARTICIPATE IN THE WAVE THAT WILL OCCUR IN ONE WEEK.
DO THESE TWO THINGS AND YOU HAVE YOUR FREEDOM.

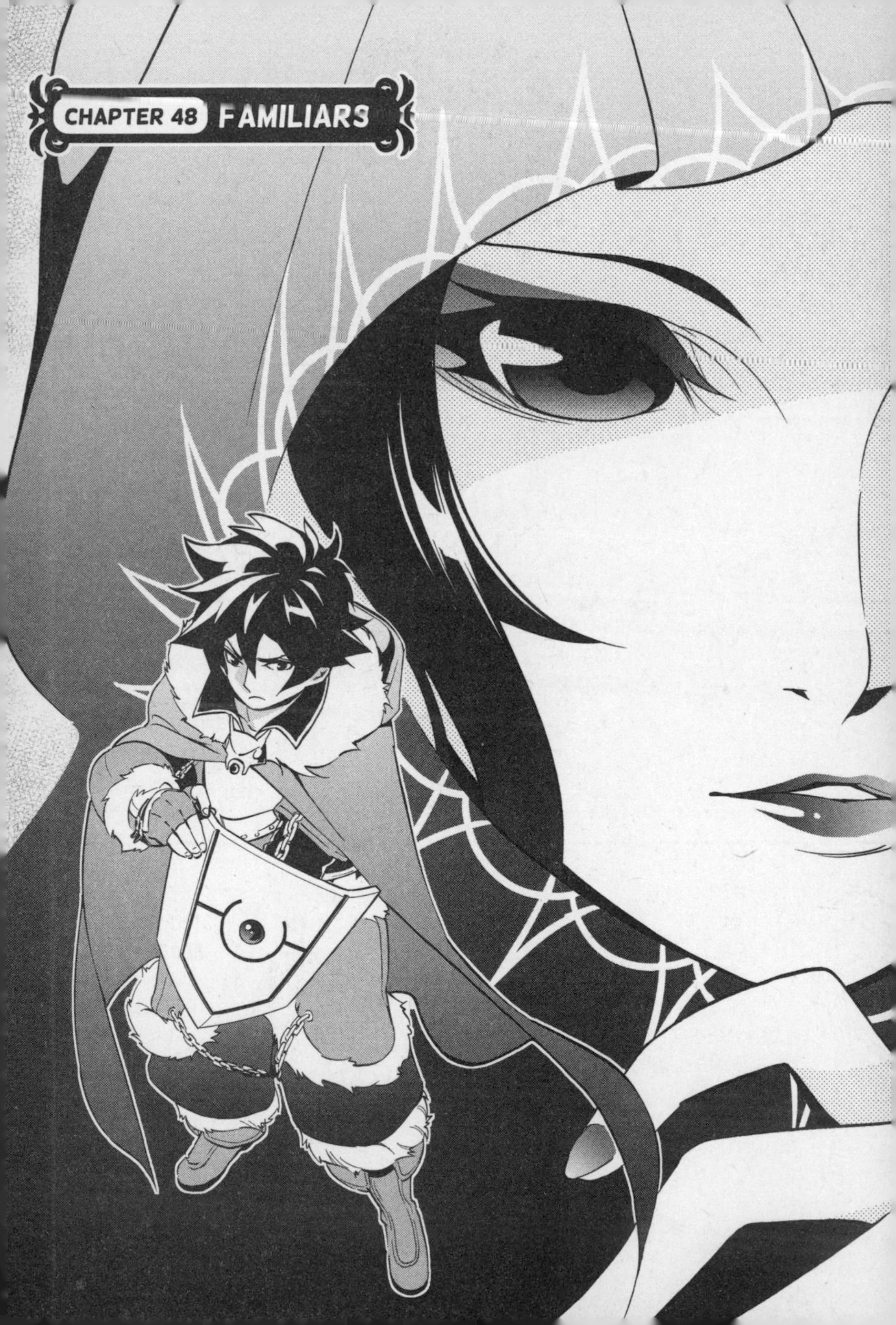
CHAPTER 48 FAMILIARS

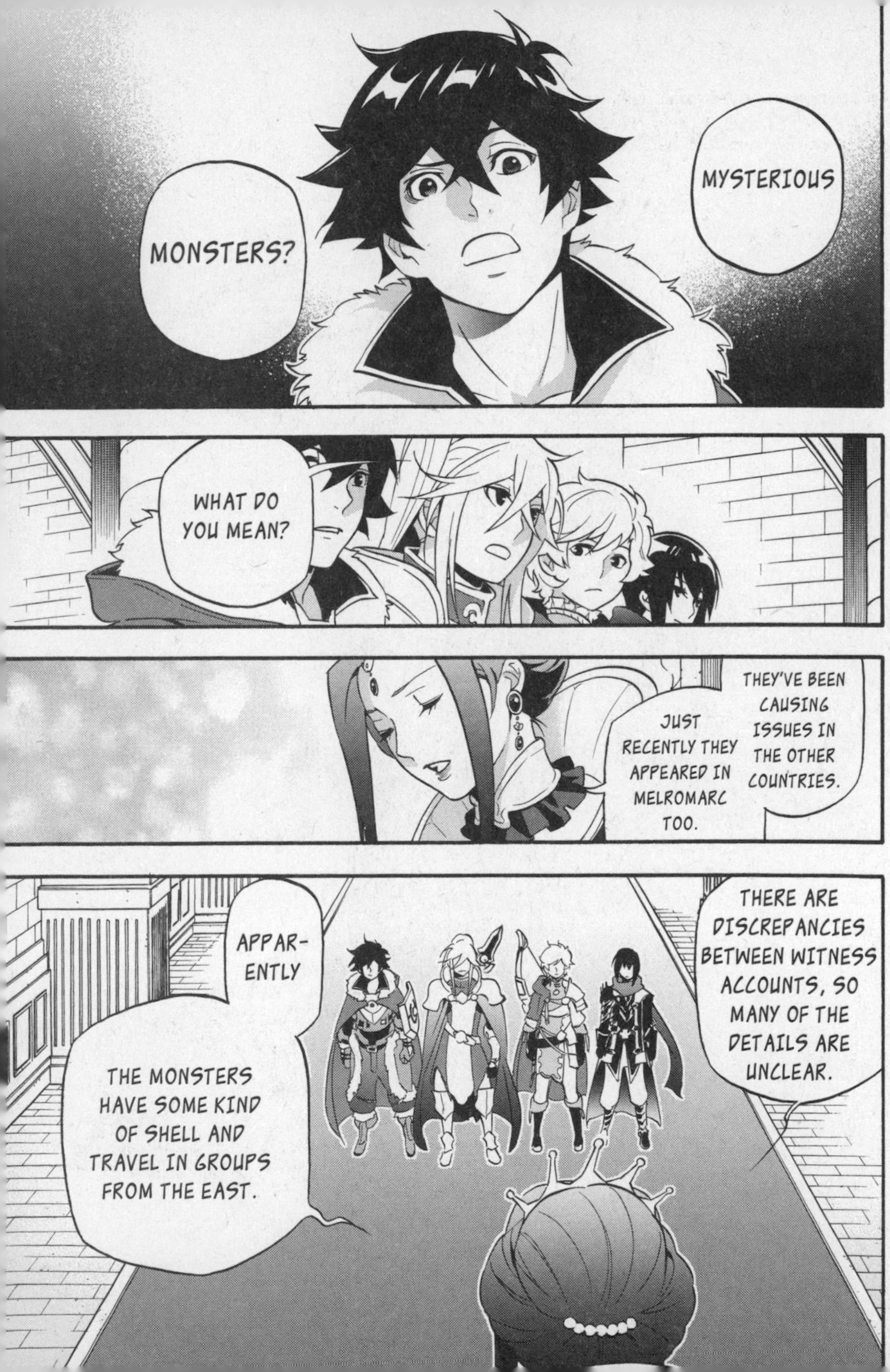
MYSTERIOUS
MONSTERS?
WHAT DO YOU MEAN?
THEY'VE BEEN CAUSING ISSUES IN THE OTHER COUNTRIES.
JUST RECENTLY THEY APPEARED IN MELROMARC TOO.
THERE ARE DISCREPANCIES BETWEEN WITNESS ACCOUNTS, SO MANY OF THE DETAILS ARE UNCLEAR.
APPAR-ENTLY
THE MONSTERS HAVE SOME KIND OF SHELL AND TRAVEL IN GROUPS FROM THE EAST.

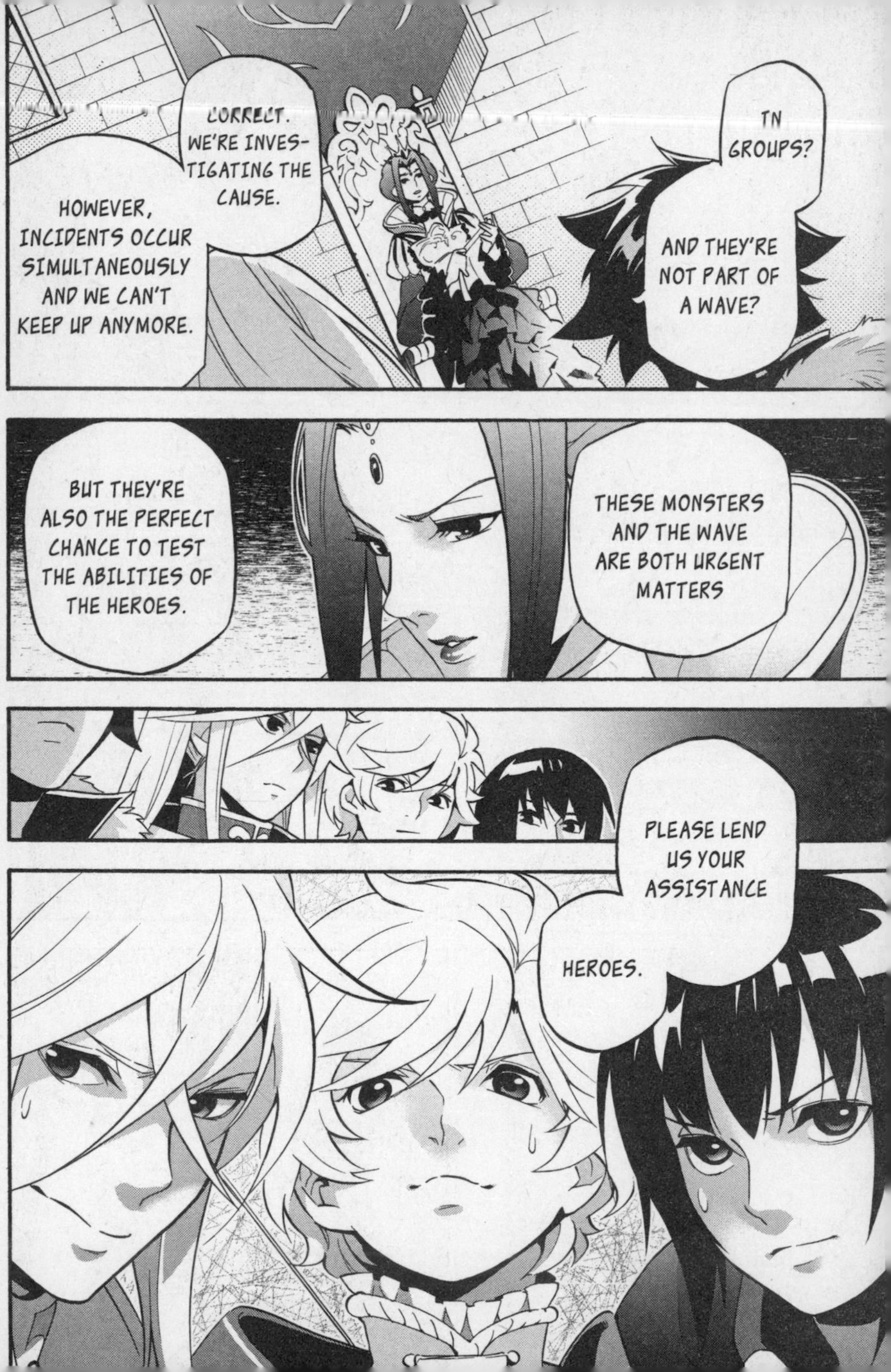
IN GROUPS?
AND THEY'RE NOT PART OF A WAVE?
CORRECT. WE'RE INVESTIGATING THE CAUSE.
HOWEVER, INCIDENTS OCCUR SIMULTANEOUSLY AND WE CAN'T KEEP UP ANYMORE.
THESE MONSTERS AND THE WAVE ARE BOTH URGENT MATTERS
BUT THEY'RE ALSO THE PERFECT CHANCE TO TEST THE ABILITIES OF THE HEROES.
PLEASE LEND US YOUR ASSISTANCE
HEROES.

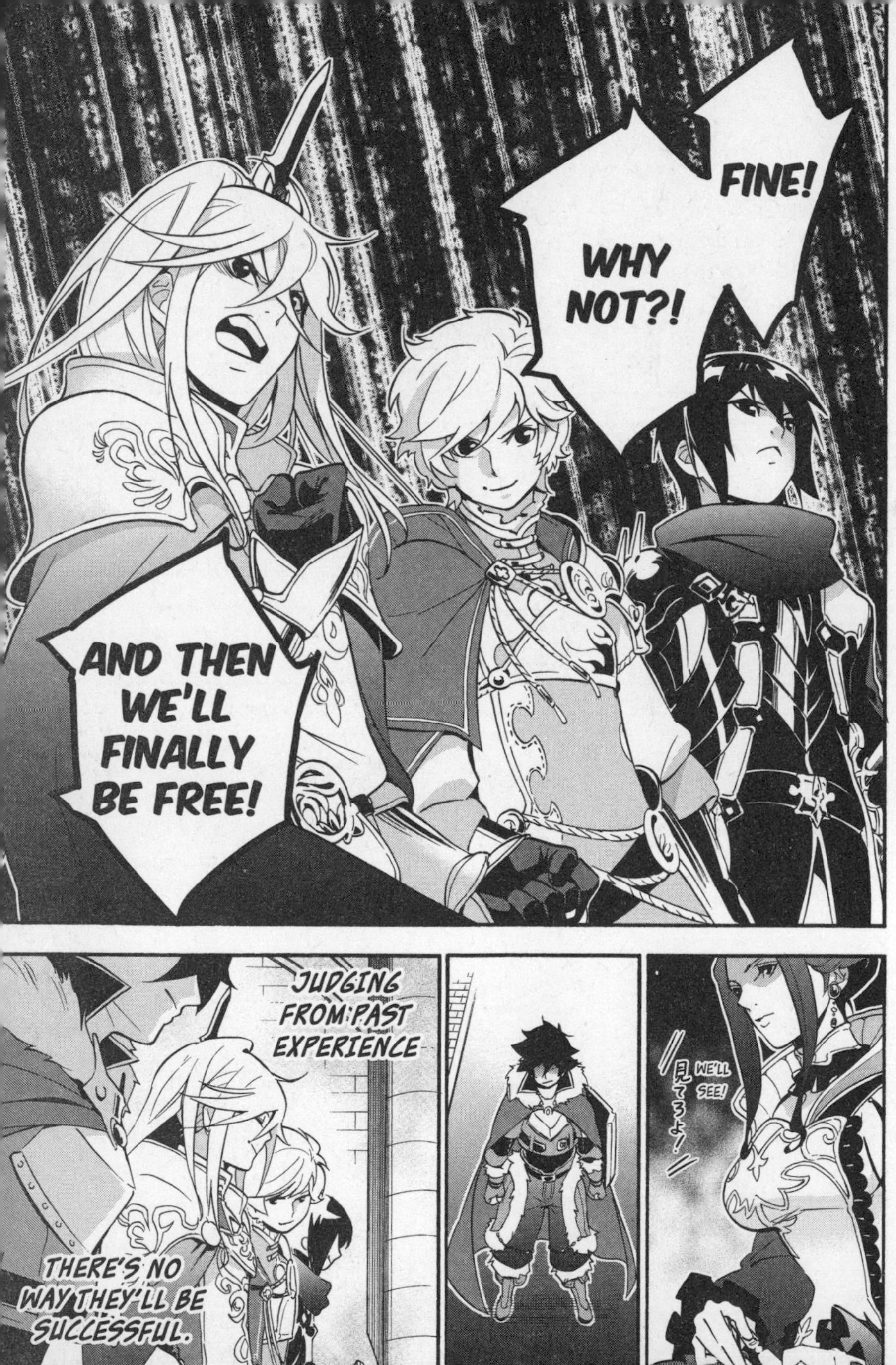
FINE!
WHY NOT?!
AND THEN WE'LL FINALLY BE FREE!
見てろよ！
WE'LL SEE!
JUDGING FROM PAST EXPERIENCE
THERE'S NO WAY THEY'LL BE SUCCESSFUL.

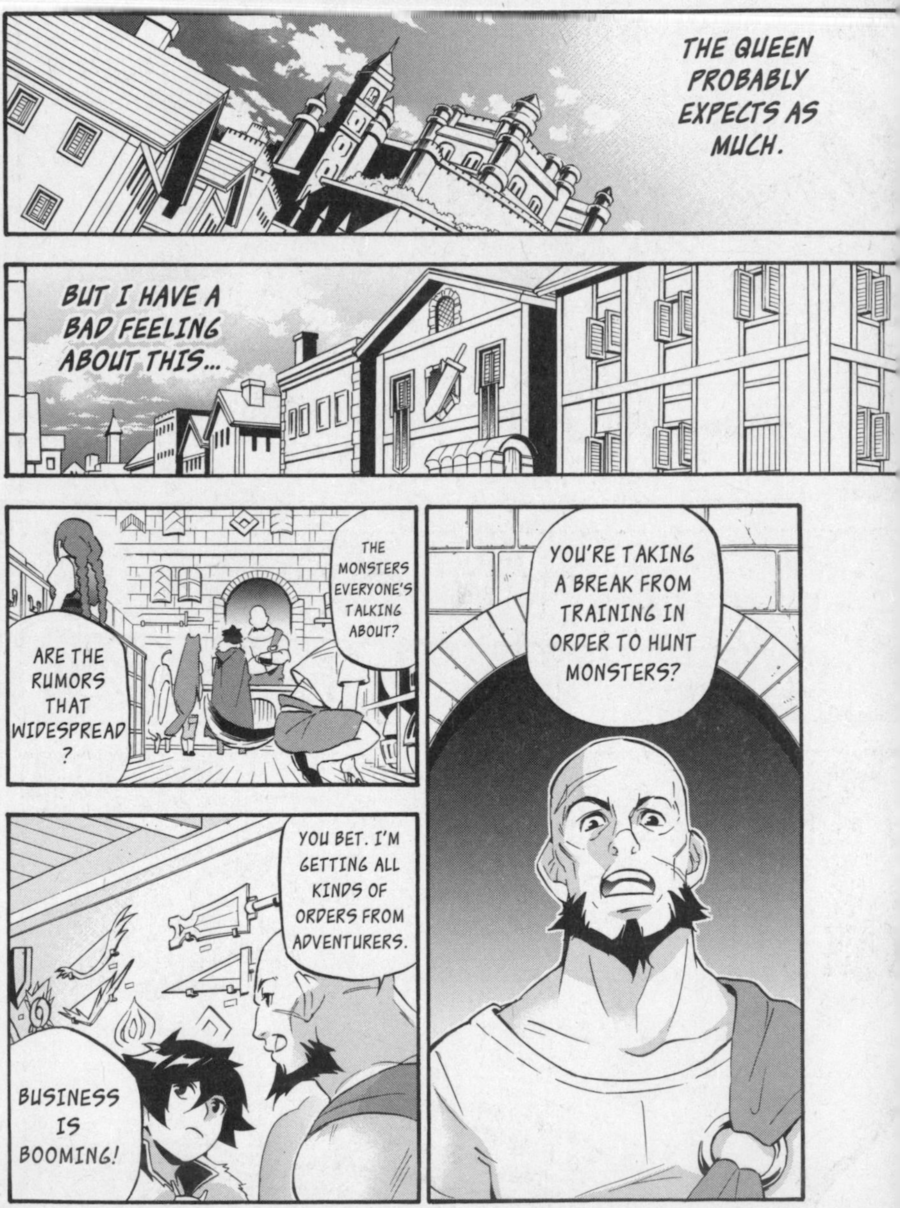
THE QUEEN PROBABLY EXPECTS AS MUCH.
BUT I HAVE A BAD FEELING ABOUT THIS...
YOU'RE TAKING A BREAK FROM TRAINING IN ORDER TO HUNT MONSTERS?
THE MONSTERS EVERYONE'S TALKING ABOUT?
ARE THE RUMORS THAT WIDESPREAD?
YOU BET. I'M GETTING ALL KINDS OF ORDERS FROM ADVENTURERS.
BUSINESS IS BOOMING!

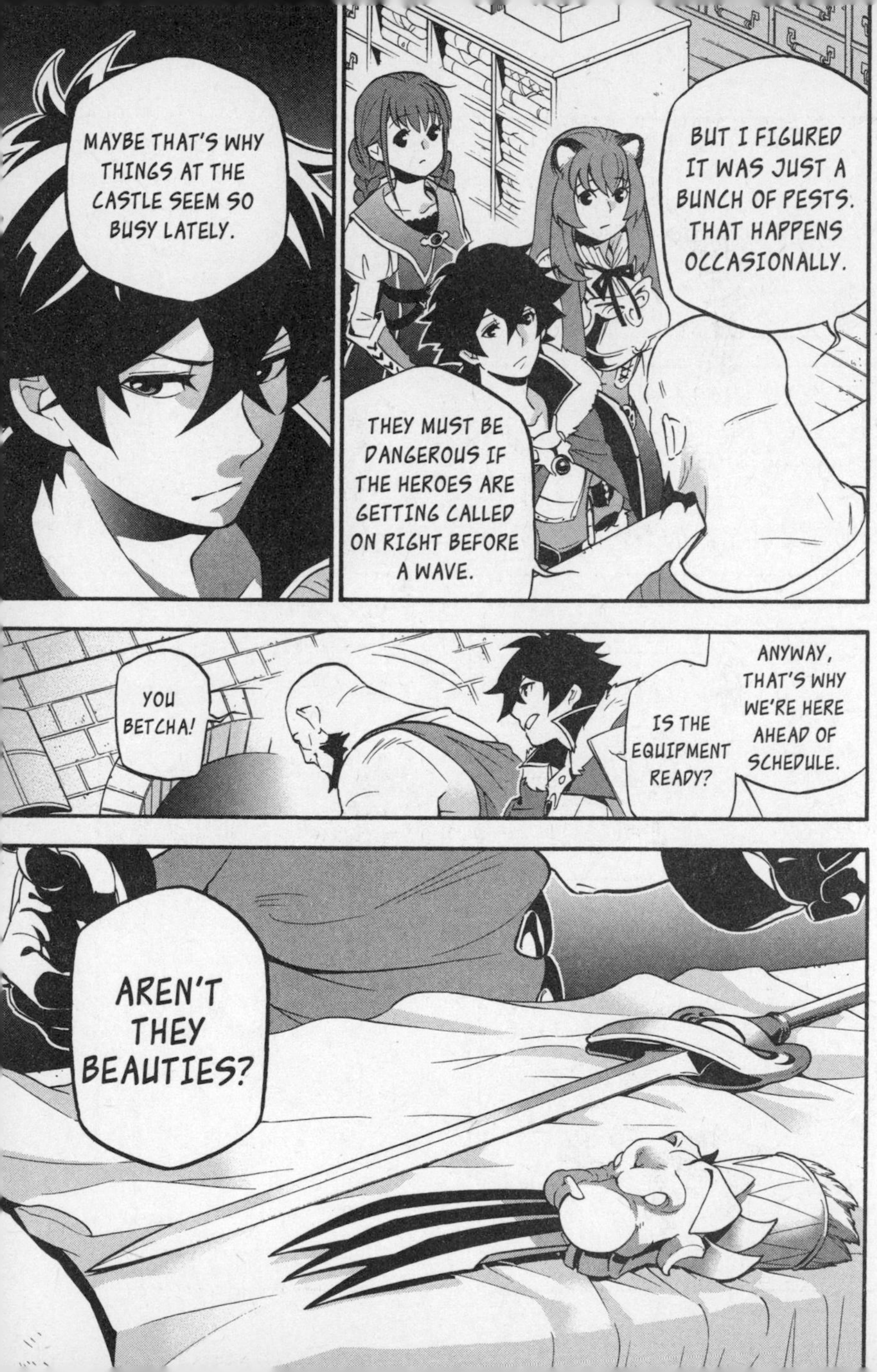
BUT I FIGURED IT WAS JUST A BUNCH OF PESTS. THAT HAPPENS OCCASIONALLY.
THEY MUST BE DANGEROUS IF THE HEROES ARE GETTING CALLED ON RIGHT BEFORE A WAVE.
MAYBE THAT'S WHY THINGS AT THE CASTLE SEEM SO BUSY LATELY.
ANYWAY, THAT'S WHY WE'RE HERE AHEAD OF SCHEDULE.
IS THE EQUIPMENT READY?
YOU BETCHA!
AREN'T THEY BEAUTIES?

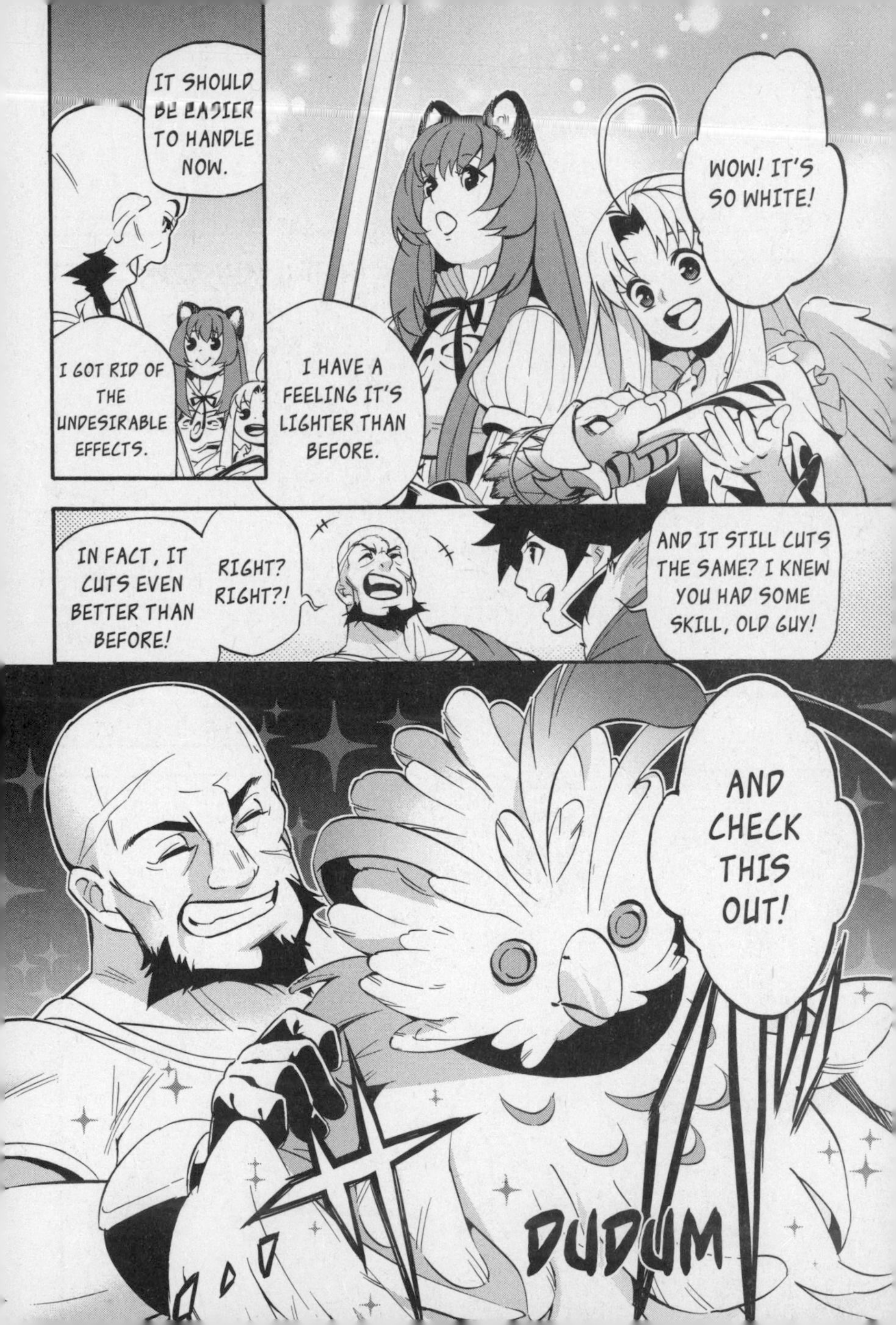
WOW! IT'S SO WHITE!
I HAVE A FEELING IT'S LIGHTER THAN BEFORE.
IT SHOULD BE EASIER TO HANDLE NOW.
I GOT RID OF THE UNDESIRABLE EFFECTS.
AND IT STILL CUTS THE SAME? I KNEW YOU HAD SOME SKILL, OLD GUY!
RIGHT? RIGHT?!
IN FACT, IT CUTS EVEN BETTER THAN BEFORE!
AND CHECK THIS OUT!
DUDUM

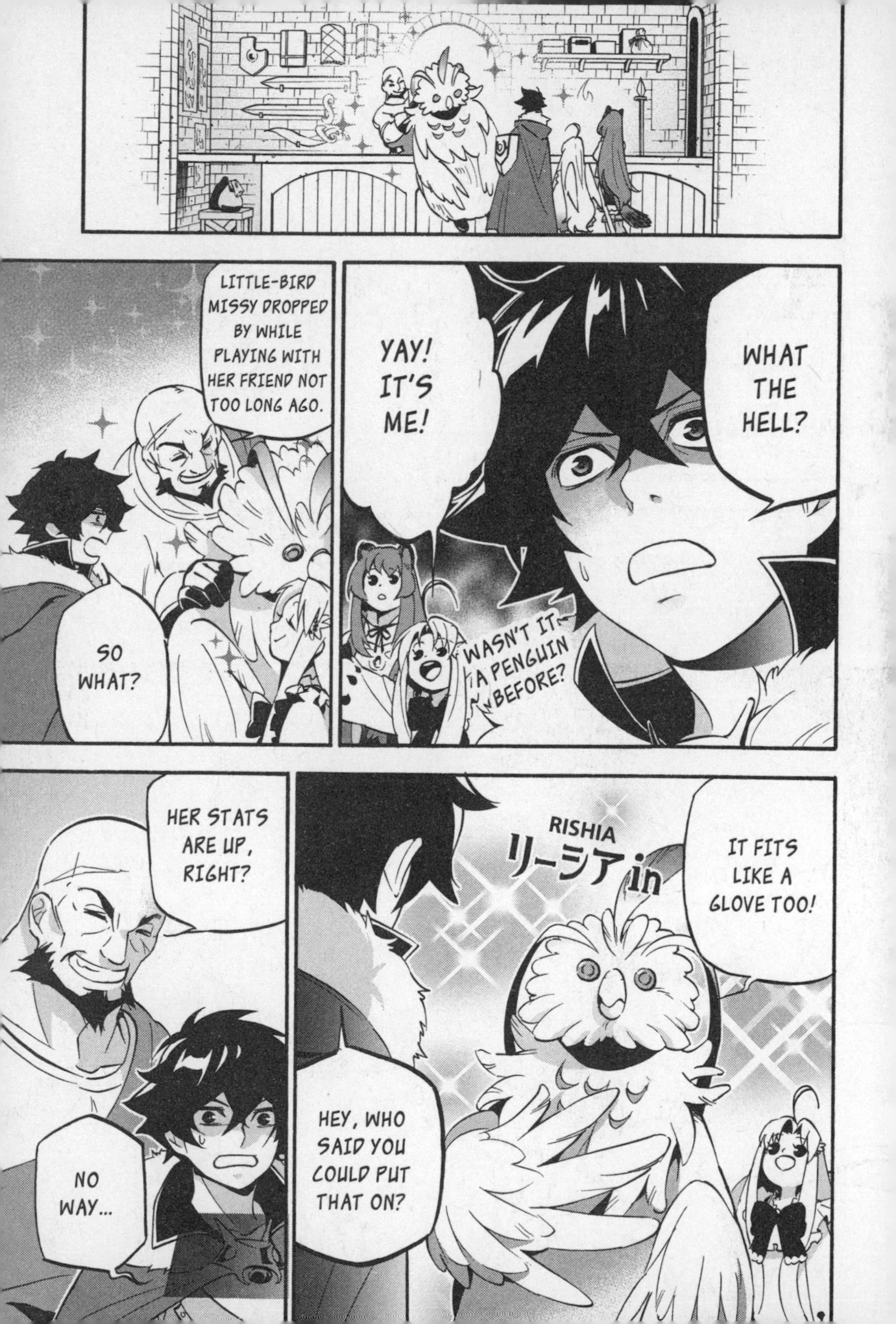
WHAT THE HELL?
YAY! IT'S ME!
WASN'T IT A PENGUIN BEFORE?
LITTLE-BIRD MISSY DROPPED BY WHILE PLAYING WITH HER FRIEND NOT TOO LONG AGO.
SO WHAT?
IT FITS LIKE A GLOVE TOO!
RISHIA
リーシア in
HEY, WHO SAID YOU COULD PUT THAT ON?
HER STATS ARE UP, RIGHT?
NO WAY...

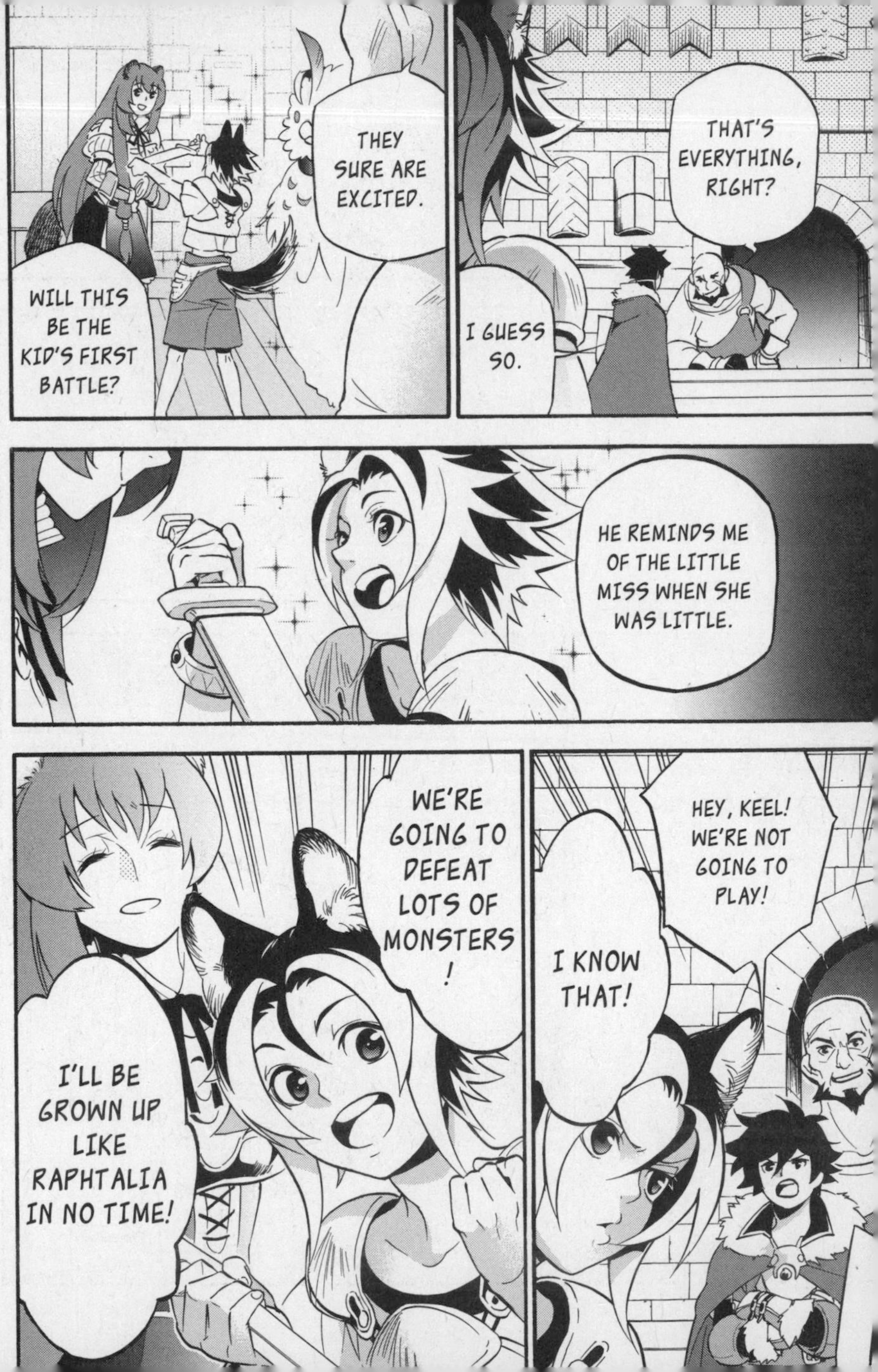
THAT'S EVERYTHING, RIGHT?
I GUESS SO.
THEY SURE ARE EXCITED.
WILL THIS BE THE KID'S FIRST BATTLE?
HE REMINDS ME OF THE LITTLE MISS WHEN SHE WAS LITTLE.
HEY, KEEL! WE'RE NOT GOING TO PLAY!
I KNOW THAT!
WE'RE GOING TO DEFEAT LOTS OF MONSTERS!
I'LL BE GROWN UP LIKE RAPHTALIA IN NO TIME!

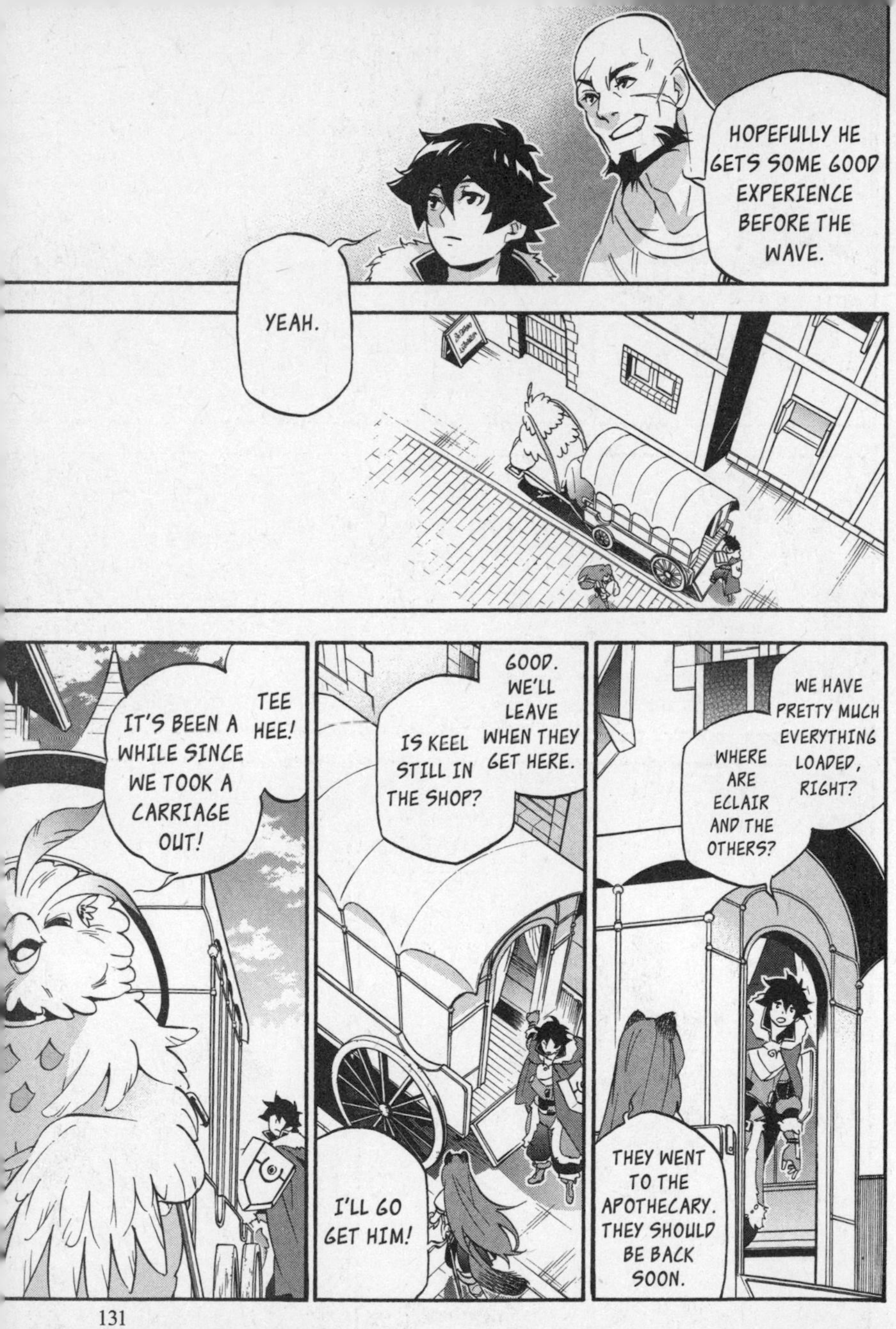
HOPEFULLY HE GETS SOME GOOD EXPERIENCE BEFORE THE WAVE.
YEAH.
WE HAVE PRETTY MUCH EVERYTHING LOADED, RIGHT?
WHERE ARE ECLAIR AND THE OTHERS?
THEY WENT TO THE APOTHECARY. THEY SHOULD BE BACK SOON.
GOOD. WE'LL LEAVE WHEN THEY GET HERE.
IS KEEL STILL IN THE SHOP?
I'LL GO GET HIM!
TEE HEE!
IT'S BEEN A WHILE SINCE WE TOOK A CARRIAGE OUT!

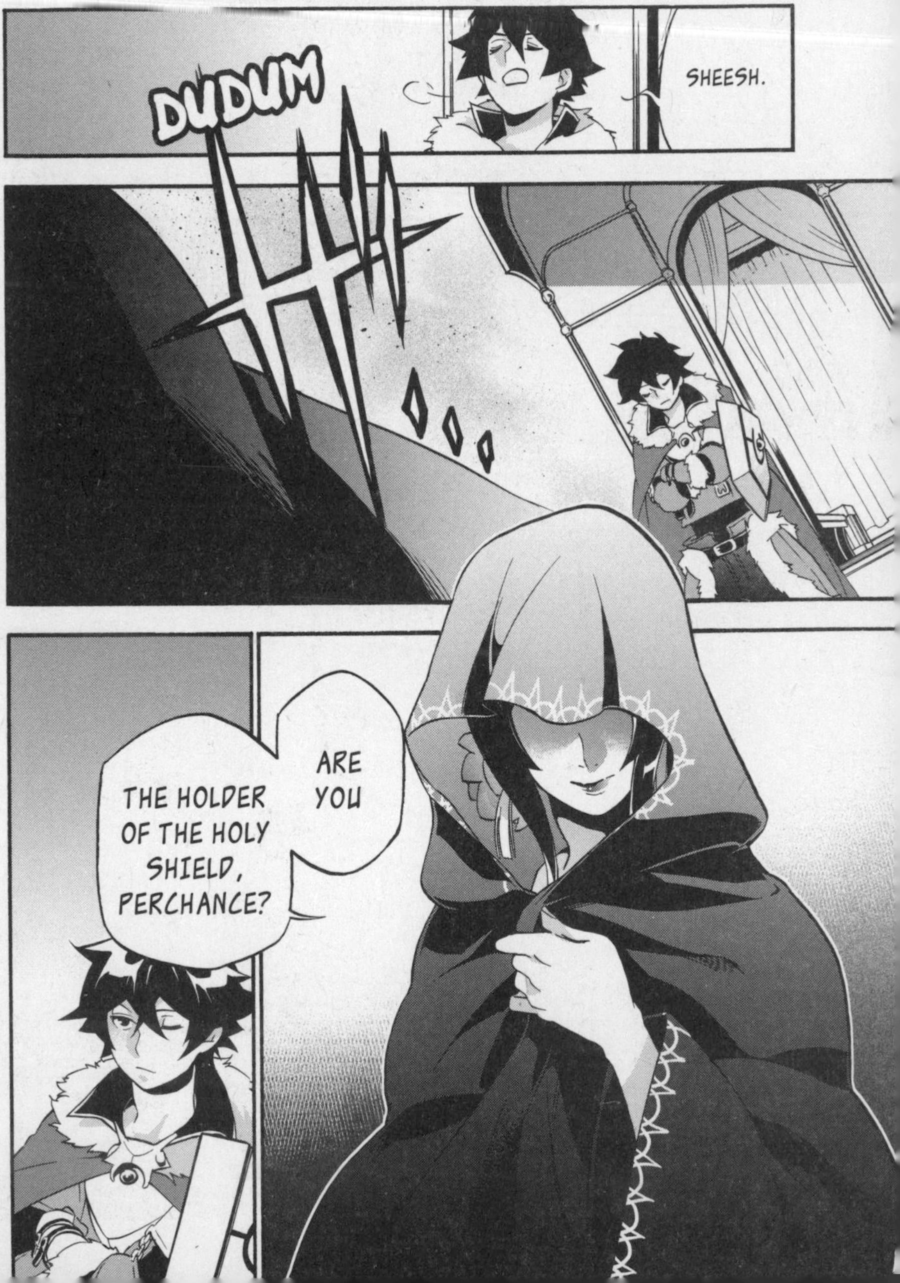
SHEESH.
DUDUM
ARE YOU THE HOLDER OF THE HOLY SHIELD, PERCHANCE?

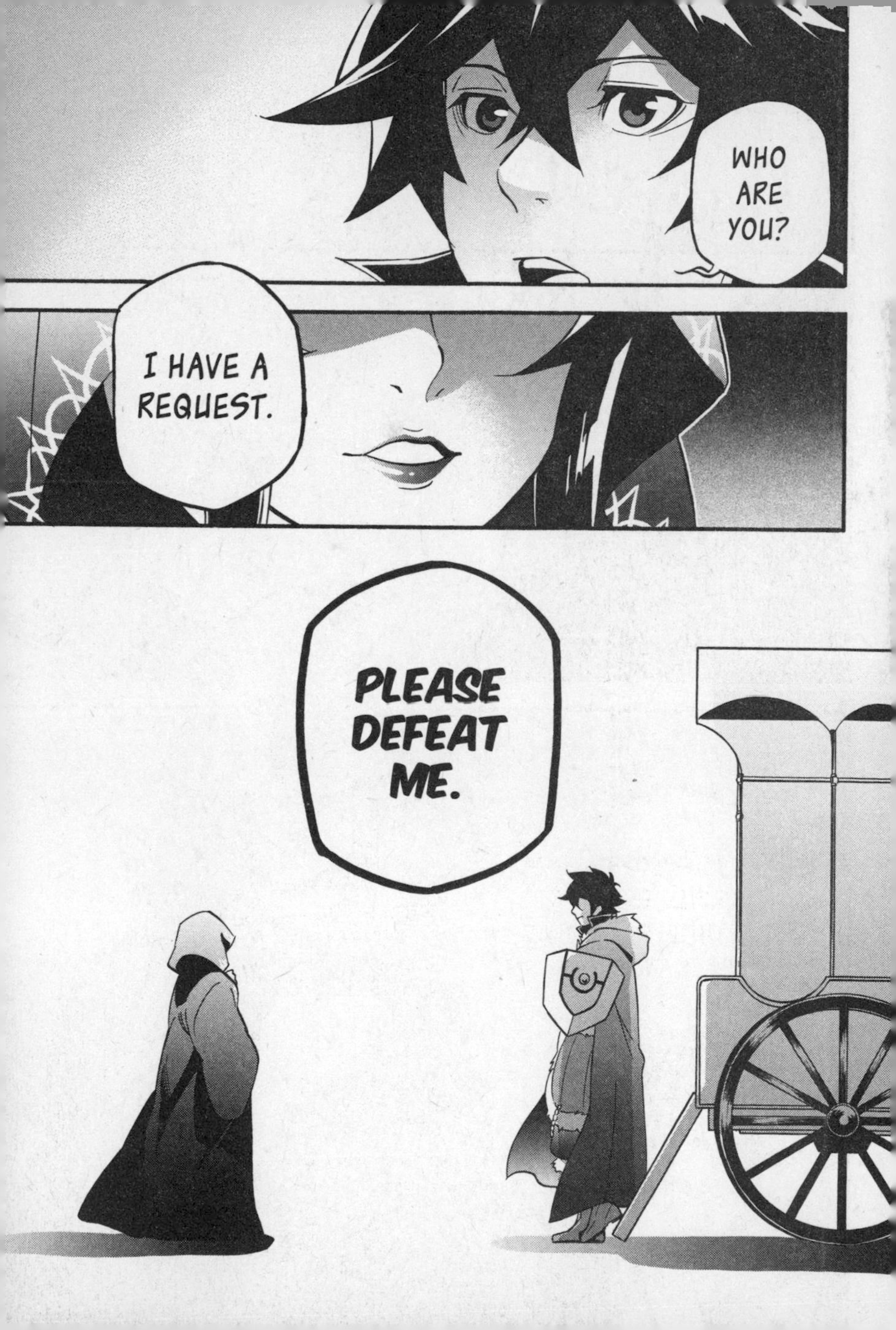
WHO ARE YOU?
I HAVE A REQUEST.
PLEASE DEFEAT ME.

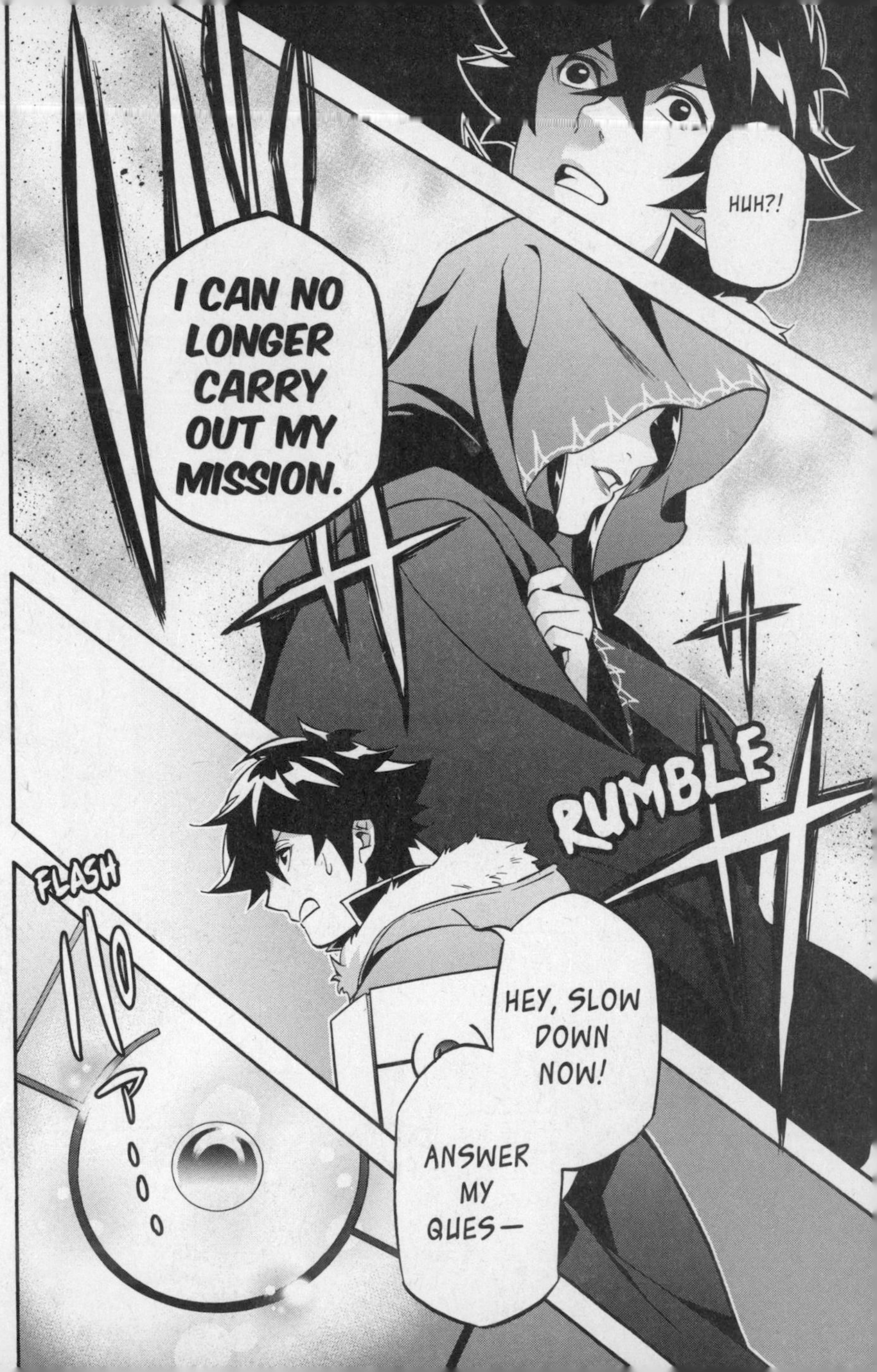
HUH?!
I CAN NO LONGER CARRY OUT MY MISSION.
RUMBLE
HEY, SLOW DOWN NOW!
ANSWER MY QUES—
FLASH

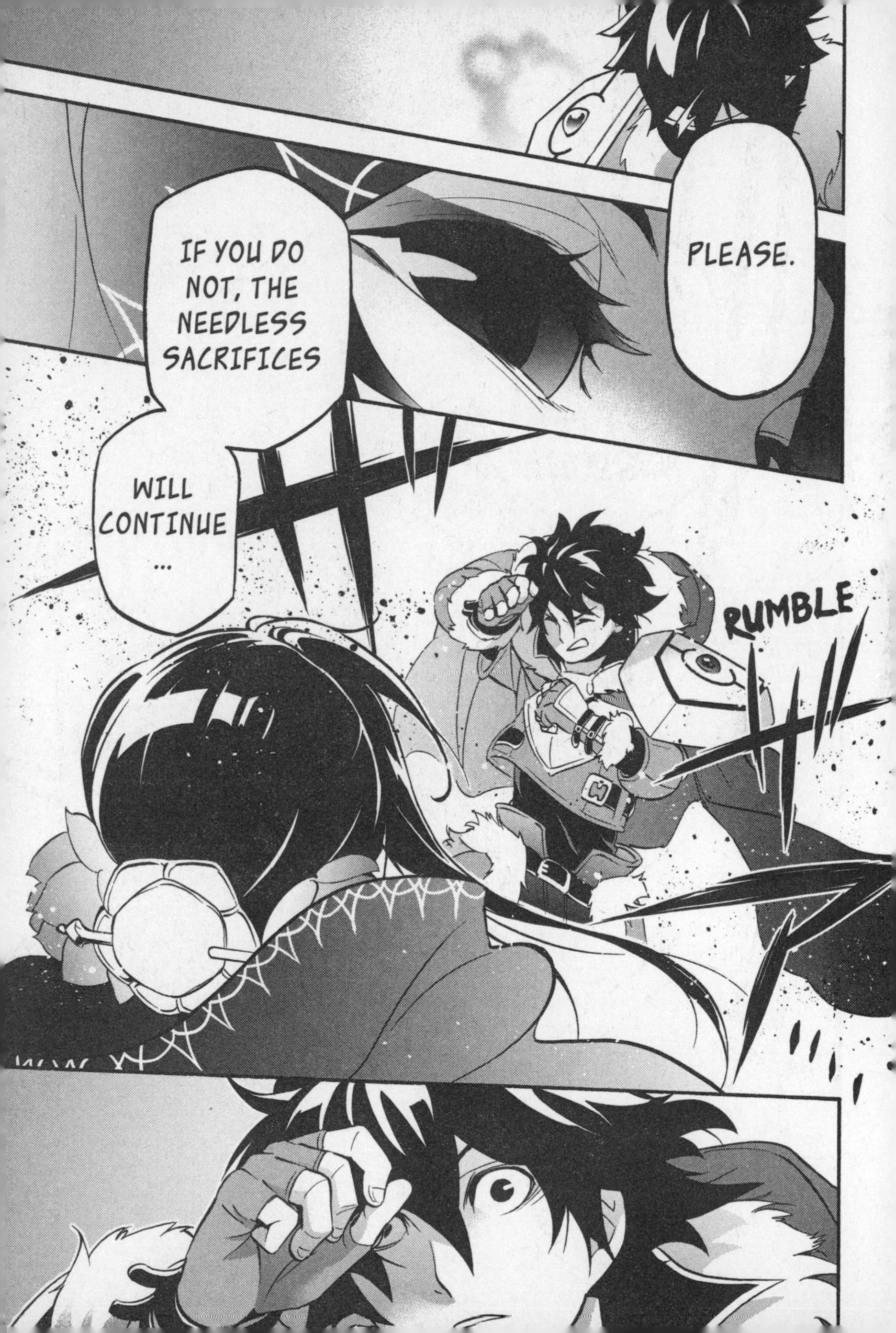
PLEASE.
IF YOU DO NOT, THE NEEDLESS SACRIFICES
WILL CONTINUE ...
RUMBLE

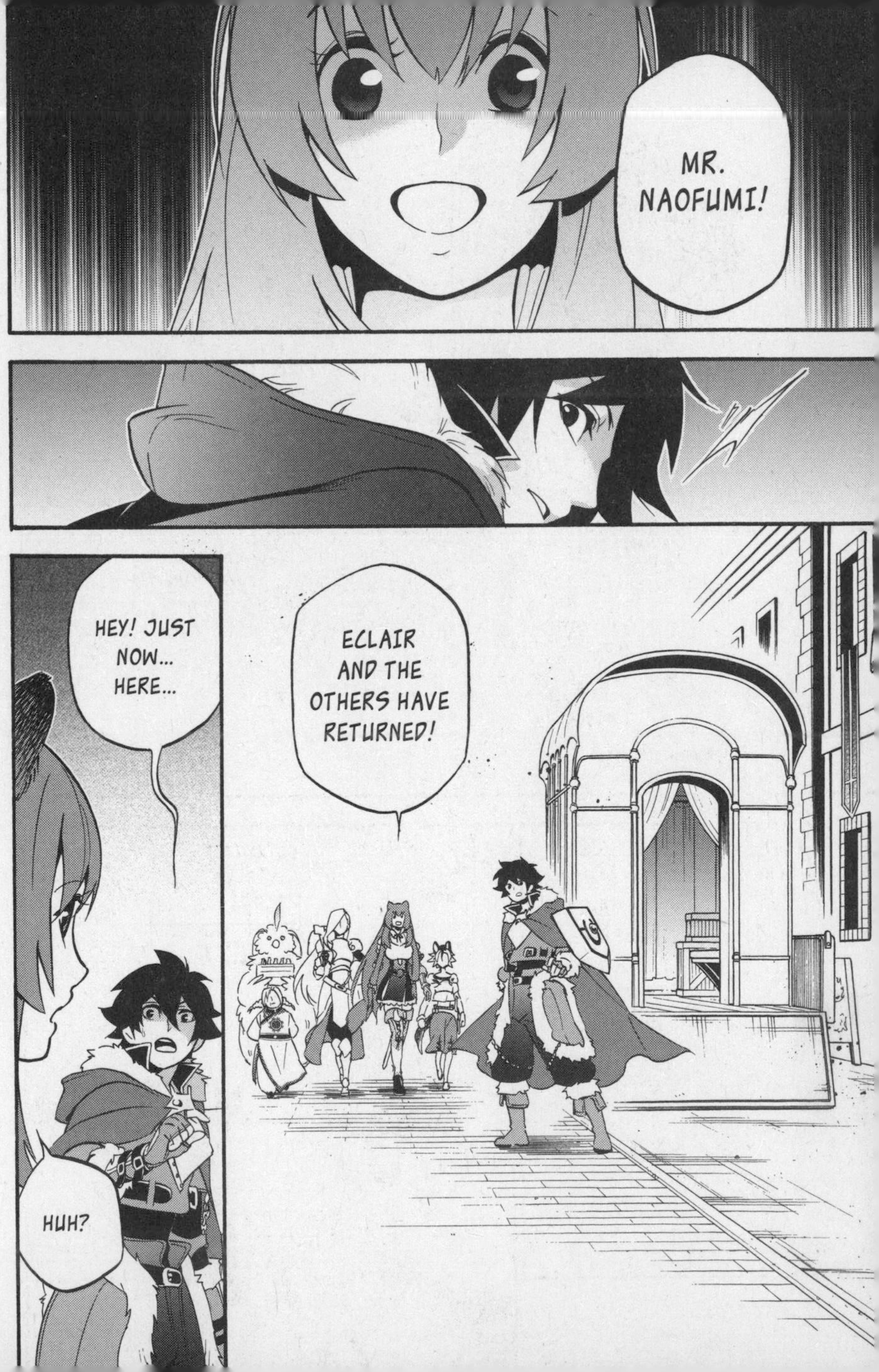
MR. NAOFUMI!
ECLAIR AND THE OTHERS HAVE RETURNED!
HEY! JUST NOW... HERE...
HUH?

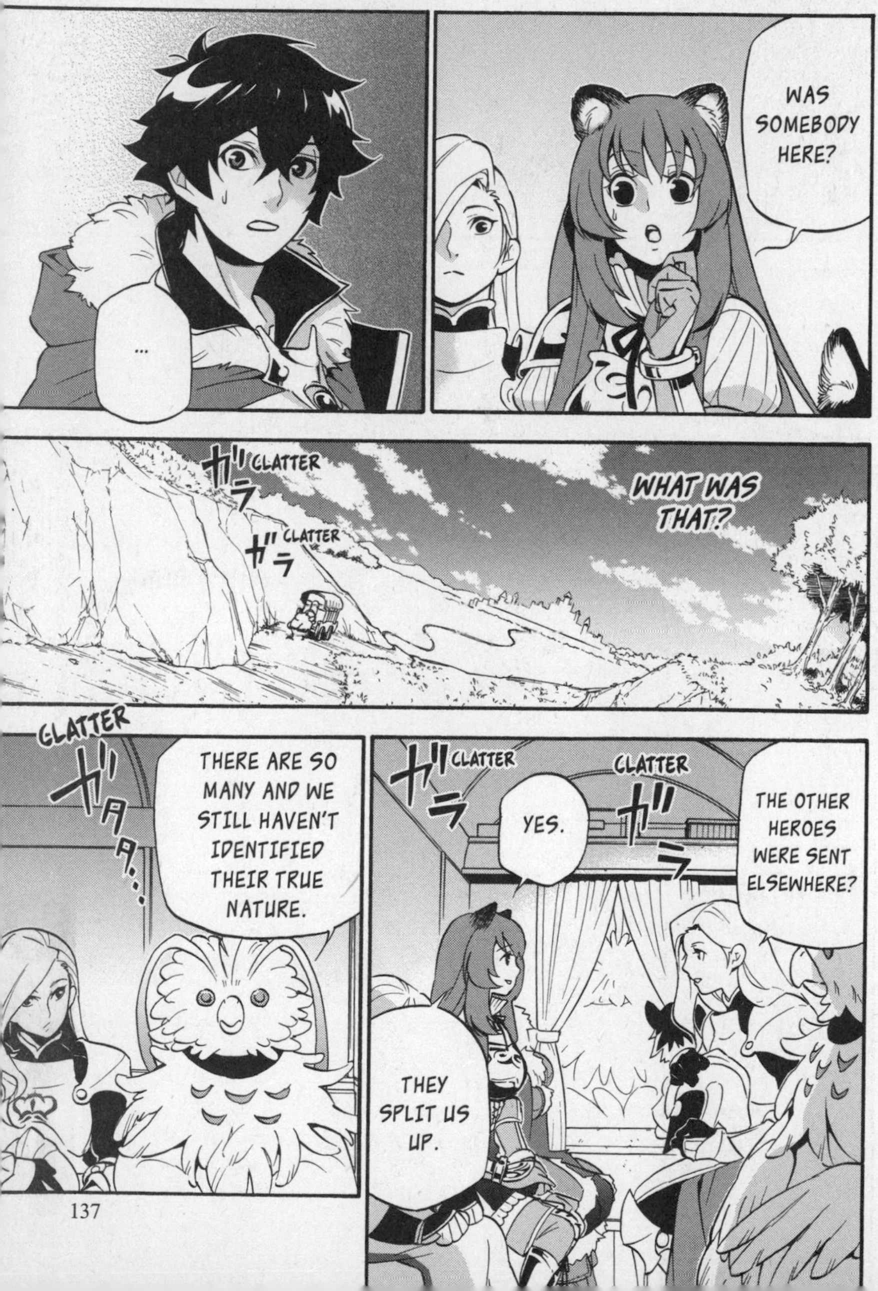
WAS SOMEBODY HERE?
...
ガラ CLATTER
ガラ CLATTER
WHAT WAS THAT?
ガラ CLATTER
ガラ CLATTER
THE OTHER HEROES WERE SENT ELSEWHERE?
YES.
THEY SPLIT US UP.
ガタタ… CLATTER
THERE ARE SO MANY AND WE STILL HAVEN'T IDENTIFIED THEIR TRUE NATURE.

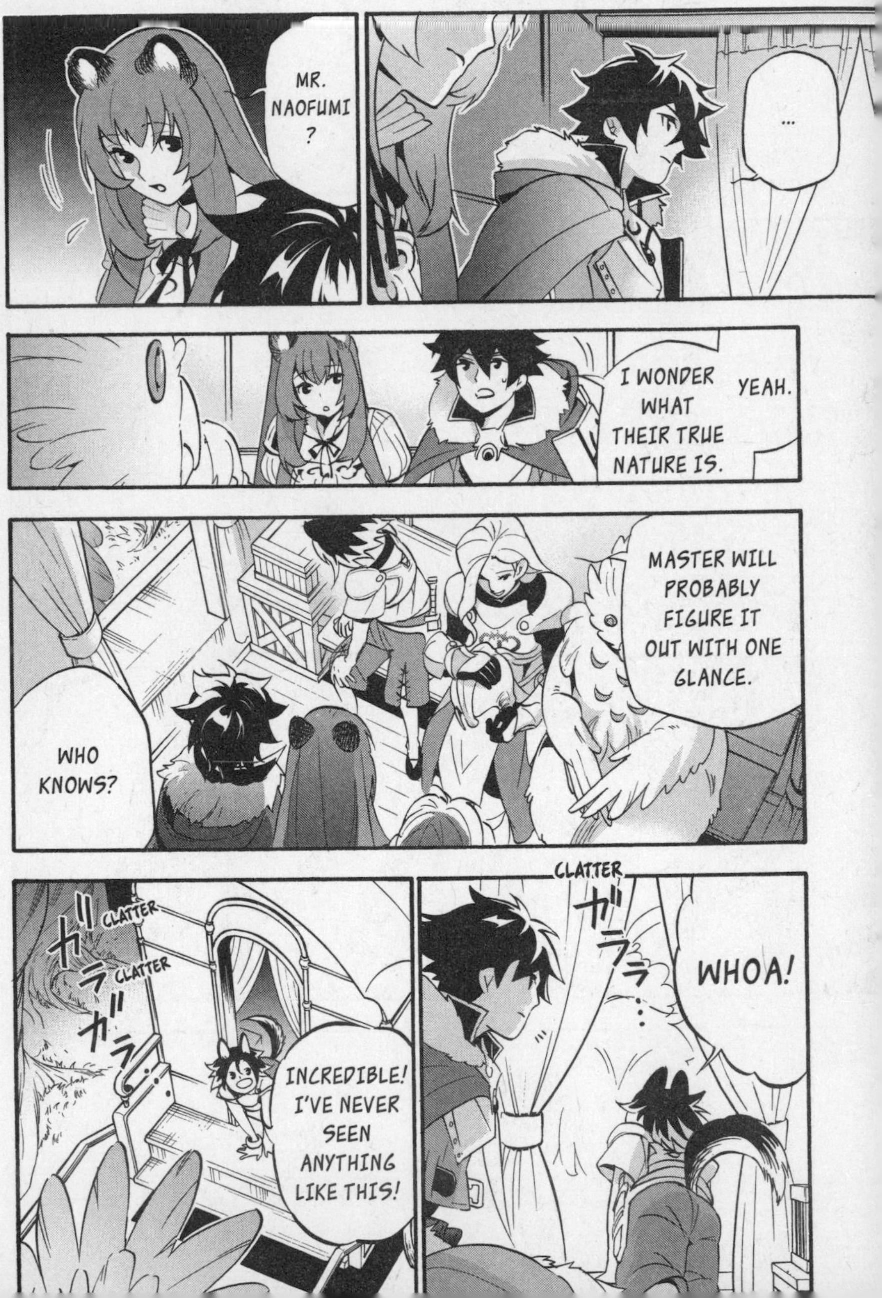
...
MR. NAOFUMI ?
YEAH.
I WONDER WHAT THEIR TRUE NATURE IS.
MASTER WILL PROBABLY FIGURE IT OUT WITH ONE GLANCE.
WHO KNOWS?
CLATTER
ガララ…
WHOA!
CLATTER
CLATTER
INCREDIBLE! I'VE NEVER SEEN ANYTHING LIKE THIS!

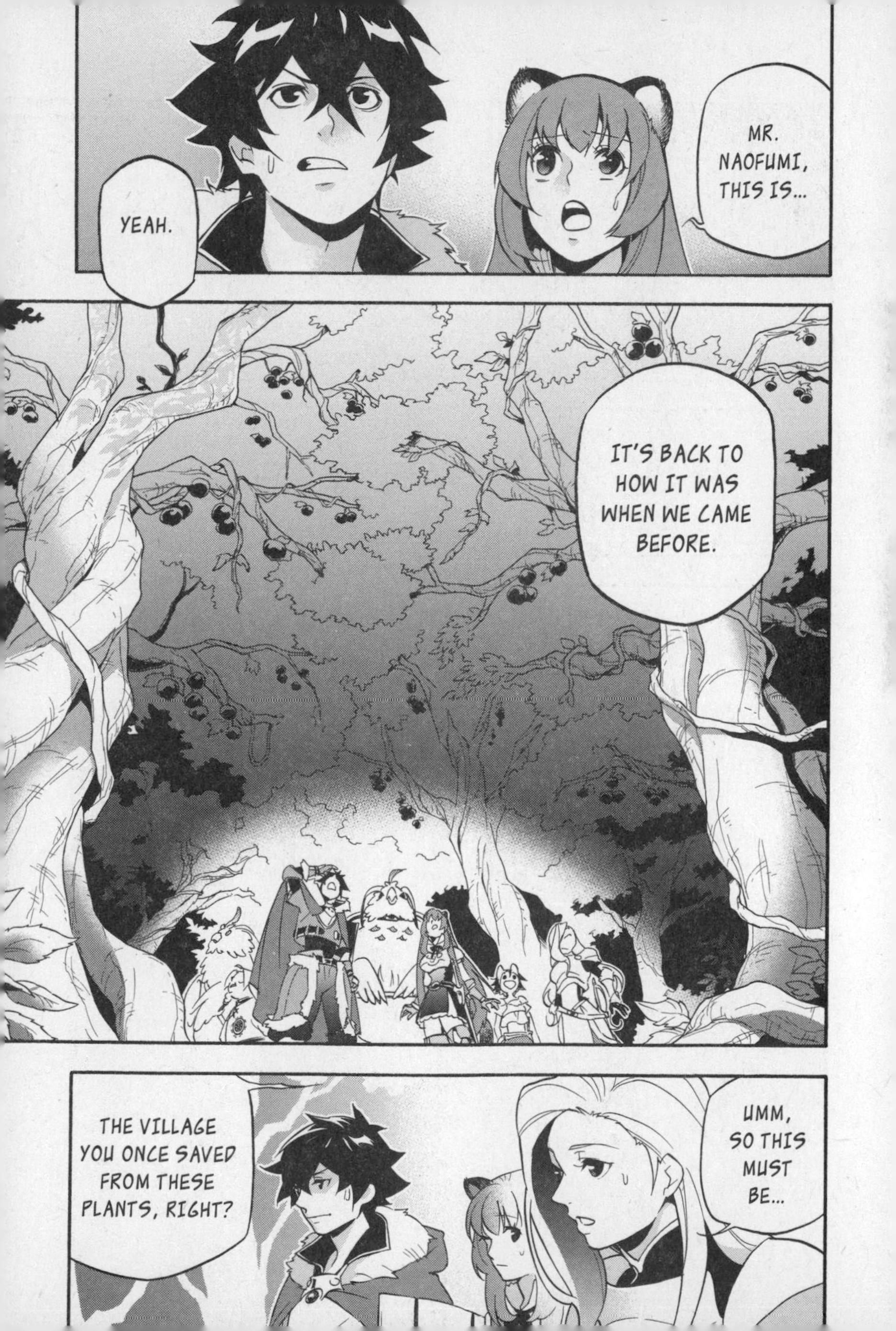
MR. NAOFUMI, THIS IS...
YEAH.
IT'S BACK TO HOW IT WAS WHEN WE CAME BEFORE.
UMM, SO THIS MUST BE...
THE VILLAGE YOU ONCE SAVED FROM THESE PLANTS, RIGHT?

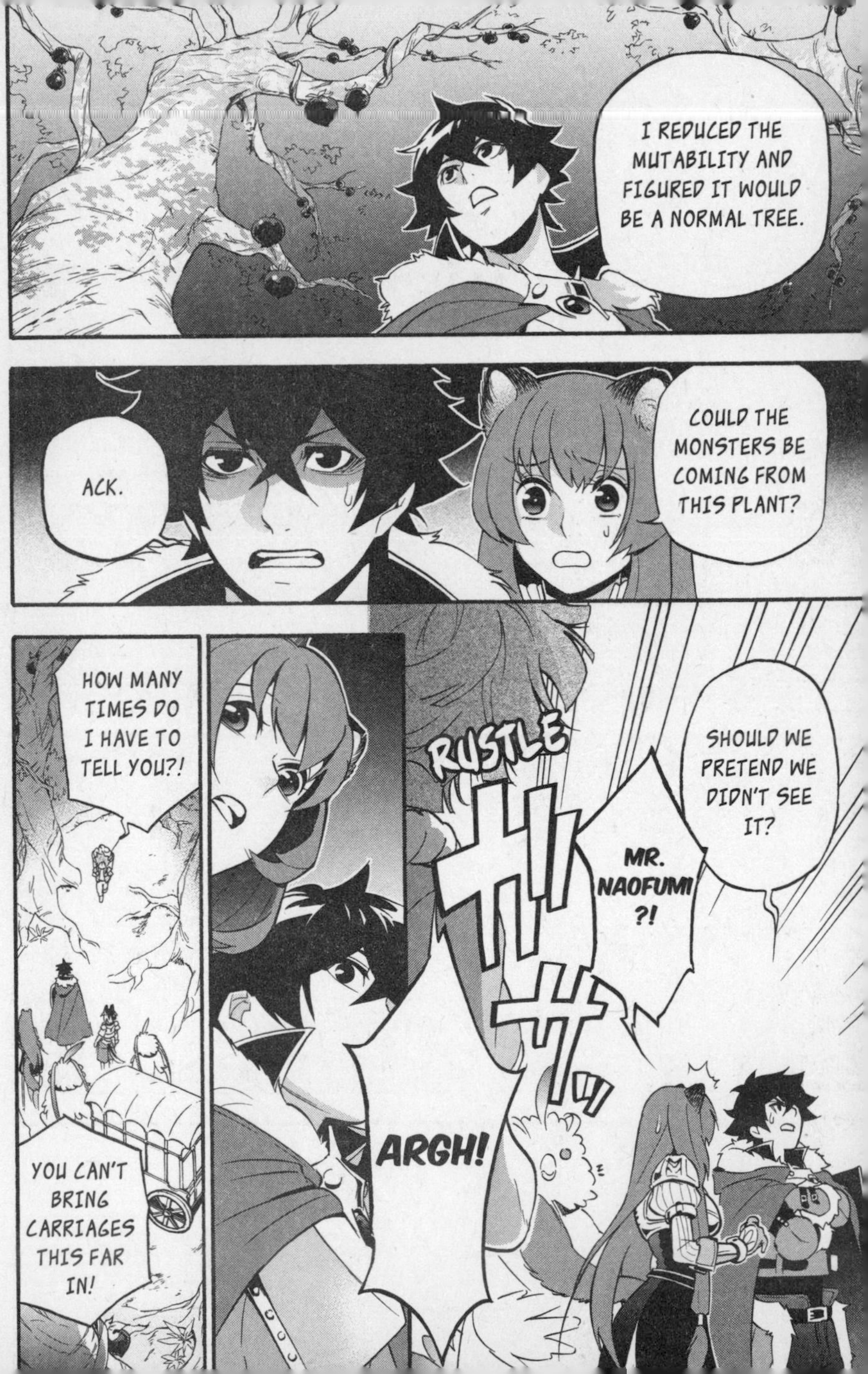
I REDUCED THE MUTABILITY AND FIGURED IT WOULD BE A NORMAL TREE.
COULD THE MONSTERS BE COMING FROM THIS PLANT?
ACK.
SHOULD WE PRETEND WE DIDN'T SEE IT?
RUSTLE
MR. NAOFUMI ?!
ARGH!
HOW MANY TIMES DO I HAVE TO TELL YOU?!
YOU CAN'T BRING CARRIAGES THIS FAR IN!

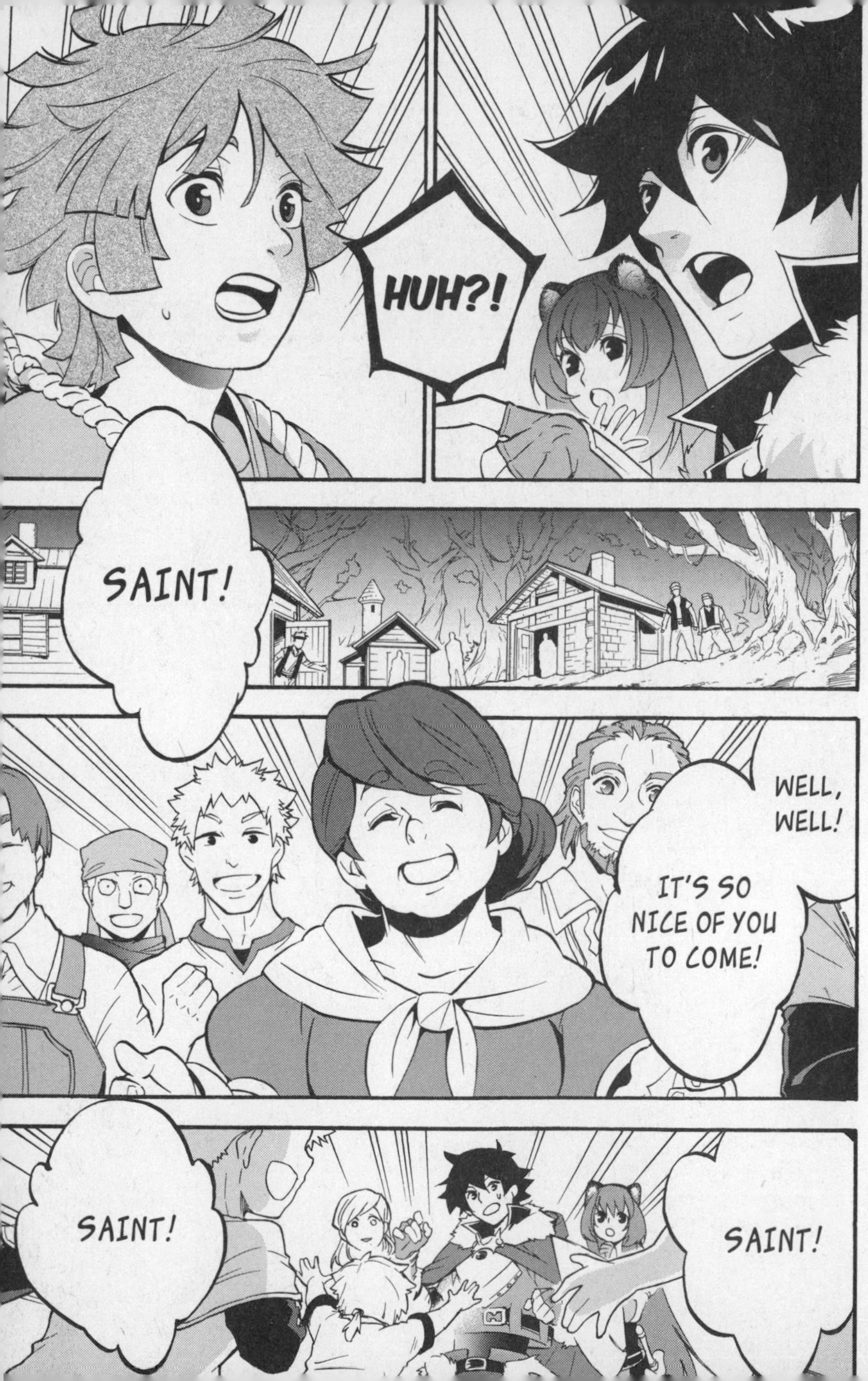
HUH?!
SAINT!
WELL, WELL!
IT'S SO NICE OF YOU TO COME!
SAINT!
SAINT!

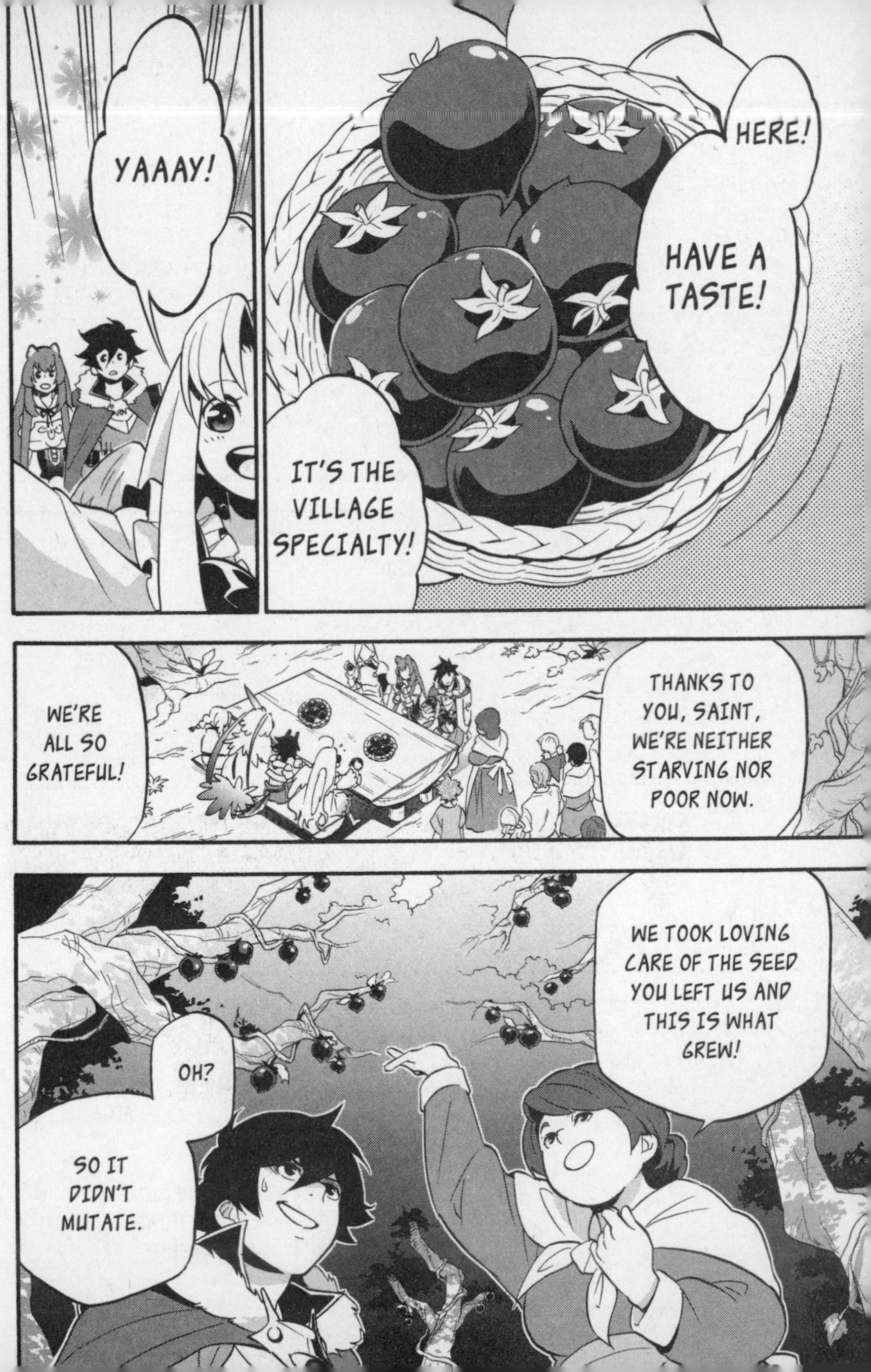
HERE!
HAVE A TASTE!
IT'S THE VILLAGE SPECIALTY!
YAAAY!
THANKS TO YOU, SAINT, WE'RE NEITHER STARVING NOR POOR NOW.
WE'RE ALL SO GRATEFUL!
WE TOOK LOVING CARE OF THE SEED YOU LEFT US AND THIS IS WHAT GREW!
OH?
SO IT DIDN'T MUTATE.

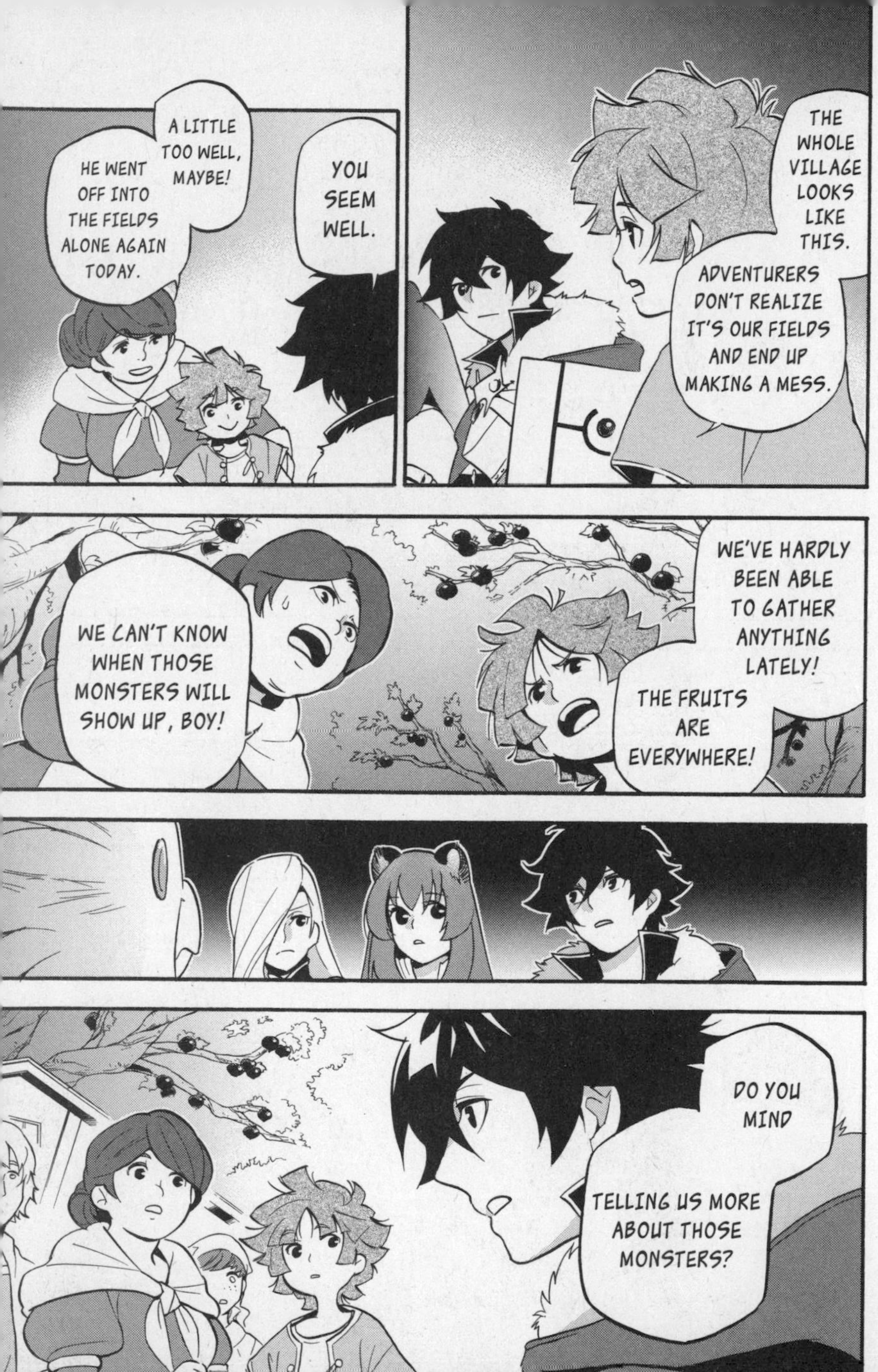
THE WHOLE VILLAGE LOOKS LIKE THIS.
ADVENTURERS DON'T REALIZE IT'S OUR FIELDS AND END UP MAKING A MESS.
YOU SEEM WELL.
A LITTLE TOO WELL, MAYBE!
HE WENT OFF INTO THE FIELDS ALONE AGAIN TODAY.
WE'VE HARDLY BEEN ABLE TO GATHER ANYTHING LATELY!
THE FRUITS ARE EVERYWHERE!
WE CAN'T KNOW WHEN THOSE MONSTERS WILL SHOW UP, BOY!
DO YOU MIND
TELLING US MORE ABOUT THOSE MONSTERS?

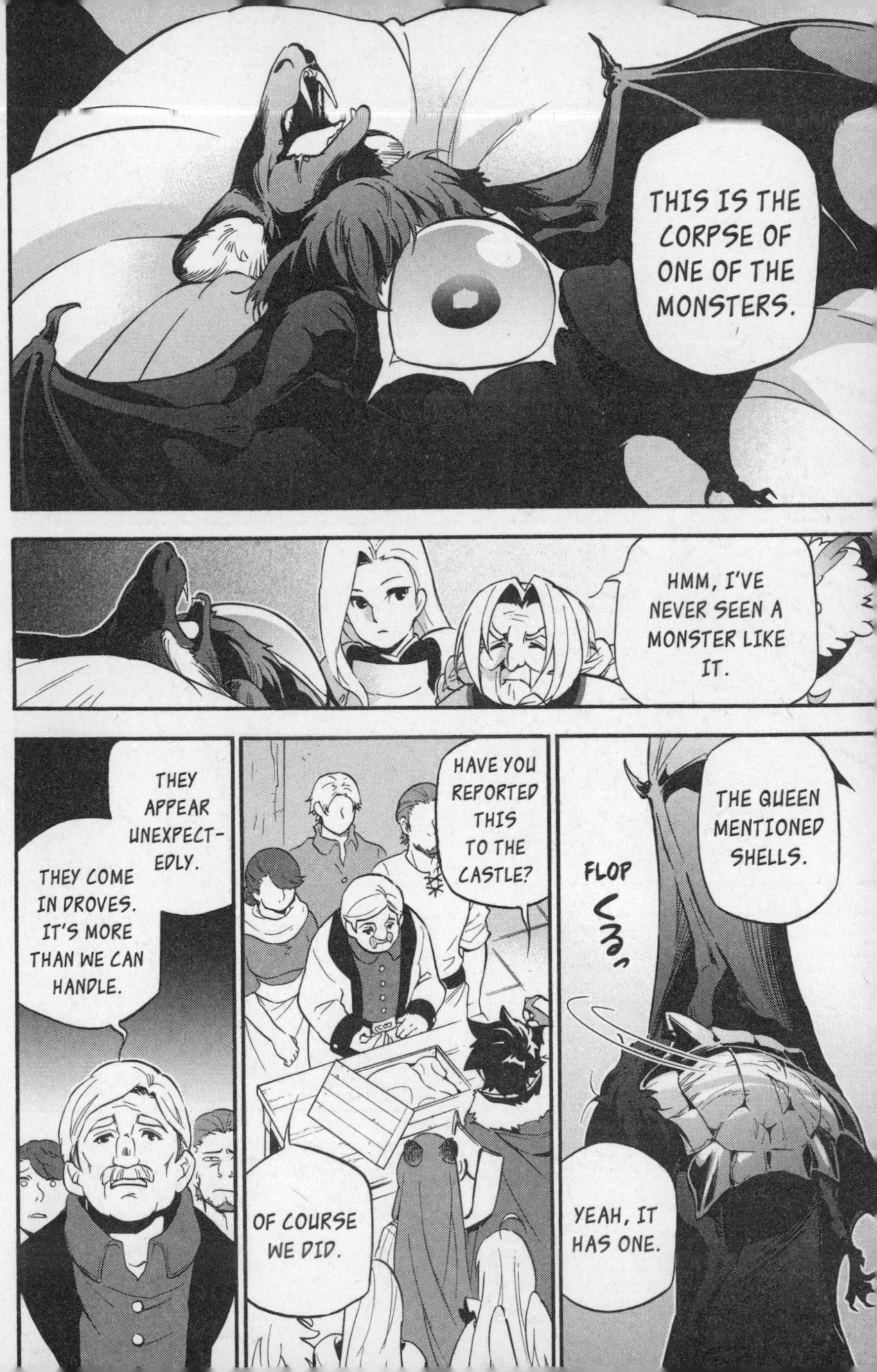
THIS IS THE CORPSE OF ONE OF THE MONSTERS.
HMM, I'VE NEVER SEEN A MONSTER LIKE IT.
THE QUEEN MENTIONED SHELLS.
FLOP
YEAH, IT HAS ONE.
HAVE YOU REPORTED THIS TO THE CASTLE?
OF COURSE WE DID.
THEY APPEAR UNEXPECT-EDLY.
THEY COME IN DROVES. IT'S MORE THAN WE CAN HANDLE.

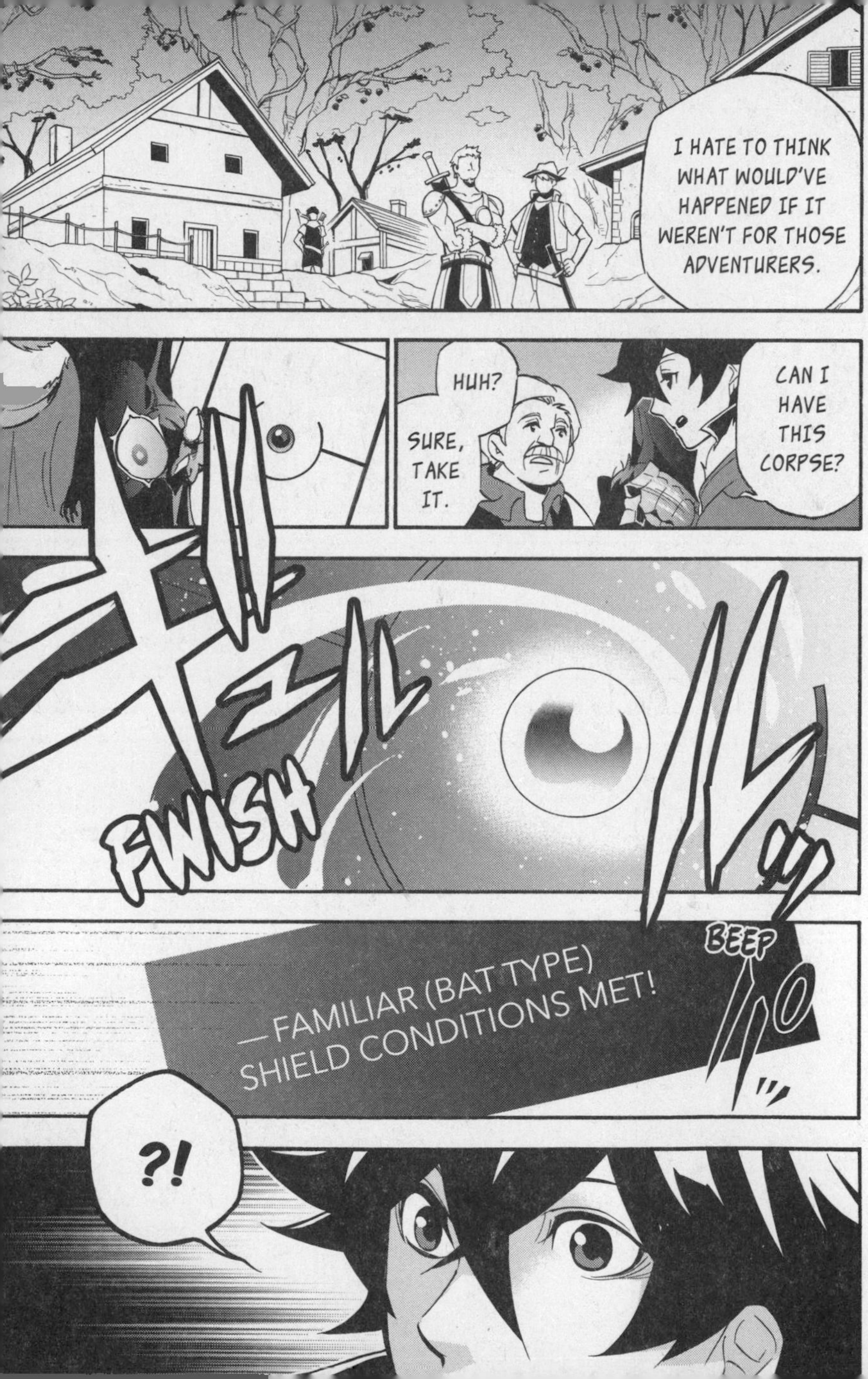
I HATE TO THINK WHAT WOULD'VE HAPPENED IF IT WEREN'T FOR THOSE ADVENTURERS.
CAN I HAVE THIS CORPSE?
HUH?
SURE, TAKE IT.
FWISH
BEEP
—FAMILIAR (BAT TYPE) SHIELD CONDITIONS MET!
?!

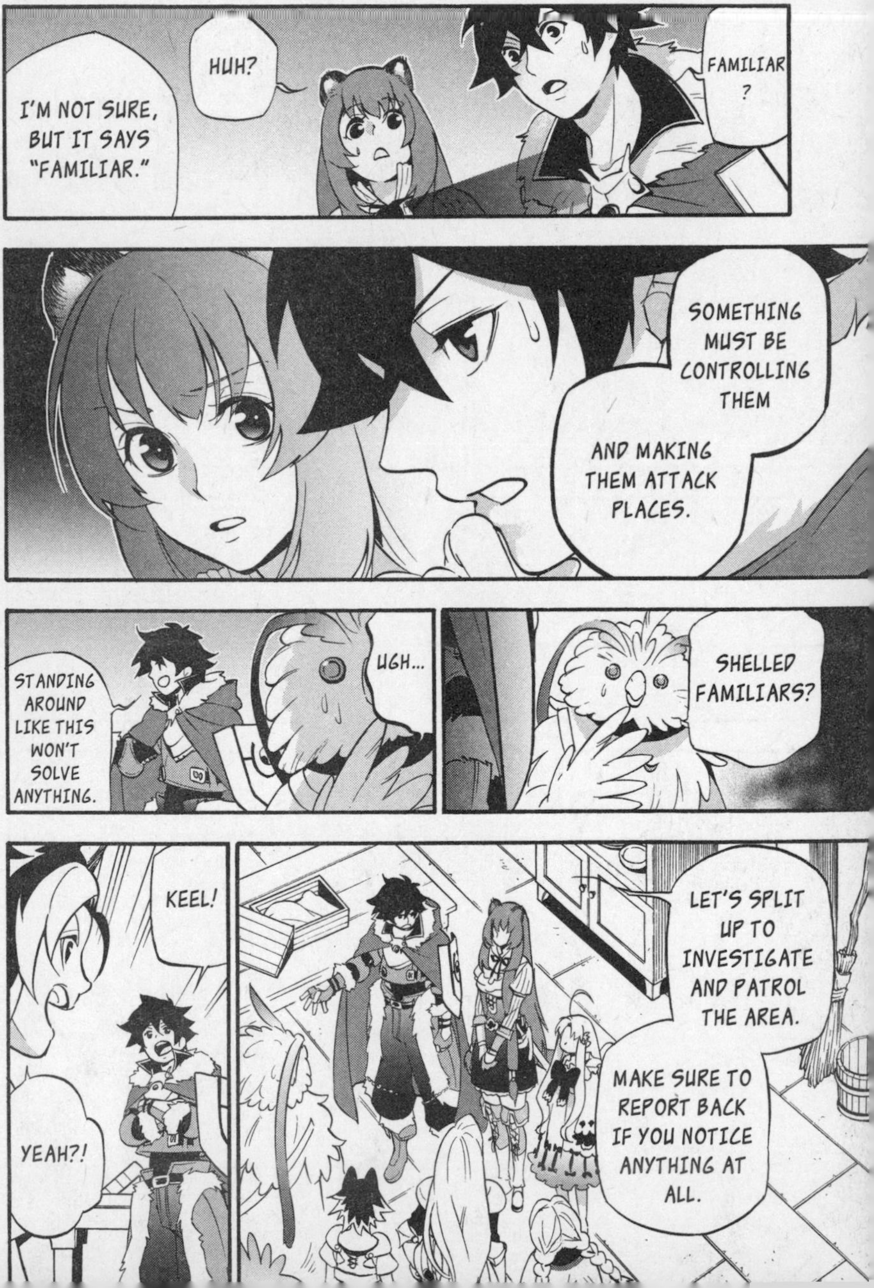
FAMILIAR ?
HUH?
I'M NOT SURE, BUT IT SAYS "FAMILIAR."
SOMETHING MUST BE CONTROLLING THEM
AND MAKING THEM ATTACK PLACES.
SHELLED FAMILIARS?
UGH...
STANDING AROUND LIKE THIS WON'T SOLVE ANYTHING.
LET'S SPLIT UP TO INVESTIGATE AND PATROL THE AREA.
MAKE SURE TO REPORT BACK IF YOU NOTICE ANYTHING AT ALL.
KEEL!
YEAH?!

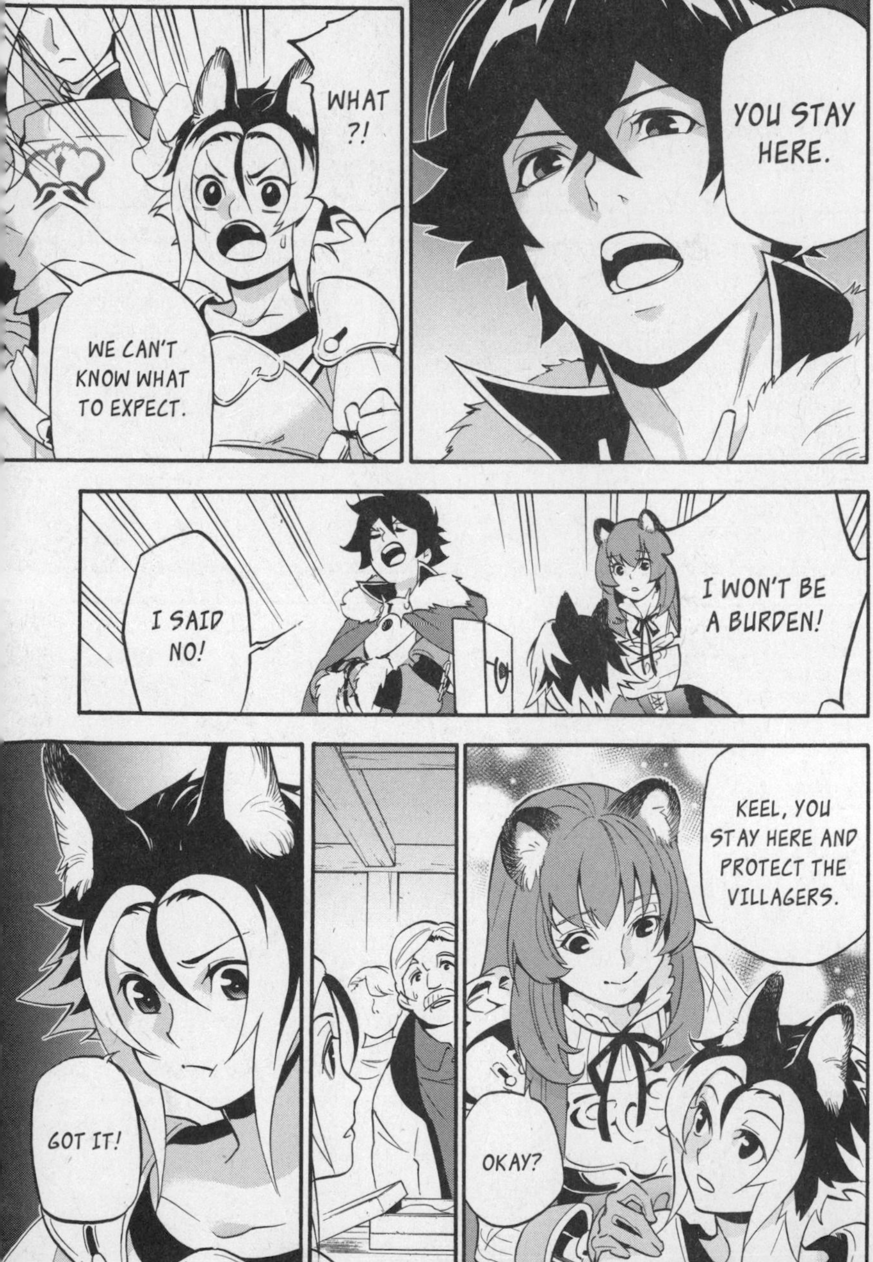
YOU STAY HERE.
WHAT ?!
WE CAN'T KNOW WHAT TO EXPECT.
I WON'T BE A BURDEN!
I SAID NO!
KEEL, YOU STAY HERE AND PROTECT THE VILLAGERS.
OKAY?
GOT IT!

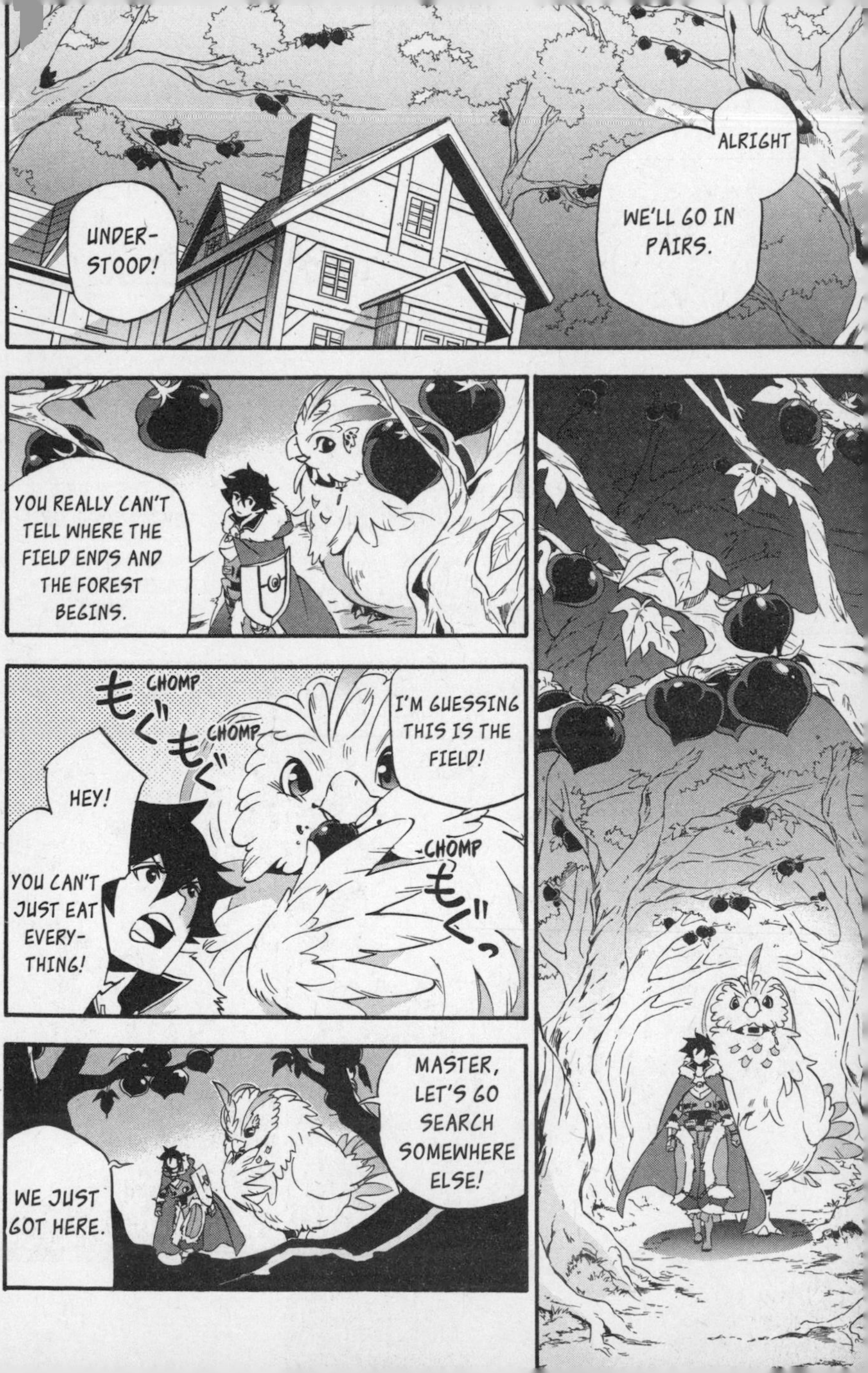
ALRIGHT
WE'LL GO IN PAIRS.
UNDER-STOOD!
YOU REALLY CAN'T TELL WHERE THE FIELD ENDS AND THE FOREST BEGINS.
I'M GUESSING THIS IS THE FIELD!
もぐもぐ CHOMP CHOMP
もぐっ CHOMP
HEY!
YOU CAN'T JUST EAT EVERY-THING!
MASTER, LET'S GO SEARCH SOMEWHERE ELSE!
WE JUST GOT HERE.

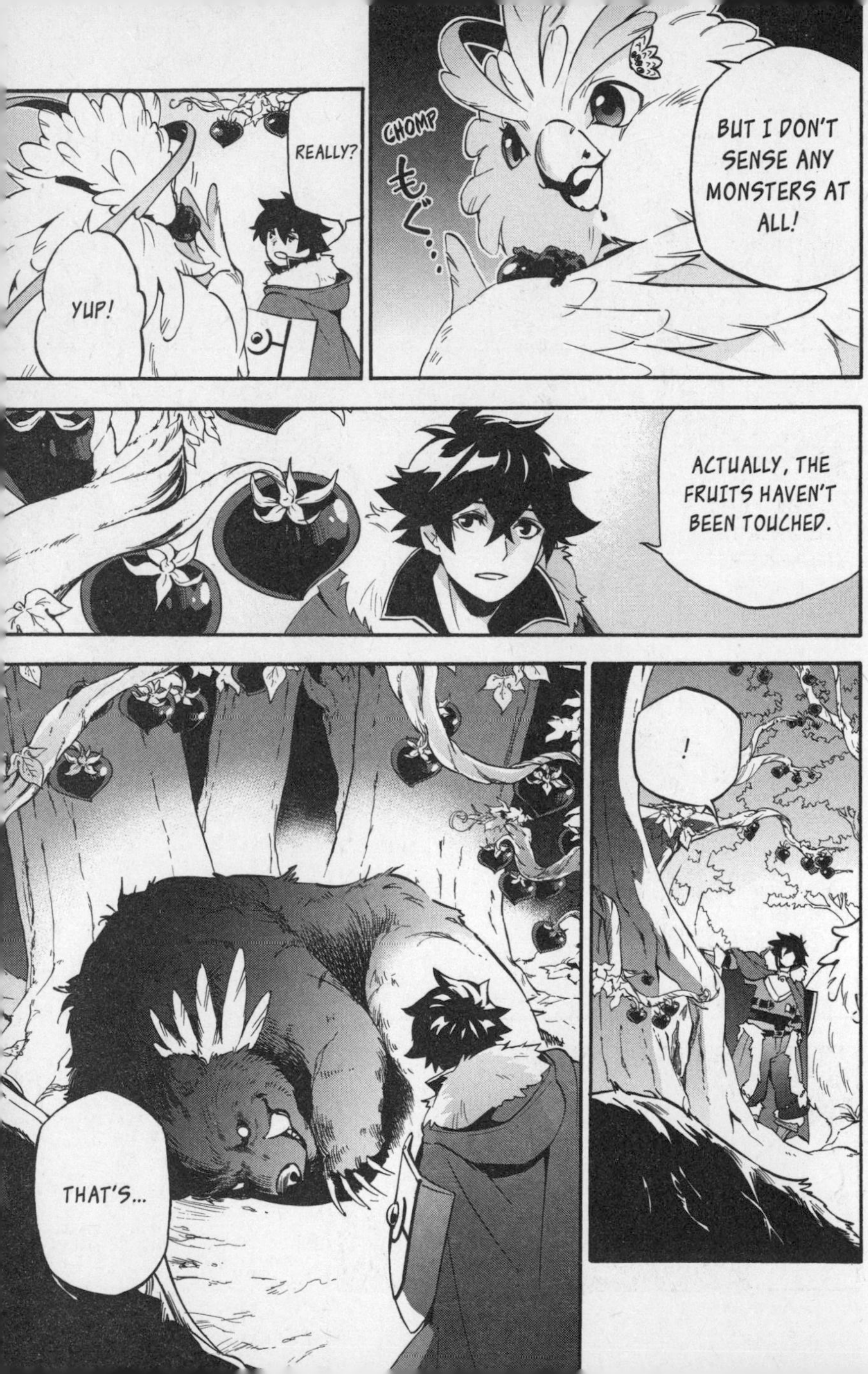
BUT I DON'T SENSE ANY MONSTERS AT ALL!
CHOMP
もぐ…
REALLY?
YUP!
ACTUALLY, THE FRUITS HAVEN'T BEEN TOUCHED.
!
THAT'S...

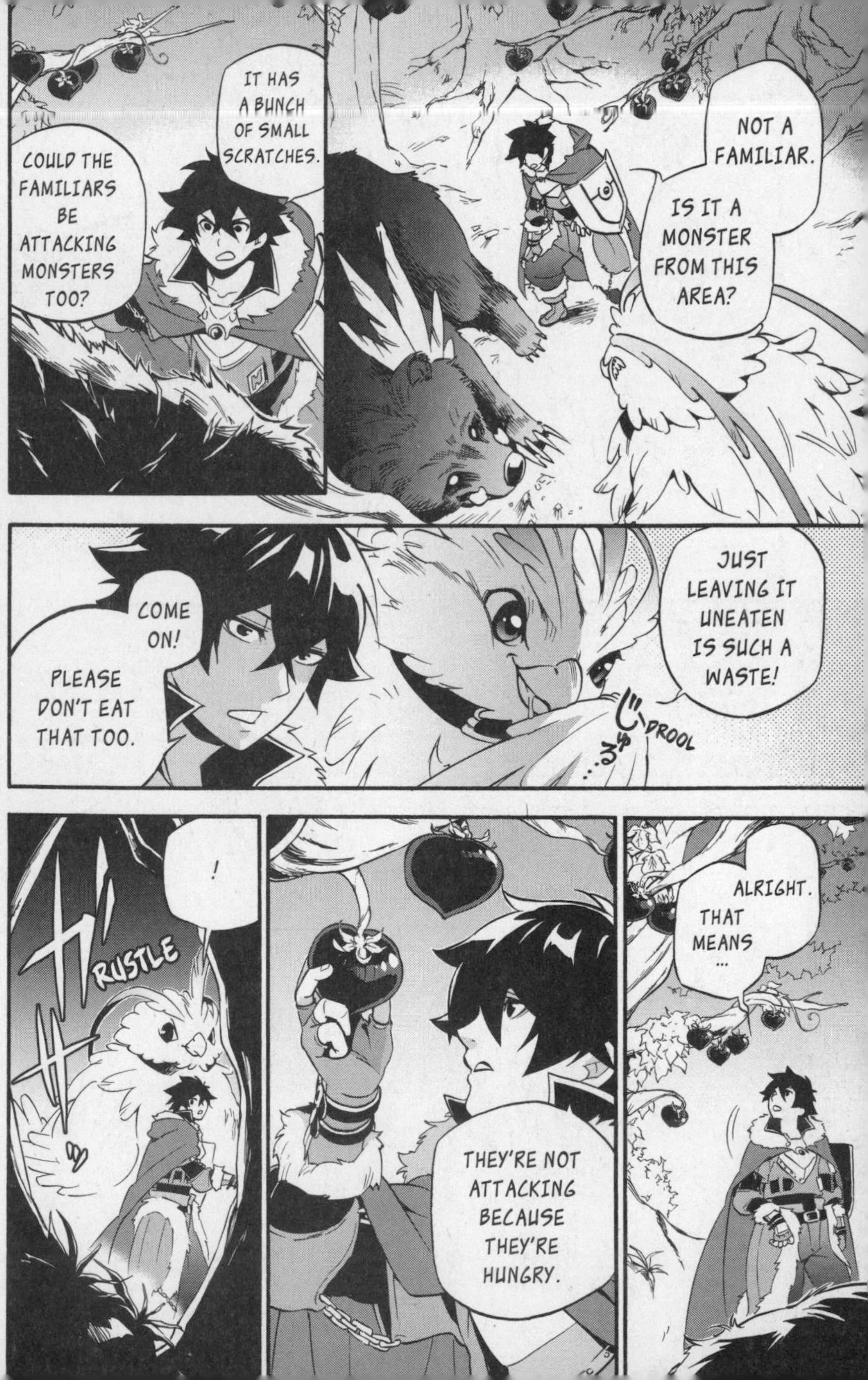
NOT A FAMILIAR.
IS IT A MONSTER FROM THIS AREA?
IT HAS A BUNCH OF SMALL SCRATCHES.
COULD THE FAMILIARS BE ATTACKING MONSTERS TOO?
JUST LEAVING IT UNEATEN IS SUCH A WASTE!
DROOL
COME ON!
PLEASE DON'T EAT THAT TOO.
ALRIGHT.
THAT MEANS ...
THEY'RE NOT ATTACKING BECAUSE THEY'RE HUNGRY.
!
RUSTLE
COME ON.

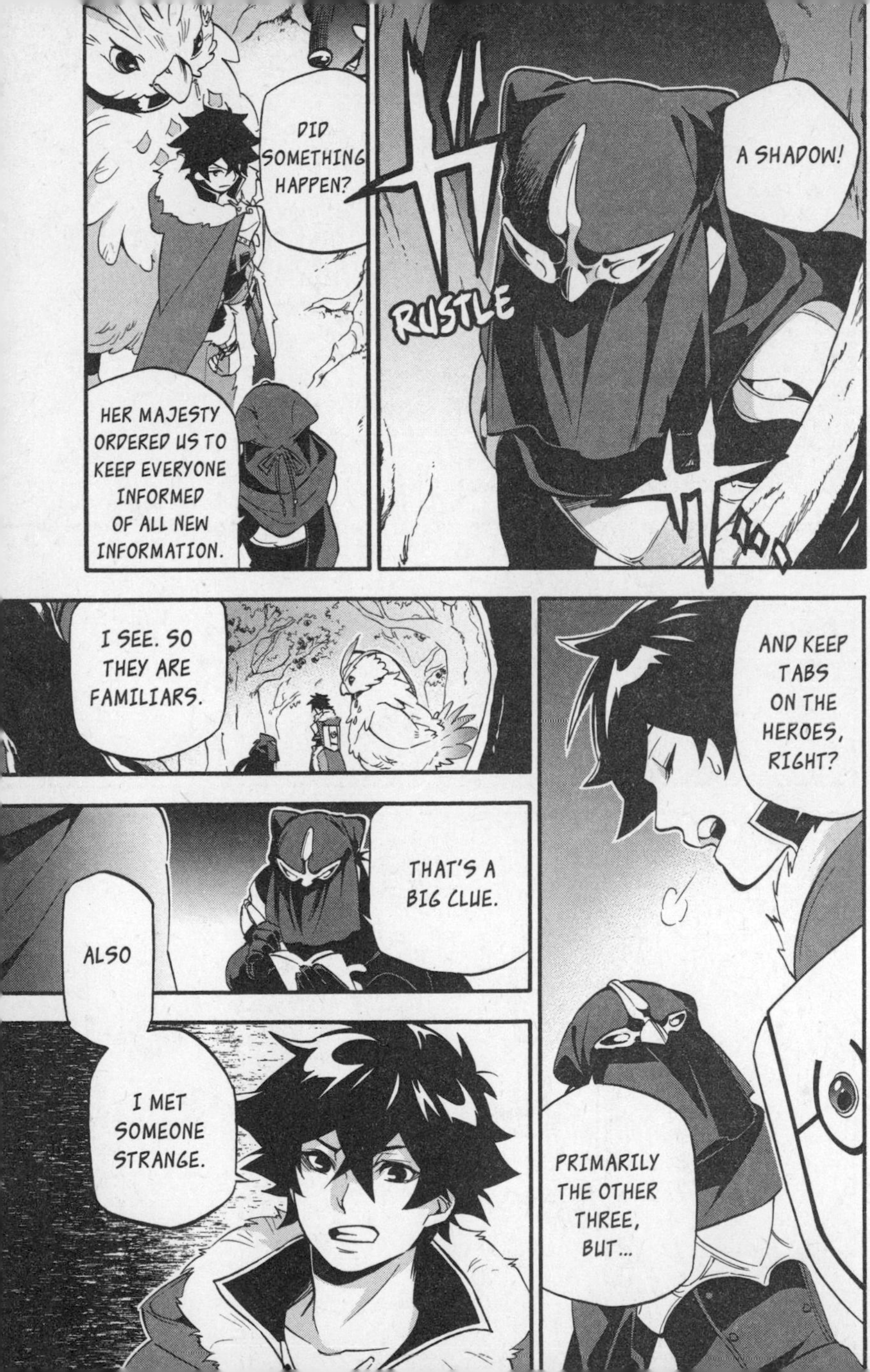
A SHADOW!
RUSTLE
DID SOMETHING HAPPEN?
HER MAJESTY ORDERED US TO KEEP EVERYONE INFORMED OF ALL NEW INFORMATION.
AND KEEP TABS ON THE HEROES, RIGHT?
I SEE. SO THEY ARE FAMILIARS.
THAT'S A BIG CLUE.
ALSO
PRIMARILY THE OTHER THREE, BUT...
I MET SOMEONE STRANGE.

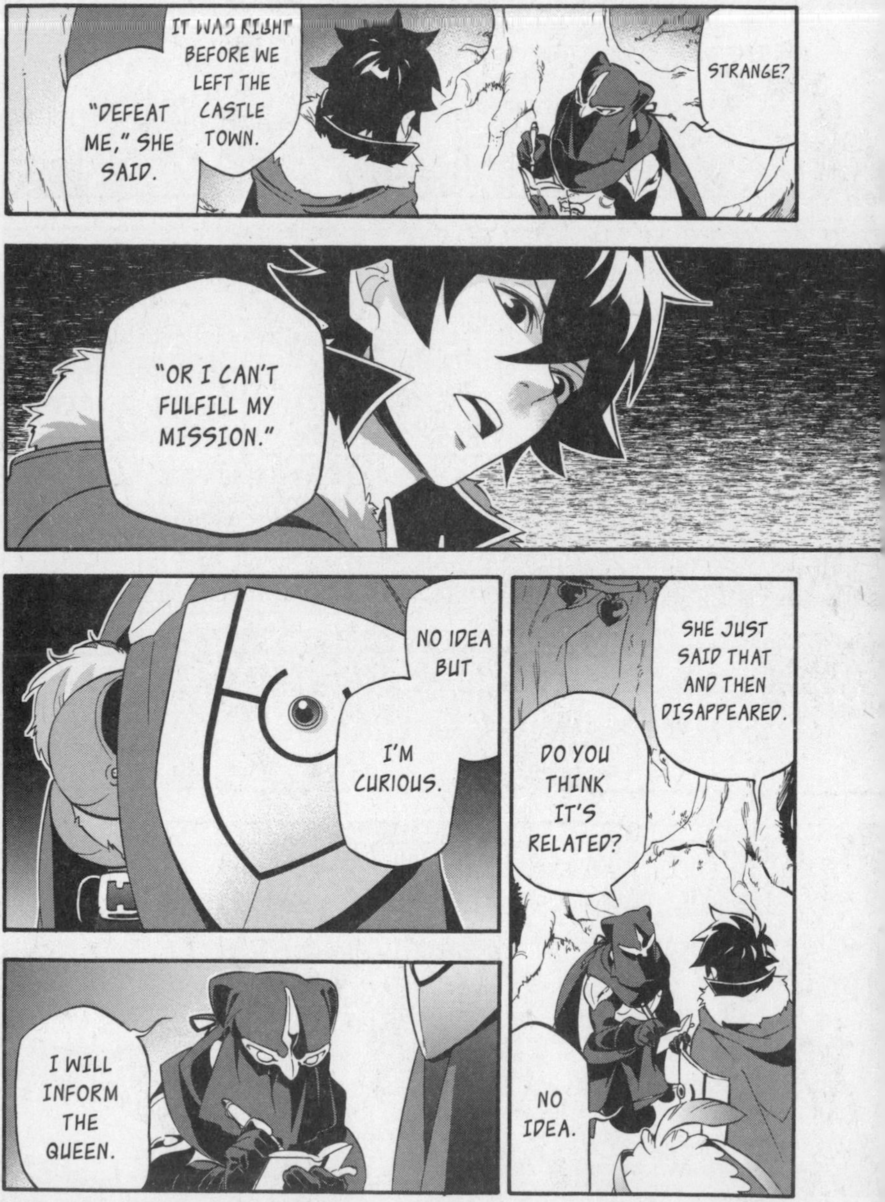
STRANGE?
IT WAS RIGHT BEFORE WE LEFT THE CASTLE TOWN.
"DEFEAT ME," SHE SAID.
"OR I CAN'T FULFILL MY MISSION."
SHE JUST SAID THAT AND THEN DISAPPEARED.
DO YOU THINK IT'S RELATED?
NO IDEA.
NO IDEA BUT
I'M CURIOUS.
I WILL INFORM THE QUEEN.

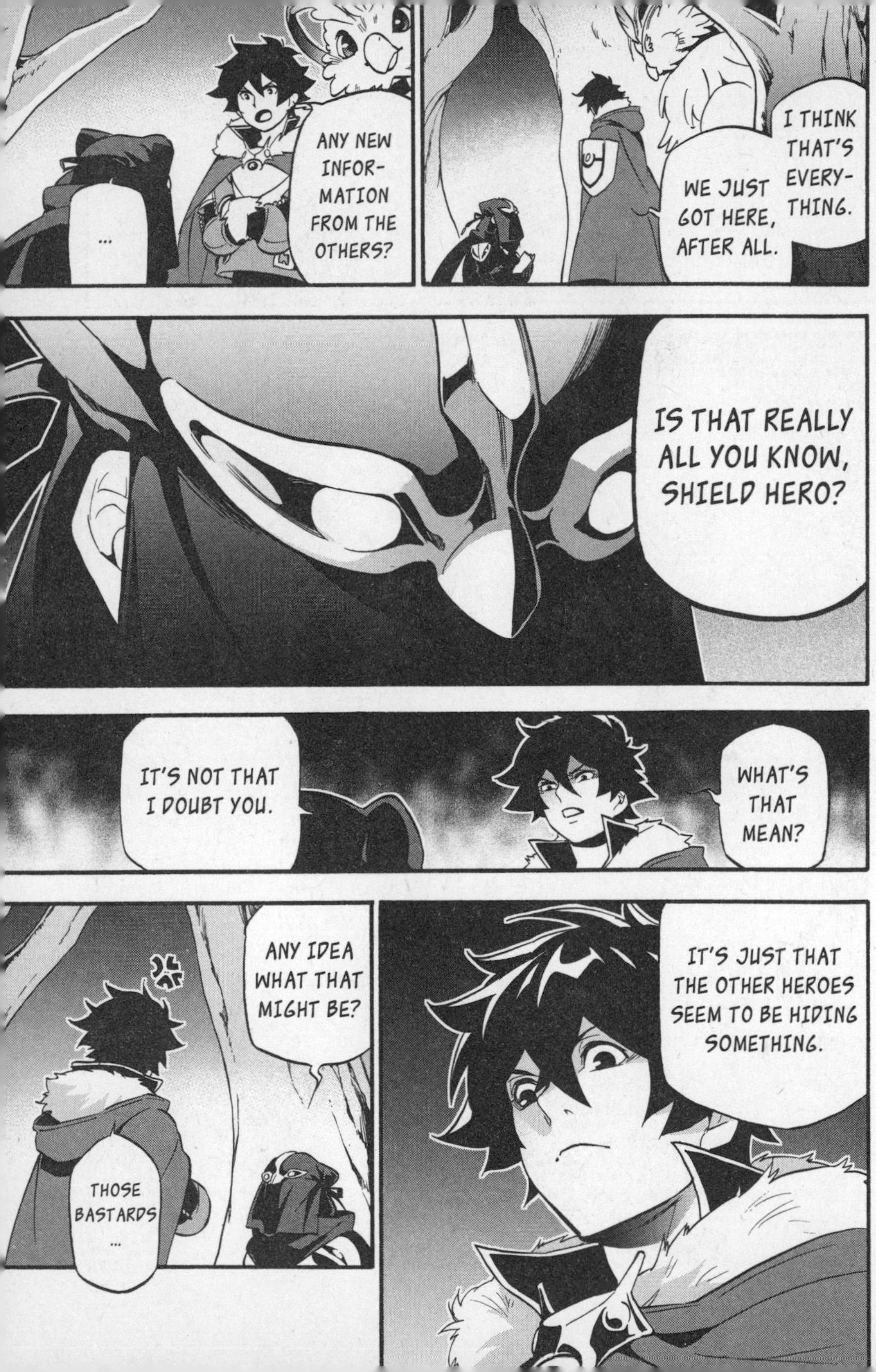
I THINK THAT'S EVERY-THING.
WE JUST GOT HERE, AFTER ALL.
ANY NEW INFOR-MATION FROM THE OTHERS?
...
IS THAT REALLY ALL YOU KNOW, SHIELD HERO?
WHAT'S THAT MEAN?
IT'S NOT THAT I DOUBT YOU.
IT'S JUST THAT THE OTHER HEROES SEEM TO BE HIDING SOMETHING.
ANY IDEA WHAT THAT MIGHT BE?
THOSE BASTARDS ...

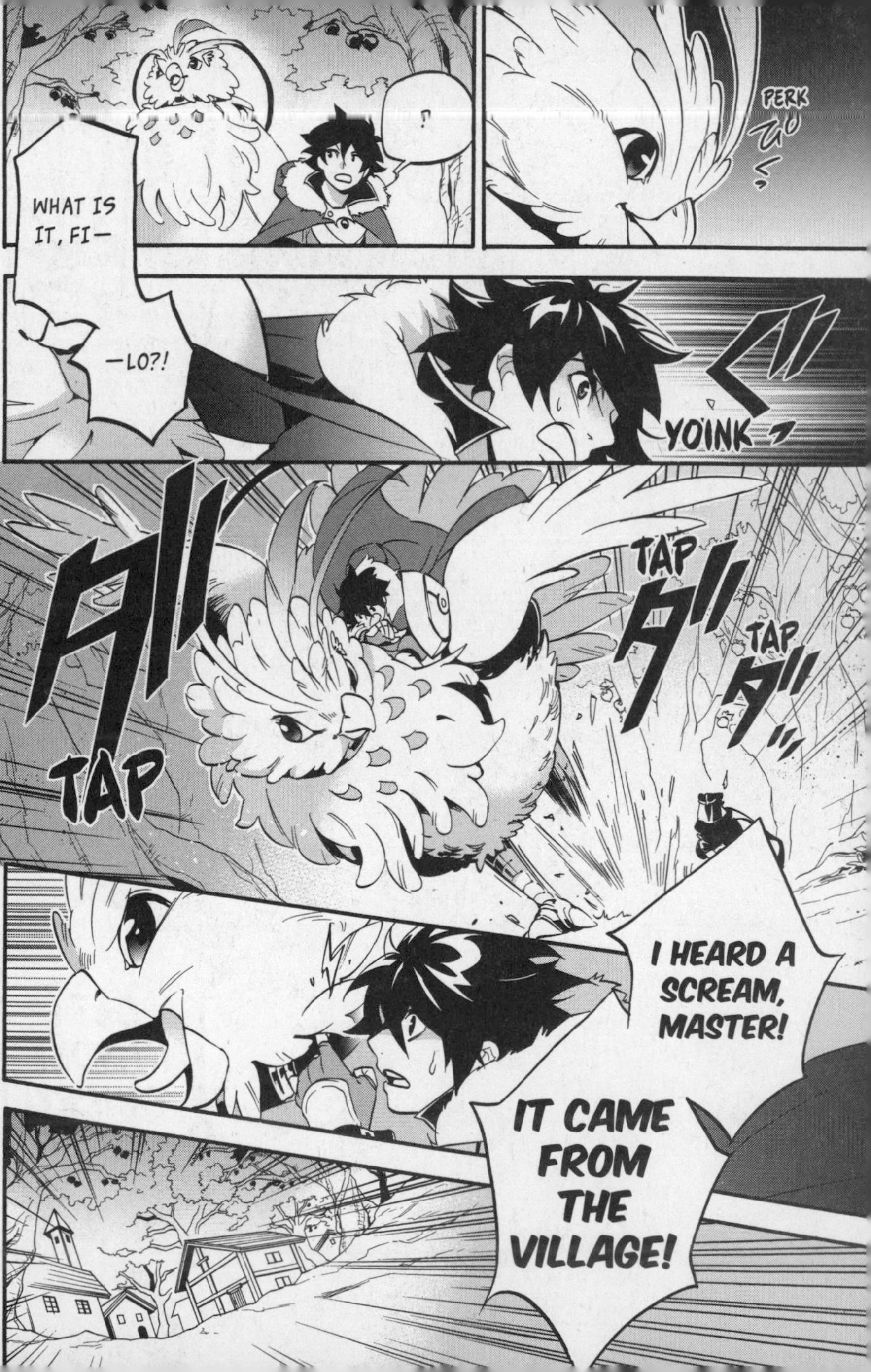
PERK
ぴくっ
!?
WHAT IS IT, FI—
—LO?!
ぐい
YOINK
TAP
ダッ
TAP
ダッ
ダッ
TAP
I HEARD A SCREAM, MASTER!
IT CAME FROM THE VILLAGE!

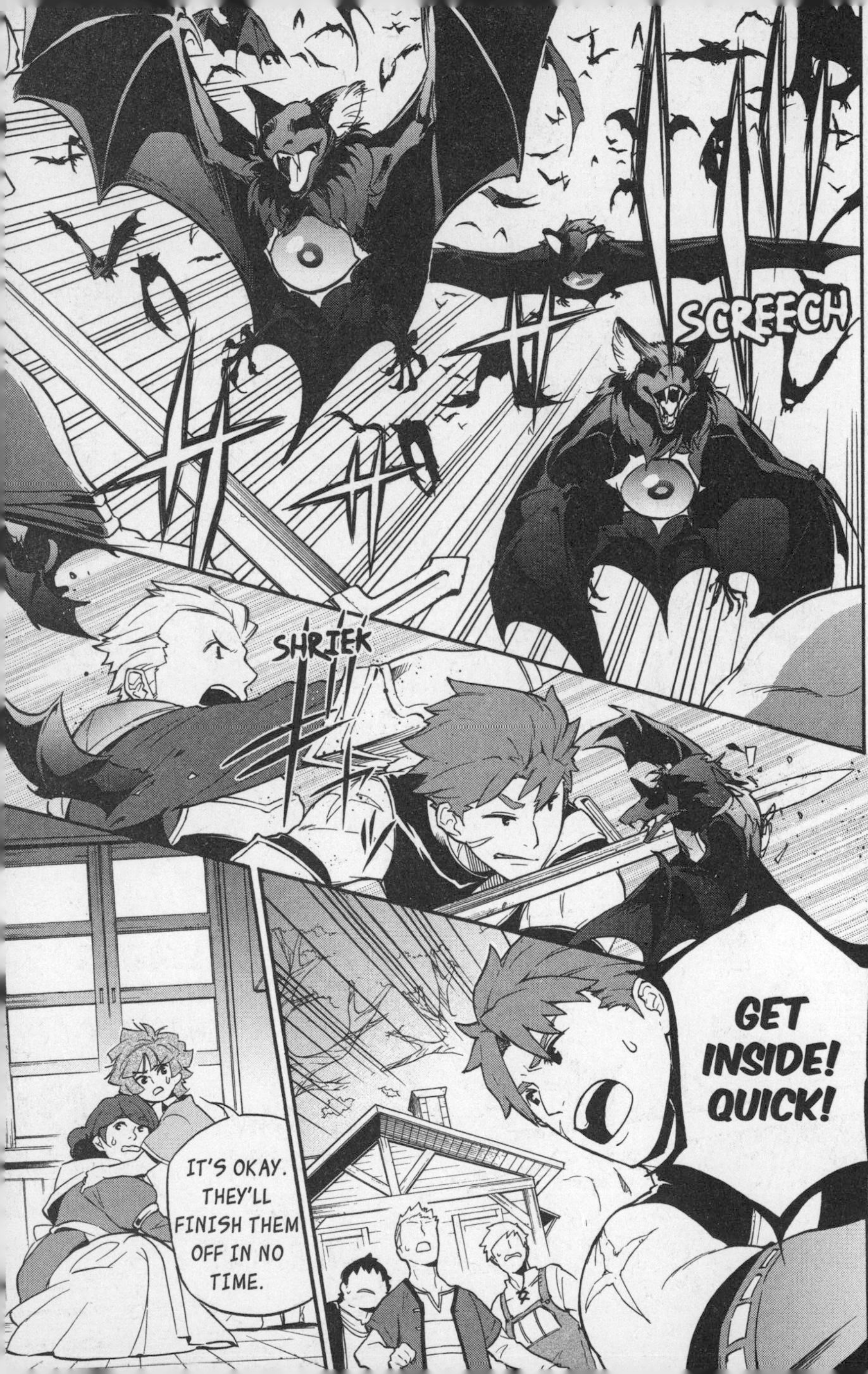
SCREECH
SHRIEK
GET INSIDE! QUICK!
IT'S OKAY. THEY'LL FINISH THEM OFF IN NO TIME.

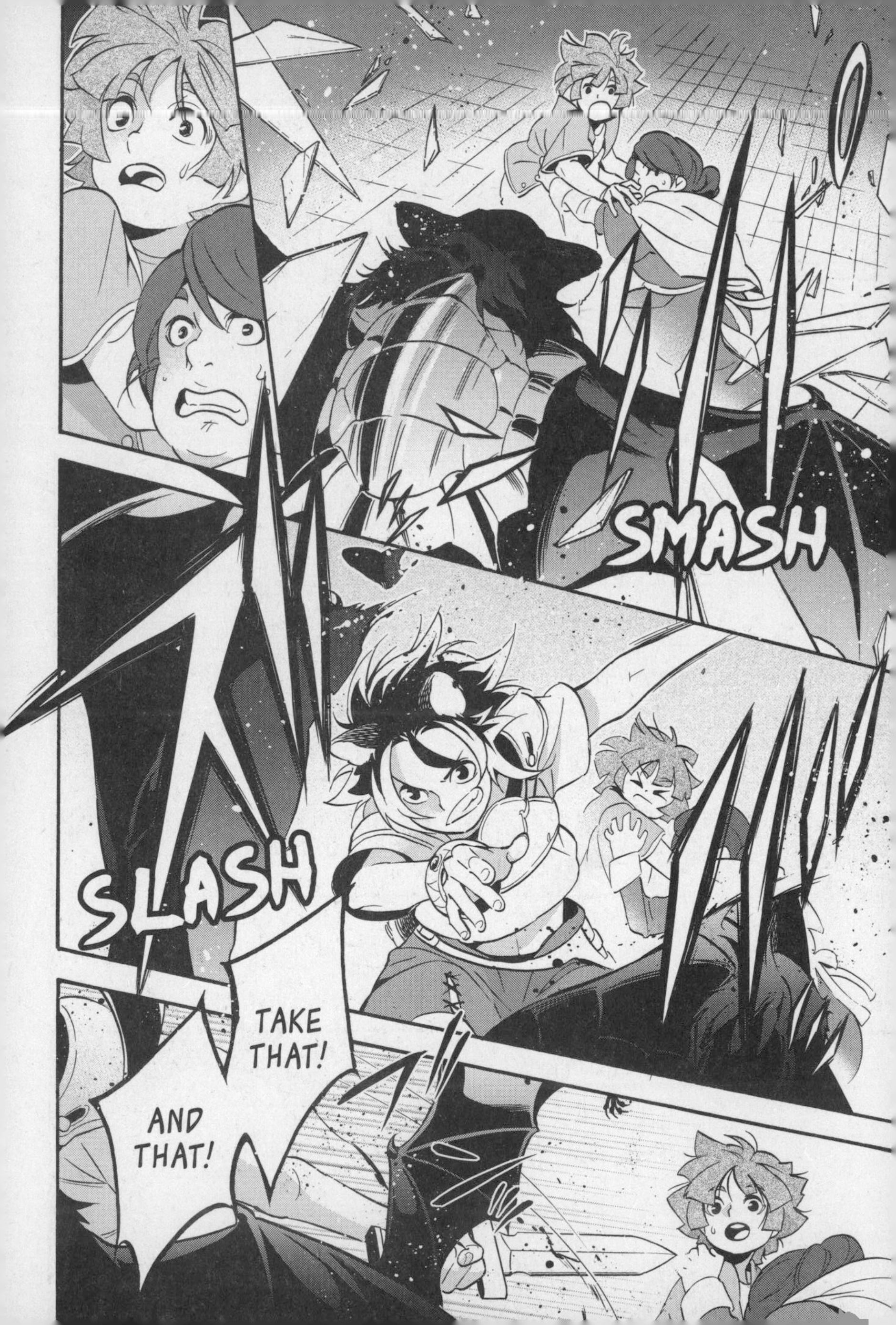
SMASH
SLASH
TAKE THAT!
AND THAT!

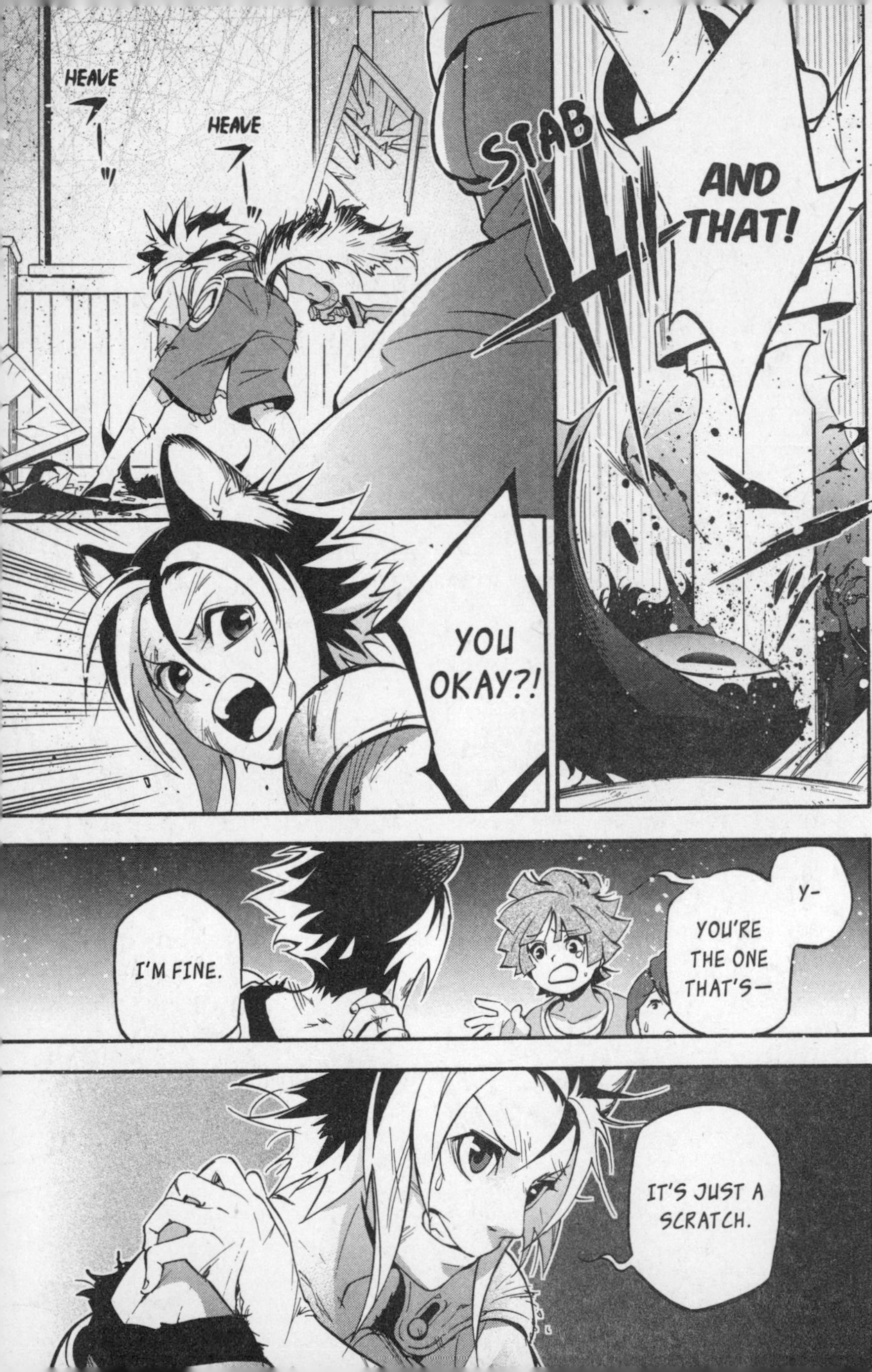
STAB
AND THAT!
HEAVE
HEAVE
YOU OKAY?!
Y- YOU'RE THE ONE THAT'S—
I'M FINE.
IT'S JUST A SCRATCH.

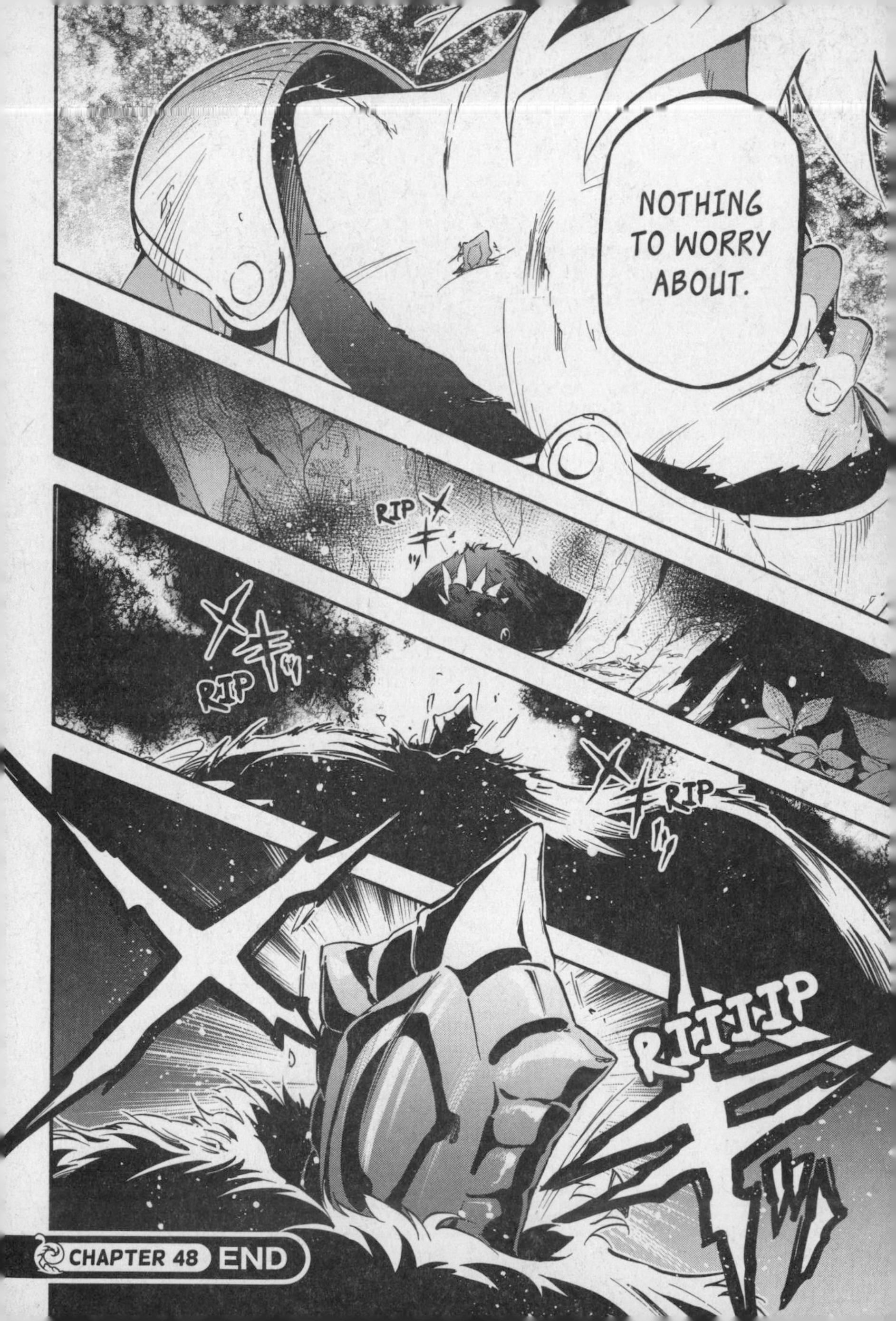
NOTHING TO WORRY ABOUT.
RIP
RIP
RIP
RIIIIP
CHAPTER 48 END

THE RISING OF THE SHIELD HERO

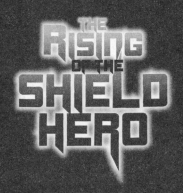

After Rishia becomes the newest member of Naofumi's party, they set out to begin a unique type of training in hopes of growing stronger. But just as they're getting started, Naofumi receives a request from the queen—mysterious monsters have begun to appear and she wants him to take care of them!

ISBN 978-1-64273-033-3

51195

9 781642 730333